Financial Analysis of Citizen Co-Operative Banks of North Gujarat

AUTHOR

Dr. Darshin R. Upadhyay

:: PUBLICATION ::

Green Flag Foundation
Sonasan
www.eternityzxy.com

ISBN 978-93-84570-96-5

ISBN 978-93-84570-96-5

First Publication

February - 2016

Typing & Design

Bharat B. Patel

Excellence Computer, Himatnagar

Printing & Binding

Manohar Book Binding, Himatnagar

: PUBLISHED BY :

Green Flag Foundation
Soasan
www.eternityzxy.com

Price: Rs.325/-

Dedicated To ....

Dadu

: INDEX :

Chapter-1

Development of Co-operative Activities and Co-operative Banking in India

1.1   Introduction

Effective banking system is an essential need of a healthy economy. The Co-operative banks are an important constituent of the Indian financial system. A co-operative bank is a financial entity which belongs to its members, who are at the same time the owners and the customers of their bank. Co-operative banks are often created by persons belonging to the same local or professional community or sharing a common interest. Co-operative banks generally provide their members with a wide range of

1

banking and financial services (loans, deposits, banking accounts etc.). The sole purpose of co-operatives have been to facilitate self-sufficiency in food grain production, creation of better employment opportunities for rural people, workers and artisans and to provide organizational strength to the persons of the limited means for their sustenance.

Earlier, in rural areas getting the credit requirement for the agricultural and its related activities was very tough. The agriculturist wholly depend for their credit requirement upon unorganized money market agencies, such as money lenders, who were providing credit often at exploitatively high rate of interest. At that time commercial banks were reluctant to enter into the field of agriculture, as good and liquid security is the main consideration by the commercial banks but agriculturist are not able to provide good securities. Land is the only security, that they can offer which is not acceptable to bank advances.

Further, the repayment of loans depends on the crop yield and the crop yield depends on the monsoon and other natural calamities which are unpredictable. If there is no crop yield or yield is unprofitable may affect the repaying of the loan by the borrower. Because of these reasons the commercial banks are trying to keep away from the fields of agricultural finance.

Therefore the co-operative banks came in to existence in 1904 to facilitate finance for agricultural activities and other related activities in order to substitute unorganized money market and money lenders.

Co-operative banks have completed 100 years of existence in India. They play a very important role in the financial system. The co-operative banks in India form an integral part of our money market today. Therefore, a brief resume of their development should be taken into account.

1.2   Definitions of Co-operation

The principle of co-operation is not new to India. The Indian joint family system is one instance of co-operation. The feeling of brotherhood and mutual help forms the basis of joint family. Panchayat in a village is another instance of co-operation. The Panchayat was mainly founded on the principle of community self-help.

Co-operation has been defined for different purposes and in different ways by co-operators, economists, lawmakers and others. It is enough to say here that the co-operative is an association of persons usually of limited means who have voluntarily joined together to fulfill a common economic need through the formation of a democratically controlled business organization making equitable contributions to the capital required and accepting a fair share of the risks and benefits of the undertaking. It denotes a special method of doing business.

Co-operation has been defined in different ways because co-operative movement developed in different countries in different forms under different social environments.Some definitions of co-operation are as follows:

- The word cooperation is derived from the Latin term 'Co-Operari' where co means 'with' and operari means 'work'. Thus, cooperation means working together for a common purpose and for mutual benefit, and it pervades in every sphere of human life.[1]

- According to Herrick, co-operation is the act of poor persons voluntarily united for utilizing reciprocally their own forces, resources or both under -mutual management to their common profit or loss.

- "Two are better than one, because they have good reward for their labour. For if they fall the one will lift up his fellow, but woe to him that is alone when he falleth and hath not another to lift up". This quotation speaks about the strength of cooperation. [2]

- According to E.R. Dowell, "Cooperation is a universal instrument of creation".

- Charles Gide considers cooperation as an economic system to supersede capitalism by mutual aid.

- In 1876, Mill in his book titled 'Principles of Political Economy' observed that cooperation transforms human life from a conflict of class struggle for opposite interests to a fair rivalry in the pursuit of common good to all.[3]

- Cooperation instil a new spirit in economic and social life; it seeks to replace competition by harmony of cooperation, for the welfare of all.

- Dr. C. R. Fay defines cooperation as, "an association for the purposes of joint trading, originating among the weak and conducted always in an unselfish spirit, on such terms that all who are prepared to assume the duties of membership share in its rewards in proportion to the degree in which they make use of their association." [4]

- Dr. E. M. Hough defines cooperation as, "In its broadest sense, cooperation may be defined simply as voluntary association in a joint undertaking for mutual benefit." [5]

- H. Calvert defines, "Cooperation is a form of organization, wherein persons voluntarily associate together as human beings, on the basis of equality, for promotion of the economic interest of themselves".[6]

- V.L. Mehta defines cooperation as, "One aspect of a vast movement which promotes voluntary association of individuals having common economic needs who combines towards the achievement of the common economic end they have in view and who bring into this combination a moral effort and a progressively developing realization of moral obligation". The underlying factor in this definition is the achievement of common ends.

- Dr. H. N. Kunzen defines cooperatives as, "Cooperative is self-help as well as mutual help. It is a joint enterprise of those who are not financially strong and cannot stand on their legs, and therefore, come together not with a view to get profits but to overcome disability arising out of the want of adequate financial resources".

- As per the International Cooperative Alliance (ICA), "A cooperative is an autonomous association of persons united voluntarily to meet their common economic, social, and cultural needs and aspirations through a jointly-owned and democratically-controlled enterprise.[7]

From the above definitions we can say that Co-operatives are based on the values of self-help, self-responsibility, democracy, equality, equity and solidarity. In the tradition of their founders, co-operative members believe in the ethical values of honesty, openness, social responsibility and caring for others. co-operation is not only result of principles but it is a mixerof principles and Practices.The Holistic meaning of co-operation is based on different co-operative principles because co-operative principles are more liberal and purposeful than definitions of co-operation.

1.3   Principles of Co-operation

Cooperative Principles, in fact, are fundamental characteristic features which determine the character of cooperation as a form of association. They are the guidelines and ground rules for cooperative enterprise. Without these principles no lasting cooperative system is possible. It is largely on their application that the success of the cooperative organization will depend.

The term 'principle' derived from the Latin word 'Princi-plum' meaning 'basis', has different meanings: the primary idea, a certain thesis, a rule of an organization.[8]A principle is a "governing law of conduct", a "settled rule of action", which describes and defines the basic and essential characteristics of a particular system or type of organization. The working definition adopted by the ICA Commission (1966) on Cooperative Principles was:

"Those practices which are essential, that is, absolutely indispensable to the achievement of the Co-operative Movement's purpose."[9]

1.3.1   Evolution of Co-operative Principles

The early nineteenth century was a period of considerable stress and strain in England. Great changes took place in the economic system that divided the society into two classes-Capitalistic and wage earners. The capitalistic system promoted social evils and this made the social thinkers like Robert Owen of England and Charles Fourier of France to think a better system of the economy. They thought of ideal form of society based on fundamental principles, i.e., association, voluntary nature of cooperation, and social motive. Many cooperatives were formed and almost all of them failed and finally in 1844 a group of 28 workers of Rochdale, an industrial town in England registered their society- "The Rochdale Society of Equitable Pioneers". The ideas of Rochdale pioneers set forth in the rules of the society make up a body of principles that have since inspired the cooperative movement throughout the world. The pioneers went on making and modifying the rules for the survival and progress and with time to look back the performance and achievements of the pioneers, these rules and ideas were considered as Rochdale Principles and these were:

1. Voluntary and open membership
2. Democratic control by "one member, one vote".
3. Division of surplus in proportion to patronage
4. Limited interest on capital
5. Political and religious neutrality
6. Cash trading
7. Promotion of education
8. Supply of pure and unadulterated goods.[10]

In course of time, cooperative movement spread to various countries and various forms of cooperation was developed. Between 1844 and 1937, the cooperative movement passed through various experiences and spread out geographically in the world. The business rules prepared by Rochdale Pioneers for conducting the operations of consumer organisations were obviously found wanting for fulfilling the needs of cooperative societies in other sections of the movement. New practices and technologies had come to be employed by cooperatives during the period. These developments demanded a second look at the cooperative principles and practices.[11] International Cooperative Alliance (ICA) was asked to appoint a special committee to examine the conditions in which Rochdale Principles were applied and to state these principles in their final form. The special committee was formed in 1934; and in 1937, the committee gave its report titled, "The Present Application of Rochdale Principles of Cooperation". The special committee listed seven principles:

    (a) Open membership
    (b) Democratic control
    (c) Limited interest on capital
    (d) Distribution of surplus to members in a proportion to their transactions
    (e) Political and religious neutrality
    (f) Cash trading and
    (g) Promotion of education.

The first four principles were granted as essential and rest as non-essential by the committee.

The social, economic and political conditions of various nations then changed and the cooperatives had to adapt themselves to the changing situations. Thus, the need for a review of the principles of cooperation was felt in 1963. Therefore, the Central Committee of ICA appointed a commission in 1964 to study cooperative principles. The commission submitted its report in 1966. The commission reaffirmed the first four principles in full form and adopted the promotion of cooperative education as the fifth principle and added a new principle - Principle of Growth: "Co-operation among Cooperatives". Thus, the commission considered the six principles as essential to genuine and effective cooperative practice both at present time and in future as far as that can be foreseen. The principles as enunciated by the commission of 1966 are as under:

1. Membership of a co-operative society should be voluntary and available without artificial restriction or any social, political or religious discrimination, to all persons who can make use of its services and are willing to accept the responsibilities of membership.

2. Co-operative societies are democratic organisations. Their affairs should be administered by persons elected or appointed in a manner agreed by the members and accountable to them. Members of primary societies should enjoy equal rights of voting (one member, one vote) and participation in decisions affecting their societies. In other than primary societies, the administration should be conducted on a democratic basis in a suitable form.

3. Share capital should only receive a strictly limited rate of interest, if any.

4. Surplus or savings, if any, arising out of the operations of a society belong to the members of that society and should be distributed in such a manner as would avoid one member gaining at the expense of others. This may be done by decision of the members as follows:

> **(a)** By provision for development of the business of the Co-operative;
>
> **(b)** By provision of common services; or
>
> **(c)** By distribution among the members in proportion to their transactions with the society.

5. All co-operative societies should make provision for the education of their members, officers and employees, and of the general public, in the principles and techniques of Co-operation, both economic and democratic.

6. All co-operative organisations, in order to best serve the interests of their members and their communities should actively co-operate in every practical way with other co-operatives at local, national and international levels.[12]

Due to changing times, a need was felt for re-affirming the values of cooperation for a deeper investigation into the relevance of the co-operative principles of 1966 to the changing environment. The ICA started the exercise in 1990 in two phases. Unlike the first two reviews of cooperative principles in 1937 and 1966 by the Special Committee and the Commission on Co-operative Principles respectively, this time it was conducted in two phases spread over as long as five years. According to the ICA statement on cooperative identity, the cooperative principles are guidelines by which cooperatives put their values into practice. These principles are given below:

1. Voluntary and Open Membership: Co-operatives are voluntary organizations, open to all persons able to use their services and willing to accept the responsibilities to membership, without gender, social, racial, political or religious discrimination.

2. Democratic Member Control: Co-operatives are democratic organizations controlled by their members, who actively participate in setting their policies and making decision. Men and women serving as elected representatives are accountable to the membership. In primary Co-operatives, members have equal voting rights (one member, one vote) and Co-operatives at other levels are also organized in a democratic manner.

3. Member's Economic Participation: Members contribute equitably to and democratically control the capital of their Co-operative. At least part of that capital is usually the common property of Cooperative. Members usually receive limited compensation, if any, on capital subscribed as a condition of membership. Members allocate surplus for any or all of the following purposes:
  ➢ Developing their Co-operative possibly by setting up reserves, part of which at least would be indivisible;
  ➢ Benefiting members in proportion to their transactions with the Cooperative; and
  ➢ Supporting other activities approved by the membership.

4. Autonomy and Independence: Co-operatives are autonomous, self-help organizations controlled by their members. If they enter into agreements with other organizations, including Government, or raise capital from external sources, they do so on terms that ensure democratic control by their members and maintain their Co-operative autonomy.

5. Education, Training and Information: Co-operatives provide education and training to their members, elected representatives, managers and employees so they can contribute effectively to the development of their Co-operative. They inform the general public particularly young people and opinion leaders about the nature and benefits of Co-operation.

6. Cooperation among Cooperatives: Co-operatives serves their members most effectively and strengthens the co-operative movement by working through local, national, regional and international structures.

7. Concern for Community: Co-operatives work for the sustainable development of their communities through policy approved by their members (RBI Occasional Papers).

These principles ought to be applied everywhere in order to set an example of honest, efficient and progressive co-operative activity. Thus, the utility of these principles lies in the fact that they attempt to avoid waste in efforts and opportunity, eliminate uneconomic competition, make proper utilization of resources and also help in exchange of ideas and experience.

1.4   Co-operative Movement in the World

This section provides a summary of major co-operative movement took place in the world at different points of time.

1.4.1 Co-operative Movement in France

Charles Fourier (1722-1837), published a Treatise on, "Domestic Agricultural Association," in 1822 for the first time on co-operation and Saint–Simon worked on various theories of 'Association'. Schulze Delitzsch (1808-1865), was the pioneer of urban co-operatives and co-operatives in handicrafts; while F.W. Raiffeisen (1818-1888), did the same for rural co-operatives.[13]

1.4.2 Co-operative Movement in England

As a modern phenomenon, the co-operative form of business organizations originated in England among the industrial workers in the mid-nineteenth century. The co-operatives started as an Urban Consumer Stores, but soon spread to rural areas amongst the farmers. During the latter half of the nineteenth century, the co-operative concept was spread to several parts of Europe and North America.

The real co-operative movement had been credited to 'Rochdale Pioneers', a person who established the Co-operative Consumer Store in North-England, at the end of 1844 which can be called as the first in the co-operative consumer movement. Robert Owen (1771-1858), is generally regarded as the founder of the modern cooperative movement with the workers of Bellers. His ideas put together had been named as, "doctrine of circumstances". Owen started his practice-work by introducing reforms in his own cotton mills of New Lanark, Scotland, as a measure to improve the conditions of workers. In Great Britain, Robert Owen established self-contained, semi-agricultural and semi-industrial communities.[14] The English Consumers Wholesale Society (CWS) was formed by the merger of many independent retail, wholesale and federal societies across Yorkshire and Lancashire by 1872.

The agricultural co-operation in England was of a comparatively recent growth. The British farmers had never been in debt, nor did they have any difficulty in the marketing of their produce but they felt some difficulty in producing farming requirements such as fertilizers, seeds, and feedstuffs. Agricultural Co-operation started with what is called "Requirement Societies". The first society, "The Agricultural and Horticultural Association", was started in 1867 with the objective of purchasing and selling of quality inputs. They also started selling agricultural machinery, petroleum and veterinary supplies. The agricultural societies organized their federations called the "Agricultural Central Co-operative Association" in 1856. William King (1757-1865), helped to spread Owens's doctrine.[15]

1.4.3 Co-operative Movement in Germany

Germany is the birthplace of co-operative credit movement in the World. Two pioneers, **Franz Schulze and F.W. Raiffeisen,** both well-known personalities in the co-operative field, moved by the miserable condition of farmers and labourers in Germany, started making experiments with various methods of relief. **Franz Schulze** (1808-1883), judge and the mayor of Delitzsch, started his efforts of co-operation after studying the conditions of famine stricken people as a chairman of the "Famine Commission". In 1849, he established his first friendly society of shoemakers with the object of making purchases of raw material in bulk and supplying it to the members.[16]In 1850, Schulze established his first credit society in his native town. Its function was to raise funds to be lent to its members. The number of his banks grew rapidly and in 1859, he called a congress of his banks which resolved to set-up "The General Union of German Industrial Societies". He remained its Director till death in 1883. He also secured the "First Co-operative Law" from Prussia in 1867, which was made applicable to the whole Germany in 1889.[17]

Raiffeisen is the one person to whom the co-operative movement owes the maximum. As the Mayor of Wyerbusch, he came across with the poverty stricken peasants and greedy money lenders. He organized the "Union in Aid of Impoverished Farmers" in 1849, in which the needy farmers joined as members.[18] At Heddesderf, Raiffeisen organized the "Heddesderf Beneficient Society". The phrase "each for all, all for each" was coined. Principles of honorary service and unlimited liability were also worked out. In 1877, "The General Union of Rural Co-operative Societies" which was known as the "Raiffeisen Union" was also set up.

After the national collapse and German defeat in 1945, the formal agricultural production co-operatives had been formed on the pattern of collective farms in Russia. These societies combined in themselves the work of providing credit, supplying agricultural requirements, marketing of crops and processing of produce.[19] In Germany, the rural co-operative movement, which started merely for the elimination of financial debility of members, covered the whole economic field in rural areas. The co-operatives are also present in growth sectors such as the service industry, in data processing and new media industries and in the education and health sectors.

1.4.4 Co-operative Movement in Sweden

The wholesalers and retailers were fixing high margin for the consumer goods, which provoked the workers to think of methods of saving themselves form this organized exploitation. Based on the Rochdale Pioneers Model, the first known cooperative enterprise in Sweden, "District Commodity Buying Company", was established in 1850.[20]

The consumer co-operative movement is a very strong force in the Swedish economy and a bulk work of protection to the Swedish consumer. The Swedish cooperative Union and Wholesale Society known as Ko-operative Farbundet (K.F.) were established in 1899 to act as a medium for publicity and an advisory body to primary co-operative stores. In 1904, K.F. began to act as a supplier of goods to the primary co-operative stores. Just after the First World War agricultural co-operatives expanded their sphere of work and societies were established in almost every sphere of agricultural activity.[21]

1.4.5 Co-operative Movement in Canada

Farmers were the first Canadian group that successfully developed cooperatives. Between 1860 and 1900 farmers in Ontario, Quebec and Atlantic Canada, developed over 1200 co-operative creameries and cheese factories to meet the needs of the rapidly growing dairy industry. Prairie farmers led by E.A. Partridge, organized the "Grain Growers' Grain Co-operative", in 1906 to market directly to millers and European buyers. In 1911 Saskatchewan farmers, aided by the provincial government, organized the "Saskatchewan Co-operative Elevator Company". Two years later, Alberta farmers organized the "Alberta Farmers' Co-operative Elevator Company". Numerous other Canadian farm groups - fruit growers, livestock producers and tobacco growers organized smaller but important supply, purchasing and marketing groups before First World War. A few from Ontario and Nova Scotia met in Hamilton in 1909 to form the Co-operative Union of Canada, a national representative body and educational institution.

In 1900 in Quebec, Alphonse Desjardins developed co-operative banking in organizing his first Caisse Populaire. Farm co-operatives expanded rapidly, including the new multipurpose Co-operative Federee (established 1910 in Quebec), and United Farmers' Co-operative (established in 1914 at Ontario). By 1919 most farmers wished to gain greater control over the marketing of their produce. They were soon drawn to "co-operative pooling," a system whereby members contracted to sell all produce through their co-operative and in return would receive dividends based on the quality of the produce they supplied. The most innovative effort was developed by the Extension Department of St. Francis Xavier University in Antigorrish, Nova Scotia. The Antigorrish movement was particularly effective in developing study clubs, which became the basis of Credit Unions, Fishing and Housing Co-operatives, and Cooperative Stores. Other forms of co-operatives appearing during the 1930s included handicraft co-operatives in Atlantic Canada, fishing co-operatives on both coasts and on inland lakes, recreation co-operatives, co-operative health facilities, co-operative film clubs, petroleum co-operative and a farm-implement co-operative organized by prairie farmers. Since the 1950s the co-operative movement has continued to grow. Today, it consists of related organizations with significant influence in agriculture, finance, insurance, fishing, retail and housing industries. The grain- and dairy marketing co-operatives dominate their industries and the retail co-operatives play significant roles on the Prairies and in Atlantic Canada.

1.4.6 Co-operative Movement in Russia

The co-operative movement in Russia began in 1864 when some co- operative stores and credit societies were organized. By 1914, the movement had become strong enough and the consumers' stores in the country handled more than half the country's supplies.[22]The earliest form of co-operative movement is Russia was "Labor Artels". Labor Artel means an association formed to carry on certain industries or render personal services on the joint responsibility of the members of the Artel and their joint account. Such Artels were organized by carpenters, masons, handicrafts-men and other artisans. The Artels were financed through deposits obtained from the members and non-members. These Artels flourished for some time but when large-scale industry came into being, their important declined. The Russian farmers organized their own association in the last decade of the 19th century. An important association of this nature was organized in1895 by the 'butter producers' in Siberia. These societies soon multiplied and in 1908, they organized their federation called, "The Union of Siberian Creameries Association". The primary units set up creameries and sold their butter through the union. The union still exists and is very strong. In Russia,Credit Co-operative Societies were set up to fight the evils of moneylenders. Their object was to create the habit of thrift among members and grant loans to them for agricultural requirements. On the contrary, there was a second type of co-operative organization, called 'Credit Associations'. These societies were fully supported by the government, especially after 1905. They provided the credit needs of their members who were mostly cultivators.[23]

1.4.7 Co-operative Movement in Japan

The co-operative movement in Japan was introduced in the form of consumers' co-operatives, the first of which was established in 1879, with the object of controlling prices. In 1900, the Industrial Co- operative Law was passed on the lines of the German Law. In 1905, a non-official body named "Co-operative Union" was established which made extensive propaganda for the promotion of co-operative societies and by 1909; the number of societies had risen to 5690 with about 3.8 lac members.[24] The primary societies soon felt the need for organizing their secondary societies and in 1923 the "National Purchase Co-operative Federation" and the "Central Co-operative Bank" were established.[25] The Japanese agricultural cooperatives cover 91 per cent farmers as members, and they provide an integrated system of marketing, supply, credit and insurance for the whole rural economy.In fiscal 2007, the Ministry of Japan considered the system of direct payment subsidies, under the farm income stabilization policy and the government decided to include community farming collectively of more than 20 hectares, even if they comprised primarily of part-time farmers.[26]

1.4.8 Co-operative Movement in Italy

In Italy, due to the great depression in 1880, the poor could not repay their loans taken from the money lenders, and as a consequence of which whatever little assets they possessed, began to pass into the hands of the money lenders. In such a situation, Luigi Luzzati and Leone Wallenberg began to think of ways and means to improve the conditions of the people who were suffering from poverty.

Luzzati started his work by organizing a friendly society at Lodi in 1864-65. Later it became a regular co-operative bank. In 1866, he started his first co-operative bank at Milan named "Banca Popular". Luzzati insisted on honorary management to reduce the rate of interest on loans. He pleaded for limited liability. He kept smaller shares, which were payable in ten months. Wallenberg started co-operative activities in the rural areas. It was in 1883 that he started a bank in his home village Loreggia with 32 members.[27]

1.4.9 Co-operative Movement in Denmark

In Denmark, the farmers were most affected because of the lack of finance and the existence of tenancies. In order to escape from these difficulties, at the end of the 19th century, the co-operative movement started in Denmark. The first co-operative dairy was established in Hjedding, with the efforts of a young dairyman named Stilling Andersen in 1882. In 1884, "Dairy Society Denmark" was established, which coordinated the production and marketing of dairy business in the country. The Consumer Co-operative movement in Denmark was introduced by H.C.Sonne, who was impressed by the successful example of consumers' co-operative societies of England by Rochdale Pioneers who convinced a number of persons to form "Thirsted Workers Society" which was established in 1886. In 1895, the "Co-operative Egg Export Association" was established. It introduced the system of grading and stamping of eggs to ensure quality of the eggs exported to England. In Denmark, cooperation also spread in other spheres such as Co-operative Poultry Killing Stations, Co-operative Cattle Sale Societies, Co-operative Seed Supply Societies, Fruit Growers Co-operative Association, Co-operative Feeding Stuff Societies and Co-operative Fertilizer Purchase Society. The Promotion of the member education has always been considered as one of the important jobs of the co-operative movement. In 1932, the Danish Co-operative College was established by the Danish Co-operative Wholesale Society at Middleport. It was realized that in Denmark Agricultural Marketing and Processing Co-operatives were beneficial and thereby in the beginning of the 20th century, virtually all the needs of the rural communities were met by co-operatives. In 1990s the Danish Consumer Co-operatives represented a market share of roughly 33 per cent of the national foodstuff and beverage consumption.[28] The co-operative movement also resulted in a series of co-operative stores known as Brugsen, under the administration of the Danish Consumer Co-operative Society.

1.4.10 Co-operative Movement in Israel

The most important contribution towards the co-operative movement was "The First Agricultural Collective Settlement" at Dagania in the Jordan Valley in 1908. In 1923, Hevrat Ovdim was registered under the Co-operative Societies Act. Co-operative farming and living was adopted in Israel because of a desire of mutual aid actuated by national affinity, pioneering zeal in the immigrants to uplift their homeland, lack of technical and farming knowledge in the immigrants, lack of resources and experience necessary to reclaim large areas of barren land and mutual protection from hostile Arabs. The co-operative sector contributes 70 per cent of the country's entire agricultural output; whereas the contribution of the private sector is only 30 per cent, as on July 2009.

1.5 History of co-operative movement in India

The history of cooperatives in India is more than a hundred years old. The Indian cooperative movement was initiated by the government. It spread and diversified with the encouragement and support of the government. Its present condition is also to a great extent because of the intrusive involvement of, and interference by the government. The following is only a brief attempt to recapture the major events that led to the cooperatives as we see them today.

The history of co-operative movement in India is broadly divided into two phases as under:

1.5.1) Co-operative movement in pre-independence era.
1.5.2) Co-operative movement in post-independence era.

These two phases are briefly discussed below:-

1.5.1) Co-operative Movement in pre-independence era:

The pages of Indian history cite many evidences of co-operative activities from earliest times. During the beginning of the 20th century, officials of the colonial government perceived the Indian farmer's dependence on usurious moneylenders to be major causes of their indebtedness and poverty. At that time the co-operative movement had become well established in Europe and achieved remarkable success there. This convinced that co-operative movement offered the best means of liberating Indian farmers from the crushing burden of debt and the tyranny of money lenders.

The first experiment in urban co-operative credit was made in the then Baroda State. On February 5, 1889, Prof. Vithal Laxman alias Bhausaheb Kavathekar arranged a dinner at his residence in Baroda and the party ended with the decision to set up **'Anyonya Sahakari Mandali'** was the object of promoting thrift and providing relief among Maharashtrian residents in Baroda city. The 21 Maharashtrians attending the dinner became founder-members on the spot by agreeing to subscribe at least Rs. two each month. It was the mutual aid society of subscriber-members, its funds were deposited in the Postal Bank, and it had no assistance from the Boarda State. Inspired by the experiments in the Baroda State,' such voluntary associations, for the twin purposes, were set up in the Bombay presidency by public-spirited men without Government assistance. At this juncture, Indian opinion had been impressed by the success of small village banks in Germany and Italy.

The Government of Madras was the first to grasp the possibilities of the cooperative movement in India and appointed, in 1892, F.H. Nicholson as the Special Officer to study the theory and practice of the co-operative movement in Europe, with special reference to the organization of cooperative credit in Germany, and to suggest means for its introduction in India. In his two reports issued in 1885 and 1897, he gave exhaustive information about the development in Europe, and recommended the model of Raiffeisen Societies. His emphasis was, however, on the man whom they had discovered 'and not on the system and, therefore, 'Find Raiffeisen' was the crux of his advice.

The Madras Government decided to set up two village banks as an experiment; but the Bombay Government was not enthusiastic about his recommendations. At the same time the States like U.P., Punjab and Bengal started cooperatives societies on the Italian model. Those were registered, in the absence of special legislation, either under the Societies Registration Act or the Companies Act.

During the contemporary period, the Famine Commission in 1898 and Dupernex in his book "People's Bank for Northern India" in 1900 argued for co- operation among Indian farmers to insulate them from many of their problems. Lord Curzon followed the famine commission's recommendations and appointed the Edward Law Committee in 1901 and the first Co-operative Societies Act was passed in 1904 which began the era of co-operation in the Indian Economy. The enactment of Co-operative Credit Societies Act, 1904 conferred legal status on credit societies and the first urban co-operative credit society was registered in 1904 at Conjeevaram in Madras Province. Subsequently, the Betegri Co-operative Credit Society in Dharwar district in the undivided Bombay Province (now in north Karnataka) and the Bangalore city the co-operative credit societies, in the erstwhile Mysore State were registered in October 1905 and December 1905 respectively. However, the real beginning was after the amendment in 1911, enhancing its scope to the formation of non-agricultural credit societies.

With the developments in terms of growth in the number of co-operatives, far exceeding anticipation, the Co-operative Societies Act of 1912 became a necessity and co-operatives could be organized under this Act for providing non-credit services to their members. The Act also provided for federations of cooperatives. The Maclagan Committee was appointed in 1914 to review the growth of themovement. It made far reaching proposals for the future development ofco-operative creation. The committee recommended three tier structure ofco-operative credit.

Under the Reforms Act 1919, co-operation became a Provincial subject under a minister with whose zeal and guidance, the movement made rapid progress. Bombay gave a lead to other provinces by passing a separate Co-operative Societies Act in 1925.

The agricultural credit scenario was a matter of concern and various committees looked into the problems of co-operative banks in various provinces. In 1928, the Royal Commission on Agriculture submitted a report emphasising the importance of co-operative sector and observed that "ifco-operation fails; there will be failure of the best hope of rural India". In 1934, the setting up of RBI was a major development in the thrust for agricultural credit. It had agriculture credit as part of its basic mandate. By extending refinance facilities to the co-operative credit system it played an important role in spreading the co-operative movement to far corners of the country.

The Mehta Committee appointed in 1937 specifically recommended reorganization of Cooperative Credit Societies as multi-purpose co-operatives. In 1942, the government enacted the Multi Unit Co-operative Act which was an enabling instrument for incorporation and winding up of co-operative societies.

The period between 1939 -1945 provided a further stimulus to the growth of the Urban Co-operative Credit structure. Many societies had started banking functions and had grown in size and operations over a period of time, with substantial diversification of activities. The Co-operative movement gathered momentum. The all India Co-operative planning Committee in 1945 also worked a lot in this direction.

1.5.2) Co-operative movement in Post-independence Era:

After independence, the Constitution came into operation on 26th January 1950. The blueprint for the growth and development of the country was being formulated. In this blueprint, the co-operatives held an extremely important position in the development of the rural and agricultural economy of the country. Mahatma Gandhi and Jawaharlal Nehru encouraged the development of the co-operative sector for the rural prosperity. Jawaharlal Nehru provided a fillip to the movement and made special provisions in thefive year plans. The successive five year plans looked upon the co-operation movement as the balancing sector between public sector and the private sector.

- **The First Five Year Plan, (1951-56)**

The first five year plan was launched in 1950-51. The plan focused on the credit aspect of the co-operatives or it described the co-operative movement as an instrument of planned economic action in democracy. In 1951 RBI constituted a committee named as All India Rural Credit Survey Committee. The committee observed that the poorer and weaker section could not get loans mainly because of their poor credit worthiness. In order to have an all-round improvement, it was felt necessary that these sections were also lifted up and provided credit to perform better. The First Plan also recommended for training of personnel's and setting up of Cooperative Marketing Societies.

- **The Second Five Year Plan, (1956-61)**

The focus of the second five year plan was organizing the co-operative at the village and primary level. This was done mainly to make it a movement at the grass roots level and create self-awareness among the people. The plan drew up programs of co-operative development based on the recommendations of the All India Rural Credit Survey Committee. The committee considered that the role of co-operative development is very important in increasing the agricultural production and making the rural economy stronger.

The plan also recommended the establishment of a National Agricultural Credit Long-term Operations Fund. The National Co-operative Development Fund was also established by the Central Government, to enable states to borrow for the purpose of subscribing share capital of non credit co-operative institutions in the country during this plan.

- **The Third Five Year Plan (1961-1969)**

In this plan, various objectives were set up to bring the entire country under the fold of the co-operative movement. It was noticed that about Rs. 30 crores should be made available for short term loans which was successfully done. The state governments also provided excellent support and assistance to the societies for creating reserves against bad debts. The co-operative movement was again boosted with a large number of primary and wholesale societies coming up during the plan period. Various panchayat working groups and societies came together for the development of the co-operatives.

Several other significant organizational developments also took place during this period such as the setting up of various National Cooperative Federations and re-organization of the National Cooperative Union of India (NCUI). In 1967, the Vaikunth Mehta National Institute of Cooperative Management was set up in Pune. Growth of consumer cooperatives was also an important development of this period. Simultaneously, the growth of Land Development Banks also accelerated and rural electric cooperatives and programmes for dairy, poultry, fishery and labour cooperatives were set up.

- **The Fourth Five Year Plan (1969-1974)**

Growth and stability was expected to be the key note of the cooperative movement during the fourth plan. The plan stated, "It is important for a planned development to bring out growth of co-operative in all the parts of the county to ensure the co-ordinate operation of various types of co-operative organisations"

The plan gave high priority to re-organization of co-operatives to make co-operative short term and medium term structure viable. The plan also made necessary provisions to provide co-operatives with management subsidy and store capital contribution, as well as for the rehabilitation of central co-operative banks. It also emphasized the need to orient policies in favor of small cultivators.

- **The Fifth Five Year Plan (1974-1979)**

The Fifth Plantook note of the high level of over-dues. In its recommended strategy for cooperative development, the correction of regional imbalances and reorienting the cooperatives towards the under-privileged was to receive special attention. Based on the recommendations of an Expert Group appointed by the Planning Commission in 1972, structural reform of the cooperative set-up was envisaged. The

Plan recommended the formulation of Farmers' Services Cooperative Societies as had been envisaged by the National Commission on Agriculture and stressed the need for professional management of cooperatives.

- ## The Sixth Five Year Plan (1980-1985)

The Sixth Planalso emphasized the importance of cooperative efforts being more systematically directed towards ameliorating the economic conditions of the rural poor. The Plan recommended steps for re-organizing Primary Agricultural Credit Societies into strong and viable multi-purpose units. It also suggested strengthening the linkages between consumer and marketing cooperatives. Consolidation of the role of Cooperative Federal Organizations, strengthening development of dairy, fishery and minor irrigation cooperatives, manpower development in small and medium cooperatives were some of the planned programs.

The National Bank for Agriculture and Rural Development (NABARD) Act was passed in 1981 and NABARD was set up to provide re-finance support to Cooperative Banks and to supplement the resources of Commercial Banks and Regional Rural Banks to enhance credit flow to the agriculture and rural sector.

With the objective of introducing a comprehensive central legislation to facilitate the organization and functioning of genuine multi-state societies and to bring uniformity in their administration and management, the MSCS Act of 1984 was enacted. The earlier Multi-Unit Cooperative Societies Act of 1942 was repealed.

- ## The Seventh Five Year Plan (1985-1990)

The Seventh Plan pointed out that while there had been all round progress in credit, poor recovery of loans and high level of overdues were matters of concern. The Plan recommended amongst others development of Primary Agricultural Credit Societies as multiple viable units; realignment of policies and procedures to expand flow of credit and ensure inputs and services particularly to weaker sections; special programmes for the North Eastern Region; strengthening of consumer co-operative movement in urban as well as rural areas and promoting professional management.

In 1989 the Agricultural Credit Review Committee under the chairmanship of Prof. A.M. Khusro examined the problems of agricultural and rural credit and recommended a major systemic improvement. The Committee recommended that the Eighth Plan should become the plan for revival of weak agricultural credit societies.

- ## The Eighth Five Year Plan (1992-1997)

The Eighth Plan laid emphasis on building up the cooperative movement as a self-managed, self-regulated and self-reliant institutional set-up, by giving it more autonomy and democratizing the movement. It also spoke of enhancing the capability of cooperatives for improving economic activity and creating employment opportunities for small farmers, labourers, artisans, women and emphasized development and training of cooperative functionaries in professional management.

- **The Ninth Five Year Plan (1997-2002)**

From the ninth plan onwards, there has been no specific mention about cooperatives as a part of the Plan. The Multi-State Cooperative Societies (MSCS) Act, enacted in 1984, was modified in 2002, in keeping with the spirit of the Model Cooperatives Act. The Ninth Plan put a targeted annual growth rate of 4.7 percent, in order to achieve the objective of removing the incidence of poverty and unemployment and ensuring food and nutritional security. In 2002, the Government of India enunciated a National Cooperative Policy. The objective of the Policy is to facilitate an all-round development of cooperatives in the country. The policy promises to provide cooperatives with the necessary support, encouragement and assistance, to ensure their functioning as autonomous, self-reliant and democratically managed institutions, accountable to their members, and making a significant contribution to the national economy.

- **The Tenth Five Year Plan (2002-2007)**

In the Tenth plan to achieve high-targeted annual agricultural growth rate and export, massive expansion and up gradation of agricultural marketing, storage and distribution infrastructure are given priority. Facilities for packaging, grading, and certification of agricultural commodities and development of future agricultural markets would be given special attention with adequate funds. To nurse the rural cooperative credit system back to health, to ensure that the rural credit doubled over three years and that the coverage of small and marginal farmers by institutional lending was expanded substantially, the Government of India in August 2004 set up a Task Force to suggest an action plan for reviving rural cooperative credit institutions and legal measures necessary for facilitating this process. The Task Force, chaired by Prof. A. Vaidyanathan, recommended that any financial restructuring which did not address the root causes of the weaknesses of the system would not result in its sustained revival and would require legal measures.

- **The Eleventh Five Year Plan (2007-2012)**

During the Eleventh Five Year Plan many important schemes, especially in cooperative credit sector, computerization, human resource development and public awareness were formulated and implemented to facilitate the public in general, especially the farmers.

1.6 The Structure of Co-Operative Banking System In India

The cooperative banking system in India comprises of:
* Primary Agricultural Credit Societies **(PACSs)**.
* Central Cooperative Banks **(CCBs)**.
* State Cooperative Banks **(SCBs)**.

FIGURE 1.1: CO-OPERATIVE BANKING SYSTEM

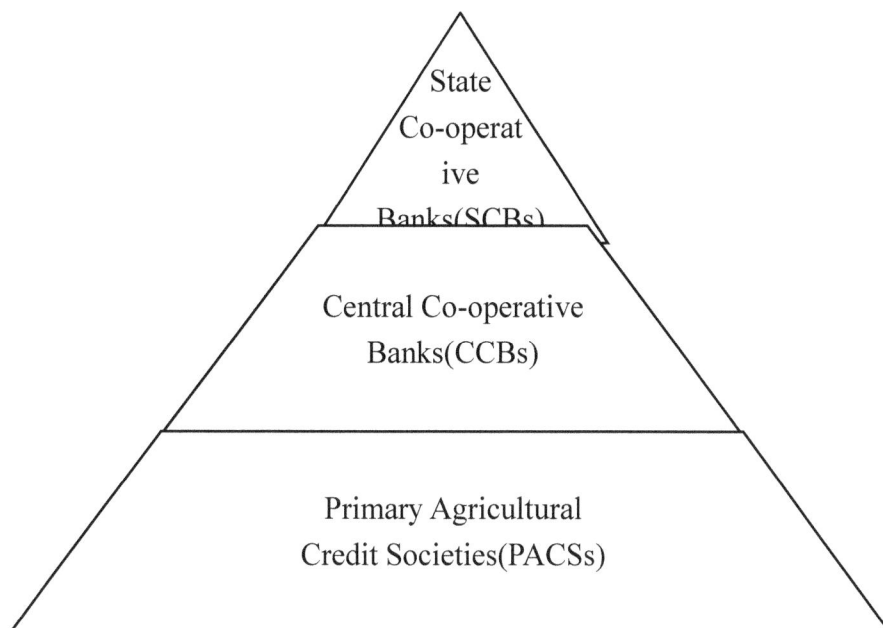

The cooperatives provide short & medium-term credit and the long-term credit. The short & medium-term credit is provided by the three-tier structure consisting of PACSs at the grass root level, CCBs at the district level and SCBs at the state level. There are urban cooperative banks functioning in towns and cities. The long-term credit is provided by two-tier structure having Primary Land Development Banks (Primary Cooperative Agricultural and Rural Development Bank) at tehsil level and Central Land Development Banks (Central Cooperative Agricultural and Rural Development Bank) at the state level.

FIGURE 1.2: ORGANISATIONAL STRUCTURE OF CO-OPERATIVE CREDIT SYSTEM IN INDIA (As at the end-March 2012)

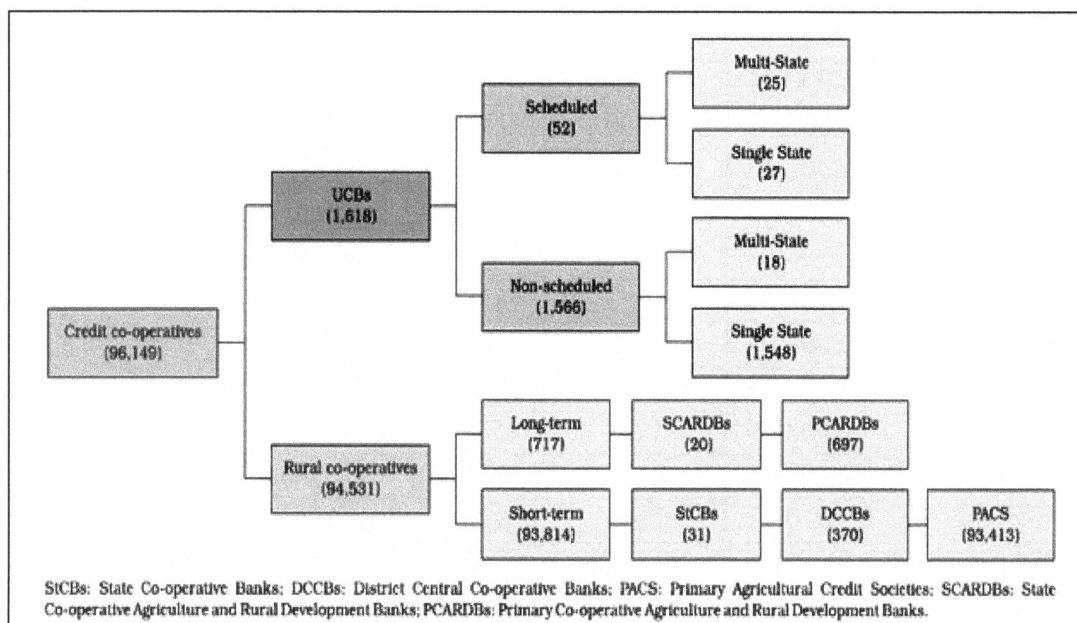

StCBs: State Co-operative Banks; DCCBs: District Central Co-operative Banks; PACS: Primary Agricultural Credit Societies; SCARDBs: State Co-operative Agriculture and Rural Development Banks; PCARDBs: Primary Co-operative Agriculture and Rural Development Banks.

The co-operative banking structure in India which shown in above figure comprises two main components, viz, urban co-operative banks and rural co- operative credit institutions.

A.) Citizen (Urban) Co-operative Banks (CCBs):

Co-operative credit societies established in urban areas are referred asCitizen (Urban) Cooperative Banks. The urban areas of the country are served by the urban co-operative banks, which are further sub-divided into scheduled and non-scheduled CCBs. Scheduled CCBs form a small proportion of the total number of CCBs. The operations of both scheduled and non-scheduled CCBs are limited to either one state or multi state. Most of the non-scheduled CCBs are primary single state CCBs having single tier structure.

Citizen Cooperative Banks are confined to the municipal area of the town. They are of two types:

(i) Unit banking

(ii) Branch banking

Citizen Cooperative Banks usually meet the needs of specific types or groups of members pertaining to certain trade, profession, community or even locality. CitizenCooperative Banks are also called Primary Cooperative Banks (PCBs) by the Reserve Bank of India.

In the following table, an attempt has been made to study the performance of CCBs at national level.

Table 1.1
Key Financial Indicators of CCBs

(Amount in Crores)

Year	No. of Banks	Deposits	Advances
1967	1106	153	167
1992-93	1399	13531	10132
2000-01	1762	71703	45856
2001-02	2090	93069	62060
2002-03	2104	100757	64022
2003-04	2105	110256	67930
2004-05	1872	105017	66905
2005-06	1853	114060	71641
2006-07	1813	121391	79733
2007-08	1770	138496	88981
2008-09	1721	157041	96234
2009-10	1674	182862	110303
2010-11	1645	212031	136341

| 2011-12 | 1618 | 238521 | 158026 |

Source: Report on Trend and Progress of Banking in India, various issues.

No. of Banks: In June 1967, there were 1106 CCBs in India and by the year 1993, the number increased to 1399. In 2002-03, there were 2104 CCBs and by the year 2011-12, the number decreased to 1618. The number of CCBs for the period 1967-1993 increased by 293 banks (26.49%) and it increased by 705 banks (50.39%) during 1993-2003. However, unfortunately the number of CCBs for the period 2002-03 to 2011-12 decreased by 396 banks (19.66%).

Deposits: From 1966-93, the recoveries mobilized by way of deposits by the CCBs have registered a phenomenal growth. In June 1967 the total deposits with these banks were around Rs.153 crores and by the year 1992-93 deposits increased to Rs.13531 crores. In 2002-03, the total deposits were Rs.100757 crores and by the year 2011-12 deposits increased to Rs.238521 crores. The deposits of these banks increased by Rs.10004 crores (6538.56%) in the period 1967-1993. The deposits of these banks increased by Rs.87226 crores (645%) in the period 1993-2003 and deposits of these banks increased by Rs.137764 crores (136.72%) in the 2011-12 in comparison of 2002-03.

Advances: In June 1967 the total advances of these banks amounted to Rs.167 crores and by the year 1992-93 advances increased to Rs.10132 crores. In 2002-03, the total advances amounted to Rs.64022 crores and by the year 2011-12, advances increased to Rs.158026 crores. The advances of these banks increased by Rs.9965 crores (5967.07%) in the period 1967-1993. The advances of these banks increased by Rs.53890 crores (531.88%) in the period 1993-2003 and advances of these banks increased by Rs.94004 crores (146.83%) in 2011-12 in comparison of 2002-03.

B.)Rural Co-operative Credit Institutions: UCBs have a single tier structure, while rural co-operatives have a complex structure. Rural co-operatives credit institutions have two distinct structure viz., the Short Term Co-operative Credit Structure (STCCS) and Long Term Co-operative Credit Structure (LTCCS).

- **The Short Term Co-Operative Credit Structure (STCCS):**

    It provides crop and other working capital loans primarily for a short period to farmers and rural artisans. The Short Term Co-operative Credit Structure is a three tier structure having State Co-operative Banks, Districts Central Co-operative Banks and Primary Agricultural Credit Societies. In each state, there is State Cooperative Bank at the apex level. In each district, there is a Central Cooperative Bank and at the base level, there are Primary Agricultural Credit Societies.

(a) PRIMARY AGRICULTURAL CREDIT SOCIETIES

PACS lie at the root of the co-operative credit structure of the country. They are at the local or base level. In rural areas, they cater to short and medium term credit needs of the farmers. They directly deal with the farmers. PACS is linked to a Central Co-operative Bank for its own requirements of finance, which in turn is linked to a State Co-operative Bank. Now in India PACS exist on an average one for six villages, this ensures mutual knowledge of the members who can exercise mutual control.

PACS operates at the village level and maintains direct contact with the farmers. The main functions PACS are to provide short and medium term credit to its members. It may supply agricultural and other production inputs and undertake marketing of agricultural produce. In addition to these, the co-operative may help in formulating and implementing a plan for agricultural production for the village and undertake such educative, advisory and welfare functions as the members might be willing to take up.

According to the committee on co-operative credit (1959), the credit society should undertake the following functions;

1) To associate itself with program of production

2) To lend adequate amount to its members for consumption purposes limited to their paying capacity.

3) To barrow adequate fund from the central financial agencies for helping the members adequately for the above purposes;

4) To protect the farmers from the clutches of money lenders and from the alienation of land and help them in effecting permanent improvement in their lands.

5) To attract local savings for share capital and fixed deposits.

6) To supervise use of loans (especially medium-term loans) and to see that they are paid punctually.

7) To distribute fertilizers, seeds, insecticides, agricultural implements etc., either on its own behalf or through agent;

8) To supply certain consumer goods in common demand such as kerosene; sugar etc.

9) To store the produce of the members till it is sold; to collect or purchase produce, where necessary on behalf of a consumer's society, marketing society or government.

10) To associate itself with programmers of economic and social welfare, for the village.

PACS raise their fund by way of share capital, membership fees, deposits of members and non-members, and loans from DCCBs and the government. The members who contributed to capital elect the president, chairman, secretary and other members of the managing committee among themselves. All elected bodies work on an honorary basis.

In the following table, an attempt has been made to study the performance of PACS at national level.

Table 1.2
PROGRESS OF PRIMARY AGRICULTURE CREDIT SOCIETIES
IN INDIA(2005-06 TO 2011-12)

(Amount in Crores)

Particulars	2005-06	2006-07	2007-08	2008-09	2009-10	2010-11	2011-12
No. of PACS	106384	93225	94950	95633	94647	93413	92432
Total Members	125197	125792	131530	132350	126419	121225	113596
Capital	5644	6138	6596	7007	7148	7551	8280
Reserve	3647	4900	4387	4888	5330	6904	7715
Owned Fund	9292	1103	10983	11805	12478	14455	15995
Deposits	19562	23484	25449	26245	35286	37238	50252
Borrowings	41017	43714	47847	48938	51763	54000	88835
Working Fund	73386	79958	88106	94584	135191	144221	160507
Loans & Advances Issued	42919	49612	57642	58786	74937	91303	107300
Loans & Advances Outstanding	51778	58620	6566	64044	76479	87767	91243
Demand	50979	54112	67292	84633	95496	90240	90747
Collection	35503	38360	43289	46697	55972	67543	66444
Balance of Overdue	15476	15752	24003	37936	39524	22697	24303
% of Over Due to Loan Outstanding	29.9	26.87	36.55	59.23	51.68	25.86	26.64
Total No. of Employees	241609	229007	278842	222173	215529	290540	208697
No.of Borrowers	46076	47910	51074	46219	59800	52388	44886

Source: NAFSCOB-(http://nafscob.org/basicdata/pacs-2012.pdf)

The above table reveals that number of PACS stood at 106384 at the end of the March 2006 declined to 92432 at the end of the March 2012. Capital and Reserve which constitutes as owned fund increased in all the years of the study period. The increased figure indicates PACS are moving towards self-reliance of the fund. Total deposits of PACS which were around Rs.19562 Crores as on 31 March 2006 increased to Rs.50252 Crores as on 31 March 2011. The increased performance in deposits indicates that PACS have increased trends in mobilizing the deposits. The percentage of over due to total loans outstanding, which is a rough indicator of the non-performing assets of PACS, witnesses a fluctuating trend in the study.

(b) DISTRICT CENTRAL CO-OPERATIVE BANKS

In the beginning of the formation of Primary Co-operative CreditSocieties (PACS), they could not function effectively without gainingfinancial support from an outside agency. Apart from this, they were in needof technical guidance and administrative support. At the same time, therewere some societies which have gained strength and possess surplus fund aswell as talents. As a precondition to get mutual help it became necessary thatall these primary societies form a federation for ensuring rational use of theirfund and provide a common place to meet and exchange of ideas and getco-operative experience. Thus the formation of DCCBs was in need for mutual help and it occupied middle level position in the three tier co-operative credit structure of the country.

PACS functioning in specified areas federated themselves into collective banking activities, giving birth to central co-operative banks with the prime objective to mobilize fund from urban outlets and divert the same to the village societies.

DCCBs are formed mainly with the objective of meeting the credit requirements of member societies. As an institution for helping the societies in times of need, they finance agricultural credit societies for production purposes, marketing societies for marketing operations, industrial societies for supply operations and other societies for working expenses. In short, the major objectives of DCCBs are to provide loans to affiliated societies, to act as a balancing Centre of finance for primary societies, to arrange for the supervision and control of the affiliated societies, to raise deposits from members and non-members, to convene conferences of the member societies and also prescribe uniform procedure for the working of primary societies, to open branches of the bank at important places with the permission of the Registrar of Co-operative Societies and to maintain and utilize state partnership.

Reserve Bank Standing Advisory Committee on Agricultural Credit and All India Rural Credit Survey Committee has expressed their view that there should be one district as an area of operation for DCCB. The norm for the area of operation of a DCCB would be most convenient to enable the bank to become a strong and powerful unit and to discharge its responsibilities towards the lower tiers in the co-operative credit structure sufficiently.

The main source of working fund is the share capital, reserve fund, deposits from members and public, surplus fund of the affiliated co-operative banks, loans from state bank of India, other commercial banks, National Bank for Agriculture and Rural Development, other co-operative banks and borrowings from the RBI, State Co-operative Bank, Government.

In the following table, an attempt has been made to study the performance of DCCBs at national level.

Table 1.3

PROGRESS OF DISTRICT CENTRAL CO-OPERATIVE BANKS IN INDIA (2005-06 TO 2011-12)

(RS.IN LAKHS)

Particulars	2005 -06	2006 -07	2007 -08	2008 -09	2009 -10	2010 -11	2011-12
NO OF D.C.C. BANKS	370	371	372	373	372	371	371
TOTAL MEMBERSHIP(NO.)	2267850	3264849	3396881	3528802	3975660	3146070	3659385
PAID UP CAPITAL	451147	509813	582923	607141	777653	725768	818892
TOTAL RESERVES	1408294	1550512	1643573	1780801	2013296	2069202	2292034
TOTAL DEPOSITS	8665222	9218136	10599372	12372182	14630314	16130882	17682238
TOTAL BORROWINGS	2320213	2794060	3053334	2847764	3035483	3910116	5048131
TOTAL LOANS ISSUED	6041849	7670381	8722909	8802869	11052929	13775717	16255432
TOTAL LOANS OUTSTANDINGS	6548656	8545975	9597423	9720682	10499715	12279548	14476115
TOTAL DEMAND	5722694	6494337	7412146	8088960	8889616	10611864	12437600
TOTAL COLLECTION	3909087	4355755	4658268	5444608	6513284	7706922	9716686
BALANCE(OVERDUES)	1813607	2138582	2753878	2644352	2376332	2904942	2720914
NUMBER OF EMPLOYEES	105885	91768	90035	89259	87554	87928	85996

Source: NAFSCOB-(http://nafscob.org)

The above table indicates that the number of DCCBs during the study period slightly improved. The number of DCCBs found during the year 2005-06 was 370. This number increased to 371 during 2008-09. Further number of DCCBs found declined to 372 and decreased to 371 during 2010-11 and 2011-12.

The deposits mobilized by DCCBs in India showed Rs.8665222 lakhs in 2005-06 which was increased to Rs.17682238 lakhs in 2011-12. Increased amount of deposits were found almost double during the study period which indicates DCCBs is able to attract various kinds of deposits from individuals and institutions.The amount of borrowings of DCCBs in India showed increasingtrend during the study period except 2008-09. The increase in borrowings shows that DCCBs dependencyon borrowings along with the deposits for their lending operation. Releasing loans and advances increased every year in the study period. Increase in loans and advance shows increased efficiencies of DCCBs distribution of loan and advances. But outstanding loans and advance figure shows that DCCBs inefficiency in recovery of loans and advance.

(c) STATE CO-OPERATIVE BANKS

State Co-operative Bank (StCB) means the principle society in a state which is registered or deemed to be registered under the Co-operative Societies Act, 1912, or any other law for the time being in force in India related to co-operative societies. StCBs are formed by federating all District Central Co-Operative Banks (DCCBs) in a particular state. If there is no such society in a state, the State Government may declare one or

25

more co-operative societies carrying on business in that state to be a State Co-operative Bank (or Banks).

The StCB is also called as Apex Bank which stands at the top of the credit structure in each State. It furnishes finance to the central co-operative banks in order to enable them to help in promoting the leading activities of the primary credit societies. Thus, StCBs serve as the final link between the money market and the co-operative sector. The StCBs not only finances but also controls and regulates the working of central co-operative banks in each State.

The StCB is interested in helping the co-operative credit movement and also in promoting other co-operative ventures and in extending the principles of co-operation. In the absence of DCCBs in a state, StCB may give direct financial assistance to the primary credit societies. The main features of StCBs are they serves as the balancing Centre in the state, organize provision of credit for credit worthy farmers, carry out banking business and leads the co-operative movement as a leader of the co-operatives in the state.

All apex banks have been given the status of a "Scheduled Bank". It acts as a link between central co-operative banks, primary co-operative societies and RBI from which it borrows. They accept deposit from member societies, non-members, individuals and institutions for their working capital. Special deposits are accepted from local boards, educational institutions and municipalities. Borrowings constitute the major source of working fund for StCBs and it is borrowed from Reserve Bank of India, the state Government, the State Bank of India and subsidiaries. The state co-operative bank enjoys an overdraft facility with the State Bank of India. Sometimes, StCBs borrow from one another. But borrowings from the Reserve Bank of India are the main source of loans to StCBs. State Co-operative Banks do not lend fund directly to farmers. Funds are sanctioned to Central Co-operative Banks and they further distribute to primary credit societies. All these societies, in turn, lend the fund to borrowers. The lending operations of StCBs cover loans, cash credit and Overdraft facilities made available to member banks. A certain limit is fixed for each central co-operative bank, up to which it can borrow from State Co-operative Banks. Short-term loans are given for a period of less than 12 months and medium-term loans for less than three year.

The main source of working fund of StCB is the share capital, reserve fund, deposits from members, surplus fund of the affiliated central co-operative bank's, loans from state bank of India, other commercial banks, National Bank for Agriculture and Rural Development, inter bank borrowings and borrowings from the RBI.

In the following table, an attempt has been made to study the performance of State Co-operative Banks at national level.

Table 1.4
PROGRESS OF STATE CO-OPERATIVE BANKS IN INDIA
(2005-06 TO 2011-12)

(RS.IN LAKHS)

Particulars	2005 -06	2006 -07	2007 -08	2008 -09	2009 -10	2010 -11	2011-12
No. of Co-operative Banks	30	31	31	31	31	31	31
Owned fund	843675	958158	994796	1015443	1039239	1162543	1317526
Deposits	4767221	4846961	5628692	7131507	8483773	8166424	8665296
Borrowings	1687166	2215024	2160638	2158221	2363252	3260686	4271362
Loans and Advances issued	4880354	4706898	5331376	5186621	5978395	6848063	8152345
Loans and Advances Outstanding	3896099	4667581	4910142	4620084	4910353	6508182	7563187
Total Demand	2438956	2770663	3179454	3960751	3454955	3227299	4791169
Total Collection	2103349	2403133	2633473	3617093	3171662	2979191	4606103
Balances(Overdues)	335607	367530	545981	343658	283293	248108	185066
Total Number Of Employees	14742	14748	14857	14635	13781	13461	13288

Source: NAFSCOB-(http://nafscob.org)

The above table shows that there were 30 StCBs in 2005-06 and then it remained 31 during the study period from 2006-07 to 2011-12.The StCBs owned fund in India increased in all the years of the study Period. StCBs owned funds were increased from Rs.843675 lakhs in2005-06 to Rs.1317526lakhs in 2011-12.It indicates the improved efficiencyof generating internal resources of finance which helps StCBs to get self-reliance of fund for fund mobilisation.

The deposits in StCBs stood at Rs.4767221 lakhs in 2005-06 and increased to Rs.8483773 lakhs in 2009-10, it shows that progress made by StCBs in deposit mobilization. It was slightly declined to Rs.8166424 lakhs in 2010-11 and increased to Rs.8665296 lakhs in 2011-12. The total borrowings of StCBs found fluctuating during the study period. It stood around Rs.1687166 lakhs during 2005-06 which increased to Rs.4271362 lakhs during 2011-12.The increase in borrowings shows that StCBs dependency on borrowings along with the deposits for their lending operation.

As a major part of the loans from StCBs being apex level institutions go towards the lower tier institutions in short-term credit structure, a decline in the growth of loans from StCBs implies reduced lending to the lower tier institutions and increased in the growth of loans and advances indicates increased lending to the lower tier institutions. The increase in loans and advance shows that increased efficiencies of bank in distribution of loan and advances.

- **The Long Term Co-operative Credit Structure (LTCCS):**

Indian farmers need three types of credit, viz. short-term, medium term and long-term. Their short-term and medium-term credit requirements are fulfilled by the cooperative banking institutions like PACSs, CCBs and SCBs. The ordinary cooperative credit structure cannot afford to lock up their funds for long periods. In view of this, Land Development Banks (LDBs) were organized for providing long term credit to agriculturists. The long-term credit requirements of Indian farmers are fulfilled by the Land Development Banks for buying pump sets, tractors and for other development purposes.

The LT co-operative credit structure has only two tiers, one at the state level and the other at the taluka/tehsil level. Some states have unitary structure with the state level banks operating through their own branches.

The long term co-operative credit structure consists of the State Co-operative Agriculture and Rural Development Banks (SCARDBs) and Primary Co-operative Agriculture and Rural Development Banks (PCARDBs) which are affiliated to SCARDBs. There are total 19 SCARDBs of which 10 have Federal Structure, 7 have Unitary Structure and 2 have Mixed Structure incorporating both the unitary and federal systems (Himachal Pradesh and West Bengal). An integrated structure providing all types of agricultural credit (both short term and long term) under 'single window' credit system is present in Andhra Pradesh. In the North-Eastern Region, only three states (Assam, Manipur and Tripura) have LT structure. Generally, the states which do not have the LT structure, separate sections of the State Co-operative Banks look after long term credit needs together with other Rural Financial Institutions (RFIs) i.e. branches of Regional Rural Banks and rural/semi-urban branches of Commercial Banks.

❖ **Working Capital**

The working capital of LDBs is raised from:

☐Share Capital

☐Deposits and Borrowings

☐Borrowings from State Bank of India, Commercial Banks and
   State Cooperative Bank

☐Long-term debentures.

Table 1.5
The Long Term Co-operative Credit Structure at a Glance- 31-03-2012

No. of SCARDBs	19
No. of PCARDBs	714
No. of Branches of PCARDBs	1,056
No. of Branches of Unitary SCARDBs	761
Annual Lending	Rs.17,603.42 Cr
Total Membership	13.65 Million

Source: Report on trend and progress of banking in India of RBI.

1.7 Concept of Citizen Co-operative banks (CCBs)

As the name suggests, a bank operating in urban areas on the basis of co-operative principles is known as an Urban (Citizen) Co-operative Bank. There was not clearly defined concept of Citizen co-operative bank before 1939. Initially Citizen co-operative banks were organized as credit societies in India and later converted into urban banks. It was the Mehta Bhansali Committee (1939) which made the first attempt to define a Citizen Co-operative Bank. Subsequently in 1966, when banking laws were made applicable to co-operative banks, Provision of section 5(CCV) of Banking Regulation Act 1949 defined a Citizen Co-operative Bank as a primary Agricultural Credit Society. " Citizen Co-operative Bank means a society registered under act and doing the business of banking, as defined in clause(b) of section 5 of the Banking Regulation Act "From the above definition the characteristics are as under.

1. The primary object or principal business of which is the transaction of banking business
2. The paid up share capital and reserves of which are not less than one lack Rupees;
3. The bye laws of which do not permit admission of any other Co-operative society as a member.

Provided that this sub-clause shall not apply to the admission of a co-operative bank as a members by reason of such a co-operative bank subscribing to the share capital of such co-operative Society out of funds provided by the State Government for the purpose.

In short, Citizen Co-operative Banks are Primary Co-operative Banks organized on Co-operative basis, operating in metropolitan, urban and semi-urban areas to cater the needs of specific types or groups of members pertaining to certain class of community, small scale industrial units, trade, professions, etc. They are of two types:
a) Unit banking type and
b) Branch banking type

Besides providing main banking service to their customers, they also provide various other banking and subsidiary services to their customers and have developed a nice market for them to survive and thrive.

❖ Objectives of the Citizen Co-operative Bank:

The Citizen Co-operative Banks are generally considered as "Small People's Bank" and they are organized for promoting thrift and co-operation among the lower and middle strata of the society. The objectives of the Citizen Co-operative Banks are summarized in two categories, which are as follow:

[A] Principal objectives:
1. to promote thrift, self-help and mutual co-operation among the members,

2. to mobilize resources i.e. to borrow funds form members and non-members to utilize for giving loans to their members,
3. to provide credit to the members at reasonable rates for productive purposes,
4. to undertake collection of bills drawn, cheques, drafts, etc. accepted or endorsed by members and approved constituents, to remit funds and to discount cheques and bills of approved members subject to rules and by laws on their behalf,
5. to arrange for safe custody of valuables and documents of members and constituents, and
6. to provide all other banking and subsidiary services.

[B] Subsidiary Objectives:

1. to give possible help and necessary guidance to traders, artisans etc. who are members of the bank,
2. to do every kind of trust and agency business and particularly do the work of investment of funds, sale of properties and of recovery and acceptance of money,
3. to undertake every kind of banking and sharaffi business and also give bank guarantee and letters of credit on behalf of members.

❖ Problems & Prospects Of CCBs :-

CCBs were setup with the objective of promoting saving habits amongst the middle-income group of the urban population 2004 is golden jubilee of Citizen co-operative banks celebrated by govt. of Gujarat. During the 100 years of their inception they have attracted considerable attention and large number of them has shown creditable performance but fair number of them have simultaneously shown discernible signs of weakness too because of the problems they could not overcame some important factors, Which are barriers to the progress of the CCBs are as given below.

1. Dual Control:-

A major problem faced by CCBs is the duality of control by the State Government and the RBI. The CCBs are supervised by RBI and also issued for license while regarding administrations like, registration, administration constitution and administration and selection etc. This had negative impact on the functioning of the CCBs. Duality in command hampers effective supervision. The Narsimhan committee suggests removing dual control system which is affected to CCBs.

2. Limited Area of Operations:-

The CCBs have to function within restricted framework in the context of mobilization of deposits. The need for heavy industrial advances and trade finance for industrial units as well as for commercial enterprises is here but the CCBs are not able to meet with it is they have to serve as per the RBI directives. But to survive in the competitive world the CCBs should enhance their area of operation and start providing loans as per local needs.

3. Violation of Prudential Financial Norms:-

It is found that many CCBs Violate norms governing advances. Top officials of the banks receive loans without documents. The failure of Visangar Co-operative Bank (Mehsana) and Madhavpura Mercantile Co-operative Bank (A'bad) are the example of violation of prudential norms. The CCBs must adopt a system of internal audit and inspection of branches and department, the RBI should follow strict supervision and to stop such malpractices.

4. Poor Management: -

The necessity of the financial institution has a good corporate financial management and articles. The Madhavrav committee insisted to appoint two directors who are professional or experience persons. But in CCBs directors are politician or illiterate. Due to this reasons management of the CCBs are poor. The RBI advise to directors about it by letter dated 05-04-2002.

5. Poor Quality Services: -

The services of the CCBs are not significant enough in terms of quality and have failed to attract deposits from individuals and institutions other than the co-operative sectors. Hence they should try to improve the quality of services by providing required facilities like waiting space; customer information counter, complain box, banking information chart, easy accessibility to higher officials at the banking promises ect. At the same time they should maintain good customer relations and keep positive attitude towards customer. Besides this; they should start providing door to door services.

6. Lack of Modernization: -

In today's world of technological advancement, still manual form of work followed in some of the CCBs which cause delay and increase operational cost. Most of the CCBs failed to provide service through use of modern techno log except some CCBs. It has become inevitable now on part of the CCBs to have computerized system of banking and adopt latest banking technique like ATM, Credit Card, Internet Banking, Branch Banking, Tele Banking etc.

7. Increasing Overdoes: -

The CCBs suffer from dangerously. Low or weak quality of loans assets and highly unsatisfactory recovery of loans, which enhance the proportion of overdue. Due to this situation, CCBs must have to develop a separate recovery department for quick recoveries.

8. Political Interference: -

Political interference in affairs of the CCBs leads to faulty lending and poor recovery. It compels, to pressure on the banks to provide loan to parties whose repaying capacity is doubtful. Visanagar co-operative bank is a example of this situation. Though banks take to legal action against the defaulter it often interferes by putting an end or postponing such an action. Hence political interferes is damage to CCBs administration.

9. Staff Problems and prospects: -

The CCBs have not trained and professional staff. The CCBs do not select staff on professional basis. External pressures are a cause of untrained and low standard staff which directly affect on quality work. At least appointment of chief executive officer (like Manager or Managing director) should be made on professional lines and provide training to untrained or fresh staff members or employees.

10. Some Other Problems of CCBs are as under: -
- ❖ Low capital adequacy ratio etc.
- ❖ Lack of transparency in financial statement.
- ❖ The Balance sheet of most of CCBs are not finalized in time due to non-completion of audit purpose.
- ❖ Lack of planning and co-ordination.
- ❖ Lack of standardization in data reported by ratio etc.

1.8   Growth & Development of CCBs in Gujarat

Gujarat holds second position in the development of the CCBs in India and is known as the "Mother Land" of the co-operative as the first co-operative body of India was formed in 1889 in Baroda named "ANYONYA SAHKARI MANDLI " Similarly the first registered CCBs of India named "THE SURAT PEOPLE'S CO-OPERATIVE BANK LTD." was established in Surat city of Gujarat on March 1922. That was the dawn of Co-operative banking. Inspired by the success of this bank, similar CCBs developed very fast in other parts of Gujarat State. By the year ended 31st March 2008, out of 1721 CCBs of India, 274 CCBs alone provided service in Gujarat having a network of about 601 branches spread over 18 districts of the state. The progress of the CCBs in Gujarat is shown in the table 1.6 below:

Table 1.6
PROGRESS OF CITIZEN CO-OPERATIVE BANKS IN GUJARAT

(Rs. In Crores)

Sr. No.	Particulars	31/03/2000	31/03/2001	31/03/2002	31/03/2003	31/03/2004	31/03/2005	31/03/2006	31/03/2007	31/03/2008
1	No. of Banks	341	350	351	351	352	306	295	293	274
2	No. of Branches	728	800	762	779	736	690	603	624	601
3	Deposits	16703	17791	16506	16345	15894	14804	14353	15006	15983
4	Share Capital	363	418	436	451	425	405	395	442	474
5	Total Reserves	2271	2487	2968	3332	5053	4247	3632	3723	3799
6	Working Capital	21120	23520	21633	22833	22087	20905	N.A.	19022	19801
7	Advances	10468	11864	11004	11304	9825	9198	8420	9084	9413
8	Profit	294	273	241	213	201	147	137	131	178
9	No. of Members	3242829	3303662	3245699	3321357	3251276	3178360	2862866	3037879	3095742
10	No. of Depositors	11009558	11634435	10998814	10641234	10284650	11541410	N.A.	8966502	8855443
11	No. of Borrowers	997619	1091005	1006030	935198	804860	757716	N.A.	626483	631524
12	No. of Staff Members	17393	17473	17190	16692	15538	14209	12443	12628	11905

Source : Statistical Hand Book – 2008 – GUCBS Federation, Ahmedabad, Pg. 11.

It is apparent form the above table that the CCBs in Gujarat have recorded commendable achievement in the entire sphere of banking operations. Further more, out of the 53 scheduled CCBs by the end of March 2008, 29 of them were registered in Gujarat itself, having deposits of more than 100 crores. In addition, 14 Mahila CCBs also marked a regional imbalance in Gujarat as out of 274 CCBs, about 219 are located in 9 districts of Gujarat, viz. Ahmedabad, Kheda, Baroda, Mehsana, Surat, Panchmahal, Sabarkantha, Bhavnagar and Rajkot - as shown in table as under:

Table 1.7

STATEMENT OF DISTRICT WISE STATISTICAL DATA OF CITIZEN CO-OPERATIVE BANKS AS ON 31/03/2008

Table 1.7

STATEMENT OF DISTRICT WISE STATISTICAL DATA OF CITIZEN CO-OPERATIVE BANKS AS ON 31/03/2008

(Rs. In Lakhs)

Sr. No.	District	Total Banks	No. of Branches	Paid up Share Capital	Deposits	Reserves and Other Funds	Advances	Investments	Working Capital	Profits	No. of Members	No. of Depositors	No. of Borrowers	No of Staff
1	Ahmedabad	48	171	10878.99	490599	126741.4	306904.1	230564.6	543144.9	5209.25	481114	1885696	118159	2839
2	Kheda	32	7	1523.07	55354.55	20853.17	26511.65	45170.66	85071.4	384.87	214417	491673	34323	551
3	Baroda	31	54	3519.96	92704.67	24649.37	50385.14	55859.88	126455.1	1154.11	300496	747216	49879	931
4	Mehsana	31	76	6202.79	166596.8	28708.13	99369.45	84506.33	171547.4	1712.58	296695	1007053	55134	1100
5	Surat	22	98	7763.62	270908.3	27340.03	152097.3	146909.2	352471.3	3215.74	320369	1207458	67972	2123
6	Panchmahal	19	10	2118.5	46256.38	11238.91	25651.19	28534.55	64642.58	335.42	152767	388652	32578	405
7	Sabarkantha	14	7	1039.78	35036.83	7247.43	19789.44	21914.56	48444.28	282.99	111606	327814	32528	363
8	Bhavnagar	11	13	1577.77	27927.13	13506.37	20730.19	21528.76	51923.7	158.69	129973	351628	38027	436
9	Rajkot	11	67	5057.56	217614.1	47659.77	132411.7	71602.92	276580	2354.32	565907	1220432	75003	1158
10	Bharuch	9	1	626.28	12594.55	3881.94	7050.19	7488.94	18310.2	186.06	100121	110055	12795	132
11	Junagadh	9	15	590.03	15878.6	2790.51	8832.21	9424.16	21097.7	91.31	34660	159685	13835	238
12	Banaskantha	6	23	782.51	25276.36	4550.08	15471.92	12899.56	32828.91	242.87	66072	150417	20961	365
13	Amreli	6	1	507.33	9882.71	1725.58	6414.6	4481.08	13247.74	189.02	25927	59104	23325	123
14	Surendranagar	6	14	799.24	15752.64	3452.66	10392.07	5002.75	18521.94	29.79	131618	178256	14314	276
15	Jamnagar	6	10	2060.14	42247.58	6706.16	24633.8	18888.28	55480.33	1219.4	32716	166106	9290	232
16	Kutch	5	17	654.27	33461.06	9473.72	11104.91	29408.23	45367.74	605.14	21042	137707	7544	297
17	Valsad	5	5	582.01	11696.55	1090.62	6463.64	7302.93	15254.09	133.42	51321	70715	6744	135
18	Gandhinagar	3	12	1122.3	28564.71	8237.6	17079.32	17544.82	39713.76	249.46	58921	195776	19113	201
	TOTAL	274	601	47406.15	1598353	379853.5	941292.8	819032.2	1980103	17745.44	3095742	8855443	631524	601

Source: Statistical Hand Book – 2008 – GUCBS Federation, Ahmedabad Pg. 12-13

In spite of regional imbalance, it can be said that the CCBs in Gujarat have established themselves as an integral part of the state economy by providing effective service to weaker section of the semi urban population in their respective areas of operations. During the last ten years, these banks have been moving towards modernization of banking operations through computerized working, namely tele banking, mobile banking, automatic teller machine (ATM) etc. and there by is helping in the development of the Indian economy.

1.9 Development of CCBs in North Gujarat.

Kalol is known as the birth place of the CCBs of North Gujarat. First registered CCB named The Kalyan Co-operative Bank LTD. Was established in 1949 at Kalol. However the large numbers of banks were established after the year 1960. The Progress of the CCBs in North Gujarat took place slowly and steady. No any bank was registered in north Gujarat before 1947. While during the 1949 to 1962 only ten CCBs were established in north Gujarat. But majority of CCBs were registered during the 1963 to 1990 i.e. around 42 new CCBs were established in 25 years and after 1990, seven CCBs were established. During last 10 years by the year ended 31st March 2004, there were 60 CCBs having 105 branches, Rs.473 crores owned funds, Rs.1372 crores deposits, Rs.1151 advances, Rs.2273 crores working capital and 2197 No. of staff-members in the north Gujarat. The comparative position of the CCBs in India, Gujarat and North Gujarat on March 31st 2004 is shown in table 1.8.

Table 1.8
Position of CCBs as on 31st March 2003 (Rs. In Crores)

Particulars	India *	Gujarat *	North Gujarat* *	Gujarat:N.Gujrat
No. of Reproby CCBs	2104	352	60	17%
Owned Funds	18236	5478	473	8.63%
Deposits	100000	15894	1372	8.60%
Advances	65000	9825	1151	11.71%
Working Capital	121556	22087	2273	10.29%

Source:- *Statistical handbook of 2004 GUCBs Federation A'bad
　　　　**Calculation based on annual Report of 60 CCBs

1.10　Conclusion

Now, It is very much clear that co-operative banks have very much importance in national development. Without the help of co-operative banks, millions of people in India would be lacking the much needed financial support. Co-operative banks take active part in local communities and local development with a stronger commitment and social responsibilities. These banks are best vehicles for taking banking to doorsteps of common men, unbanked people in urban and rural areas. Their presence in the social, economic and democratic structure of the country is essential to bring about harmonious development and that perhaps is the best justification for nurturing them and strengthening their base. These banks are sure to win in the race because they are from the people, by the people and of the people.

References

1. K.R. Kulkarni, and V.L. Mehta, "Theory & Practice of Co-operation in India and Abroad" Bombay, Co-operator's Book Depot. (1958) p.1.

2. C.B. Mamoria, and R.D. Saksena, "Co-operation in India" Allahabad, Kitab Mahal. (1973) p.65.

3. G.S. Kamat, "New Dimensions of Cooperative Management" Mumbai, Himalaya Publishing House. (1978) p.1.

4. C.R. Fay, "Co-operation at Home and Abroad" Vol II. 1908-1938, London, Staples Press Limited. (1948) p.5.

5. Eleanor M. Hough; Horace Plunkeet,; and K. Madhava Das, "The Co-operative Movement in India" Bombay, Oxford University Press. (1959) p.40

6. H. Calvert, "The Law and Practice of Co-operation" Calcutta, Thacker, Spink & Co., (1933)p.11.

7. Campbell Dennis, "Comaprative Law Year Book of International Business" Vol. 31, Wolters Kluwer, (2009) p. 282.

8. O.R. Krishnaswami, "Fundamentals of Co-operation" New Delhi, Sultan Chand & Company Ltd. (1978) p.7.

9. *Ibid.,*p.10.

10. *Ibid.,*p.11.

11. G.S. Kamat, *op. cit.,* p.12.

12. K.K. Tamini, "Cooperative Organisation and Management" New Delhi, WAFM, Farmers Welfare Trust Society.(1976) p.4.

13. C.B. Mamoria, and R.D. Saksena, *op. cit.,* p.110.

14. R.D. Bedi, "Theory, History and Practice of Co-operation" Meerut, Loyal Book Depot.(1971) P.81.

15. *Ibid.*

16. C.B. Mamoria, and R.D. Saksena, *op. cit.,* p.110.

17. R.D. Bedi, *op. cit.,* p.73.

18. R.D. Bedi, *op. cit.,* p.72.

19. C.B. Mamoria, and R.D. Saksena, *op. cit.,* p.109.

20. R.D. Bedi, *op. cit.,* p.180.

21. R.D. Bedi, *op. cit.,* p.188.

22. Website:www.Co-op.Societies_Russian history.encyclopedia.com.htm.2004.

23. R.D. Bedi, *op. cit.,* pp.124-125

24. Miyahara Yukinori, "The Development and Role of Co-op Societies in Japan-Special Reference to Agricultural Co-operatives". Edited by Chinchankar P.Y.

& Namjoshi M.V., "Co-operation and the Dynamics of Change", Bombay, Somaiya Pub. (1977). P.194.

25. "History of Consumer Co-op Movement in Japan", (http://jccu.coop/eng/aboutus/history.php), Assessed on 2014.

26. "The Agricultural Co-operatives and Farming Reforms in Japan (1 & 2)", The Tokyo Foundation, Jan.14, 2009.

27. R.D. Bedi, *op. cit.,* pp.155-159.

28. http://en.wikipedia.org/wiki/Danish_cooperative_movement

Chapter-2
Conceptual Framework of Financial Analysis

2.1   Introduction

2.2   Concept and need of Financial Analysis

2.3   Objectives of Financial Analysis

2.4   Significance of Financial Analysis

2.5   Process of Analysis of financial statements

2.6   Tools and Techniques of Financial Analysis

2.7   Precautions in financial Statement Analysis

2.8   Conclusion

2.1   Introduction

Financial analysis or analysis of financial statements, viz., balance sheet and profit and loss account aimed at diagnosing the liquidity, profitability, productivity, activity and financial condition of a business concern. Satisfactory diagnosis can rarely be made on the basis of such an information which are included in these financial statements alone because figure are dumb, But, if they are analysed, they get a tongue and therefore they help the bank management and other interested parties in assessing the financial adventure of a bank.

2.2   Concept and need of Financial Analysis

Figures are dumb. However, they may tell a vivid story of financial adventures of an enterprise, if analyzed. Financial analysis is a scientific evaluation of the profitability and financial strength of any business concern. "Financial statement analysis attempts to unveil the meaning and significance of the items composed in profit and loss account and balance sheet so as to assist the management in the formulation of sound operating financial policies." [1]

A great deal of knowledge can be had about business performance and financial position through an appraisal of financial statements. Financial analysis is the process of making an analytical study of the financial and operational data contained in the profit and loss account and the balance sheet of a given concern and thereby satisfying the information needs of the internal and external users of such data. "An analysis of both these statements gives a comprehensive understanding of business operations and their impact on the financial health." [2]

"The appraisal or analysis of financial statements spotlights the significant facts and relationship concerning managerial performance, corporate efficiency, financial strength and weakness and credit worthiness that would have otherwise been buried in a maze of detail." [3]

Thus, financial analysis is a preliminary step towards the financial evaluation of the results drawn by the analysts. The analysis of such results is made by the management for decision making process.

Financial analysis is the end of that continuous flow of accounting cycle which starts from classification, Recording, summarizing, presentation and analysis of data and ends with the interpretation of the results obtained from such an analysis.

Thus, "the analysis and interpretation of financial statements are an attempt to determine the meaning and significance of the financial statement data so that a forecast may be made of the prospects for future earnings, ability to pat interest and debt maturities (both current and long-term) and profitability of a sound dividend policy." [4]

These statements are valuable in the sense that they depict hoe the financial data of the related enterprise fit into the fabric of its accounting system. It aids in decision making to various users interested in the financial status and operating results of the business. According to Moore, "Financial analysis is a process synthesis and summarization of erative data embodied in the financial statements with view to get an insight into the operative activities of a business enterprise." [5]

"It is a technique of xraying the financial position as well as the progress of the company."

As stated earlier, the major and most significant financial statements of a business concern are the profit and loss account and the balance sheet.

A careful examination of profit and loss account throws ample light on the operating efficiency, inventory management, control over indirect overheads and dividend policies perused by the concern. Moreover a study of the major individual items of a statement in relation to some other items of other statement will measure the activity and the profitability of the enterprise. As both the major financial statements are interrelated, the analysis of only either of them is devoid of the purpose.

2.3   Objectives of Financial Analysis

Analysis of financial statements is an attempt to assess the efficiency and performance of an enterprise. Thus, the analysis and interpretation of financial statements is very essential to measure the efficiency, profitability, financial soundness and future prospects of the business units. Financial analysis serves the following purposes:

a) Measuring the profitability

The main objective of a business is to earn a satisfactory return on the funds invested in it. Financial analysis helps in ascertaining whether adequate profits are being earned on the capital invested in the business or not. It also helps in knowing the capacity to pay the interest and dividend.

b) Indicating the trend of Achievements

Financial statements of the previous years can be compared and the trend regarding various expenses, purchases, sales, gross profits and net profit etc. can be ascertained. Value of assets and liabilities can be compared and the future prospects of the business can be envisaged.

c) Assessing the growth potential of the business

The trend and other analysis of the business provide sufficient information indicating the growth potential of the business.

d) Comparative position in relation to other firms

The purpose of financial statements analysis is to help the management to make a comparative study of the profitability of various firms engaged in similar businesses. Such comparison also helps the management to study the position of their firm in respect of sales, expenses, profitability and utilizing capital, etc.

e) Assess overall financial strength

The purpose of financial analysis is to assess the financial strength of the business. Analysis also helps in taking decisions, whether funds required for the purchase of new machines and equipment are provided from internal sources of the business or not if yes, how much? and also to assess how much funds have been received from external sources.

f) Assess solvency of the firm

The different tools of an analysis tell us whether the firm has sufficient funds to meet its short term and long term liabilities or not.

2.4   Significance of Financial Analysis

The significance and requirement of financial analysis rise from the viewpoint of all live participants who are interested in the routine of the unit. Various parties like management, investors, creditors, government, employees and research scholars are interested in analysis of financial statements. These statements supply a valuable information regarding p's- progress, position and prospectus of the company to the above mentioned parties. An unbiased and scientific analysis provides clues to the progress and financial position of a business enterprise. As such, the importance of the analysis of the financial statements has been discussed for various parties in the following pages:

1. Importance to Management

Financial analysis plays a vital role in providing such information to the management, which it needs for planning, decision making and control e.g. operational analysis provides gross margin, operating expense analysis and profit margin. Asset management outlines asset turnover, working capital under inventory turnover, accounts receivable and payable. Profitability position shows return on assets, Earning before interest and tax (EBIT) and return on assets. Gresternberg stated that, "Management can measure the effectiveness of its own policies and decisions, determine the advisability of adopting new policies and procedures and documents to owners as a result of their managerial efforts." Thus, management should examine a great deal of information in the context of various resources placed at the disposal of an undertaking.

2. Importance to Investors

An investor is primarily concerned with the safety of their investment and the ability of the company to earn profit. By analyzing the financial statements the prospective investor can take investment decision.

3. Importance to Creditors

"To the creditor, they act as a magic eye highlighting the credit worthiness i.e. assurance whether the company will honour obligations as and when they mature."[6]

4. Importance to Government

Government have significance of financial analysis of an individual organisation or industry as a whole by the means of various taxes, revenues, financial assistance, sanctioning subsidy to a unit or industry as well as price fixing policies frame outlines. The key role of financial analysis for the government lies in planning, decision making and control process.

5. Importance to Employees and Trade Unions

Employees are resources of the company and are interested to know the financial position and profits of the company. Generally, they analyse by the comparison between past and present performance, profit margin and cash flow of the company. Trade unions are interested to know the data of financial performance pertaining to their demands for increase in wages, salaries, facilities and social welfare.

6. Importance to Society and Others

Society and Others are including in external environment of the company and every business organisation has a greater responsibility towards society. In this context, performance appraisal should be appraised through various types of elements such as customers, investors, media, credit institutions, labour bureaus, taxation authorities, economists are interested for the appraisal of a business organisation. The society as a whole also looks forward to know about the social performance i.e. environmental obligations, social welfare, etc.

2.5   Process of Analysis of Financial Statements

"The process of analysis of financial statements involves the compilation, comparison and study of financial data and the preparation, study and interpretation of measuring devices such as ratios, trends and percentages."[7]

The initial step in this direction is the reorganization and rearrangement of the entire financial data as embodied in the financial statements. By such reclassification, the profit and loss account and the balance sheet are completely recast and presented in condensed form, entirely different from their original shape. A heap of financial data is thus reduced to a simple, analytical and standard form. The next step is the establishment of significant relationships between the individual components of profit and loss account and balance sheet through the application of tool of financial analysis. Finally, the significance of comparative data obtained by applying by tools of financial analysis is evaluated. It requires establishment of standards with which the comparative data can be measured and evaluated. The standards so established guide the analyst in understanding the sound as well as unsound relationship as reflected by comparative data. The relative magnitude is judged in the light of these standards. A probe is then made in the deviation which portrays the financial and operating policies perused by the management during the accounting period. Specific conclusions arrived at as a result of financial analysis are presented in the form of a report which highlights the financial situation. However, precision in the results of financial analysis depends upon the skill, judgment and experience of the analyst.

2.6   Tools and Techniques of Financial Analysis

Financial statements are only the means of providing general information regarding operational results and financial position of business enterprise. Financial statements convey only information about the financial position and profitability of the business in absolute figures. But figures in their original form do not convey any meaningful information and are not useful in financial analysis. Financial analysis is a multipurpose and multidimensional technique which involves a systematic and careful examination of information contained in the financial statement for a certain period. To make financial analysis more meaningful the following accounting techniques are used by the analysts:

1) Comparative Financial Statement Analysis
2) Common Size Statement Analysis
3) Trend Analysis
4) Ratio Analysis
5) Fund Flow Analysis
6) Break Even Analysis

1. Comparative Financial Statement Analysis: -

Comparative financial statements are statements of financial position of a concern so designed as to facilitate comparison of different accounting variables and thereby draw useful conduciveness. According to the M.R. Agrawal, "Comparative financial statements are those statements which summarize and present related accounting data for a number of years incorporating therein the changes (absolute or relative or both) in individual item.[8]

In these statements, the financial data for two or more years are placed and presented in adjacent columns. So that it may provide a true perspective in order to facilitate period comparison. It is also comparative financial statements are usually prepared with special columns indicating absolute data for each of the period and changes in it terms of rupees as well as in terms of percentages. The comparative financial statements is to ascertain the changes accruing year by year in each item of assets, liabilities and net worth shown in the financial statements of a business firm and whether such changes are favorable or adverse. Thus it focuses on the trends and direction of changes in different items of financial statements.

2. Common Size Statement Analysis: -

Financial statements that depict financial data in the shape of vertical percentages are known as common size statements. A common size statement is used as an important by converting absolute figures into percentage. Thus expressing each monetary item of the financial statement as a percentage of some total of which that item is a part, transforms a financial statement, what is referred as, "Common size statement include common size balance sheet and common size profit and loss account". In short common size statements are those in which figures reported in financial statement are converted in to percentage to some common base, which equals to 100. On the basis of common size statement, common size analysis can be done which facilitates comparison between amounts in the same statement and also between similar expenses in successive statement and further, enables the analyst to measure the relationship of each item within the statement. The ratio that each item bears to the total is ascertained by dividing the individual money amount by the total amount as contained in the statement and multiplying the quotient by 100. In vertical analysis, the common size statement are used for inter firm comparison of firms and relevant industry, while in horizontal analysis financial statement of different years are converted into common size statements and trend is analyzed. Comparison of common size statement over a number of years would highlight the relative changes in each group of expenses, assets and liabilities; while comparison of common size statement of two or more enterprises will assist in corporate evaluation and ranking.

3. Trend Analysis: -

A study based on trend percentage is known as trend analysis. Trend analysis indicates the trend of progress during past several years. Trend percentages are helpful in making a comparative study of financial statements for several years as it indicates increase or decrease in an item along with the magnitude of change in percentage. According to R. A. Kennedy and S. Y. Mc Mullen, " For the purpose of financial appraisal, an effective use of financial ratios can be made by observing the behavior of ratios over period of time."[9]

As one of the management tools, the importance of looking into tendency of events between financial statements prepared at different period cannot be lost sight of where the business was? Where the business is ? And where the business will be? All these uses being clearly revealed through trend analysis. According to M.R. Agrawal, "The trend analysis is the method of analyzing financial position of a business on the basis of changes in the items of financial statement of successive years in comparison a specific date or period commencement of study". Thus trend analysis, facilitates an effective comparative study of the financial performance of a concern. This method involves the calculation of percentage relationship that each statement bears to the same item in the base year. All items in the base year are assumed to be 100. By looking at the trend of ratios one may have insight into the past, present and future of the business enterprise. Thus trend analysis facilitates a long run view but does not express the cause of change in the item. Trend analysis can also be defined as "Index Analysis" or "Dynamic Analysis"

4. Ratio Analysis: -

Analysis of financial statement based on ratios is known as ratio analysis. Ratio analysis is a technique of presenting internal and external events affecting the business transaction relating to its operations, operating results and attainment of pre-determined goals and objectives of a business in brief and summary form.

According to Belverd-E-Needless, "Ratio guides or short cuts that are useful in evaluating the financial position and operations of a company and in comparing them with previous years or with other companies. The primary purpose of ratio is to point out areas for further investigations. They should be used in connection with a general understanding of the company and its environment."[10]

In short ratio analysis is the process of determining and presenting is the relationship of items or group of items in the financial statement. It is an expression of one number in relation to other while ratio analysis is the method by which the relationship of items or groups of items in the financial statements are computed, determined and presented through accounting ratios. Ratio analysis is used as a technique for evaluating financial position and performance of a firm. It points out areas of weakness and strength. But the analysis will be useful only when ratios are compared with past or future ratios or with ratio of another company, engaged in a similar business with the help of these ratios, the liquidity position, long term solvency, operating efficiency, or profitability and efficiency of a concern can be evaluated.

➢ Financial Ratios and their Interpretation

Table 2.1
Different Financial Ratios

Sl.No.	CATEGORY	TYPES OF RATIO	INTERPRETATION
1.	Liquidity ratios	**Net Working Capital** = Current assets- current liabilities	• It measures the liquidity of a firm.
		Current ratio = $\dfrac{\text{Current Assets}}{\text{Current Liabilities}}$	• It measures the short term liquidity of a firm. A firm with a higher ratio has better liquidity. • A ratio of 2:1 is considered safe.
		Acid test or Quick ratio = $\dfrac{\text{Quick assets}}{\text{Current Liabilities}}$	• It measures the liquidity position of a firm. • A ratio of 1:1 is considered safe.

2.	Turnover ratios	**Inventory Turnover ratio** = $\dfrac{\text{Costs of goods sold}}{\text{Average inventory}}$	• This ratio indicates how fast inventory is sold. • A firm with a higher ratio has better liquidity.
		Debtor Turnover ratio = $\dfrac{\text{Net credit sales}}{\text{Average debtors}}$	• This ratio measures how fast debts are collected. • A high ratio indicates shorter time lag between credit sales and cash collection.
		Creditor's Turnover ratio = $\dfrac{\text{Net credit purchases}}{\text{Average Creditors}}$	• A high ratio shows that accounts are to be settled rapidly.

3.	Capital Structure Ratios	**Debt-Equity ratio** = $\dfrac{\text{Long term debt}}{\text{Shareholder's Equity}}$	• This ratio indicates the relative proportions of debt and equity in financing the assets of a firm. • A ratio of 1:1 is considered safe.

		Debt to Total capital ratio = $$\frac{\text{Long term debt}}{\text{Permanent Capital}}$$ or $$\frac{\text{Total debt}}{\text{Permanent capital} + \text{Current liabilities}}$$ or $$\frac{\text{Total Shareholder's Equity}}{\text{Total Assets}}$$	• It indicates what proportion of thePermanent capital of a firm consists of long-term debt. • A ratio 1:2 is considered safe. • It measures the share of the total assets financed by outside funds. • A low ratio is desirable for creditors. • It shows what portion of the total assets is financed by the owners' capital. • A firm should neither have a high ratio nor a low ratio.

4.	Coverage Ratios	Interest Coverage $=$ $\dfrac{\text{Earning before Interests and Tax}}{\text{interest}}$	• A ratio used to determine how easily a company can pay on outstanding debt. • A ratio of more than 1.5 is satisfactory.
		Dividend Coverage $=$ $\dfrac{\text{Earning after tax}}{\text{Preference Dividend}}$	• It measures the ability of firm to pay dividend on preference shares. • A high ratio is better for creditors.
		Total Coverage ratio $=$ $\dfrac{\text{Earning before interests and tax}}{\text{Total fixed charges}}$	• It shows the overall ability of the firm to fulfill the liabilities. • A high ratio indicates better ability.
		Gross Profit margin $=$ $\dfrac{\text{Gross profit} * 100}{\text{Sales}}$	• It measures the profit in relation to sales. • A firm should neither have a high ratio nor a low ratio.

5.	**Profitability Ratios**	**Net Profit margin** $=$ $$\frac{\text{Net profit after tax}}{\text{Sales}}$$ before interest or $$\frac{\text{Net Profit after tax}}{\text{Sales}}$$ and Interest or $$\frac{\text{Net profit after}}{\text{Sales}}$$ Tax and Interest	• It measures the net profit of a firm with respect to sale. • A firm should neither have a high ratio nor a low ratio.
6.	**Expenses Ratios**	**Operating ratio** $=$ $$\frac{\text{Cost of Goods sold + other expenses}}{\text{Sales}}$$	• Operating ratio shows the operational efficiency of the business. • Lower operating ratio shows higher operating profit and vice versa.
		Cost of Goods sold ratio $=$ $$\frac{\text{Cost of Goods sold}}{\text{Sales}}$$	• It measures the cost of goods sold per sale.
		Specific Expenses ratio $=$ $$\frac{\text{Specific Expenses}}{\text{Sales}}$$	• It measures the specific expenses per sale.

7.	**Return on Investments**	**Return on Assets (ROA) =** $\dfrac{\text{Net Profit after Taxes} * 100}{\text{Total Assets}}$ Or $\dfrac{(\text{Net Profit after Taxes} + \text{Interest}) * 100}{\text{Total Assets}}$ Or $\dfrac{(\text{Net profit after Taxes} + \text{Interest}) * 100}{\text{Tangible Assets}}$ Or $\dfrac{(\text{Net Profit after Taxes} + \text{Interest}) * 100}{\text{Total Assets}}$ Or $\dfrac{(\text{Net Profit after Taxes} + \text{Interest}) * 100}{\text{Fixed Assets}}$	• It measures the profitability of the total funds per investment of a firm.
		Return on Capital Employed (ROCE) = $\dfrac{(\text{Net Profit after Taxes}) * 100}{\text{total capital employed}}$ Or $\dfrac{(\text{Net Profit after Taxes} + \text{Interest}) * 100}{\text{Total Capital Employed}}$ Or $\dfrac{(\text{Net Profit after Taxes} + \text{Interest}) * 100}{\text{Total Capital Employed} - \text{Intangible assets}}$	• It measures profitability of the firm with respect to the total capital employed. • The higher the ratio, the more efficient use of capital employed.

		Return on Total Shareholder's Equity = $\dfrac{\text{Net Profit after Taxes} * 100}{\text{Total shareholder's equity}}$	• It reveals how profitably the owner's fund has been utilized by the firm.
		Return on ordinary shareholder's equity = $\dfrac{\text{Net profit after taxes and Pref. dividend} * 100}{\text{Ordinary Shareholder's Equity}}$	• It determines whether the firm has earned satisfactory return for its equity holders or not.
8.	Shareholdr's Ratios	**Earnings per Share (EPS)** = $\dfrac{\text{Net Profit of Equity holders}}{\text{Number of Ordinary Shares}}$	• It measures the profit available to the equity holders on a per share basis.
		Dividend per Share (DPS) = $\dfrac{\text{Net profits after interest and preference dividend paid to ordinary shareholders}}{\text{Number of ordinary shares outstanding}}$	• It is the net distributed profit belonging to the Shareholder's divided by the number of ordinary shares.
		Dividend Payout ratio (D/P) = $\dfrac{\text{Total Dividend To Equity holders}}{\text{Total net profit of equity holders}}$ Or $\dfrac{\text{Dividend per Ordinary Share}}{\text{Earnings per Share}}$	• It shows what percentage share of the net profit after taxes and preference dividend is paid to the equity holders. • A high D/P ratio is preferred from investor's point of view.

		Earnings per Yield = $\dfrac{\text{Earnings per Share}}{\text{Market Value per Share}}$	• It shows the percentage of each rupee invested in the stock that was earned by the company.

		Dividend Yield = $$\frac{\text{Dividend per share}}{\text{Market Value per share}}$$	• It shows how much a company pays out in dividends each year relative to its share price.
		Price-Earnings ratio (P/E) = $$\frac{\text{Market value per Share}}{\text{Earnings per Share}}$$	• It reflects the price currently paid by the market for each rupee of EPS. • Higher the ratio better it is for owners.
		Earning Power = $$\frac{\text{Net profit after Taxes}}{\text{Total Assets}}$$	• It measures the overall profitability and operational efficiency of a firm.
9.	Activity Ratios	Inventory turnover = $$\frac{\text{Sales}}{\text{Closing Inventory}}$$	• It measures how quickly inventory is sold. • A firm should neither have a high ratio nor a low ratio.
		Raw Material turnover = $$\frac{\text{Cost of Raw Material used}}{\text{Average Raw Material Inventory}}$$	

		Work in Progress turnover = $$\frac{\text{Cost of Goods manufactured}}{\text{Average Work in process inventory}}$$	
		Debtors turnover = $$\frac{\text{Cost of Goods manufactured}}{\text{Average Work in Process Inventory}}$$	• It shows how quickly current assets i.e receivables or debtors are converted to cash. • A firm should neither have a high ratio nor a low ratio.

10.	Assets Turnover Ratios	Total Assets turnover = $\dfrac{\text{Cost of Goods Sold}}{\text{Total Assets}}$	• It measures the efficiency of a firm in managing and utilizing its assets.
		Fixed Assets turnover = $\dfrac{\text{Cost of Goods Sold}}{\text{Fixed Assets}}$	• Higher the ratio, more efficient is the firm in utilizing its assets.
		Capital turnover = $\dfrac{\text{Cost of Goods Sold}}{\text{Capital Employed}}$	
		Current Assets turnover = $\dfrac{\text{Cost of Goods Sold}}{\text{Current Assets}}$	

5. Funds Flow Analysis: -

In financial statements, balance sheet shows assets, liabilities and equity of the firm at a certain moment of time. Profit and loss account depicts operating results over a period of time. Fund Flow analysis is an analysis of sources and uses of funds. It highlights the changes in the financial composition of an undertaking between two dates.

As per Accounting Standard Board of ICAI "A statement which summaries for the period covered by it the changes in financial position including the sources from which the funds were obtained by the enterprise and the specific uses to which the funds were applied."

Thus funds flow statement is not a statement of financial position at a particular date, but it is a report of financial operations, changes, flows and movement of funds. It is an important financial technique widely used by financial analysts, investors and bankers for judging.

6. Break Even Analysis:-

Break Even Analysis is another tool for financial appraisal. It determines the relationship between sales volume and total costs. As stated by Weston and Brigham, "Break even analysis is useful in studying the relations among volume, prices and cost structure; it is thus helpful in pricing, cost control and other financial decisions."[11]

In the words of L.R.Amey and D.A.Egginton the break even analysis is, ".......an examination of price and cost of output (volume) in relation to the profit outcome."[12]

According to N.K.Kulshrestha, "It magnifies a set of inter-relationships of fixed costs, variable costs, level of activity to the profitability of the concern." [13]

Thus, it is a tool of financial analysis in a specific way of presenting and studying the inter-relationship between costs, volume and profits.

2.7 Precautions in financial Statement Analysis

The objective of analysis of financial statement is achieved only if the analysis is rightly done. In order to be successful the analyst should be well-versed in the art of analysis, he should take the following precautions in the analysis of financial statements:

1) He should see that the financial statements have been prepared by following the same concepts and conventions of book-keeping and accounting. If there has been any change in the depreciation policy, inventory valuation method or any other variable affecting profit figure and assets and liabilities, the analyst should first make the data comparable by making necessary adjustments in the concerning items.

2) If two or more companies are being compared, it should be seen that their nature and size do not widely differ.

3) In the computation of trend the base year, with which the data of other years are compared should be compared carefully. The base year in any case should be a normal year.

4) Sometimes a percentage figure is misleading. Therefore, the analysis of statements submitted to management should contain absolute figures along with their percentages.

5) The relationship should be established only between the relevant figures. For example, the profitability should be interpreted only in terms of sales or capital employed.

2.8 Conclusion

Financial statements are formal records of the financial activities of a business, person, or other entity and provide an overview of a business or person's financial condition in both short and long term. They give an accurate picture of a company's condition and operating results in a condensed form. Analysis and interpretation of financial statements help in determining the liquidity position, long term solvency, financial viability and profitability of a firm. Ratio analysis shows whether the company is improving or deteriorating in past years. Moreover, Comparison of different aspects of all the firms can be done effectively with this. It helps the clients to decide in which firm the risk is less or in which one they should invest so that maximum benefit can be earned. Thus, an effective analysis and interpretation of financial statements is required.

References

1. Tentative conclusions on objectives of Financial Statements of Business Enterprise.p.5.

2. R.D. Kennedy, and S.Y. McMllen, "Financial statements form Analysis and interpretation" Illinois, Richard D. Irwin Inc. (1968) p.17.

3. J.F.Weston, and E.F.Brigham, "Essentials of Managerial Finance" 2nd ed., New York, Holt, Rinehart and Winston.(1971) p.67.

4. V.L.Gole, "Fitzerald's Analysis and Interpretation of Financial Statements" Butterworth's.(1966)p.2.

5. Carl L. Moore, "Managerial Accounting" 1st Ed., London, Anold Publishers Ltd.p.119.

6. Charles W.Gerstenberg, "Financial Organisation and Management of Business" IVth Ed., New Delhi, Asia Publishing House.p.365.

7. N.K. Kulshrestha , "Theory and Practice of Management Accounting" 1st Ed., Aligarh, Navman Prakashan.p.236.

8. M.R. Agrawal, "Financial Management" RBSA Publishers.(2003) p.32.

9. R.D. Kennedy and S.Y. McMllen, *op. cit.,*pp.344-345.

10. Belverd E. Needless, "Financial and Management accounting" Honghton Mittin Co. (1988) p.1081.

11. J.F.Weston, and E.F.Brigham, *op. cit.,*p.80

12. L.R.Amey, and D.A.Egginton, "Management Accounting- A Conceptual Approach'' London, longman Group Ltd. (1975) p.271.

13. N.K. Kulshrestha , "An Approach to Management Accounting" Aligarh, Navman Prakashan.(1970)p.368.

Chapter-3
Research Methodology

3.1   Introduction

3.2   Statement of the problem

3.3   Review of related literature

3.4   Research gaps identified

3.5   Objectives of the study

3.6   Hypothesis of the study

3.7   Population and sampling

3.8   Data collection

3.9   Data analysis

3.10   Scope of the study

3.11   Rationale of the study

3.12   limitations of the study

3.1   Introduction

Banking industry has been changed after reforms process. The government has taken this sector in a basic priority and this service sector has been changed according to the need of present days. Today they have become an important constituent of the Indian financial system and cover a large segment of society because of their prompt and personalized service. We are living in a society, in which we care for each and every person of the society. Co-operation is an important aspect of the society. For the development of society land, labour, capital and technology are the important components. Insufficient development of these components leads to problems in economy. Bank is an important organisation in the terms of financial liquidity. Bank utilizes the unused deposits in the development of the country. For the economic development of the country mobility of the production equipments is necessary, in which financial management plays a great role. If the bank manages their funds properly, financial liquidity is preserved in the country.

"The special interests of economists in the activities of banks is due to the monetary nature of the deposit liabilities of the banks. Like any other business, the activities of banks are direct personal interest to the people who use them and to the people who work in them."[1]

The banks are the heart of our financial system. Banking is very useful field for the short and long term credit. Co-operative banks play major role for not only the large

56

industrialists but also for the small industrialists. Co-operative banks fulfil the facility of credit for the Co-operative societies also. Citizen Co-operative banks play very important role in providing banking services to common man in their area of co-operation. A small depositor or a small borrower feels comfortable in dealing with the local staff of co –operative bank than to the staff of nationalized banks and private sector banks.

Thus it can be stated that though organized on a small scale primarily to meet the need of the poor or weaker sections of society, the Co-operative banks have proved that they occupy a key position in semi-urban and urban areas so far as the national banking structure is concerned. Now a days Citizen Co-operative banks are loosing their reliability. So the researcher has tried to find out the financial position of the Citizen Co-operative banks of North Gujarat region.

3.2   Statement of the problem

Reserved bank of India had accepted the citizen co-operative banks as an important element in the structure of co-operative banking. Also; RBI had considered citizen co-operative banks as an effective factor for urban development. Citizen co-operative banks have been set up to promote banking habits among lower and middle income groups in urban areas and to provide credit to small borrowers including weaker sections of the society.

The performance of the citizen Co-operative bank largely depends on deposit mobilization, lending operations, repayment performance and utilization of funds.

Citizen co-operative banks of North Gujarat has played effective role in the development of co-operative sector and rural sector. So; in present research, researcher has selected citizen co-operative banks from four districts of North Gujarat for the study of their financial position.

Hence, the title of the problem selected for the study is **"FINANCIAL ANALYSIS OF CITIZEN CO-OPERATIVE BANKS OF NORTH GUJARAT"**

3.3   Review of related literature

The review of literature is aimed to find out the literature work done in the area of banking sector with special reference to the financial analysis of the Citizen co-operative banks. The studies carried out in the area of banking sector were reviewed as below.

❖   **Rao, J. J. (1982)** conducted a study on **"Working of PrimaryCo-operative Societies in Orissa - a case study of the Balasore PrimaryCo-operative Credit Society"**. The study observed that the net earnings of the cooperative societies in Orissa have declined during 1979-81 as compared to previous years. The main reason for such trend was attributed to cost escalation in almost all heads.[2]

❖ **Sardhara, B. L. (2005)** in his study titled **"Financial Analysis of District Co-operative Banks"** (With special reference to Saurashtra Region) evaluated the performance of district co-operative banks by analysing income, expenses, profitability, productivity, assets & debts of the selected Co-operative banks. By analysis of financial statements of six banks with the help of ratio analysis, statistical mean and "F" test he found that there is no Uniformity in income, expenses, profitability, productivity, assets & debts of the selected Co-operative banks. He suggested that all selected banks have to decrease their administrative expenses for better performance. They have to invest their funds in secured high interest rated securities for better interest income.[3]

❖ **Vashist, A.K. (1987)** in his study titled **"Performance appraisal of commercial banks in India"** evaluated the performance of public sectorcommercial banks with regard to six key indicators i.e. branch expansion,deposits, credit, priority sector, advances, DRI advances and net profit.He developed the composite weighted growth index, which is used forranking the banks. For improving the performance of commercial banks, he suggested (I) the developing of marketing strategy for depositmobilization (II) profit planning and strength, weaknesses, opportunities and threat analysis in commercial banks.[4]

❖ **Kshatriya, A.B. (2012)** conducted a study on **"A Comparative Analysis on Performance Appraisal of Mahila Co-operative Banks of Gujarat".** To study the growth, performance, profitability, financial efficiency and productivity of the mahila co-operative banks she had selected five mahila co-operative banks and 100 members from selected banks. She analyzed five year's data (2005-06 to 2009-10) of the selected banks with the help of ratio analysis, correlation, chi-square test and "t" test.In the whole research she observed that the growth of mahila co-operative banks on the whole was satisfactory, though there were imbalances in the various factors. She found that all the sample banks have financed more than 70 percent of their loans to the priority sector. She suggested that mahila co-operative banks has to open their branches in the uncovered districts of Gujarat as well as in the rural area. They should develop more efficient training programmes for the employees.[5]

❖ **Vyas, M.R.(1991)** studied **"Financial performance of regional rural banksin Rajasthan".** He analyzed the financial performance with the help ofquick ratio, credit deposit ratio, profit to proprietors, capital ratio andworking capital analysis. He concluded that regional rural banks had abright future as an effective instrument in the economic growth andupliftment of down trodden sections of Indian society particularly in ruralarea.[6]

❖ **Patel, R.R. (2005)** in her study titled **"Operational Efficiency of District Central Co-operative Banks in Gujarat - A Comparative Study"** evaluated the Operational Efficiency of District Central Co-operative Banks by analysing deposits, lending recovery, profitability, customers views on working of the banks and marketing of banking services rendered by the banks. For this purpose she had selected four District Central Co-operative Banks and data of the period 1996 to 2001. By the analysis of the views of total 250 individuals taken by a questionnaire she found that the ratio of short term agricultural finance was about 70 % of total advances and the non-farm sector finance was only about 9 %. Remaining 21 % finance on re-financing basis. She suggested that the funds management in District Central Co-operative Banks requires efficient handling. Also, the effective marketing services should be made available to the farmers at their door steps.[7]

❖ **Padmini,E.V.K. (1997)** conducted a study on **"Funds Management of District Co-operative Banks in Kerala".** To examine trend and pattern in sources and uses of funds and to analyse efficiency with respect to resources mobilisation and utilisation, she selected 6 district co-operative banks and the data from those banks of the period 1989 to 1993-94. With the help of ratio analysis, opportunity cost and X-efficiency analysis, she found that though funds mobilisation is done reasonably well in most district co-operative banks, sufficient attention is not given for efficient utilisation of these funds. She suggested that for recovery of over dues recovery cell may be properly utilized. Setting up of a national co-operative bank is also desirable to have an efficient co-ordination in remittance and transfer of funds.[8]

❖ **Koringa, N.H. (2008)** conducted a study on **"A Study of Operational Performance and Efficiency Management of District Co-operative Purchase-Sales Unions Limited"** (With special reference to Saurashtra region) In this study, the researcher analysed income, expenses, profitability, productivity, assets & debts of the five District Co-operative Purchase-Sales Unions, during the period 1997-98 to 2006-07, with the help of ratio analysis, statistical mean and "F" test. Researcher observed that there is no equality in income, expenses, profitability, productivity, assets & debts of the selected five District Co-operative Purchase-Sales Unions. Researcher suggested that District Co-operative Purchase-Sales Unions should reduce their administrative and miscellaneous expenses and debt. They should increase sales by promotion efforts.[9]

❖ **Nathwani, Nirmal (2004)** in his research on"**The Study of Financial Performance of Banking Sector of India"**has evaluated the financial performance of the Indian banking sector for the purpose to analyse operational efficiency, profitability, productivity and credit efficiency of the banks, during the period 1997-98 to 2001-02, with the help of statistical tools like ratios, trends, co relation, regression and F test. Researcher found that the operational efficiency, profitability, productivity and Credit efficiency in all the banking groups was significantly differing during the study. Researcher suggested various strategies like technology upgradation, human resource management and innovation should be implemented for restructuring banking sector.[10]

❖   **Ramani, V.K. (2009)** conducted a study on **"Financial Performance of selected Foreign Banks in India".** He had analysed financial performance of the selected five foreign banks, for the period 2001-02 to 2005-06, with the help of cash flow, ratio analysis, fund flow, trend analysis, comparison, common size statement analysis, statistical mean and "F" test. He found that deposits, investments, loans and income of the selected banks are increasing during the study period. He suggested that foreign banks should open their branches in the small cities and rural areas of India. For expanding their services they should apply policy of amalgamation or absorption with private Indian banks.[11]

❖   A Ramachandran and D.Siva Shanmugam (2012) conducted study on **"An Empirical Study on the Financial Performance of Selected Scheduled Urban Cooperative Banks in India".** The researcher aims to analyze the financial performance and progress of 10 Urban Cooperative banks for sample study.For this purpose data from these 10 banks was collected for the period 2001-2002 to 2009-2010 (9 Years).The relative performance of each bank has been assessed in the context of Resources Deployed, Assets Quality, Management Productivity and Earning Capacity variables. Analysis of data is made using certain tools and techniques such as Ratio Analysis, Averages andMin-Max.They conclude that urban cooperative banks have to put maximum efforts to attract term deposits, which contribute significantly towards the enhancement of bank profitability. [12]

❖   Agale S.V. (2012) in his Article **"Progress of District Central Cooperative Banks in Maharashtra",** evaluated the progress of the district central Co-operative Banks of Maharashtra.For the purpose of evaluationof progress of 31 District CentralCo-Operative Banks in Maharashtra he takes data from these banks during sevenyears from 2001 to 2007. He found that amount of share capital, amount of owned funds, deposits and working capital of selected DCCBs shows increasing trend during the study period. [13]

❖   Bhatt M.S. and Showkat Ahmad Bhat (2013) in their paper titled **"Financial Performance and Efficiency of Cooperative Banks in Jammu & Kashmir",** tries to investigate the technical efficiency and financial performance of cooperative banks operating in Jammu & Kashmir. The study has employed Data Envelopment Analysis (DEA) to estimate the relative efficiency of 8 cooperative banks operating in Jammu & Kashmir during the period 2000-01 to 2006- 07. They have used four parameters--deposits, number of employees as inputs and loans advanced and investments as outputs. The estimated results show that three banks are relatively efficient when their efficiency is measured in terms of constant returns to scale and five banks are relatively efficient when their efficiency is measured in terms of variable returns to scale. They have suggested that by improving management of deposits, number of employees, loan advances and investment operations the less efficient banks can successfully achieve efficiency in resource utilization. [14]

❖   Chander Ramesh and Chandel Jai Kishan (2011) attempted to study "**An Evaluation of Financial Performance and Viability of Four DCCBs in Haryana.**" They have made an attempted to analyze the financial performance and viability of four District Central Cooperative Banks (DCCBs) operating in Hisar division in Haryana for a period of twelve years (1997-98 to 2008-09) by financial analysis with different parameters and z-score analysis. The financial parameters here taken are profitability, liquidity, efficiency, solvency, risk and bankruptcy. The results reveal that four DCCBs with approximately fifty branches have not been performing well on all financial parameters taken for study. The banks performed well on one parameter but deteriorated on another and in different years as well. All the banks have been a part of bankruptcy zone (weak performance zone) throughout the study period. The banks need to visualize their operations, policies and strategies for effective utilization of available financial and human resources. [15]

❖   Das S.K. (2012) evaluates "**Financial and Operational Viability ofState Cooperative Banking in Northeast India.**" The paper explores and evaluates the growth and progressof State Cooperative Banks in the Northeastern region of India. It isfound that all the financial variables (capital, reserves, deposits, advances, demand,collection and over dues) increased with higher growth rate during 2002-2009 onthe basic of Compound Annual Growth Rate. Further, thispaper focuses on several pitfalls and shortcomings faced by State CooperativeBanks in region. Finally, it is observed that the State Cooperative Banks in theNortheastern region are not at par with the all India level which is evidenced fromthe study of some selected financial indicators. [16]

❖   Deshmukh P.V. (2013)tries to study, "**The Performance of Cooperative Banking in India.**" He has studied performance of Indian cooperative banking sector on the basis of income, expenditure, NPA, borrowers etc. He analyze thatthe movements to upward directionwere relatively more in loan amount in case of numberof borrowers.The amountof total expenditure was more to the income during 1996-97 and 2009-10. He also suggested that there is an urgent need for a significant reduction in NPAs because the NarasimhamCommittee-II also highlighted the need for 'zero' non-performingassets for all Indian banks with International presence.Therefore there is more scope to improve financialfunctioning and efficiency to Co-operative Banks in India.The number of urban co-operativebanks has increasing trend so It is need to improve theservices and profitability of Urban Co-operative banks forthe development of Indian banking sector. [17]

❖ Dimitrios P. Petropoulos and George Kyriazopoulos (2010) evaluated **"Profitability, Efficiency and Liquidity of the Co-Operative Banks in Greece".** In order to achieve this purpose they presentedthe course of the co-operative banks in Greece and analyzed a series of basic arithmetic indexes. A comparative analysis of the cooperativebank indexes with those of the Greek banking system as a whole was attempted as well.For the analysis of the economic magnitudes of the co-operative banks the groups of indexes such as: of profitability, of efficiencyand of liquidity were being implemented. With the help of the above indexes the values of the corresponding magnitudes for the cooperativebanks as a whole through the years was compared. Finally, through the above analysis the reasons for these changes through time werepointed out. From the analysis was revealed that profitability and efficiency for the co-operative banks turn out to be very satisfactory.More specifically these indexes for the co-operative banks were better compared to the equivalent ones of the banks as a whole whilethe liquidity indexes for the co-operative banks are worse compared to the equivalent ones of the banks as a whole. [18]

❖ E.Gnanasekaran, M.Anbalgan and N.Abdul Nazar (2012) examines UCBs through **"A study on the Urban Cooperative Banks Success and growth in Vellore District-Statistical Analysis."** With the help of the correlation analysis, chi-square test and multiple regression analysis of the selective variables for the period 2003-04 to 2008-09, the study predicted the future growth of the UCB's. The overall financial performance of the UCB's in all fronts namely, Membership, Share Capital, Deposits, Loans and Advances, Profit and Reserve Funds, Working capital, Overdues, Loans issued etc., were showing a significantly and undistrubing trend through the application of different statistical tools applied in the study. Therefore they undoubtfuly concluded that the UCB's are the road of progress. This also clears that, the UCB's are enjoying a predominant position in the banking industry occupied in eighth place in the banking institution serving in Vellore District. [19]

❖ Gupta Jyoti and Jain Suman(2012)conducted **"A study on Cooperative Banks in India with special reference to Lending Practices."** The study wasbased on some successful co-op banks in Delhi (India). The study of the bank's performance along with thelending practices provided to the customers was undertaken. The Study population includes the customers of bank and Sampling Unit for Study wasIndividual 200 Customer. They found that there is a very simple procedure followed by bank for loan and Average time for the processing of loan is less i.e. approx 7 days. The customers have taken more than one typeof loan from the banks. Moreover customers suggested that the bank should adopt the latest technology of the bankinglike ATMs, internet / online banking, credit cards etc. so as to bring the bank at par with the private sector banks. [20]

❖ Gupta V.K., Pawan kumar, and Goyal, A. (2013)have done **"Financial Analysis of Indian Oil Corporation Limited."** They judged financial analysis of Indian Oil Corporation Limited and its financial position by profitability ratios (Gross profit ratio, Net profit ratio andReturn on investment ratio), liquidity ratio (Current ratio and Quick ratio), Solvency ratio (Debt-Equity ratio, Debt to Total Assets Ratio and proprietary ratio) andInvestment ratio (Earning per share and Dividend payout ratio). The study was based on secondary data collected from the Annual Reports for the period 2005-06 to 2011-12 of Indian Oil CorporationLimited, Annual Reports of the Ministry of Petroleum and other secondary sources.After the study of financial analysis of Indian Oil Corporation Limited from various financial aspects like profitability, liquidity and solvency, activity andinvestment, they concluded that the profitability position of the company cannot be said satisfactory. They suggested that company need to improve the qualityof financial decision so that the wealth of equity shareholder' can be maximized. [21]

❖ Jagtap P.A. (2013) has made A Case Study on**"Financial Analysis of Rajarambapu Co-Op. Bank Ltd., Peth, Dist. Sangli."**The paper was an attempt made to evaluate financial performance of Rajarambapu Co-operative Bank Ltd., Peth, Dist-Sangli, State-Maharashtra as a empirical case study. To appraise the financial performance of the bank they covered a period from 2000-01 to 2010- 11. For studying growth of this bank, some financial aspects like membership, share capital, deposits, working capital, loans and advances, investments etc. were analyzed. Related data was collected from annual reports of bank and some websites.The statistics of the bank clearly indicates that Rajarambapu Bank is doing good service and it has tremendous market potential in areas like credit expansion and credit marketing. [22]

❖ Khandare V.B. (2012) has studied **"Some Issues in Customers Services of Urban Cooperative Banks."** To examine the overall growth performance of urban cooperative banks in Beeddistrict the study covers period of13 years from 1991-92 to 2003-04.The primary data was collected from 200 customers that were taken 50 from each selected urban cooperative banks inBeed district. In general the progress of urban cooperative banks in Beed district is satisfactory.It was observed from the study thatlocker and overdraft facility utilization was very low in urbancooperative banks. It was found from the study that the customers of urban cooperative banks in Beeddistrict excepted from these banks to provide more modern facilities to them. [23]

❖ K.V.S.N Jawahar Babu and B.Muniraja Selkhar (2012) in their paper on **"The Emerging Urban Co-Operative Banks (UCBs) In India: Problems and Prospects"** reviewed the progress made by the urban co-operative banks during the last 10 years (2001 to 2011). They found that Net profits of UCBs improved in 2010-11 as compared to the previous year owing to higher growth oftheir total income. But the gross as well as net NPA ratio of UCB sector declined.It wasobserved that the performance has by and large been satisfactory. Though there has been reductionin the number of UCBs from 2004 onwards, the total banking business (deposits plus advances) of UCBs hasshown steady increase signifying that the banks have been able to garner more business. There has been a gradual fall of the share of UCBs' business in the overall business of the banking sector. They suggested that UCbs should make changes in their regulatory frame work for strengthening recovery mechanism and also should maintain computerized reporting system for ready information and competing the commercial banks.[24]

❖   Narayana Gowd Talla, Anand Bethapudi, and Reddeppa Reddy G.conducted **"An Analytical Study on Financial Performance of Dharmavaram Urban Cooperative Bank, A.P. India."**The study employs exploratory research design which relies on secondary data. The analyzed data reveals that there was significant growth in the deposits mobilization, membership, loans and advances, working capital, reserves, owned funds, Total income, Total expenditure and over dues with reference to DUCB.Therefore the performance of DUCB was moderately satisfactory. For improving its performance, it has to concentrate on recovery performance, controlling expenses, robust risk management practices and diversifying their operations.[25]

❖   Padmaja, B., BhanuKiran, C. and Rama Prasada Rao, C.H.(2013)conducted **"An Empirical Study on Financial Performance of Anantapur Urban Cooperative Bank."**The study used exploratory research design which relies on secondary data.Secondarydata such as Balance sheets with schedule and profit and loss accountof Anantapur Urban Cooperative Bank were collected for the period2005-06 to 2009-2010 (5 Years). Analysis of data was made using certain tools and techniques such asRatio Analysis, Averages, Standard deviation and t -test. The analyzeddata reveals that there was significant growth in the deposits mobilization, loans and advances, working capital, reserves and owned funds.The total profits and the profits per share have beenshowing positive trend. Therefore the performance of AUCB was satisfactory.[26]

❖   Pandya B.H. (2012) in his case study on **"Financial Analysis of Tata Steel Ltd."**attempted to evaluate and judge the performance of Tata Steel during the research period.The reference period for the study is 10 years beginning from year 2001-02 to 2010-11.Datafor the study has been taken from the annual report of Tata steel for the year 2010-11. The study reveals that Tata Steel performed well in terms of returnavailable to all the investors measured as return on average capital employed. It also revealed that Tata steel offered a higher return to equity shareholdersmeasured in terms of return on equity and earnings per share during the reference period .However, declining return on average net worth on year on year basisis a cause of concern for TSL. Besides, this it was also found that debt policy of the company is very conservative as it uses lower degree of risk to avoid financialrisk and insolvency risk. Though, TSL is performing well at least in terms of book value measures as highlighted above, markets don't seem to be favoring thestock of TSL as it is offering lower premium on its share in terms of low P/E Ratio which also offers an opportunity to conduct further research. [27]

❖   Pareek Shachi (2012) has done "**Profitability Performance Analysis of Urban Co-operative Banks in Jaipur District.**" The researcher has taken period for the study is 5 years beginning from year 2005-06 to 2009-10. Total eight Urban Co-operative Banks in Jaipur district were selected for the study. Datafor the study has been taken from the annual reports of the selected Urban Co-operative Banks. Analysis of data was made using certain tools and techniques such asRatio Analysis and Average.The analysis reveals that theUCBs in Jaipur are in a positive state of health withsatisfactory level of profitability. Even being small insize, they have got a great potential to cater the marginalclients. The pace with which these banks wereable to reduce the burden was higher than the pace ofincreasing the spread. The same will help in liftingtheir profits automatically. The researcher suggested that UCBs in Jaipur should undertakesome promotional campaigns to attract more clientsand thus broaden their customer base. This will helpin increasing their deposits and will increase the interestincome too. The outperformingUCBs should be set as a "benchmark",against which the performance of other UCBs shouldbe measured. This will increase the competitivenessof these banks and will thus improve their profitabilityperformance. [28]

❖   Patel R.K. (2012)conducted study on "**Financial Performance of Urban Co-operative Bank.**"The period of this study for key financialindicators was confined to 1967 to 2011. Ratio Analysistechnique has been used for the analysis of Non-Performing Assets (NPA). He concluded that during the period1991-2004 the urban co-operative banking sectorwitnessed substantial growth, possibly encouragedby the liberalized policy environment in post reformperiod. The study also shows that overallfinancial performance of UCBs improved during thestudy period. He suggested that UCBs should proactively adoptCorporate Governance and should not wait for itsimposition by statute for the development of UCBsector. [29]

❖   Patel R.K. (2012) has made a study on "**Growth Of Urban Co-Operative Banks In India.**"In this Paper he analysed the growth of UCBs in India during 1966-67 to 2010-11. This paper also analysed the financial performance of UCBs in India during 2000-01 to 2010-11. Secondary data has been used for the study. Ratio Analysis technique has been used for the data analysis. This paper concluded that Urban Co-operative Banks developed only in five states of India. The growth of UCBs on owned funds, deposits and advances in the post reform period (after 1991) was more than pre reform period. Due to number of scams have taken place in UCBs in 2001-02, number of UCBs became weak. These banks lost the confidence of the depositors. He suggested that the Board of Directors of UCBs should implement professional management approach. Reserve Bank of India and government should co-operate to UCBs for their development. [30]

❖ Patel R.K. (2012) attempted to make **"Multi-Factor Evaluation and Forecasting of the Performance of Urban Co-Operative Banks in Ahmedabad."** This paper analyses Urban Co-operative Banks (UCBs) in Ahmedabad with respect to their financialperformance during the period of 1995-96 to 2004-05. The study through factor analyses brought out themost important six factors on which a bank should pay attention and deliberate on. Grade-I banks give importance to profitability ratios, operational efficiency and interestmanagement. Grade-II banks give prior importance to establishment expenses and interest expenses andthen to profitability and financial management. Due to lack of public trust, Grade-III banks maintain moreliquidity and due to excess staff in comparison to workload, higher establishment expenses (staff cost) inGrade-III banks. He concluded that there is no proper fund management in UCBs. It is time for the UCBs to concentrate onfund management, human resources and customer service to become sound and cope with challengingenvironment in the banking sector. Grade-III banks should improve their financial performance or mergewith stronger banks. [31]

❖ Rasal R.G. (2011)in his study on **"Performance of District Central Cooperative Banks during Post-reform period with special reference to Ahmednagar District Central Cooperative Bank,"** attempted to study the sources and uses of finance, growth and future prospects of the Ahmednagar District CentralCooperative Bank. The type of research was applied research based on primary and secondarydata collected for the study. Thesecondary data used for the study was collected from the Annual Reports andstatements of ADCC bank from 1990-91 to 2004-05. He found that the number of branches of ADCC Bank increased more than the 1.24times during the period under study. The educational level shows that 48.21 percent borrowers were educatedand 51.79 percent were illiterates. He suggested that there should be major policy changes in the cooperativelaw and practices. [32]

❖ R.Renuka and C.Elamathi (2013) attempted to study **"Development of Cooperative Banking in India".** The specific objective of the study was to analyses the performanceof urban cooperative bank. The study has analyzed the functioning of the bank with regard to deposit mobilisation, issueof loans and advances, recovery of loans, regarding the working performance of the Bank. The data required for this study were collected through secondary sources. They concluded that reforms pertaining to the urban co-operative andshort-term rural co-operative sectors seem to have set inmotion a process of revival in these sectors. In the coming years, it needs to be seenwhether the revival is sustained and broad-based. [33]

❖ Sanjay Kantidas (2012) **Operational and Financial Performance Analysis of Meghalaya Cooperative apex Bank.** Theobjectives of this paper were to access the growth and structure of cooperativecredit societies in the North Easter Region of India. It also aims to study the financial performance andfinancial health of Meghalaya

Cooperative Apex Bank through descriptivestatistics and ratio analysis of some selected financial indicators. The paper was exploratoryresearch in nature. The nature of data which were collected and used for thisresearch article was secondary. The study covers 8 years from 2002-03 to 2009-10.The researcher observed that Low Credit-Deposit (C-D) ratios, high over dues, high volume of Non-Performing Assets etc. were common to all State Cooperative Banks in the NorthEastern Region of India. But among the rest of all State Cooperative Banks inNorth Eastern Region, the Meghalaya Cooperative Apex Bank was performing verywell in terms of profitability and operational efficiency. [34]

❖ Sant Seema and Chaudhari P.T. (2012) in their paper on **"A Study of the Profitability of Urban Cooperative Banks"** attempted to evaluate the performance of Urban Cooperative banks for the period 2004-2009. Financial ratios were employed to measure the profitability, liquidity and credit quality performance of Ten Urban Cooperative banks from Jalgaon and Greater Mumbai. They found that overall bank performance increased considerably in the years of the analysis. A significant change in trend was noticed at the onset of the global financial crisis in 2007, reaching its peak during 2008-2009. This resulted in falling profitability, less liquidity and deteriorating credit quality in the Indian Banking sector. [35]

❖ Shirasi R.S. (2012) conducted a study titled **"A Study of Financial Working and Operational Performance of Urban Co-operative Banks in Pune District."**The main purpose of the research work was to study the financial working andoperational performance of UCBs in Pune district. 6 UCBs were selected by the random sampling procedure.To examine the experiences and expectations of the customers of UCBs, 120 customers from 6 UCBs wereselected for the study.The research study was an imperical research based on survey method. The researcher observed that number of branches of the sample UCBs increased from 32 to 59 during the period of1998-99 to 2003-04.It was observed that out of the total sample customers, 70% customers expressed that they receivedpolite treatment from the bank employees. The researcher suggested that there is need forextending the banking facilities in different regions of the country. In order to take advantages of new opportunities created by liberalization and globalization, the UCBsshould work towards improving their position. [36]

❖ Solanke S.S. and Agrawal S.R. (2012) conducted a study on **"Problems faced by co-operative banks and perspectives in the Indian Economy."** To elaborate the growth and development of cooperativeBanks the secondary data was collected through various newspapers, journals,Souvenir, Internet and Books. They found that Co-operative banks till now have to depend heavily onrefinancing facilities from the govt., RBI andNABARD. They were not able to become self-reliantthrough their own resources of deposits. They suggested that the higher authorities of thebanking should help the lower authorities in the way of motherinstitutions. The deposit mobilization profit andreserves should be commonly shared. [37]

❖   Soni Anilkumar and Saluja Harjinder Singh(2013)in their paper on **"Financial Ratio Analysis of DCC Bank Limited Rajnandgaon A Case Study"**, attempts to analyze the financial ratios of DCC Bank Rajnandgaon duringthe period 2008-2009 to 2010-2011. An analytical research design (Financial Ratio Analysis) was followed in the study. The study was based on secondary data. Empirical results show positive and sufficient growth of DCC BankRajnandgaon. The liquidity and solvency position of the bank was found to be sound. They recommended that the DCC Bank Rajnandgaon should try to increase their deposits by opening branches in business areas, improvethe services to clients, introduce different types of deposit schemes and offer competitive rates of interest. [38]

❖   Thirupathi Kanchu (2012)has made a case study on **"Performance Evaluation of DCCBs in India."** He attemptsto examine the growth of DCCBs in India through selective indicators; it analyzes the Deposits,Credits and C/D Ratios of DCCBs. The researcher also studies the growth of investment, workingCapital and Cost of Management position in DCCBs. To achieve the objectives of the paper data were collected for period of tenyears from 2001-02 to 2011-12. For analysis of the data, various statistical tools (Mean, S.D, C.V, Trend analysis) have been used to arrive at conclusion in a scientific way. It was concluded that the capital, reserves, and borrowings increased almost double during the study period, with a nominal percentage of variation. It was suggested that government should formulate specific policies and they should be implemented for the upliftment of District Central Cooperative Banks in India. [39]

3.4   Research gaps identified

According to the researcher, there have been few researches already done on the topic Citizen Co-operative banks of Gujarat. Co-operative banks of particular North Gujarat region were not covered in any of the reviewed studies. Period covered in all of the studies reviewed was till the year 2010. But, the five years study from the year 2007-08 to 2011-12 for the Citizen Co-operative banks of North Gujarat has not been found so far. So, the need felt by the researcher to focus on the latest development and financial performance till the year 2012 for the Citizen Co-operative banks of North Gujarat.

3.5   Objectives of the study

The specific objectives of the study were as follows:

1) To do the comparative evaluation of financial statements of Citizen Co-operative banks of North Gujarat.

2) To analyse income and expenses of the Citizen Co-operative banks of North Gujarat.

3) To study the various aspects affecting profitability of the Citizen Co-operative banks of North Gujarat.

4) To examine the productivity of the Citizen Co-operative banks of North Gujarat.

5) To study the assets of the Citizen Co-operative banks of North Gujarat.

6) To study the debts of the Citizen Co-operative banks of North Gujarat.

7) To give suggestions for effective financial management of the Citizen Co-operative banks of North Gujarat.

3.6 Hypothesis of the study

The Researcher has selected broader Hypothesis as under:

Hypothesis between the banks:

1) H_0 : There is no significant difference in the income and expenses of different Citizen Co-operative banks of North Gujarat for every financial year.

   H_1 : There is significant difference in the income and expenses of different Citizen Co-operative banks of North Gujarat for every financial year.

2) H_0: There is no significant difference in the profitability of different Citizen Co-operative banks of North Gujarat for every financial year.

   H_1 : There is significant difference in the profitability of different Citizen Co-operative banks of North Gujarat for every financial year.

3) H_0 : There is no significant difference in the productivity of different Citizen Co-operative banks of North Gujarat for every financial year.

   H_1 : There is significant difference in the productivity of different Citizen Co-operative banks of North Gujarat for every financial year.

4) H_0 : There is no significant difference in the assets and debts of different Citizen Co-operative banks of North Gujarat for every financial year.

   H_1 : There is significant difference in the assets and debts of different Citizen Co-operative banks of North Gujarat for every financial year.

Hypothesis between the years:

1) H_0 : There is no significant difference in the income and expenses of every Citizen Co-operative bank of North Gujarat for different financial years.

   H_1 : There is significant difference in the income and expenses of every Citizen Co-operative bank of North Gujarat for different financial years.

2) H_0 : There is no significant difference in the profitability of every Citizen Co-operative bank of North Gujarat for different financial years.

   H_1 : There is significant difference in the profitability of every Citizen Co-operative bank of North Gujarat for different financial years.

3) H_0 : There is no significant difference in the productivity of every Citizen Co-operative banks of North Gujarat for different financial year.

   H_1 : There is significant difference in the productivity of every Citizen Co-operative bank of North Gujarat for different financial years.

4) H_0 : There is no significant difference in the assets and debts of every Citizen Co-operative bank of North Gujarat for different financial years.

H_1 : There is significant difference in the assets and debts of every Citizen Co-operative bank of North Gujarat for different financial years.

3.7 Population and sampling

The population or universe has been consisted of all Citizen Co-operative banks of North Gujarat region.

Sample is the representative of the whole universe. The researcher had collected data from randomly selected two Citizen Co-operative banks from every district of North Gujarat. So the researcher had selected total eight Citizen Co-operative banks from four districts (Sabarkantha, Mehsana, banaskantha and Patan) of North Gujarat region. Comparison of these eight banks had been done by researcher. For this purpose last five years (i.e.,2007-2008 to 2011-2012) data was collected from these banks. Randomly selected two Citizen Co-operative banks from four district of North Gujarat were mentioned in the table 3.1 as follows:

Table 3.1
Citizen Co-operative Banks (CCBs) selected for the study

No.	Name of Bank	District
1.	Himmatnagar Nagarik Sahakari Bank Ltd., Himmatnagar	Sabarkantha
2.	The Modasa Nagarik Sahakari Bank Ltd., Modasa	
3.	The Mehsana Nagarik Sahakari Bank Ltd., Mehsana	Mehsana
4.	The Co-operative Bank of Mehsana Ltd., Mehsana	
5.	The Chhapi Nagarik Sahakari Bank Ltd., Chhapi	Banaskantha
6.	The Banaskantha Mercantile Co-operative Bank Ltd., Palanpur	
7.	The Chanasma Nagarik Sahakari Bank Ltd., Chanasma	Patan
8.	Patan Nagarik Sahakari Bank Ltd., Patan	

3.8 Data collection

Data has been collected in following two forms:

I. Published information: Related published annual reports, audited reports has been collected from Citizen Co-operative banks of North Gujarat. Researcher has collected bulletins of reserve bank of India, economic times, magazines, articles related to Citizen Co-operative banks and newspapers and also had attended banking related seminars.

II. Primary information: Primary information has been gathered through interview with bank managers and employees of selected banks by questioning on the routine problems and their solutions in the field of co-operative banking.

3.9   Data analysis

Data analyses have been done by ratio analysis as well as with the help of statistical method i.e. "F" test (ANOVA).

3.10   Scope of the study

➢ The study covers only those Citizen Co-operative banks which are registered in North Gujarat. It does not cover those Citizen Co-operative banks which are working in North Gujarat but registered elsewhere.

➢ This study enables researcher to improve knowledge about the banking sector, specifically on financial statements analysis of Citizen Co-operative banks.

➢ This study also enables the banks to know its actual position on income, expenses, profitability, productivity, assets and debts in last five years.

3.11   Rationale of the study

1) Citizen Co-operative banks have been social organisations so the balance between profitability and welfare activities is the subject of the study.

2) Research is needed to find out reasons behind increasing management expenses of Citizen Co-operative banks and also to minimize those expenses.

3) Since last several years Citizen Co-operative banks' deposits are decreasing this is also the point to worry.

4) Reliability for the customer care services is also decreasing in Citizen Co-operative banks.

5) How much devotion is given to the farmers and small industries from the Citizen Co-operative banks is point of talk.

6) There are differences in the profit (or loss) of different Citizen Co-operative banks.

7) It is important to understand the role of Citizen Co-operative banks for the development of rural areas through loans from these banks.

8) The structure to give loans should be well defined and the proper utilisation of deposits is expected.

9) Ratio of N.P.A. is increasing which is also the point to worry.

3.12   limitations of the study

➢ Only North Gujarat region was selected for the study.

➢ From all Citizen Co-operative banks of North Gujarat only eight banks were selected for the research purpose.

➢ From all selected Citizen Co-operative banks of North Gujarat only five years data (i.e., 2007-08 to 2011-12) have been collected for research purpose.

> From all the methods of financial analysis only ratio analysis and F-test was selected for the present study.

> The limitations of the analysis methods i.e., ratio analysis and statistical methods were also affected the study.

> The limitation of published information was also affected the study.

References

1. R.S. Sayers, "Modern Banking" 7th Edition, London, Oxford University Press, (1972) p.2.

2. J.J. Rao, "A study of Personnel Management in Selected Primary Agricultural Cooperative Societies in Orissa" Indian Journal of Commerce (1982) Vol. XXXI No. 11.

3. B. L. Sardhara, "Financial Analysis of District Co-operative Banks" An Unpublished Ph.D. Thesis, Submitted to Rajkot, Saurashtra University, (2005).

4. A.K. Vashist, "Performance appraisal of commercial banks in India" An Unpublished Ph.D. Thesis, Submitted to Shimla, Himachal Pradesh University, (1987).

5. A.B. Kshatriya, "A Comparative Analysis on Performance Appraisal of Mahila Co-operative Banks of Gujarat" An Unpublished Ph.D. Thesis, Submitted to Rajkot, Saurashtra University, (2012).

6. M.R. Vyas, "Financial performance of rural banks" Jaipur, Arihant Publishers, (1991).

7. R.R. Patel, "Operational Efficiency of District Central Co-operative Banks in Gujarat - A Comparative Study" An Unpublished Ph.D. Thesis, Submitted to Rajkot, Saurashtra University, (2005).

8. E.V.K. Padmini, "Funds Management of District Co-operative Banks in Kerala" An Unpublished Ph.D. Thesis, Submitted to Cochin, Cochin University of science and technology, (1997).

9. N.H. Koringa, "A Study of Operational Performance and Efficiency Management of District Co-operative Purchase-Sales Unions Limited" An Unpublished Ph.D. Thesis, Submitted to Rajkot, Saurashtra University, (2008).

10. Nirmal Nathwani, "The Study of Financial Performance of Banking Sector of India"An Unpublished Ph.D Thesis, Submitted to Rajkot, Saurashtra University, (2004).

11. V.K. Ramani, "Financial Performance of selected Foreign Banks in India" An Unpublished Ph.D. Thesis, Submitted to Rajkot, Saurashtra University, (2009).

12. A Ramachandran and D. Siva Shanmugam, "An Empirical Study on the Financial Performance of Selected Scheduled Urban Cooperative Banks in India" Asian Journal of Research in Banking and Finance Volume 2, Issue 5 (May, 2012), pp.1-24, ISSN: 2249-7323.

13. S.V. Agale, "Progress of District Central Cooperative Banks in Maharashtra" International Referred Research Journal, (February, 2012), Vol. III, Issue-29, pp.14-15, ISSN-0975-3486, RNI-RAJBIL 2009/30097.

14. M.S. Bhatt and Ahmad Bhat Showkat,"Financial Performance And Efficiency of Cooperative Banks In Jammu & Kashmir"Journal of Co-Operative Accounting and Reporting, V2, N1, (summer 2013) pp.16-36.

15. Ramesh Chander and Jai Kishan Chandel, "An Evaluation of Financial Performance and Viability of Cooperative Banks - A Study of Four DCCBs in Haryana"Kaim Journal of Management and Research vol.3, No.2, (2011, Nov.-Apr.) pp.1-12.

16. S.K. Das, "State Cooperative Banking in Northeast India: Financial and Operational Viability Analysis"Journal of North East India Studies, Vol. 2, No. 1, (2012, Jul.-Dec.) pp. 13-32.

17. P.V. Deshmukh, "The Performance of Cooperative Banking in India" Indian Journal Of Applied Research, Vol. 3, Issue 5, (2013, May) pp.160-162.

18. Dimitrios P. Petropoulos and George Kyriazopoulos, "Profitability, Efficiency and Liquidity of the Co-Operative Banks in Greece"International Conference On Applied Economics, (2010) pp.603-607.

19. E.Gnanasekaran, M.Anbalgan and N.Abdul Nazar, "A study on the Urban Cooperative Banks Success and growth in Vellore District-Statistical Analysis" International Journal of Advanced Research in Computer Science and Software Engineering, Vol. 2, Issue 3, (2012, March) pp.434-437.

20. Jyoti Gupta and Suman Jain,"A study on Cooperative Banks in India with special reference to Lending Practices"European Journal of Education and Learning, Vol.12, (2012) pp.1-9.

21. V.K. Gupta, Pawan kumar, and A. Goyal, "Financial Analysis of Indian Oil Corporation Limited"International Journal of Research In Commerce & Management, Vol. 4, Issue no. 07, (2013, July) pp.46-52.

22. P.A. Jagtap, "Financial Analysis of Rajarambapu Co-Op. Bank Ltd., Peth, Dist. Sangli-A Case Study"Advances In Management, Vol. 6 (6), (2013, June) pp.60-64.

23. V.B. Khandare, "Some Issues in Customers Services of Urban Cooperative Banks: A Case Study of Beed District" International Journal of Social Science & Interdisciplinary ResearchVol.1 Issue 10, (2012, October) pp.145-152.

24. Jawahar Babu K.V.S.N and Muniraja B. Selkhar, "The Emerging Urban Co-Operative Banks (Ucbs) In India: Problems and Prospects" Journal of Business and Management, Vol. 2, Issue 5, (2012, July-Aug) PP 01-05.

25. Narayana Gowd Talla, Anand Bethapudi, and Reddeppa Reddy G, "An Analytical Study on Financial Performance of Dharmavaram Urban Cooperative Bank, A.P. India"Abhinav,Vol. NO.2, Issue no.8, pp.1-13.

26. Padmaja, B., BhanuKiran, C. and Rama Prasada Rao, C.H.,"An Empirical Study on Financial Performance of Anantapur Urban Cooperative Bank" International Journal of Current Research,Vol. 5, Issue, 06, (2013, June) pp.1451-1456.

27. B.H. Pandya, "Financial Analysis of Tata Steel Ltd.- A Case Study" International Journal of Research In Commerce & Management, Vol. 3, Issue NO. 1, (2012, January) pp.93-97.

28. Shachi Pareek, "Profitability Performance Analysis of Urban Co-operative Banks in Jaipur District"International Indexed & Referred Research Journal, Vol. III, Issue-33, (2012, June) pp.24-25.

29. R.K. Patel, "Financial Performance of Urban Co-operative Bank"Contemporary Research In India, Vol.: 2, Issue: 2, (2012, June) pp.263-266.

30. R.K. Patel, "Growth Of Urban Co-Operative Banks In India"The Clute Institute International Academic Conference Las Vegas, Nevada, USA, (2012) pp. 882-891.

31. R.K. Patel, "Multi-Factor Evaluation and Forecasting of the Performance of Urban Co-Operative Banks in Ahmedabad"Contemporary Research in India, Vol. 2, Issue: 2, (2012, June) pp.71-80.

32. R.G. Rasal, "Performance of District Central Cooperative Banks During Post-reform period with special reference to Ahmednagar District Central Cooperative Bank"Indian Streams Research Journal, Vol. - I, ISSUE-V, (2011, July).

33. Renuka R. and Elamathi C., "Development of Cooperative Banking in India"Indian Journal Of Applied Research, Vol. 3, Issue 8, (2013, Aug.) pp.115-118.

34. Sanjay Kantidas, "Operational and Financial Performance Analysis of Meghalaya Cooperative apex Bank"Journal on Banking Financial Services & Insurance Research. Vol.2, Issue 3, (2012, March) pp.20-39.

35. Seema Sant and P.T. Chaudhari, "A Study of the Profitability of Urban Cooperative Banks"International Journal of Multidisciplinary Research, Vol.2 Issue 5, (2012, May) pp.124-134.

36. R.S. Shirasi, "A Study of Financial Working and Operational Performance of Urban Co-operative Banks in Pune District" Indian Streams Research Journal. Vol.1, (2012, June) pp.1-4.

37. S.S. Solanke and S.R. Agrawal, "Problems faced by co-operative banks and perspectives in the Indian Economy"International Journal of Commerce, Business and Management, Vol. 1, No.2, (2012, October) pp.53-54.

38. Anilkumar Soni and HarjinderSingh Saluja, "Financial Ratio Analysis of DCC Bank Limited Rajnandgaon A Case Study"International Journal of Accounting and Financial Management Research, Vol. 3, Issue 1, (2013, March) pp.93-105.

39. Kanchu Thirupathi, "Performance Evaluation of DCCBs in India-A Study"Asia Pacific Journal of Marketing & Management Review, Vol.1, No. 2, (2012, October) pp.169-180.

Chapter-4
Analysis of Income and Expenses

4.1 Introduction

4.2 Analysis of Income

    4.2.1 Interest Income to Total Income Ratio

    4.2.2 Non-Interest Income to Total Income Ratio

4.3 Analysis of Expenses

    4.3.1 Interest Expense to Total Expense Ratio

    4.3.2 Operating Expense to Total Expense Ratio

    4.3.3 Other Expense to Total Expense Ratio

4.4 Net Profit

    4.4.1 Net Profit to Total Income Ratio

4.5 Conclusion

4.1 Introduction

In this chapter researcher has tried to analyze income and expenses of Citizen co-operative banks of North Gujarat. For this Purpose income statement of CCBs has been taken for the study by the researcher. Income Statement, also known as Profit & Loss Account, is a report of income, expenses and the resulting profit or loss earned during an accounting period. It is based on a <u>fundamental</u> <u>accounting equation</u> (Income = Revenue - Expenses) and shows the <u>rate</u> at which the <u>owners' equity</u> is changing for better or worse. According to **H.G. Guthmann**, "This statement singles out and summarizes those transactions in which there is a loss or gain for the owners of the business."[1] As **kennedy** and **Mcmullen** observe, "It is statement of activity and the results of that activity."[2] Similarly, **Paton and Paton** say that, "The income statement is accountant's major report of activity."[3]

Income and expenditure indicates the financial health of citizen cooperative banks. The citizen cooperative banks derive majority of their income from interest on credit deployment and income from investment as well. The term expenditure refers to the interest paid on deposits and other borrowings, if any, establishments expenses including management cost and miscellaneous expenses incurred towards operations. In this chapter data on the income and expenditure is analyzed for the years 2007-08 to 2011-12 of the sample citizen cooperative banks.

4.2 Analysis of Income

The major sources of income of Citizen Co-operative Banks are interest and discount earned on loans and advances, interest on deposits kept with other bank branches and commission on services provided to customers, exchange and brokerage, subsidies and donations, income from non-banking assets and profit from sale of or dealing with such assets, other miscellaneous sources of income. In the income analysis; income side particulars of profit and loss account has analyzed for the period 2007-08 to 2011-12 of selected citizen cooperative banks of North Gujarat.Analysis of Income has been done by the following ratios:

1. Interest Income to Total Income Ratio
2. Non-Interest Income to Total Income Ratio

4.2.1 Interest Income to Total Income Ratio

Income received from interest and discount is the main source of income of Citizen Co-operative Banks. Interest earning in banks refer to fund based income and represent the return on pure banking business. Generally, interest income is the main part of bank's total income. By this ratio we can know proportion of interest income in bank's total income. Formula for the ratio of interest income to total income is as follows:

$$\text{Interest Income to Total Income Ratio} = \frac{\text{Interest Income}}{\text{Total Income}} *100$$

Higher ratio shows the improved earning capacity of the bank.

Interest Income to Total Income Ratio of selected citizen cooperative banks of North Gujarat for the study period 2007-08 to 2011-12 is presented in the table 4.1as follows:

Table 4.1
Interest Income to Total Income Ratio

YEAR	HIMNSB	MODNSB	MEHNSB	COBMEH	CHHNSB	BANMCB	CHANSB	PATNSB	AVERAGE
2007-08	94.80	97.97	97.63	98.74	98.50	95.93	98.77	98.75	97.64
2008-09	98.44	98.57	97.53	99.04	96.45	97.44	99.17	99.18	98.23
2009-10	98.69	98.44	97.67	99.16	98.51	97.58	99.13	99.29	98.56
2010-11	98.49	99.20	97.42	99.38	98.67	98.27	99.33	98.93	98.71
2011-12	98.67	99.63	97.90	99.13	99.37	98.75	98.44	99.40	98.91
AVERAGE	97.82	98.76	97.63	99.09	98.30	97.59	98.97	99.11	98.41

Source: Annual reports of CCBs during year 2007-08 to 2011-12.

It can be observed from the above table 4.1 for himmatnagar nagarik sahakari bank that Interest Income to Total Income Ratio was 94.80% in the year 2007-08 which was the lowest during all the study period. In the year 2008-09 and 2009-10 this ratio was increased to 98.44% and 98.69% respectively. In the year 2009-10 it was the highest during all the study period. In the year 2010-11 this ratio decreased to 98.49% and in the year 2011-12 it was increased to 98.67%. During all the study period average of this ratio was 97.82%. For all the five years of the study this ratio was lower than its average for one year and higher than its average in all the remaining years.

It is obvious from the above table 4.1 for modasa nagarik sahakari bank that Interest Income to Total Income Ratio was 97.97% in the year 2007-08 which was the lowest during all the study period. In the year 2008-09 this ratio was increased to 98.57% and in 2009-10 it was decreased to 98.44%. In the year 2010-11 and 2011-12 this ratio was increased to 99.20% and 99.63% respectively. In the year 2011-12 it was the highest during all the study period. During all the study period average of this ratio was 98.76%. For all the five years of the study this ratio was lower than its average for three years and higher than its average for remaining two years.

It is apparent from the above table 4.1 for mehsana nagarik sahakari bank that Interest Income to Total Income Ratio was 97.63% in the year 2007-08 which was equal to average of all the study period. In the year 2008-09 this ratio decreased to 97.53% and in the year 2009-10 it was increased to 97.67%. In the year 2010-11 this ratio decreased to 97.42% which was the lowest during all the study period. In the year 2011-12 it was increased to 97.90% which was the highest during all the study period. During all the study period average of this ratio was 97.63%. For all the five years of the study this ratio was lower than its average for two years, higher than its average for two years and equal to its average for one year.

It is cleared from the above table 4.1 for co-operative bank of mehsana that Interest Income to Total Income Ratio was 98.74% in the year 2007-08 which was the lowest during all the study period. In the year 2008-09 to 2010-11 this ratio was continuously increased to 99.04%, 99.16% and 99.38% respectively. In the year 2010-11 it was the highest during all the study period. In the year 2011-12 it was decreased to 99.13%. During all the study period average of this ratio was 99.09%. For all the five years of the study this ratio was lower than its average for two years and higher than its average for remaining three years.

It isevident from the above table 4.1 for chhapi nagarik sahakari bank that Interest Income to Total Income Ratio was 98.50% in the year 2007-08. In the year 2008-09 this ratio was decreased to 96.45% which was the lowest during all the study period. In the year 2009-10 and 2010-11 this ratio was increased to 98.51% and 98.67% respectively. In the year 2011-12 it was increased to 99.37% which was the highest during all the study period. During all the study period average of this ratio was 98.30%. For all the five years of the study this ratio was lower than its average for one year and higher than its average in all the remaining years.

It can be observed from the above table 4.1 for banaskantha mercantile co-operative bank that Interest Income to Total Income Ratio was 95.93% in the year 2007-08 which was the lowest during all the study period. In the year 2008-09 to 2011-12 this ratio was increased to 97.44%, 97.58%, 98.27% and 98.75% respectively. In the year 2011-12 it was the highest during all the study period. During all the study period average of this ratio was 97.59%. For all the five years of the study this ratio was lower than its average for three years and higher than its average in remaining two years.

It is obvious from the above table 4.1 for chanasma nagarik sahakari bank that Interest Income to Total Income Ratio was 98.77% in the year 2007-08. In the year 2008-09 this ratio was increased to 99.17% and in the year 2009-10 it was decreased to 99.13%. In the year 2010-11 this ratio increased to 99.33% which was the highest during all the study period. In the year 2011-12 it was decreased to 98.44% which was the lowest during all the study period. During all the study period average of this ratio was 98.97%. For all the five years of the study this ratio was lower than its average for two years and higher than its average in remaining three years.

It is apparent from the above table 4.1 for patan nagarik sahakari bank that Interest Income to Total Income Ratio was 98.75% in the year 2007-08 which was the lowest during all the study period. In the year 2008-09 and 2009-10 this ratio was increased to 99.18% and 99.29% respectively. In the year 2010-11 this ratio decreased to 98.93% and in the year 2011-12 it was increased to 99.40%. In the year 2011-12 it was the highest during all the study period. During all the study period average of this ratio was 99.11%. For all the five years of the study this ratio was lower than its average for two years and higher than its average in remaining three years.

It can be seen from the above table 4.1 for all Citizen co-operative banks that average of Interest Income to Total Income Ratio during 2007-08 to 2011-12 was 98.41%. In the year 2007-08 average ratio of all banks was 97.64% which was the lowest during all the study period. In the year 2008-09 to 2011-12 this ratio was increased to 98.23%, 98.56%, 98.71% and 98.91% respectively. In the year 2011-12 it was the highest during all the study period. For all the five years of the study average ratio of all banks was lower than its average for two years and higher than its average in remaining three years.

❖ **F test (ANOVA) Analysis**

The statements of hypothesis are as under:
- **Hypothesis between the banks:**

H_0:   There is no significant difference in the interest income to total income ratio of different Citizen Co-operative banks of North Gujarat for every financial year.

H_1:   There is significant difference in the interest income to total income ratio of different Citizen Co-operative banks of North Gujarat for every financial year.

- **Hypothesis between the years:**

H_0:   There is no significant difference in the interest income to total income ratio of every Citizen Co-operative bank of North Gujarat for different financial years.

H₁: There is significant difference in the interest income to total income ratio of every Citizen Co-operative bank of North Gujarat for different financial years.

Table 4.1-A

Source of Variation	SS	df	MS	F
Between Banks	15.12	07	2.16	3.85
Between years	07.96	04	1.99	3.55
Error	15.71	28	0.56	
Total	38.78	39		

Table Value for df (7,28) is 2.36 at 5% level of significance.
Table Value for df (4,28) is 2.71 at 5% level of significance.

Table 4.1-A represents the difference for the banks is significant because the table value for df (7,28) is (2.36) which is lower than calculated value of 'F' (3.85). So, null hypothesis (H₀) is rejected and alternative hypothesis (H₁) is accepted. i.e. There is significant difference in the interest income to total income ratio of different Citizen Co-operative banks of North Gujarat for every financial year.

Same way the difference for the years is significant because the table value for df (4,28) is (2.71) which is lower than the calculated value of 'F' (3.55) for years and so here also null hypothesis(H₀) is rejected and alternative hypothesis (H₁) is accepted. i.e. There is significant difference in the interest income to total income ratio of every Citizen Co-operative bank of North Gujarat for different financial years.

4.2.2 Non-Interest Income to Total Income Ratio

Non-interest income includes commission, exchange and brokerage and other receipts including income from non-banking assets. Generally, proportion of non-interest income remains negligible in the bank's total income. By this ratio we can know proportion of non-interest income in bank's total income. Formula for the ratio of non-interest income to total income is as follows:

$$\text{Non-Interest Income to Total Income Ratio} = \frac{\text{Non-Interest Income}}{\text{Total Income}} * 100$$

Non-interest income to total income ratio of selected citizen co-operative banks of North Gujarat for the study period 2007-08 to 2011-12 is presented in the table 4.2 as follows:

Table 4.2
Non-Interest Income to Total Income Ratio

YEAR	HIMNSB	MODNSB	MEHNSB	COBMEH	CHHNSB	BANMCB	CHANSB	PATNSB	AVERAGE
2007-08	5.20	2.03	2.37	1.26	1.50	4.07	1.23	1.25	2.36
2008-09	1.56	1.43	2.47	0.96	3.55	2.56	0.83	0.82	1.77
2009-10	1.31	1.56	2.33	0.84	1.49	2.42	0.87	0.71	1.44

2010-11	1.51	0.80	2.58	0.62	1.33	1.73	0.67	1.07	1.29
2011-12	1.33	0.37	2.10	0.87	0.63	1.25	1.56	0.60	1.09
AVERAGE	2.18	1.24	2.37	0.91	1.70	2.41	1.03	0.89	1.59

Source: Annual reports of CCBs during year 2007-08 to 2011-12.

It can be observed from the above table 4.2 for himmatnagar nagarik sahakari bank that Non-Interest Income to Total Income Ratio was 5.20% in the year 2007-08 which was the highest during all the study period. In the year 2008-09 and 2009-10 this ratio was decreased to 1.56% and 1.31% respectively. In the year 2009-10 it was the lowest during all the study period. In the year 2010-11 this ratio increased to 1.51% and in the year 2011-12 it was decreased to 1.33%. During all the study period average of this ratio was 2.18%. For all the five years of the study this ratio was lower than its average for four years and higher than its average in remaining one year.

It is obvious from the above table 4.2 for modasa nagarik sahakari bank that Non-Interest Income to Total Income Ratio was 2.03% in the year 2007-08 which was the highest during all the study period. In the year 2008-09 this ratio was decreased to 1.43% and in 2009-10 it was increased to 1.56%. In the year 2010-11 and 2011-12 this ratio was decreased to 0.80% and 0.37% respectively. In the year 2011-12 it was the lowest during all the study period. During all the study period average of this ratio was 1.24%. For all the five years of the study this ratio was lower than its average for two years and higher than its average for remaining three years.

It is apparent from the above table 4.2 for mehsana nagarik sahakari bank that Non-Interest Income to Total Income Ratio was 2.37% in the year 2007-08 which was equal to average of all the study period. In the year 2008-09 this ratio increased to 2.47% and in the year 2009-10 it was decreased to 2.33%. In the year 2010-11 this ratio increased to 2.58% which was the highest during all the study period. In the year 2011-12 it was decreased to 2.10% which was the lowest during all the study period. During all the study period average of this ratio was 2.37%. For all the five years of the study this ratio was lower than its average for two years, higher than its average for two years and equal to its average for one year.

It is cleared from the above table 4.2 for co-operative bank of mehsana that Non-Interest Income to Total Income Ratio was 1.26% in the year 2007-08 which was the highest during all the study period. In the year 2008-09 to 2010-11 this ratio was continuously decreased to 0.96%, 0.84% and 0.62% respectively. In the year 2010-11 it was the lowest during all the study period. In the year 2011-12 it was increased to 0.87%. During all the study period average of this ratio was 0.91%. For all the five years of the study this ratio was lower than its average for three years and higher than its average for remaining two years.

It isevident from the above table 4.2 for chhapi nagarik sahakari bank that Non-Interest Income to Total Income Ratio was 1.50% in the year 2007-08. In the year 2008-09 this ratio was increased to 3.55% which was the highest during all the study period. In the year 2009-10 and 2010-11 this ratio was decreased to 1.49% and 1.33%

respectively. In the year 2011-12 it was decreased to 0.63% which was the lowest during all the study period. During all the study period average of this ratio was 1.70%. For all the five years of the study this ratio was lower than its average for four years and higher than its average in the remaining one year.

It can be observed from the above table 4.2 for banaskantha mercantile co-operative bank that Non-Interest Income to Total Income Ratio was 4.07% in the year 2007-08 which was the highest during all the study period. In the year 2008-09 to 2011-12 this ratio was decreased to 2.56%, 2.42%, 1.73% and 1.25% respectively. In the year 2011-12 it was the lowest during all the study period. During all the study period average of this ratio was 2.41%. For all the five years of the study this ratio was lower than its average for two years and higher than its average in remaining three years.

It is obvious from the above table 4.2 for chanasma nagarik sahakari bank that Non-Interest Income to Total Income Ratio was 1.23% in the year 2007-08. In the year 2008-09 this ratio was decreased to 0.83% and in the year 2009-10 it was increased to 0.87%. In the year 2010-11 this ratio decreased to 0.67% which was the lowest during all the study period. In the year 2011-12 it was increased to 1.56% which was the highest during all the study period. During all the study period average of this ratio was 1.03%. For all the five years of the study this ratio was lower than its average for three years and higher than its average in remaining two years.

It is apparent from the above table 4.2 for patan nagarik sahakari bank that Non-Interest Income to Total Income Ratio was 1.25% in the year 2007-08 which was the highest during all the study period. In the year 2008-09 and 2009-10 this ratio was decreased to 0.82% and 0.71% respectively. In the year 2010-11 this ratio increased to 1.07% and in the year 2011-12 it was decreased to 0.60%. In the year 2011-12 it was the lowest during all the study period. During all the study period average of this ratio was 0.89%. For all the five years of the study this ratio was lower than its average for three years and higher than its average in remaining two years.

It can be seen from the above table 4.2 for all Citizen co-operative banks that average of Non-Interest Income to Total Income Ratio during 2007-08 to 2011-12 was 1.59%. In the year 2007-08 average ratio of all banks was 2.36% which was the highest during all the study period. In the year 2008-09 to 2011-12 this ratio was decreased to 1.77%, 1.44%, 1.29% and 1.09% respectively. In the year 2011-12 it was the lowest during all the study period. For all the five years of the study average ratio of all banks was lower than its average for three years and higher than its average in remaining two years.

❖ **F test (ANOVA) Analysis**

The statements of hypothesis are as under:
- **Hypothesis between the banks:**

H$_0$:   There is no significant difference in the non-interest income to total income ratio of different Citizen Co-operative banks of North Gujarat for every financial year.

H$_1$:   There is significant difference in the non-interest income to total income ratio of different Citizen Co-operative banks of North Gujarat for every financial year.

- **Hypothesis between the years:**

H$_0$:   There is no significant difference in the non-interest income to total income ratio of every Citizen Co-operative bank of North Gujarat for different financial years.

H$_1$:   There is significant difference in the non-interest income to total income ratio of every Citizen Co-operative bank of North Gujarat for different financial years.

Table 4.2-A

Source of Variation	SS	df	MS	F
Between Banks	15.12	07	2.16	3.85
Between years	07.96	04	1.99	3.55
Error	15.71	28	0.56	
Total	38.78	39		

Table Value for df (7,28) is 2.36 at 5% level of significance.

Table Value for df (4,28) is 2.71 at 5% level of significance.

Table 4.2-A represents the difference for the banks is significant because the table value for df (7,28) is (2.36) which is lower than calculated value of 'F' (3.85). So, null hypothesis (H$_o$) is rejected and alternative hypothesis (H$_1$) is accepted. i.e. There is significant difference in the non-interest income to total income ratio of different Citizen Co-operative banks of North Gujarat for every financial year.

Same way the difference for the years is significant because the table value for df (4,28) is (2.71) which is lower than the calculated value of 'F' (3.55) for years and so here also null hypothesis(H$_o$) is rejected and alternative hypothesis (H$_1$) is accepted. i.e. There is significant difference in the non-interest income to total income ratio of every Citizen Co-operative bank of North Gujarat for different financial years.

4.3   Analysis of Expenses

The major elements of expenses are interest on deposits/ borrowings, salaries, allowances and provident fund, fees and allowances paid to directors, auditor's fees etc. In the expense analysis; expense side particulars of profit and loss account has analyzed for the period 2007-08 to 2011-12 of selected citizen co-operative banks of North Gujarat.Analysis of Expenses has been done by the following ratios:

1. Interest Expense to Total Expense Ratio
2. Operating Expense to Total Expense Ratio
3. Other Expense to Total Expense Ratio

4.3.1 Interest Expense to Total Expense Ratio

Interest expenses by banks refer to fund based expenditure which consist of interest paid on deposits and borrowings. This is one of the major components of total expenses. Generally, interest expense is the main part of bank's total expense. By this ratio we can know proportion of interest expense in bank's total expense. Formula for the ratio of interest expense to total expense is as follows:

$$\text{Interest Expense to Total Expense Ratio} = \frac{\text{Interest Expense}}{\text{Total Expense}} *100$$

deposits. Similarly, decreasing ratio indicates efficiency of bank in obtaining low cost deposits.

Interest Expense to Total Expense Ratio of selected citizen co-operative banks of North Gujarat for the study period 2007-08 to 2011-12 is presented in the table 4.3 as follows:

Table 4.3

Interest Expense to Total Expense Ratio

YEAR	HIMNSB	MODNSB	MEHNSB	COBMEH	CHHNSB	BANMCB	CHANSB	PATNSB	AVERAGE
2007-08	59.03	62.72	77.07	61.58	76.92	63.41	69.74	69.69	67.52
2008-09	63.73	66.15	74.24	69.49	74.69	66.45	73.28	67.44	69.43
2009-10	62.12	66.17	72.81	72.27	67.52	68.34	71.59	67.21	68.50
2010-11	58.51	66.87	62.33	70.38	66.57	65.75	70.09	66.74	65.90
2011-12	55.68	66.36	61.22	75.40	63.61	66.92	68.47	63.56	65.15
AVERAGE	59.81	65.65	69.53	69.82	69.86	66.17	70.63	66.93	67.30

Source: Annual reports of CCBs during year 2007-08 to 2011-12.

It can be observed from the above table 4.3 for himmatnagar nagarik sahakari bank that Interest Expense to Total Expense Ratio was 59.03% in the year 2007-08. In the year 2008-09 this ratio was increased to 63.73% which was the highest during all the study period. In the year 2009-10 to 2011-12 it was decreased to 62.12%, 58.51% and 55.68% respectively. In the year 2011-12 it was the lowest during all the study period. During all the study period average of this ratio was 59.81%. For all the five years of the study this ratio was lower than its average for three years and higher than its average in remaining two years.

It is obvious from the above table 4.3 for modasa nagarik sahakari bank that Interest Expense to Total Expense Ratio was 62.72% in the year 2007-08 which was the lowest during all the study period. In the year 2008-09 to 2010-11 this ratio was increased to 66.15%, 66.17% and 66.87% respectively. In the year 2011-12 it was the highest during all the study period. In the year 2011-12 this ratio was decreased to

66.36%. During all the study period average of this ratio was 65.65%. For all the five years of the study this ratio was lower than its average for one year and higher than its average for remaining four years.

It is apparent from the above table 4.3 for mehsana nagarik sahakari bank that Interest Expense to Total Expense Ratio was 77.07% in the year 2007-08 which was the highest during all the study period. In the year 2008-09 to 2011-12 this ratio shows continuously decreasing trend. In the year 2008-09 to 2011-12 this ratio was decreased to 74.24%, 72.81%, 62.33% and 61.22% respectively. In the year 2011-12 it was the lowest during all the study period. During all the study period average of this ratio was 69.53%. For all the five years of the study this ratio was lower than its average for two years and higher than its average for remaining three years.

It is cleared from the above table 4.3 for co-operative bank of mehsana that Interest Expense to Total Expense Ratio was 61.58% in the year 2007-08 which was the lowest during all the study period. In the year 2008-09 and 2009-10 this ratio was continuously increased to 69.49% and 72.27% respectively. In the year 2010-11 it was the lowest during all the study period. In the year 2010-11 it was decreased to 70.38%. In the year 2011-12 it was increased to 75.40% which was the highest during all the study period. During all the study period average of this ratio was 69.82%. For all the five years of the study this ratio was lower than its average for two years and higher than its average for remaining three years.

It isevident from the above table 4.3 for chhapi nagarik sahakari bank that Interest Expense to Total Expense Ratio was 76.92% in the year 2007-08 which was the highest during all the study period. In the year 2008-09 to 2011-12 this ratio shows continuously decreasing trend. In the year 2008-09 to 2011-12 this ratio was decreased to 74.69%, 67.52%, 66.57% and 63.61% respectively. In the year 2011-12 it was the lowest during all the study period. During all the study period average of this ratio was 69.86%. For all the five years of the study this ratio was lower than its average for three years and higher than its average in remaining two years.

It can be observed from the above table 4.3 for banaskantha mercantile co-operative bank that Interest Expense to Total Expense Ratio was 63.41% in the year 2007-08 which was the lowest during all the study period. In the year 2008-09 and 2009-10 this ratio was increased to 66.45% and 68.34% respectively. In the year 2009-10 it was the highest during all the study period. In the year 2010-11 this ratio was decreased to 65.75% and in the year 2011-12 it was increased to 66.92%. During all the study period average of this ratio was 66.17%. For all the five years of the study this ratio was lower than its average for one year and higher than its average in remaining four years.

It is obvious from the above table 4.3 for chanasma nagarik sahakari bank that Interest Expense to Total Expense Ratio was 69.74% in the year 2007-08. In the year 2008-09 this ratio was increased to 73.28% which was the highest during all the study period. In the year 2009-10 to 2011-12 this ratio was decreased to 71.59%, 70.09% and 68.47% respectively. In the year 2011-12 it was the lowest during all the study period.

During all the study period average of this ratio was 70.63%. For all the five years of the study this ratio was lower than its average for three years and higher than its average in remaining two years.

It is apparent from the above table 4.3 for patan nagarik sahakari bank that Interest Expense to Total Expense Ratio was 69.69% in the year 2007-08 which was the highest during all the study period. In the year 2008-09 to 2011-12 this ratio shows continuously decreasing trend. In the year 2008-09 to 2011-12 this ratio was decreased to 67.44%, 67.21%, 66.74% and 63.56% respectively. In the year 2011-12 it was the lowest during all the study period. During all the study period average of this ratio was 66.93%. For all the five years of the study this ratio was lower than its average for two years and higher than its average in remaining three years.

It can be seen from the above table 4.3 for all Citizen co-operative banks that average of Interest Expense to Total Expense Ratio during 2007-08 to 2011-12 was 67.30%. In the year 2007-08 average ratio of all banks was 67.52%. In the year 2008-09 this ratio was increased to 69.43% which was the highest during all the study period. In the year 2009-10 to 2011-12 this ratio was decreased to 68.50%, 65.90% and 65.15% respectively. In the year 2011-12 it was the lowest during all the study period. For all the five years of the study average ratio of all banks was lower than its average for two years and higher than its average in remaining three years.

❖ **F test (ANOVA) Analysis**

The statements of hypothesis are as under:

- **Hypothesis between the banks:**

H_0:   There is no significant difference in the interest expense to total expense ratio of different Citizen Co-operative banks of North Gujarat for every financial year.

H_1:   There is significant difference in the interest expense to total expense ratio of different Citizen Co-operative banks of North Gujarat for every financial year.

- **Hypothesis between the years:**

H_0:   There is no significant difference in interest expense to total expense ratio of every Citizen Co-operative bank of North Gujarat for different financial years.

H_1:   There is significant difference in the interest expense to total expense ratio of every Citizen Co-operative bank of North Gujarat for different financial years.

Table 4.3-A

Source of Variation	SS	df	MS	F
Between Banks	446.08	07	63.73	4.05
Between years	100.93	04	25.23	1.60
Error	441.01	28	15.75	
Total	988.01	39		

Table Value for df (7,28) is 2.36 at 5% level of significance.

Table Value for df (4,28) is 2.71 at 5% level of significance.

Table 4.3-A represents the difference for the banks is significant because the table value for df (7,28) is (2.36) which is lower than calculated value of 'F' (4.05). So, null hypothesis (H_o) is rejected and alternative hypothesis (H_1) is accepted. i.e. There is significant difference in the interest expense to total expense ratio of different Citizen Co-operative banks of North Gujarat for every financial year.

Same way the difference for the years is not significant because the table value for df (4,28) is (2.71) which is higher than the calculated value of 'F' (1.60) for years and so here null hypothesis(H_o) is accepted and alternative hypothesis (H_1) is rejected. i.e. There is no significant difference in the interest expense to total expense ratio of every Citizen Co-operative bank of North Gujarat for different financial years.

4.3.2 Operating Expense to Total Expense Ratio

Operating expenses include salary, pension, gratuity, and other allowances/ expenses pertaining to staff.[4]These appear as the second largest expenses after the interest and discount paid by the banks on deposits and borrowings.[5]By this ratio we can know proportion of operatingexpense in bank's total expense. Formula for the ratio of operatingexpense to total expense is as follows:

$$\text{Operating Expense to Total Expense Ratio} = \frac{\text{Operating Expense}}{\text{Total Expense}} *100$$

Higher ratio indicates inefficiency in the management of operating expenses.

Operating Expense to Total Expense Ratio of selected citizen cooperative banks of North Gujarat for the study period 2007-08 to 2011-12 is presented in the table 4.1as follows:

Table 4.4

Operating Expense to Total Expense Ratio

YEAR	HIMNSB	MODNSB	MEHNSB	COBMEH	CHHNSB	BANMCB	CHANSB	PATNSB	AVERAGE
2007-08	26.77	19.26	14.14	9.72	10.44	20.19	16.96	23.68	17.65
2008-09	25.87	17.94	15.02	9.01	10.38	19.68	15.56	22.33	16.97
2009-10	27.95	18.73	14.66	8.98	13.32	19.71	15.96	22.78	17.76
2010-11	33.70	20.96	17.11	9.99	12.55	22.29	15.26	20.96	19.10
2011-12	30.99	20.68	18.00	8.87	18.12	21.22	13.39	19.38	18.83
AVERAGE	29.06	19.51	15.79	9.31	12.96	20.62	15.43	21.83	18.06

Source: Annual reports of CCBs during year 2007-08 to 2011-12.

It can be observed from the above table 4.4 for himmatnagar nagarik sahakari bank that Operating Expense to Total Expense Ratio was 26.77% in the year 2007-08. In the year 2008-09 this ratio was decreased to 25.87% which was the lowest during all the study period. In the year 2009-10 and 2010-11 this ratio was increased to 27.95%

and 33.70% respectively. In the year 2010-11 it was the highest during all the study period. In the year 2011-12 this ratio was decreased to 30.99%. During all the study period average of this ratio was 29.06%. For all the five years of the study this ratio was lower than its average for three years and higher than its average in remaining two years.

It is obvious from the above table 4.4 for modasa nagarik sahakari bank that Operating Expense to Total Expense Ratio was 19.26% in the year 2007-08. In the year 2008-09 this ratio was decreased to 17.94% which was the lowest during all the study period. In the year 2009-10 and 2010-11 this ratio was increased to 18.73% and 20.96% respectively. In the year 2010-11 it was the highest during all the study period. In the year 2011-12 this ratio was decreased to 20.68%. During all the study period average of this ratio was 19.51%. For all the five years of the study this ratio was lower than its average for three years and higher than its average for remaining two years.

It is apparent from the above table 4.4 for mehsana nagarik sahakari bank that Operating Expense to Total Expense Ratio was 14.14% in the year 2007-08 which was the lowest during all the study period. In the year 2008-09 this ratio was increased to 15.02% and in the year 2009-10 it was decreased to 14.66%. In the year 2010-11 and 2011-12 this ratio was increased to 17.11% and 18% respectively. In the year 2011-12 it was the highest during all the study period. During all the study period average of this ratio was 15.79%. For all the five years of the study this ratio was lower than its average for three years and higher than its average for remaining two years.

It is cleared from the above table 4.4 for co-operative bank of mehsana that Operating Expense to Total Expense Ratio was 9.72% in the year 2007-08. In the year 2008-09 and 2009-10 this ratio was decreased to 9.01% and 8.98% respectively. In the year 2010-11 it was the lowest during all the study period. In the year 2010-11 it was increased to 9.99% which was the highest during all the study period. In the year 2011-12 it was decreased to 8.87% which was the lowest during all the study period. During all the study period average of this ratio was 9.31%. For all the five years of the study this ratio was lower than its average for three years and higher than its average for remaining two years.

It isevident from the above table 4.4 for chhapi nagarik sahakari bank that Operating Expense to Total Expense Ratio was 10.44% in the year 2007-08. In the year 2008-09 this ratio was decreased to 10.38% which was the lowest during all the study period. In the year 2009-10 it was increased to 13.32% and in the year 2010-11 it was decreased to 12.55%. In the year 2011-12 this ratio was increased to 18.12% which was the highest during all the study period. During all the study period average of this ratio was 12.96%. For all the five years of the study this ratio was lower than its average for three years and higher than its average in remaining two years.

It can be observed from the above table 4.4 for banaskantha mercantile co-operative bank that Operating Expense to Total Expense Ratio was 20.19% in the year 2007-08. In the year 2008-09 this ratio was decreased to 19.68% which was the lowest during all the study period. In the year 2009-10 and 2010-11 it was increased to 19.71%

and 22.29% respectively. In the year 2010-11 it was the highest during all the study period. In the year 2011-12 this ratio was decreased to 21.22% which was the highest during all the study period. During all the study period average of this ratio was 20.62%. For all the five years of the study this ratio was lower than its average for three years and higher than its average in remaining two years.

It is obvious from the above table 4.4 for chanasma nagarik sahakari bank that Operating Expense to Total Expense Ratio was 16.96% in the year 2007-08 which was the highest during all the study period. In the year 2008-09 this ratio was decreased to 15.56%. In the year 2009-10 this ratio was increased to 15.96% and in the year 2010-11 it was decreased to 15.26%. In the year 2011-12 this ratio was decreased to 13.39% which was the lowest during all the study period. During all the study period average of this ratio was 15.43%. For all the five years of the study this ratio was lower than its average for two years and higher than its average in remaining three years.

It is apparent from the above table 4.4 for patan nagarik sahakari bank that Operating Expense to Total Expense Ratio was 23.68% in the year 2007-08 which was the highest during all the study period. In the year 2008-09 this ratio was decreased to 22.33%. In the year 2009-10 this ratio was increased to 22.78% and in the year 2010-11 it was decreased to 20.96%. In the year 2011-12 this ratio was decreased to 19.38% which was the lowest during all the study period. During all the study period average of this ratio was 21.83%. For all the five years of the study this ratio was lower than its average for two years and higher than its average in remaining three years.

It can be seen from the above table 4.4 for all Citizen co-operative banks that average of Operating Expense to Total Expense Ratio during 2007-08 to 2011-12 was 18.06%. In the year 2007-08 average ratio of all banks was 17.65%. In the year 2008-09 this ratio was decreased to 16.97% which was the lowest during all the study period. In the year 2009-10 and 2010-11 this ratio was increased to 17.76% and 19.10% respectively. In the year 2010-11 it was the highest during all the study period. In the year 2011-12 this ratio was decreased to 18.83%. For all the five years of the study average ratio of all banks was lower than its average for three years and higher than its average in remaining two years.

❖ F test (ANOVA) Analysis

The statements of hypothesis are as under:

- **Hypothesis between the banks:**

H_0: There is no significant difference in the Operatingexpense to total expense ratio of different Citizen Co-operative banks of North Gujarat for every financial year.

H_1: There is significant difference in the Operatingexpense to total expense ratio of different Citizen Co-operative banks of North Gujarat for every financial year.

- **Hypothesis between the years:**

H₀: There is no significant difference in Operatingexpense to total expense ratio of every Citizen Co-operative bank of North Gujarat for different financial years.

H₁: There is significant difference in the Operatingexpense to total expense ratio of every Citizen Co-operative bank of North Gujarat for different financial years.

Table 4.4-A

Source of Variation	SS	df	MS	F
Between Banks	1291.90	07	184.56	52.26
Between years	24.96	04	6.24	1.77
Error	98.88	28	3.53	
Total	1415.73	39		

Table Value for df (7,28) is 2.36 at 5% level of significance.

Table Value for df (4,28) is 2.71 at 5% level of significance.

Table 4.4-A represents the difference for the banks is significant because the table value for df (7,28) is (2.36) which is lower than calculated value of 'F' (52.26). So, null hypothesis (H₀) is rejected and alternative hypothesis (H₁) is accepted. i.e. There is significant difference in the Operatingexpense to total expense ratio of different Citizen Co-operative banks of North Gujarat for every financial year.

Same way the difference for the years is not significant because the table value for df (4,28) is (2.71) which is higher than the calculated value of 'F' (1.77) for years and so here null hypothesis(H₀) is accepted and alternative hypothesis (H₁) is rejected. i.e. There is no significant difference in the Operatingexpense to total expense ratio of every Citizen Co-operative bank of North Gujarat for different financial years.

4.3.3 Other Expense to Total Expense Ratio

Other expenses include rent, rates and taxes, postage, telephone and telegraph, stationery and printing, commission and exchange paid, sitting fees and allowances of the directors etc. By this ratio we can know proportion of otherexpense in bank's total expense. Formula for the ratio of otherexpense to total expense is as follows:

$$\text{Other Expense to Total Expense Ratio} = \frac{\text{Other Expense}}{\text{Total Expense}} *100$$

Higher ratio indicates inefficiency in the management of other expenses.

Other Expense to Total Expense Ratio of selected citizen cooperative banks of North Gujarat for the study period 2007-08 to 2011-12 is presented in the table 4.1as follows:

90

Table 4.5

Other Expense to Total Expense Ratio

YEAR	HIMNSB	MODNSB	MEHNSB	COBMEH	CHHNSB	BANMCB	CHANSB	PATNSB	AVERAGE
2007-08	14.20	18.03	8.79	28.70	12.64	16.40	13.30	6.63	14.84
2008-09	10.40	15.91	10.74	21.51	14.93	13.87	11.16	10.23	13.59
2009-10	9.93	15.10	12.52	18.75	19.16	11.96	12.44	10.00	13.73
2010-11	7.79	12.17	20.56	19.63	20.87	11.97	14.66	12.30	14.99
2011-12	13.33	12.97	20.78	15.73	18.27	11.86	18.14	17.06	16.02
AVERAGE	11.13	14.84	14.68	20.86	17.18	13.21	13.94	11.24	14.63

Source: Annual reports of CCBs during year 2007-08 to 2011-12.

It can be observed from the above table 4.5 for himmatnagar nagarik sahakari bank that Other Expense to Total Expense Ratio was 14.20% in the year 2007-08 which was the highest during all the study period. In the year 2008-09 this ratio was decreased to 10.40%. In the year 2009-10 and 2010-11 this ratio was decreased to 9.93% and 7.79% respectively. In the year 2010-11 it was the lowest during all the study period. In the year 2011-12 this ratio was increased to 13.33%. During all the study period average of this ratio was 11.13%. For all the five years of the study this ratio was lower than its average for three years and higher than its average in remaining two years.

It is obvious from the above table 4.5 for modasa nagarik sahakari bank that Other Expense to Total Expense Ratio was 18.03% in the year 2007-08 which was the highest during all the study period. In the year 2008-09 to 2010-11 this ratio was decreased to 15.91%, 15.10% and 12.17% respectively. In the year 2010-11 it was the lowest during all the study period. In the year 2011-12 this ratio was increased to 12.97%. During all the study period average of this ratio was 14.84%. For all the five years of the study this ratio was lower than its average for two years and higher than its average for remaining three years.

It is apparent from the above table 4.5 for mehsana nagarik sahakari bank that Other Expense to Total Expense Ratio was 8.79% in the year 2007-08 which was the lowest during all the study period. In the year 2008-09 to 2011-12 this ratio shows continuously increasing trend. In the year 2008-09 to 2011-12 this ratio was decreased to 10.74%, 12.52%, 20.56% and 20.78% respectively. In the year 2011-12 it was the highest during all the study period. During all the study period average of this ratio was 14.68%. For all the five years of the study this ratio was lower than its average for three years and higher than its average for remaining two years.

It is cleared from the above table 4.5 for co-operative bank of mehsana that Other Expense to Total Expense Ratio was 28.70% in the year 2007-08 which was the highest during all the study period. In the year 2008-09 and 2009-10 this ratio was decreased to 21.51% and 18.75% respectively. In the year 2010-11 it was increased to 19.63%. In the year 2011-12 it was decreased to 15.73% which was the lowest during all the study period. During all the study period average of this ratio was 20.86%. For all the five years of the study this ratio was lower than its average for three years and higher than its average for remaining two years.

It isevident from the above table 4.5 for chhapi nagarik sahakari bank that Other Expense to Total Expense Ratio was 12.64% in the year 2007-08 which was the lowest during all the study period. In the year 2008-09 to 2010-11 this ratio was increased to 14.93%, 19.16% and 20.87% respectively. In the year 2010-11 this ratio was the highest during all the study period. In the year 2011-12 this ratio was decreased to 18.27%. During all the study period average of this ratio was 17.18%. For all the five years of the study this ratio was lower than its average for two years and higher than its average in remaining three years.

It can be observed from the above table 4.5 for banaskantha mercantile co-operative bank that Other Expense to Total Expense Ratio was 16.40% in the year 2007-08 which was the highest during all the study period. In the year 2008-09 and 2009-10 this ratio was decreased to 13.87% and 11.96% respectively. In the year 2010-11 this ratio was increased to 11.97%. In the year 2011-12 this ratio was decreased to 11.86% which was the lowest during all the study period. During all the study period average of this ratio was 13.21%. For all the five years of the study this ratio was lower than its average for three years and higher than its average in remaining two years.

It is obvious from the above table 4.5 for chanasma nagarik sahakari bank that Other Expense to Total Expense Ratio was 13.30% in the year 2007-08. In the year 2008-09 this ratio was decreased to 11.16% which was the lowest during all the study period. In the year 2008-09 to 2011-12 this ratio was increased to 12.44%, 14.66% and 18.14% respectively. In the year 2011-12 it was the highest during all the study period. During all the study period average of this ratio was 13.94%. For all the five years of the study this ratio was lower than its average for three years and higher than its average in remaining two years.

It is apparent from the above table 4.5 for patan nagarik sahakari bank that Other Expense to Total Expense Ratio was 6.63% in the year 2007-08 which was the lowest during all the study period. In the year 2008-09 this ratio was increased to 10.23%. In the year 2009-10 this ratio was increased to 10.00% and in the year 2010-11 it was increased to 12.30%. In the year 2011-12 this ratio was increased to 17.06% which was the highest during all the study period. During all the study period average of this ratio was 11.24%. For all the five years of the study this ratio was lower than its average for three years and higher than its average in remaining two years.

It can be seen from the above table 4.5 for all Citizen co-operative banks that average of Other Expense to Total Expense Ratio during 2007-08 to 2011-12 was 14.63%. In the year 2007-08 average ratio of all banks was 14.84%. In the year 2008-09 this ratio was decreased to 13.59% which was the lowest during all the study period. In the year 2009-10 to 2011-12 this ratio was increased to 13.73%, 14.99% and 16.02% respectively. In the year 2011-12 it was the highest during all the study period. For all the five years of the study average ratio of all banks was lower than its average for two years and higher than its average in remaining three years.

❖ F test (ANOVA) Analysis

The statements of hypothesis are as under:

• Hypothesis between the banks:

H_0: There is no significant difference in the otherexpense to total expense ratio of different Citizen Co-operative banks of North Gujarat for every financial year.

H_1: There is significant difference in the otherexpense to total expense ratio of different Citizen Co-operative banks of North Gujarat for every financial year.

• Hypothesis between the years:

H_0: There is no significant difference in otherexpense to total expense ratio of every Citizen Co-operative bank of North Gujarat for different financial years.

H_1: There is significant difference in the otherexpense to total expense ratio of every Citizen Co-operative bank of North Gujarat for different financial years.

Table 4.5-A

Source of Variation	SS	df	MS	F
Between Banks	357.88	07	51.13	3.71
Between years	31.85	04	7.96	0.58
Error	385.71	28	13.78	
Total	775.44	39		

Table Value for df (7,28) is 2.36 at 5% level of significance.

Table Value for df (4,28) is 2.71 at 5% level of significance.

Table 4.5-A represents the difference for the banks is significant because the table value for df (7,28) is (2.36) which is lower than calculated value of 'F' (3.71). So, null hypothesis (H_o) is rejected and alternative hypothesis (H_1) is accepted. i.e. There is significant difference in the otherexpense to total expense ratio of different Citizen Co-operative banks of North Gujarat for every financial year.

Same way the difference for the years is not significant because the table value for df (4,28) is (2.71) which is higher than the calculated value of 'F' (0.58) for years and so here null hypothesis(H_o) is accepted and alternative hypothesis (H_1) is rejected. i.e. There is no significant difference in the otherexpense to total expense ratio of every Citizen Co-operative bank of North Gujarat for different financial years.

4.4   Net Profit

Generally, interest income is the main part of citizen co-operative bank's total income and interest expense is the main part of bank's total expense. Proportion of other income and expense remains lower than interest income and expense. Net profit is a deduction of total expenses, depreciation and taxes from total income from which other reserves can be raise up.

4.4.1 Net Profit to Total Income Ratio

Generally, Net Profit Ratio is calculated on the basis of total income. With the help of this ratio we can do evaluation of bank's annual activities. A higher ratio indicates handsome return on funds employed and the bank's ability to maintain reserves and provide dividend to its members. While a lower ratio indicates inefficient utilization of funds and increasing proportion of operating cost.

$$\text{Net Profit to Total Income Ratio} = \frac{\text{Net Profit}}{\text{Total Income}} * 100$$

Net Profit to Total Income Ratio of selected citizen cooperative banks of North Gujarat for the study period 2007-08 to 2011-12 is presented in the table 4.1as follows:

Table 4.6
Net Profit to Total Income Ratio

YEAR	HIMNSB	MODNSB	MEHNSB	COBMEH	CHHNSB	BANMCB	CHANSB	PATNSB	AVERAGE
2007-08	6.44	10.18	3.07	10.84	7.09	5.10	8.99	6.25	7.25
2008-09	6.65	9.87	4.55	10.27	4.71	5.07	8.21	7.92	7.16
2009-10	7.19	10.01	6.21	9.69	6.49	4.79	7.93	7.93	7.53
2010-11	8.02	9.45	4.75	12.09	4.76	4.65	8.04	7.16	7.37
2011-12	8.09	10.55	7.84	11.20	4.97	5.53	6.55	7.09	7.73
AVERAGE	7.28	10.01	5.28	10.82	5.60	5.03	7.94	7.27	7.41

Source: Annual reports of CCBs during year 2007-08 to 2011-12.

Chart 4.1
Chart showing Net Profit to Total Income Ratio

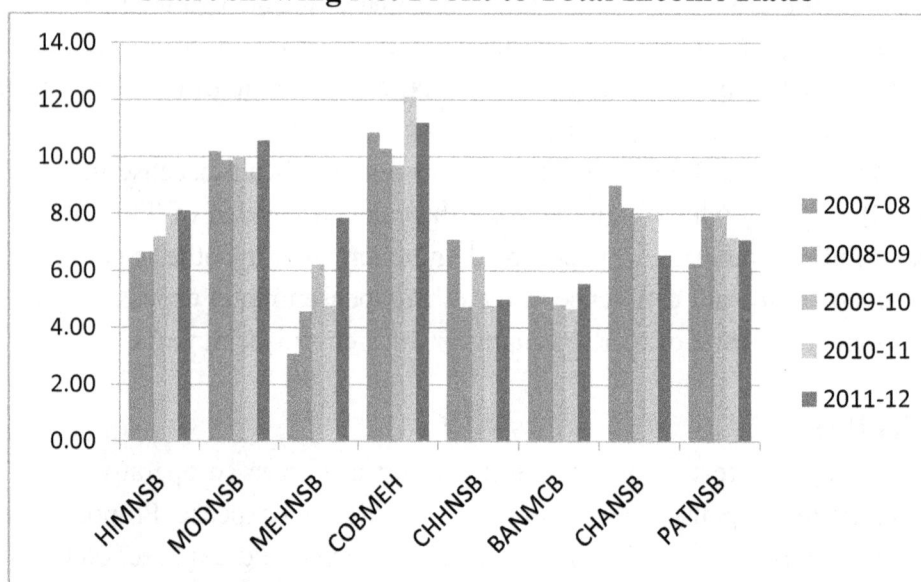

94

It can be observed from the above table 4.6 for himmatnagar nagarik sahakari bank that Net Profit to Total Income Ratio was 6.44% in the year 2007-08 which was the lowest during all the study period. In the year 2008-09 to 2011-12 this ratio shows continuously increasing trend. In the year 2008-09 to 2011-12 this ratio was decreased to 6.65%, 7.19%, 8.02% and 8.09% respectively. In the year 2011-12 it was the highest during all the study period. During all the study period average of this ratio was 7.28%. For all the five years of the study this ratio was lower than its average for three years and higher than its average in all the remaining two years.

It is obvious from the above table 4.6 for modasa nagarik sahakari bank that Net Profit to Total Income Ratio was 10.18% in the year 2007-08. In the year 2008-09 this ratio was decreased to 9.87% and in 2009-10 it was increased to 10.01% which was equal to the average of all the study period. In the year 2010-11 this ratio was decreased to 9.45% which was the lowest during all the study period. In the year 2011-12 this ratio was increased to 10.55%. In the year 2011-12 it was the highest during all the study period. During all the study period average of this ratio was 10.01%. For all the five years of the study this ratio was lower than its average for two years, higher than its average for two years and equal to its average for one year.

It is apparent from the above table 4.6 for mehsana nagarik sahakari bank that Net Profit to Total Income Ratio was 3.07% in the year 2007-08 which was the lowest during all the study period. In the year 2008-09 and 2009-10 this ratio was increased to 4.55% and 6.21% respectively. In the year 2010-11 this ratio decreased to 4.75%. In the year 2011-12 it was increased to 7.84% which was the highest during all the study period. During all the study period average of this ratio was 5.28%. For all the five years of the study this ratio was lower than its average for three years and higher than its average in all the remaining two years.

It is cleared from the above table 4.6 for co-operative bank of mehsana that Net Profit to Total Income Ratio was 10.84% in the year 2007-08. In the year 2008-09 and 2009-10 this ratio was continuously decreased to 10.27% and 9.69% respectively. In the year 2009-10 it was the lowest during all the study period. In the year 2010-11 this ratio increased to 12.09% which was the highest during all the study period. In the year 2011-12 it was decreased to 11.20%. During all the study period average of this ratio was 10.82%. For all the five years of the study this ratio was lower than its average for two years and higher than its average for remaining three years.

It isevident from the above table 4.6 for chhapi nagarik sahakari bank that Net Profit to Total Income Ratio was 7.09% in the year 2007-08 which was the highest during all the study period. In the year 2008-09 this ratio was decreased to 4.71% which was the lowest during all the study period. In the year 2009-10 this ratio was increased to 6.49% and in the year 2010-11 it was decreased 4.76%. In the year 2011-12 it was increased to 4.97%. During all the study period average of this ratio was 5.60%. For all the five years of the study this ratio was lower than its average for three years and higher than its average in all the remaining two years.

It can be observed from the above table 4.6 for banaskantha mercantile co-operative bank that Net Profit to Total Income Ratio was 5.10% in the year 2007-08. In the year 2008-09 to 2010-11 this ratio was decreased to 5.07%, 4.79% and 4.65% respectively. In the year 2010-11 it was the lowest during all the study period. In the year 2011-12 this ratio was increased to 5.53% which was the highest during all the study period. During all the study period average of this ratio was 5.03%. For all the five years of the study this ratio was lower than its average for two years and higher than its average in remaining three years.

It is obvious from the above table 4.6 for chanasma nagarik sahakari bank that Net Profit to Total Income Ratio was 8.99% in the year 2007-08% which was the highest during all the study period. In the year 2008-09 and 2009-10 this ratio was decreased to 8.21% and 7.93% respectively. In the year 2010-11 this ratio increased to 8.04%. In the year 2011-12 it was decreased to 6.55% which was the lowest during all the study period. During all the study period average of this ratio was 7.94%. For all the five years of the study this ratio was lower than its average for two years and higher than its average in remaining three years.

It is apparent from the above table 4.6 for patan nagarik sahakari bank that Net Profit to Total Income Ratio was 6.25% in the year 2007-08 which was the lowest during all the study period. In the year 2008-09 and 2009-10 this ratio was increased to 7.92% and 7.93% respectively. In the year 2009-10 it was the highest during all the study period. In the year 2010-11 and 2011-12 this ratio was decreased to 7.16% and 7.09% respectively. During all the study period average of this ratio was 7.27%. For all the five years of the study this ratio was lower than its average for three years and higher than its average in remaining two years.

It can be seen from the above table 4.6 for all Citizen co-operative banks that average of Net Profit to Total Income Ratio during 2007-08 to 2011-12 was 7.41%. In the year 2007-08 average ratio of all banks was 7.25%. In the year 2008-09 this ratio was decreased to 7.16% which was the lowest during all the study period. In the year 2009-10 it was increased to 7.53% and in the year 2010-11 it was decreased to 7.37%. In the year 2011-12 this ratio was increased to 7.73% which was the highest during all the study period. For all the five years of the study average ratio of all banks was lower than its average for three years and higher than its average in remaining two years.

❖ **F test (ANOVA) Analysis**

The statements of hypothesis are as under:

- **Hypothesis between the banks:**

H_0: There is no significant difference in the net Profit to total income ratio of different Citizen Co-operative banks of North Gujarat for every financial year.

H_1: There is significant difference in the net Profit to total income ratio of different Citizen Co-operative banks of North Gujarat for every financial year.

- **Hypothesis between the years:**

H₀: There is no significant difference in the net Profit to total income ratio of every Citizen Co-operative bank of North Gujarat for different financial years.

H₁: There is significant difference in the net Profit to total income ratio of every Citizen Co-operative bank of North Gujarat for different financial years.

Table 4.6-A

Source of Variation	SS	df	MS	F
Between Banks	160.84	07	22.98	22.83
Between years	1.67	04	0.42	0.41
Error	28.18	28	1.01	
Total	190.69	39		

Table Value for df (7,28) is 2.36 at 5% level of significance.
Table Value for df (4,28) is 2.71 at 5% level of significance.

Table 4.6-A represents the difference for the banks is significant because the table value for df (7,28) is (2.36) which is lower than calculated value of 'F' (22.83). So, null hypothesis (H₀) is rejected and alternative hypothesis (H₁) is accepted. i.e. There is significant difference in the net Profit to total income ratio of different Citizen Co-operative banks of North Gujarat for every financial year.

Same way the difference for the years is not significant because the table value for df (4,28) is (2.71) which is higher than the calculated value of 'F' (0.41) for years and so here also null hypothesis(H₀) is accepted and alternative hypothesis (H₁) is rejected. i.e. There is no significant difference in the net Profit to total income ratio of every Citizen Co-operative bank of North Gujarat for different financial years.

4.5 Conclusion

In this chapter researcher has tried to analyze income and expenses of selected Citizen co-operative banks of north Gujarat. For this purpose researcher has calculated total six ratios i.e. Interest Income to Total Income Ratio, Non-Interest Income to Total Income Ratio, Interest Expense to Total Expense Ratio, Operating Expense to Total Expense Ratio, Other Expense to Total Expense Ratio and Net Profit to Total Income Ratio of selected Citizen co-operative banks of north Gujarat.

In the analysis of income and expenses, profit and loss account of selected Citizen co-operative banks has been analyzed with the help of above six ratios and "F" test (ANOVA) of all ratios proves that there is no uniformity in income and expenses of different Citizen Co-operative banks of North Gujarat for every financial year. Majority ratios also prove that there is uniformity in income and expenses of every Citizen Co-operative banks of North Gujarat for different financial year.

References

1. Harry G. Guthmann, "Analysis of Financial Statements" New Delhi, Prentice Hall of India Pvt. Ltd. (1976) p.46.
2. R.D. Kennedy and S.Y. Mcmullen, "Financial Statements-Form Analysis and Interpretation, 6th ed., (Richard D. Irwin : Homewood, Illinois). (1968) p.5.
3. Paton and Paton, "Corporation Accounts and Statements" New York, McMillan. (1964) p.362.
4. R.K. Uppal, "Profitability Behaviour of Major Banks in the Post Economic Reforms Era" A Research Journal of Humanities & Social Sciences, Vol. 3, June, (2005) pp.103-118
5. Amandeep, "Profits and Profitability of Indian Nationalised Banks" Doctoral Thesis, Chandigarh, Panjab University, (1991).

Chapter-5
Analysis of Profitability

5.1   Introduction

Profit - the soul of any business - is the fundamental objective of the business. It is the ultimate test of the firm's wellbeing. It is a comprehensive indicator of the management's ability to coordinate the functions of planning and decision-making. Business is lifeless without profit. Failure to make profit results in erosion of capital that ultimately leads to closure of the business. Profit is the only alternative available to attract and retain the required capital. Further, investment decisions are largely affected by profit. Whether it is production, marketing or investment, it is the profit figure which is in the driving seat and that makes decision-making easier. Hence for a banker, profit has become very significant. **J.M. Keynes** remarked; "the profit is the engine that drives the business Enterprise."[1]

According to **Peter Drucker**, "profit in business serves three purposes: (I) it measures the net effectiveness and soundness of business effort; (II) it is the premium that covers the cost of staying in the business, replacements, obsolescence, market and technical risk and uncertainty; and (III) it ensures the supply of future capital, either by providing means for ploughing back of profit or by attracting new outside capital."[2]

In the modern business world, emergence of new concepts like strategic alliance and 'co-opetition' are mainly due to the desire for earning more profits. In a nutshell, "profit is the progressive report card of the past, inventive gold star of the future, and also the grab stake for new ventures."[3]

The word profit has been defined in a number of ways. **Kohler** defined profits as "A general term for the excess of revenue proceeds or selling price over related cost." [4] According to **Davidson, Stickney and Wail** "The term net income earnings and profits are synonymous used interchangeably in corporate annual report."[5]

Profitability is the most important parameter for financial analysis of any business organization. In the changing economic environment, it is very important to get idea of profitability of various banking groups. So, this chapter deals with the profitability analysis of Co-operative Banking Sector.

5.2 Concept of Profitability

Profits are the reminder available after deducting the cost of operation from the operational revenue. But profitability is the profit making ability of a business organization. It is an index of operational efficiency. "The word profitability is composed of two words profit and ability. The word profit has been defined in a number of ways. The term ability is also referred to as earning power or operating performance of the concerned investment. Profitability may be defined as the ability of a given investment to earn a return from its use."[6]

The overall objective of a business is to earn at least a satisfaction return on fund invested in it, consistent with maintaining a sound financial position. Satisfactory return depends upon several factors, including the nature of business risk. According to **Chakra borty**, "The term profitability has a sense of relatives, whereas the term profit is used in absolute sense."[7] The efficiency of a business concern is generally measured by the amount of profit earned. According to **Kuchhal S.C.,** "The profit margin is a measure of overall profitability. This measure is also referred to as the net income percentage or the return on sales."[8]

Profitability means ability to earn profit and is measured in relative terms with various factors. Profitability is an important criterion to evaluate the overall efficiency of funds management. The Citizen co-operative banks, today, have been experiencing decline in productivity and erosion in profitability. They are facing a tough challenge to deliver at high expectation in a fiercely competitive credit environment and scepticism expressed on creditworthiness of borrowers and viability of the institution. Thusprofitability analysis is one of the significant aspects of financialanalysis of individual firms, industries or Citizen co-operative banks.

5.3 Measurement of Profitability

The profitability can be measured in terms of different components of income statement or balance sheet. Measurement of profitability is of great importance to a banking enterprise because it enables the   management to ascertain the exact standing of its bank in comparison to other banks in the same locality, city or town. It also helps them to take important decision regarding expansion of area of operation, adoption of modern technology, rising of additional funds, changes in financial policies etc. The ratio analysis can make comparison between different size firms much more meaningful. One can analyze performance of bank through profitability. The ratio is the most important measure of profitability of any organization. It provides an idea about the efficiency of a management in allocating its resources and earning returns thereby. In the word of **Murthy,** "The most important measure of profitability of enterprise is ratio."[9]

Measurement of profitability to ascertain the real efficiency and performance of a bank is of utmost importance. In order to measure profitability in banks, we should relate profit to acceptable factors. In other words, profitability can be judged by expressing profit as a percentage of total income, as a percentage of total deposits, as a percentage of working capital and as a percentage of total assets. For measuring performance of Citizen co-operative banks of North Gujarat in terms of profitability three ratios have been used, viz., spread ratio, burden ratio and profitability ratio.

5.4   Analysis of Profitability

Researcher has been made an attempt to judge the profitability of the selected Citizen co-operative banks of North Gujarat through the following ratios:

5.4.1   Interest Income to Working Funds Ratio

Interest earnings relate to funds based on income and represents the income from pure banking business. The major components of interest income consist of interest earned on loans and advances granted. It shows how far working funds are effectively utilized for profit making. The working funds denote the total of the balance sheet items except contra items. Formula for the ratio of interest income to working funds is as follows:

$$\text{Interest Income to Working Funds Ratio} = \frac{\text{Interest Income}}{\text{Working Funds}} * 100$$

The higher this ratio is, higher is the interest based earnings of the bank. Thus, a high ratio is desirable.

Interest Income to Working Funds Ratio of selected citizen cooperative banks of North Gujarat for the study period 2007-08 to 2011-12 is presented in the table 5.1as follows:

Table 5.1
Interest Income to Working Funds Ratio

YEAR	HIMN SB	MODNS B	MEHNS B	COBME H	CHHNS B	BANMC B	CHANS B	PATNS B	AVERAGE
2007-08	8.67	9.19	10.84	8.41	8.43	10.29	9.25	8.16	9.15
2008-09	8.80	9.50	9.44	8.34	8.44	10.70	10.59	8.58	9.30
2009-10	9.08	9.49	8.96	8.03	10.08	9.89	10.14	8.14	9.23
2010-11	8.41	8.93	7.80	8.57	8.67	9.81	10.17	7.73	8.76
2011-12	9.62	9.40	8.80	9.06	9.75	10.50	10.66	8.30	9.51
AVERAGE	8.92	9.30	9.17	8.48	9.07	10.24	10.16	8.18	9.19

Source: Annual reports of CCBs during year 2007-08 to 2011-12.

It can be observed from the above table 5.1 for himmatnagar nagarik sahakari bank that Interest Income to Working Funds Ratio was 8.67% in the year 2007-08. In the year 2008-09 and 2009-10 this ratio was increased to 8.80% and 9.08% respectively. In the year 2010-11 this ratio decreased to 8.41% which was the lowest during all the study period. In the year 2011-12 it was increased to 9.62% which was the highest during all the study period. During all the study period average of this ratio was 8.92%. For all the five years of the study this ratio was lower than its average for three years and higher than its average in the remaining two years.

It is obvious from the above table 5.1 for modasa nagarik sahakari bank that Interest Income to Working Funds Ratio was 9.19% in the year 2007-08 which was the lowest during all the study period. In the year 2008-09 this ratio was increased to 9.50% which was the highest during all the study period. In the year 2009-10 and 2010-11 it was decreased to 9.49% and 8.93% respectively. In the year 2011-12 this ratio was increased to 9.40%. During all the study period average of this ratio was 9.30%. For all the five years of the study this ratio was lower than its average for two years and higher than its average for remaining three years.

It is apparent from the above table 5.1 for mehsana nagarik sahakari bank that Interest Income to Working Funds Ratio was 10.84% in the year 2007-08 which was the highest during all the study period. In the year 2008-09 to 2010-11 this ratio was continuously decreased to 9.44%, 8.96% and 7.80% respectively. In the year 2010-11 this ratio was the lowest during all the study period. In the year 2011-12 it was increased to 8.80%. During all the study period average of this ratio was 9.17%. For all the five years of the study this ratio was lower than its average for three years and higher than its average in the remaining two years.

It is cleared from the above table 5.1 for co-operative bank of mehsana that Interest Income to Working Funds Ratio was 8.41% in the year 2007-08. In the year 2008-09 to 2009-10 this ratio was continuously decreased to 8.34%, 99.16% and 8.03% respectively. In the year 2009-10 it was the lowest during all the study period. In the year 2010-11 to 2011-12 it was increased to 8.57% and 9.06% respectively. In the year 2011-12 this ratio was the highest during all the study period. During all the study period average of this ratio was 8.48%. For all the five years of the study this ratio was lower than its average for three years and higher than its average in the remaining two years.

It isevident from the above table 5.1 for chhapi nagarik sahakari bank that Interest Income to Working Funds Ratio was 8.43% in the year 2007-08 which was the lowest during all the study period. In the year 2008-09 and 2009-10 this ratio was increased to 8.44% and 10.08% respectively. In the year 2009-10 it was the highest during all the study period. In the year 2010-11 this ratio was decreased to 8.67% and in the year 2011-12 it was increased to 9.75%. During all the study period average of this ratio was 9.07%. For all the five years of the study this ratio was lower than its average for three years and higher than its average in the remaining two years.

It can be observed from the above table 5.1 for banaskantha mercantile co-operative bank that Interest Income to Working Funds Ratio was 10.29% in the year 2007-08. In the year 2008-09 this ratio was increased to 10.70% which was the highest during all the study period. In the year 2009-10 and 2010-11 it was decreased to 9.89% and 9.81%. respectively. In the year 2010-11 it was the lowest during all the study period. In the year 2011-12 it was increased to 10.50%. During all the study period average of this ratio was 10.24%. For all the five years of the study this ratio was lower than its average for two years and higher than its average in remaining three years.

It is obvious from the above table 5.1 for chanasma nagarik sahakari bank that Interest Income to Working Funds Ratio was 9.25% in the year 2007-08 which was the lowest during all the study period. In the year 2008-09 this ratio was increased to 10.59%. In the year 2009-10 this ratio was decreased to 10.14% and 2010-11 it was increased to 10.17%. In the year 2011-12 it was increased to 10.66% which was the highest during all the study period. During all the study period average of this ratio was 10.16%. For all the five years of the study this ratio was lower than its average for two years and higher than its average in remaining three years.

It is apparent from the above table 5.1 for patan nagarik sahakari bank that Interest Income to Working Funds Ratio was 8.16% in the year 2007-08. In the year 2008-09 this ratio was increased to 8.58% which was the highest during all the study period. In the year 2009-10 and 2010-11 this ratio was decreased to 8.14% and 7.73% respectively. In the year 2010-11 it was the lowest during all the study period. In the year 2011-12 this ratio was increased to 8.30%. During all the study period average of this ratio was 8.18%. For all the five years of the study this ratio was lower than its average for three years and higher than its average in remaining two years.

It can be seen from the above table 5.1 for all Citizen co-operative banks that average of Interest Income to Working Funds Ratio during 2007-08 to 2011-12 was 9.19%. In the year 2007-08 average ratio of all banks was 9.15%. In the year 2008-09 this ratio was increased to 9.30%. In the year 2009-10 and 2010-11 this ratio was decreased to 9.23% and 8.76% respectively. In the year 2010-11 it was the lowest during all the study period. In the year 2011-12 this ratio was increased to 9.51% which was the highest during all the study period. For all the five years of the study average ratio of all banks was lower than its average for two years and higher than its average in remaining three years.

❖ F test (ANOVA) Analysis

The statements of hypothesis are as under:

• Hypothesis between the banks:

H_0: There is no significant difference in the interest income to working funds ratio of different Citizen Co-operative banks of North Gujarat for every financial year.

H_1: There is significant difference in the interest income to working funds ratio of different Citizen Co-operative banks of North Gujarat for every financial year.

• Hypothesis between the years:

H_0: There is no significant difference in the interest income to working funds ratio of every Citizen Co-operative bank of North Gujarat for different financial years.

H_1: There is significant difference in the interest income to working funds ratio of every Citizen Co-operative bank of North Gujarat for different financial years.

Table 5.1-A

Source of Variation	SS	df	MS	F
Between Banks	18.32	07	2.62	8.29
Between years	2.42	04	0.61	1.92
Error	8.84	28	0.32	
Total	29.58	39		

Table Value for df (7,28) is 2.36 at 5% level of significance.

Table Value for df (4,28) is 2.71 at 5% level of significance.

Table 5.1-A represents the difference for the banks is significant because the table value for df (7,28) is (2.36) which is lower than calculated value of 'F' (8.29). So, null hypothesis (H_o) is rejected and alternative hypothesis (H_1) is accepted. I.e. there is significant difference in the interest income to working funds ratio of different Citizen Co-operative banks of North Gujarat for every financial year.

Same way the difference for the years is not significant because the table value for df (4,28) is (2.71) which is higher than the calculated value of 'F' (1.92) for years and so here null hypothesis(H_o) is accepted and alternative hypothesis (H_1) is rejected. I.e. there is no significant difference in the interest income to working funds ratio of every Citizen Co-operative bank of North Gujarat for different financial years.

5.4.2 Interest Expense to Working Funds Ratio

Interest expenditure relates to funds based on expenditure and represents the cost of funds to the bank. The major items of interest expenditure consist of interest paid on deposits and interest paid on borrowing. It is an indicator of the rate at which a bank incurs expenditure by borrowing funds. Formula for the ratio of interest expense to working funds is as follows:

$$\text{Interest Expense to Working Funds Ratio} = \frac{\text{Interest Expense}}{\text{Working Funds}} \times 100$$

A lower ratio is preferable for banks.

Interest Expense to Working Funds Ratio of selected citizen cooperative banks of North Gujarat for the study period 2007-08 to 2011-12 is presented in the table 5.2 as follows:

Table 5.2
Interest Expense to Working Funds Ratio

YEAR	HIMNSB	MODNSB	MEHNSB	COBMEH	CHHNSB	BANMCB	CHANSB	PATNSB	AVERAGE
2007-08	5.05	5.28	8.29	4.68	6.11	6.45	5.94	5.40	5.90
2008-09	5.32	5.75	6.86	5.25	6.23	6.93	7.19	5.37	6.11
2009-10	5.31	5.74	6.26	5.29	6.46	6.59	6.74	5.07	5.93
2010-11	4.59	5.45	4.75	5.33	5.57	6.26	6.60	4.84	5.43
2011-12	4.99	5.60	5.07	6.12	5.93	6.72	6.93	4.93	5.79
AVERAGE	5.05	5.56	6.25	5.33	6.06	6.59	6.68	5.12	5.83

Source: Annual reports of CCBs during year 2007-08 to 2011-12.

It can be observed from the above table 5.2 for himmatnagar nagarik sahakari bank that Interest Expense to Working Funds Ratio was 5.05% in the year 2007-08 which was equal to average of all the study period. In the year 2008-09 this ratio was increased to 5.32% which was the highest during all the study period. In the year 2009-10 and 2010-11 this ratio was decreased to 5.31% and 4.59% respectively. In the year 2010-11 this ratio was the lowest during all the study period. In the year 2011-12 it was increased to 4.99%. During all the study period average of this ratio was 5.05%. For all the five years of the study this ratio was lower than its average for two years, higher than its average for two years and equal to its average for one year.

It is obvious from the above table 5.2 for modasa nagarik sahakari bank that Interest Expense to Working Funds Ratio was 5.28% in the year 2007-08 which was the lowest during all the study period. In the year 2008-09 this ratio was increased to 5.75% which was the highest during all the study period. In the year 2009-10 and 2010-11 it was decreased to 5.74% and 5.45% respectively. In the year 2011-12 this ratio was increased to 5.60%. During all the study period average of this ratio was 5.56%. For all the five years of the study this ratio was lower than its average for two years and higher than its average for remaining three years.

It is apparent from the above table 5.2 for mehsana nagarik sahakari bank that Interest Expense to Working Funds Ratio was 8.29% in the year 2007-08 which was the highest during all the study period. In the year 2008-09 to 2010-11 this ratio was continuously decreased to 6.86%, 6.26% and 4.75% respectively. In the year 2010-11 this ratio was the lowest during all the study period. In the year 2011-12 it was increased to 5.07%. During all the study period average of this ratio was 6.25%. For all the five years of the study this ratio was lower than its average for two years and higher than its average in the remaining three years.

It is cleared from the above table 5.2 for co-operative bank of mehsana that Interest Expense to Working Funds Ratio was 4.68% in the year 2007-08 which was the lowest during all the study period. In the year 2008-09 to 2011-12 this ratio was continuously increased to 5.25%, 5.29%, 5.33% and 6.12% respectively. In the year 2010-11 this ratio was equal to average of all the study period and in the year 2011-12 it was the highest during all the study period. During all the study period average of this ratio was 8.48%. For all the five years of the study this ratio was lower than its average for three years, higher than its average for one year and equal to its average for remaining one year.

It isevident from the above table 5.2 for chhapi nagarik sahakari bank that Interest Expense to Working Funds Ratio was 6.11% in the year 2007-08. In the year 2008-09 and 2009-10 this ratio was increased to 6.23% and 6.46% respectively. In the year 2009-10 it was the highest during all the study period. In the year 2010-11 this ratio was decreased to 5.57% which was the lowest during all the study period. In the year 2011-12 it was increased to 5.93%. During all the study period average of this ratio was 6.06%. For all the five years of the study this ratio was lower than its average for two years and higher than its average in the remaining three years.

It can be observed from the above table 5.2 for banaskantha mercantile co-operative bank that Interest Expense to Working Funds Ratio was 6.45% in the year 2007-08. In the year 2008-09 this ratio was increased to 6.93% which was the highest during all the study period. In the year 2009-10 and 2010-11 it was decreased to 6.59% and 6.26% respectively. In the year 2009-10 this ratio was equal to average of all the study period and in the year 2010-11 it was the lowest during all the study period. In the year 2011-12 it was increased to 6.72%. During all the study period average of this ratio was 6.59%. For all the five years of the study this ratio was lower than its average for two years, higher than its average for two years and equal to its average for one year.

It is obvious from the above table 5.2 for chanasma nagarik sahakari bank that Interest Expense to Working Funds Ratio was 5.94% in the year 2007-08 which was the lowest during all the study period. In the year 2008-09 this ratio was increased to 7.19% which was the highest during all the study period. In the year 2009-10 and 2010-11 this ratio was decreased to 6.74% and 6.60% respectively. In the year 2011-12 it was increased to 6.93%. During all the study period average of this ratio was 6.68%. For all the five years of the study this ratio was lower than its average for two years and higher than its average in remaining three years.

It is apparent from the above table 5.2 for patan nagarik sahakari bank that Interest Expense to Working Funds Ratio was 5.40% in the year 2007-08 which was the highest during all the study period. In the year 2008-09 to 2010-11 this ratio was continuously decreased to 5.37%, 5.07% and 4.84% respectively. In the year 2010-11 it was the lowest during all the study period. In the year 2011-12 this ratio was increased to 4.93%. During all the study period average of this ratio was 5.12%. For all the five years of the study this ratio was lower than its average for three years and higher than its average in remaining two years.

It can be seen from the above table 5.2 for all Citizen co-operative banks that average of Interest Expense to Working Funds Ratio during 2007-08 to 2011-12 was 5.83%. In the year 2007-08 average ratio of all banks was 5.90%. In the year 2008-09 this ratio was increased to 6.11% which was the highest during all the study period. In the year 2009-10 and 2010-11 this ratio was decreased to 5.93% and 5.43% respectively. In the year 2010-11 it was the lowest during all the study period. In the year 2011-12 this ratio was increased to 5.79%. For all the five years of the study average ratio of all banks was lower than its average for two years and higher than its average in remaining three years.

❖ F test (ANOVA) Analysis

The statements of hypothesis are as under:

• Hypothesis between the banks:

H_0: There is no significant difference in the interest expense to working funds ratio of different Citizen Co-operative banks of North Gujarat for every financial year.

H_1: There is significant difference in the interest expense to working funds ratio of different Citizen Co-operative banks of North Gujarat for every financial year.

• Hypothesis between the years:

H_0: There is no significant difference in the interest expense to working funds ratio of every Citizen Co-operative bank of North Gujarat for different financial years.

H_1: There is significant difference in the interest expense to working funds ratio of every Citizen Co-operative bank of North Gujarat for different financial years.

Table 5.2-A

Source of Variation	SS	df	MS	F
Between Banks	14.76	07	2.11	6.23
Between years	2.08	04	0.52	1.54
Error	9.47	28	0.34	
Total	26.31	39		

Table Value for df (7,28) is 2.36 at 5% level of significance.
Table Value for df (4,28) is 2.71 at 5% level of significance.

107

Table 5.2-A represents the difference for the banks is significant because the table value for df (7,28) is (2.36) which is lower than calculated value of 'F' (6.23). So, null hypothesis (H$_o$) is rejected and alternative hypothesis (H$_1$) is accepted. I.e. there is significant difference in the interest expense to working funds ratio of different Citizen Co-operative banks of North Gujarat for every financial year.

Same way the difference for the years is not significant because the table value for df (4,28) is (2.71) which is higher than the calculated value of 'F' (1.54) for years and so here null hypothesis(H$_o$) is accepted and alternative hypothesis (H$_1$) is rejected. I.e. there is no significant difference in the interest expense to working funds ratio of every Citizen Co-operative bank of North Gujarat for different financial years.

5.4.3 Spread to Working Funds Ratio

The difference between interest earned and interest paid is called spread in banking terminology. It is also one of the important indicators to determine the profitability of the bank. As already mentioned, spread is calculated as the difference between the interest earned as percentage of working funds and interest paid as percentage of working funds. This ratio is useful to know how the banks are maintaining the funds to meet the expensed of management and administration.

As a matter of practice, every bank try to increase the spread volume so that it is sufficiently available to meet the non-interest expenses and the remainder contribute to the profit volume. Proper management and deployment of funds and assets available to banks is of great importance to enhance the spread volume. The larger is the spread, the higher are the profits of the bank. Here, It is computed as: Spread = Interest earned - Interest paid. Formula for the ratio of spread to working funds is as follows:

$$\textbf{Spread to Working Funds Ratio} = \frac{\textbf{Spread}}{\textbf{Working Funds}} *100$$

This ratio provides a cushion to the bank for meeting the expenses of management and administration. Thus, a higher ratio is desirable for banks.

Spread to Working Funds Ratioof selected citizen cooperative banks of North Gujarat for the study period 2007-08 to 2011-12 is presented in the table 5.3 as follows:

Table 5.3
Spread to Working Funds Ratio

YEAR	HIMNSB	MODNSB	MEHNSB	COBMEH	CHHNSB	BANMCB	CHANSB	PATNSB	AVERAGE
2007-08	3.62	3.90	2.55	3.74	2.31	3.84	3.31	2.76	3.25
2008-09	3.48	3.75	2.58	3.09	2.21	3.77	3.41	3.21	3.19
2009-10	3.78	3.75	2.69	2.74	3.62	3.29	3.40	3.07	3.29
2010-11	3.81	3.48	3.05	3.23	3.10	3.55	3.57	2.89	3.34
2011-12	4.63	3.80	3.73	2.94	3.82	3.78	3.73	3.37	3.73
AVERAGE	3.86	3.74	2.92	3.15	3.01	3.65	3.48	3.06	3.36

Chart 5.1
Chart Showing Spread to Working Funds Ratio

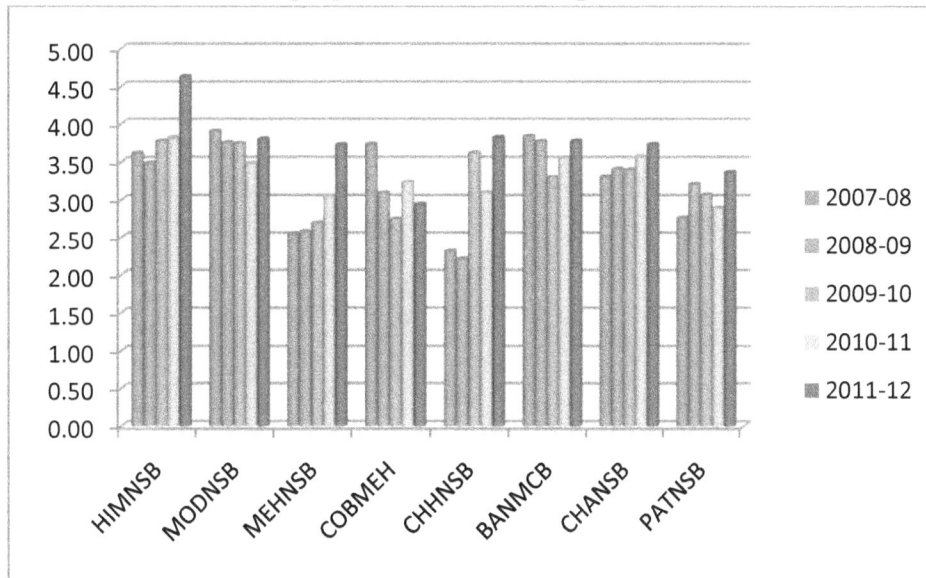

It can be observed from the above table 5.3 for himmatnagar nagarik sahakari bank that Spread to Working Funds Ratio was 3.62% in the year 2007-08. In the year 2008-09 this ratio was decreased to 3.48% which was the lowest during all the study period. In the year 2009-10 to 2011-12 this ratio was continuously increased to 3.78%, 3.81% and 4.63% respectively. In the year 2011-12 this ratio was the highest during all the study period. During all the study period average of this ratio was 3.86%. For all the five years of the study this ratio was lower than its average for four years and higher than its average for remaining one year.

It is obvious from the above table 5.3 for modasa nagarik sahakari bank that Spread to Working Funds Ratio was 3.90% in the year 2007-08 which was the highest during all the study period. In the year 2008-09 and 2009-10 this ratio was decreased to same 3.75%. In the year 2010-11 this ratio was decreased to 3.48% which was the lowest during all the study period. In the year 2011-12 this ratio was increased to 3.80%. During all the study period average of this ratio was 3.74%. For all the five years of the study this ratio was lower than its average for one year and higher than its average for remaining four years.

It is apparent from the above table 5.3 for mehsana nagarik sahakari bank that Spread to Working Funds Ratio was 2.55% in the year 2007-08 which was the lowest during all the study period. In the year 2008-09 to 2011-12 this ratio was continuously increased to 2.58%, 2.69%, 3.05% and 3.73% respectively. In the year 2011-12 this ratio was the highest during all the study period. During all the study period average of this ratio was 2.92%. For all the five years of the study this ratio was lower than its average for three years and higher than its average in the remaining two years.

It is cleared from the above table 5.3 for co-operative bank of mehsana that Spread to Working Funds Ratio was 3.74% in the year 2007-08 which was the highest during all the study period. In the year 2008-09 and 2009-10 this ratio was continuously decreased to 3.09% and 2.74% respectively. In the year 2009-10 it was the lowest during all the study period. In the year 2010-11 this ratio was increased to 3.23% and in the year 2011-12 it was decreased to 2.94%. During all the study period average of this ratio was 3.15%. For all the five years of the study this ratio was lower than its average for three years and higher than its average for remaining two years.

It isevident from the above table 5.3 for chhapi nagarik sahakari bank that Spread to Working Funds Ratio was 2.31% in the year 2007-08. In the year 2008-09 this ratio was decreased to 2.21% which was the lowest during all the study period. In the year 2009-10 this ratio was increased to 3.62% and in the year 2010-11 it was decreased to 3.10%. In the year 2011-12 it was increased to 3.82% which was the highest during all the study period. During all the study period average of this ratio was 3.01%. For all the five years of the study this ratio was lower than its average for two years and higher than its average in the remaining three years.

It can be observed from the above table 5.3 for banaskantha mercantile co-operative bank that Spread to Working Funds Ratio was 3.84% in the year 2007-08 which was the highest during all the study period. In the year 2008-09 and 2009-10 this ratio was decreased to 3.77% and 3.29% respectively. In the year 2009-10 this ratio was the lowest during all the study period. In the year 2010-11 and 2011-12 this ratio was increased to 3.55% and 3.78% respectively. During all the study period average of this ratio was 3.65%. For all the five years of the study this ratio was lower than its average for two years and higher than its average in the remaining three years.

It is obvious from the above table 5.3 for chanasma nagarik sahakari bank that Spread to Working Funds Ratio was 3.31% in the year 2007-08 which was the lowest during all the study period. In the year 2008-09 this ratio was increased to 3.41%. In the year 2009-10 this ratio was decreased to 3.40%. In the year 2010-11 and 2011-12 this ratio was increased to 3.57% and 3.73% respectively. In the year 2011-12 this ratio was the highest during all the study period. During all the study period average of this ratio was 3.48%. For all the five years of the study this ratio was lower than its average for three years and higher than its average in remaining two years.

It is apparent from the above table 5.3 for patan nagarik sahakari bank that Spread to Working Funds Ratio was 2.76% in the year 2007-08 which was the lowest during all the study period. In the year 2008-09 this ratio was increased to 3.21%. In the year 2009-10 and 2010-11 this ratio was continuously decreased to 3.07% and 2.89% respectively. In the year 2011-12 this ratio was increased to 3.37% which was the highest during all the study period. During all the study period average of this ratio was 3.06%. For all the five years of the study this ratio was lower than its average for two years and higher than its average in remaining three years.

It can be seen from the above table 5.3 for all Citizen co-operative banks that average of Spread to Working Funds Ratio during 2007-08 to 2011-12 was 3.36%. In the year 2007-08 average ratio of all banks was 3.25%. In the year 2008-09 this ratio was increased to 3.19% which was the lowest during all the study period. In the year 2009-10 to 2011-12 this ratio was continuously increased to 3.29%, 3.34% and 3.73% respectively. In the year 2011-12 it was the highest during all the study period. For all the five years of the study average ratio of all banks was lower than its average for four years and higher than its average in remaining one year.

❖ F test (ANOVA) Analysis

The statements of hypothesis are as under:

• Hypothesis between the banks:

H_0: There is no significant difference in the spread to working funds ratio of different Citizen Co-operative banks of North Gujarat for every financial year.

H_1: There is significant difference in the spread to working funds ratio of different Citizen Co-operative banks of North Gujarat for every financial year.

• Hypothesis between the years:

H_0: There is no significant difference in the spread to working funds ratio of every Citizen Co-operative bank of North Gujarat for different financial years.

H_1: There is significant difference in the spread to working funds ratio of every Citizen Co-operative bank of North Gujarat for different financial years.

Table 5.3-A

Source of Variation	SS	df	MS	F
Between Banks	4.72	07	0.67	5.08
Between years	1.44	04	0.36	2.70
Error	3.72	28	0.13	
Total	9.88	39		

Table Value for df (7,28) is 2.36 at 5% level of significance.

Table Value for df (4,28) is 2.71 at 5% level of significance.

Table 5.3-A represents the difference for the banks is significant because the table value for df (7,28) is (2.36) which is lower than calculated value of 'F' (5.08). So, null hypothesis (H_o) is rejected and alternative hypothesis (H_1) is accepted. I.e. there is significant difference in the spread to working funds ratio of different Citizen Co-operative banks of North Gujarat for every financial year.

Same way the difference for the years is not significant because the table value for df (4,28) is (2.71) which is higher than the calculated value of 'F' (2.70) for years and so here null hypothesis(H_o) is accepted and alternative hypothesis (H_1) is rejected. I.e. there is no significant difference in the spread to working funds ratio of every Citizen Co-operative bank of North Gujarat for different financial years.

5.4.4 Non-Interest Income to Working Funds Ratio

Non-interest income of bank represents income earned by way of commission, exchanges, brokerage, service charges, and other miscellaneous receipts. Non-interest income is very nominal and inadequate to meet non-interest expenses and it may cause rise in burden. Efforts should be taken to improve the non-interest income ratio, so that burden could be reduced and profitability of the bank will be improved. If the bank diversified its activity, there is a possibility to improve the profitability. Formula for the ratio of Non-Interest Income to working funds is as follows:

$$\text{Non-Interest Income to Working Funds Ratio} = \frac{\text{Non-Interest Income}}{\text{Working Funds}} *100$$

Ideally, this ratio should be as high as possible for the banks.

Non-Interest Income to Working Funds Ratioof selected citizen cooperative banks of North Gujarat for the study period 2007-08 to 2011-12 is presented in the table 5.4as follows:

Table 5.4
Non-Interest Income to Working Funds Ratio

YEAR	HIMN SB	MODNS B	MEHNS B	COBME H	CHHNS B	BANMC B	CHANS B	PATNS B	AVERAG E
2007-08	0.48	0.19	0.26	0.11	0.13	0.44	0.12	0.10	0.23
2008-09	0.14	0.14	0.24	0.08	0.31	0.28	0.09	0.07	0.17
2009-10	0.12	0.15	0.21	0.07	0.15	0.24	0.09	0.06	0.14
2010-11	0.13	0.07	0.21	0.05	0.12	0.17	0.07	0.08	0.11
2011-12	0.13	0.04	0.19	0.08	0.06	0.13	0.17	0.05	0.11
AVERAGE	0.20	0.12	0.22	0.08	0.15	0.25	0.11	0.07	0.15

Source: Annual reports of CCBs during year 2007-08 to 2011-12.

It can be observed from the above table 5.4 for himmatnagar nagarik sahakari bank that Non-Interest Income to Working Funds Ratio was 0.48% in the year 2007-08 which was the highest during all the study period. In the year 2008-09 and 2009-10 this ratio was continuously decreased to 0.14% and 0.12% respectively. In the year 2009-10 this ratio was the lowest during all the study period. In the year to 2010-11 and 2011-12 this ratio was increased to same 0.13%. During all the study period average of this ratio was 0.20%. For all the five years of the study this ratio was lower than its average for four years and higher than its average for remaining one year.

It is obvious from the above table 5.4 for modasa nagarik sahakari bank that Non-Interest Income to Working Funds Ratio was 0.19% in the year 2007-08 which was the highest during all the study period. In the year 2008-09 this ratio was decreased to 0.14% and in the year 2009-10 it was increased to 0.15%. In the year 2010-11 and 2011-12 this ratio was decreased to 0.07% and 0.04% respectively. In the year 2011-12 this ratio was the lowest during all the study period. During all the study period average of this ratio was 0.12%. For all the five years of the study this ratio was lower than its average for two years and higher than its average for remaining three years.

It is apparent from the above table 5.4 for mehsana nagarik sahakari bank that Non-Interest Income to Working Funds Ratio was 0.26% in the year 2007-08 which was the highest during all the study period. In the year 2008-09 this ratio was decreased to 0.24%. In the year 2009-10 and 2010-11 this ratio was decreased to same 0.21%. In the year 2011-12 this ratio was decreased to same 0.19% which was the lowest during all the study period. During all the study period average of this ratio was 0.22%. For all the five years of the study this ratio was lower than its average for three years and higher than its average in the remaining two years.

It is cleared from the above table 5.4 for co-operative bank of mehsana that Non-Interest Income to Working Funds Ratio was 0.11% in the year 2007-08 which was the highest during all the study period. In the year 2008-09 to 2010-11 this ratio was continuously decreased to 0.08%, 0.07 and 0.05% respectively. In the year 2008-09 this ratio was equal to average of all the study period and in the year 2010-11 it was the lowest during all the study period. In the year 2011-12 this ratio was increased to 0.08% which was equal to average of all the study period. During all the study period average of this ratio was 0.08%. For all the five years of the study this ratio was lower than its average for two years, higher than its average for one year and equal to its average for two years.

It isevident from the above table 5.4 for chhapi nagarik sahakari bank that Non-Interest Income to Working Funds Ratio was 0.13% in the year 2007-08. In the year 2008-09 this ratio was increased to 0.31% which was the highest during all the study period. In the year 2009-10 to 2011-12 this ratio was continuously decreased to 0.15%, 0.12 and 0.06% respectively. In the year 2009-10 this ratio was equal to average of all the study period and in the year 2011-12 it was the lowest during all the study period. During all the study period average of this ratio was 0.15%. For all the five years of the study this ratio was lower than its average for three years, higher than its average for one year and equal to its average for one year.

It can be observed from the above table 5.4 for banaskantha mercantile co-operative bank that Non-Interest Income to Working Funds Ratio was 0.44% in the year 2007-08 which was the highest during all the study period. In the year 2008-09 to 2011-12 this ratio was continuously decreased to 0.28%, 0.24%, 0.17% and 0.13% respectively. In the year 2011-12 this ratio was the lowest during all the study period. During all the study period average of this ratio was 0.25%. For all the five years of the study this ratio was lower than its average for three years and higher than its average in the remaining two years.

It is obvious from the above table 5.4 for chanasma nagarik sahakari bank that Non-Interest Income to Working Funds Ratio was 0.12% in the year 2007-08. In the year 2008-09 and 2009-10 this ratio was decreased to same 0.09%. In the year 2010-11 this ratio was decreased to 0.07% which was the lowest during all the study period. In the year 2011-12 this ratio was increased to 0.17% which was the highest during all the study period. During all the study period average of this ratio was 0.11%. For all the five years of the study this ratio was lower than its average for three years and higher than its average in remaining two years.

It is apparent from the above table 5.4 for patan nagarik sahakari bank that Non-Interest Income to Working Funds Ratio was 0.10% in the year 2007-08 which was the highest during all the study period. In the year 2008-09 and 2009-10 this ratio was decreased to 0.07% and 0.06% respectively. In the year 2008-09 this ratio was equal to average of all the study period. In the year 2010-11 this ratio was increased to 0.08%. In the year 2011-12 this ratio was decreased to 0.05% which was the lowest during all the study period. During all the study period average of this ratio was 0.07%. For all the five years of the study this ratio was lower than its average for two years, higher than its average for two years and equal to its average for one year.

It can be seen from the above table 5.4 for all Citizen co-operative banks that average of Non-Interest Income to Working Funds Ratio during 2007-08 to 2011-12 was 0.15%. In the year 2007-08 average ratio of all banks was 0.23% which was the highest during all the study period. In the year 2008-09 and 2009-10 this ratio was decreased to 0.17% and 0.14% respectively. In the year 2010-11 and 2011-12 this ratio was decreased to same 0.11% which was the lowest during all the study period. For all the five years of the study average ratio of all banks was lower than its average for three years and higher than its average in remaining two years.

❖ F test (ANOVA) Analysis

The statements of hypothesis are as under:

• Hypothesis between the banks:

H_0:   There is no significant difference in the non-Interest Income to working funds ratio of different Citizen Co-operative banks of North Gujarat for every financial year.

H_1:   There is significant difference in the non-Interest Incometo working funds ratio of different Citizen Co-operative banks of North Gujarat for every financial year.

• Hypothesis between the years:

H_0:   There is no significant difference in the non-Interest Incometo working funds ratio of every Citizen Co-operative bank of North Gujarat for different financial years.

H_1:   There is significant difference in the non-Interest Incometo working funds ratio of every Citizen Co-operative bank of North Gujarat for different financial years.

Table 5.4-A

Source of Variation	SS	df	MS	F
Between Banks	0.16	07	0.02	4.77
Between years	0.08	04	0.02	4.04
Error	0.14	28	0.00	
Total	0.38	39		

Table Value for df (7,28) is 2.36 at 5% level of significance.

Table Value for df (4,28) is 2.71 at 5% level of significance.

Table 5.4-A represents the difference for the banks is significant because the table value for df (7,28) is (2.36) which is lower than calculated value of 'F' (4.77). So, null hypothesis (H_o) is rejected and alternative hypothesis (H_1) is accepted. I.e. there is significant difference in the non-Interest Income to working funds ratio of different Citizen Co-operative banks of North Gujarat for every financial year.

Same way the difference for the years is significant because the table value for df (4,28) is (2.71) which is lower than the calculated value of 'F' (4.04) for years and so here also null hypothesis (H_o) is rejected and alternative hypothesis (H_1) is accepted. I.e. there is significant difference in the non-Interest Income to working funds ratio of every Citizen Co-operative bank of North Gujarat for different financial years.

5.4.5 Non-Interest Expense to Working Funds Ratio

Non-interest expenditure of banks denotes expenses on manpower and other expenses. The ratio non-interest expenditure as percentage of working funds expresses the effective management of funds. It shows the operational efficiency of the bank. Formula for the ratio of non-interest expense to working funds is as follows:

$$\text{Non-Interest Expense to Working Funds Ratio} = \frac{\text{Non-Interest Expense}}{\text{Working Funds}} * 100$$

Ideally, this ratio should be as low as possible for the banks.

Non-Interest Expense to Working Funds Ratio of selected citizen cooperative banks of North Gujarat for the study period 2007-08 to 2011-12 is presented in the table 5.5as follows:

Table 5.5
Non-Interest Expense to Working Funds Ratio

YEAR	HIMNSB	MODNSB	MEHNSB	COBMEH	CHHNSB	BANMCB	CHANSB	PATNSB	AVERAGE
2007-08	3.50	3.14	2.47	2.92	1.83	3.72	2.58	2.35	2.81
2008-09	3.03	2.94	2.38	2.31	2.11	3.50	2.62	2.59	2.68
2009-10	3.24	2.93	2.34	2.03	3.11	3.05	2.68	2.47	2.73
2010-11	3.26	2.70	2.87	2.24	2.80	3.26	2.82	2.41	2.80
2011-12	3.97	2.84	3.21	2.00	3.39	3.32	3.19	2.83	3.09
AVERAGE	3.40	2.91	2.65	2.30	2.65	3.37	2.78	2.53	2.82

Source: Annual reports of CCBs during year 2007-08 to 2011-12.

It can be observed from the above table 5.5 for himmatnagar nagarik sahakari bank that Non-Interest Expense to Working Funds Ratio was 3.50% in the year 2007-08. In the year 2008-09 this ratio was decreased to 3.03% which was the lowest during all the study period. In the year 2009-10 to 2011-12 this ratio was continuously increased to 3.24%, 3.26% and 3.97% respectively. In the year 2011-12 this ratio was the highest during all the study period. During all the study period average of this ratio was 3.40%. For all the five years of the study this ratio was lower than its average for three years and higher than its average for remaining two years.

It is obvious from the above table 5.5 for modasa nagarik sahakari bank that Non-Interest Expense to Working Funds Ratio was 3.14% in the year 2007-08 which was the highest during all the study period. In the year 2008-09 to 2010-11 this ratio was continuously decreased to 2.94%, 2.93% and 2.70% respectively. In the year 2010-11 this ratio was the lowest during all the study period. In the year 2011-12 this ratio was increased to 2.84%. During all the study period average of this ratio was 2.91%. For all the five years of the study this ratio was lower than its average for two years and higher than its average for remaining three years.

It is apparent from the above table 5.5 for mehsana nagarik sahakari bank that Non-Interest Expense to Working Funds Ratio was 2.47% in the year 2007-08. In the year 2008-09 and 2009-10 this ratio was continuously decreased to 2.38% and 2.34% respectively. In the year 2009-10 this ratio was the lowest during all the study period. In the year 2010-11 and 2011-12 it was increased to 2.87% and 3.21% respectively. In the year 2011-12 this ratio was the highest during all the study period. During all the study period average of this ratio was 2.65%. For all the five years of the study this ratio was lower than its average for three years and higher than its average in the remaining two years.

It is cleared from the above table 5.5 for co-operative bank of mehsana that Non-Interest Expense to Working Funds Ratio was 2.92% in the year 2007-08 which was the highest during all the study period. In the year 2008-09 and 2009-10 this ratio was continuously decreased to 2.31% and 2.03% respectively. In the year 2010-11 this ratio was increased to 2.24%. In the year 2011-12 this ratio was decreased to 2.00% which was the lowest during all the study period. During all the study period average of this ratio was 2.30%. For all the five years of the study this ratio was lower than its average for three years and higher than its average in the remaining two years.

It isevident from the above table 5.5 for chhapi nagarik sahakari bank that Non-Interest Expense to Working Funds Ratio was 1.83% in the year 2007-08 which was the lowest during all the study period. In the year 2008-09 and 2009-10 this ratio was increased to 2.11% and 3.11% respectively. In the year 2010-11 this ratio was decreased to 2.80%. In the year 2011-12 it was increased to 3.39% which was the highest during all the study period. During all the study period average of this ratio was 2.65%. For all the five years of the study this ratio was lower than its average for two years and higher than its average in the remaining three years.

It can be observed from the above table 5.5 for banaskantha mercantile co-operative bank that Non-Interest Expense to Working Funds Ratio was 3.72% in the year 2007-08 which was the highest during all the study period. In the year 2008-09 and 2009-10 this ratio was decreased to 3.50% and 3.05% respectively. In the year 2009-10 this ratio was the lowest during all the study period. In the year 2010-11and 2011-12it was increased to 3.26% and 3.32% respectively. During all the study period average of this ratio was 3.37%. For all the five years of the study this ratio was lower than its average for three years and higher than its average for two years.

It is obvious from the above table 5.5 for chanasma nagarik sahakari bank that Non-Interest Expense to Working Funds Ratio was 2.58% in the year 2007-08 which was the lowest during all the study period. In the year 2008-09 to 2011-12 this ratio was continuously increased to 2.62%, 2.68%, 2.82% and 3.19% respectively. In the year 2011-12 this ratio was the highest during all the study period. During all the study period average of this ratio was 2.78%. For all the five years of the study this ratio was lower than its average for three years and higher than its average in remaining two years.

It is apparent from the above table 5.5 for patan nagarik sahakari bank that Non-Interest Expense to Working Funds Ratio was 2.35% in the year 2007-08 which was the lowest during all the study period. In the year 2008-09 this ratio was increased to 2.59%. In the year 2009-10 and 2010-11 this ratio was decreased to 2.47% and 2.41% respectively. In the year 2011-12 this ratio was increased to 2.83%. In the year 2011-12 it was the highest during all the study period. During all the study period average of this ratio was 2.53%. For all the five years of the study this ratio was lower than its average for three years and higher than its average in remaining two years.

It can be seen from the above table 5.5 for all Citizen co-operative banks that average of Non-Interest Expense to Working Funds Ratio during 2007-08 to 2011-12 was 2.82%. In the year 2007-08 average ratio of all banks was 2.81%. In the year 2008-09 this ratio was decreased to 2.68% which was the lowest during all the study period. In the year 2009-10 to 2011-12 this ratio was continuously increased to 2.73%, 2.80% and 3.09% respectively. In the year 2011-12 it was the highest during all the study period. For all the five years of the study average ratio of all banks was lower than its average for four years and higher than its average in remaining one year.

❖ **F test (ANOVA) Analysis**

The statements of hypothesis are as under:
- **Hypothesis between the banks:**

H₀: There is no significant difference in the non-interest expense to working funds ratio of different Citizen Co-operative banks of North Gujarat for every financial year.

H₁: There is significant difference in the non-interest expense to working funds ratio of different Citizen Co-operative banks of North Gujarat for every financial year.

- **Hypothesis between the years:**

H₀: There is no significant difference in the non-interest expense to working funds ratio of every Citizen Co-operative bank of North Gujarat for different financial years.

H₁: There is significant difference in the non-interest expense to working funds ratio of every Citizen Co-operative bank of North Gujarat for different financial years.

Table 5.5-A

Source of Variation	SS	df	MS	F
Between Banks	5.31	07	0.76	6.41
Between years	0.82	04	0.20	1.73
Error	3.32	28	0.12	
Total	9.45	39		

Table Value for df (7,28) is 2.36 at 5% level of significance.

Table Value for df (4,28) is 2.71 at 5% level of significance.

Table 5.5-A represents the difference for the banks is significant because the table value for df (7,28) is (2.36) which is lower than calculated value of 'F' (6.41). So, null hypothesis (H₀) is rejected and alternative hypothesis (H₁) is accepted. I.e. there is significant difference in the non-interest expense to working funds ratio of different Citizen Co-operative banks of North Gujarat for every financial year.

Same way the difference for the years is not significant because the table value for df (4,28) is (2.71) which is higher than the calculated value of 'F' (1.73) for years and so here null hypothesis(H₀) is accepted and alternative hypothesis (H₁) is rejected. I.e. there is no significant difference in the non-interest expense to working funds ratio of every Citizen Co-operative bank of North Gujarat for different financial years.

5.4.6 Burden to Working Funds Ratio

The non-interest expenditure not covered by non-interest income is known as burden this helps to meet out the expenses for manpower and other expenses of banks. It is to be noted that the non-interest expense cannot be reduced. Hence the profitability of the banks depends on the spread. The profit may be defined as the difference between spread and burden, instead of difference between total income and total expenditure. Therefore, an effort to improve the bank's profitability will involve the management of burden. So, to reduce the burden, either the interest income should be increased or the non-interest expenditure should be reduced or by both.Here, It is computed as: burden = non-interest expenditure - non-interest income. Formula for the ratio of burden to working funds is as follows:

$$\text{Burden to Working Funds Ratio} = \frac{\text{Burden}}{\text{Working Funds}} * 100$$

118

Ideally, this ratio should be as low as possible for the banks.

Burden to Working Funds Ratio of selected citizen cooperative banks of North Gujarat for the study period 2007-08 to 2011-12 is presented in the table 5.6 as follows:

Table 5.6
Burden to Working Funds Ratio

YEAR	HIMNSB	MODNSB	MEHNSB	COBMEH	CHHNSB	BANMCB	CHANSB	PATNSB	AVERAGE
2007-08	3.03	2.95	2.20	2.81	1.71	3.29	2.46	2.25	2.59
2008-09	2.89	2.80	2.14	2.23	1.80	3.22	2.53	2.52	2.52
2009-10	3.12	2.78	2.13	1.96	2.96	2.81	2.59	2.42	2.59
2010-11	3.13	2.63	2.67	2.19	2.68	3.09	2.75	2.33	2.68
2011-12	3.84	2.80	3.02	1.92	3.33	3.19	3.02	2.78	2.99
AVERAGE	3.20	2.79	2.43	2.22	2.49	3.12	2.67	2.46	2.67

Source: Annual reports of CCBs during year 2007-08 to 2011-12.

Chart 5.2
Chart Showing Burden to Working Funds Ratio

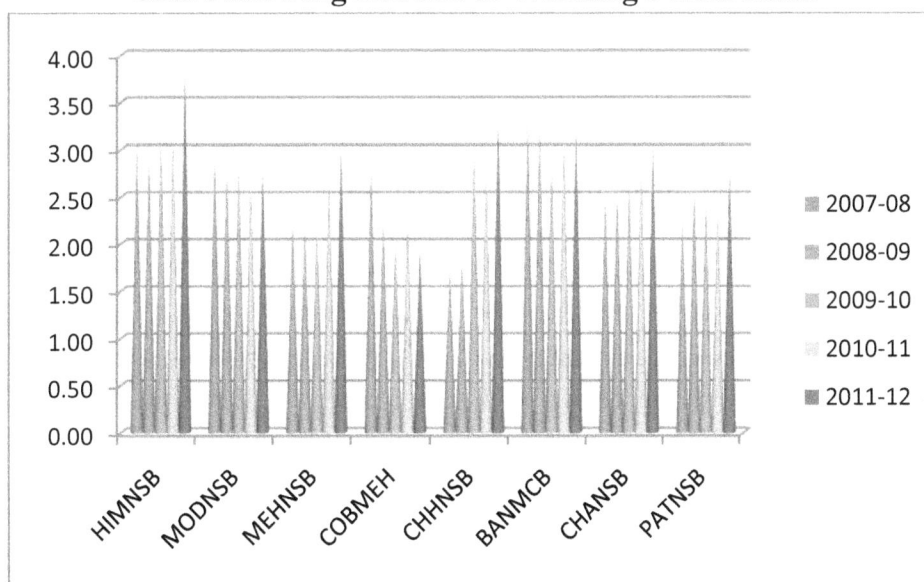

It can be observed from the above table 5.6 for himmatnagar nagarik sahakari bank that Burden to Working Funds Ratio was 3.03% in the year 2007-08. In the year 2008-09 this ratio was decreased to 2.89% which was the lowest during all the study period. In the year 2009-10 to 2011-12 this ratio was continuously increased to 3.12%, 3.13% and 3.84% respectively. In the year 2011-12 this ratio was the highest during all the study period. During all the study period average of this ratio was 3.20%. For all the five years of the study this ratio was lower than its average for four years and higher than its average for remaining one year.

It is obvious from the above table 5.6 for modasa nagarik sahakari bank that Burden to Working Funds Ratio was 2.95% in the year 2007-08 which was the highest

119

during all the study period. In the year 2008-09 to 2010-11 this ratio was continuously decreased to 2.80%, 2.78% and 2.63% respectively. In the year 2010-11 this ratio was the lowest during all the study period. In the year 2011-12 this ratio was increased to 2.80%. During all the study period average of this ratio was 2.79%. For all the five years of the study this ratio was lower than its average for two years and higher than its average for remaining three years.

It is apparent from the above table 5.6 for mehsana nagarik sahakari bank that Burden to Working Funds Ratio was 2.20% in the year 2007-08. In the year 2008-09 and 2009-10 this ratio was continuously decreased to 2.14% and 2.13% respectively. In the year 2009-10 this ratio was the lowest during all the study period. In the year 2010-11 and 2011-12 it was increased to 2.67% and 3.02% respectively. In the year 2011-12 this ratio was the highest during all the study period. During all the study period average of this ratio was 2.43%. For all the five years of the study this ratio was lower than its average for three years and higher than its average in the remaining two years.

It is cleared from the above table 5.6 for co-operative bank of mehsana that Burden to Working Funds Ratio was 2.81% in the year 2007-08 which was the highest during all the study period. In the year 2008-09 and 2009-10 this ratio was continuously decreased to 2.23% and 1.96% respectively. In the year 2010-11 this ratio was increased to 2.19%. In the year 2011-12 this ratio was decreased to 1.92% which was the lowest during all the study period. During all the study period average of this ratio was 2.22%. For all the five years of the study this ratio was lower than its average for three years and higher than its average in the remaining two years.

It isevident from the above table 5.6 for chhapi nagarik sahakari bank that Burden to Working Funds Ratio was 1.71% in the year 2007-08 which was the lowest during all the study period. In the year 2008-09 and 2009-10 this ratio was increased to 1.80% and 2.96% respectively. In the year 2010-11 this ratio was decreased to 2.68%. In the year 2011-12 it was increased to 3.33% which was the highest during all the study period. During all the study period average of this ratio was 2.49%. For all the five years of the study this ratio was lower than its average for two years and higher than its average in the remaining three years.

It can be observed from the above table 5.6 for banaskantha mercantile co-operative bank that Burden to Working Funds Ratio was 3.29% in the year 2007-08 which was the highest during all the study period. In the year 2008-09 and 2009-10 this ratio was decreased to 3.22% and 2.81% respectively. In the year 2009-10 this ratio was the lowest during all the study period. In the year 2010-11and 2011-12it was increased to 3.09% and 3.19% respectively. During all the study period average of this ratio was 3.12%. For all the five years of the study this ratio was lower than its average for three two years and higher than its average for three years.

It is obvious from the above table 5.6 for chanasma nagarik sahakari bank that Burden to Working Funds Ratio was 2.46% in the year 2007-08 which was the lowest during all the study period. In the year 2008-09 to 2011-12 this ratio was continuously increased to 2.53%, 2.59%, 2.75% and 3.02% respectively. In the year 2011-12 this ratio was the highest during all the study period. During all the study period average of this ratio was 2.67%. For all the five years of the study this ratio was lower than its average for three years and higher than its average in remaining two years.

It is apparent from the above table 5.6 for patan nagarik sahakari bank that Burden to Working Funds Ratio was 2.25% in the year 2007-08 which was the lowest during all the study period. In the year 2008-09 this ratio was increased to 2.52%. In the year 2009-10 and 2010-11 this ratio was decreased to 2.42% and 2.33% respectively. In the year 2011-12 this ratio was increased to 2.78%. In the year 2011-12 it was the highest during all the study period. During all the study period average of this ratio was 2.46%. For all the five years of the study this ratio was lower than its average for three years and higher than its average in remaining two years.

It can be seen from the above table 5.6 for all Citizen co-operative banks that average of Burden to Working Funds Ratio during 2007-08 to 2011-12 was 2.67%. In the year 2007-08 average ratio of all banks was 2.59%. In the year 2008-09 this ratio was decreased to 2.52% which was the lowest during all the study period. In the year 2009-10 to 2011-12 this ratio was continuously increased to 2.59%, 2.68% and 2.99% respectively. In the year 2011-12 it was the highest during all the study period. For all the five years of the study average ratio of all banks was lower than its average for three years and higher than its average in remaining two years.

❖ F test (ANOVA) Analysis

The statements of hypothesis are as under:

• Hypothesis between the banks:

H_0: There is no significant difference in the burden to working funds ratio of different Citizen Co-operative banks of North Gujarat for every financial year.

H_1: There is significant difference in the burden to working funds ratio of different Citizen Co-operative banks of North Gujarat for every financial year.

• Hypothesis between the years:

H_0: There is no significant difference in the burden to working funds ratio of every Citizen Co-operative bank of North Gujarat for different financial years.

H_1: There is significant difference in the burden to working funds ratio of every Citizen Co-operative bank of North Gujarat for different financial years.

Table 5.6-A

Source of Variation	SS	df	MS	F
Between Banks	4.16	07	0.59	5.19
Between years	1.11	04	0.28	2.41
Error	3.21	28	0.11	
Total	8.47	39		

Table Value for df (7,28) is 2.36 at 5% level of significance.

Table Value for df (4,28) is 2.71 at 5% level of significance.

Table 5.6-A represents the difference for the banks is significant because the table value for df (7,28) is (2.36) which is lower than calculated value of 'F' (5.19). So, null hypothesis (H₀) is rejected and alternative hypothesis (H₁) is accepted. I.e. there is significant difference in the burden to working funds ratio of different Citizen Co-operative banks of North Gujarat for every financial year.

Same way the difference for the years is not significant because the table value for df (4,28) is (2.71) which is higher than the calculated value of 'F' (2.41) for years and so here null hypothesis(H₀) is accepted and alternative hypothesis (H₁) is rejected. I.e. there is no significant difference in the burden to working funds ratio of every Citizen Co-operative bank of North Gujarat for different financial years.

5.4.7 Net Profit to Working Funds Ratio

Net profit is excess of total income over total expenses of the bank. In other wards it is the difference between spread and burden. The familiar analytical tool to determine the bank's profitability is the ratio of net profit as percentage of working funds. This ratio indicates the efficiency with which a bank deploys its total working funds so as to maximize its profits. Hence, the ratio serves as an index to the degree of asset utilization of banks. Formula for the ratio of net profit to working funds is as follows:

$$\text{Net profit to Working Funds Ratio} = \frac{\text{Net profit}}{\text{Working Funds}} *100$$

A high ratio is a positive indicator of managerial efficiency and also indicates higher profits.

Net profit to Working Funds Ratio of selected citizen cooperative banks of North Gujarat for the study period 2007-08 to 2011-12 is presented in the table 5.7 as follows:

Table 5.7
Net profit to Working Funds Ratio

YEAR	HIMNSB	MODNSB	MEHNSB	COBMEH	CHHNSB	BANMCB	CHANSB	PATNSB	AVERAGE
2007-08	0.59	0.95	0.34	0.92	0.61	0.55	0.84	0.52	0.67
2008-09	0.59	0.95	0.44	0.87	0.41	0.56	0.88	0.68	0.67
2009-10	0.66	0.96	0.57	0.78	0.66	0.49	0.81	0.65	0.70
2010-11	0.68	0.85	0.38	1.04	0.42	0.46	0.82	0.56	0.65
2011-12	0.79	1.00	0.71	1.02	0.49	0.59	0.71	0.59	0.74
AVERAGE	0.66	0.94	0.49	0.93	0.52	0.53	0.81	0.60	0.69

Source: Annual reports of CCBs during year 2007-08 to 2011-12.

Chart 5.3
Chart Showing Net profit to Working Funds Ratio

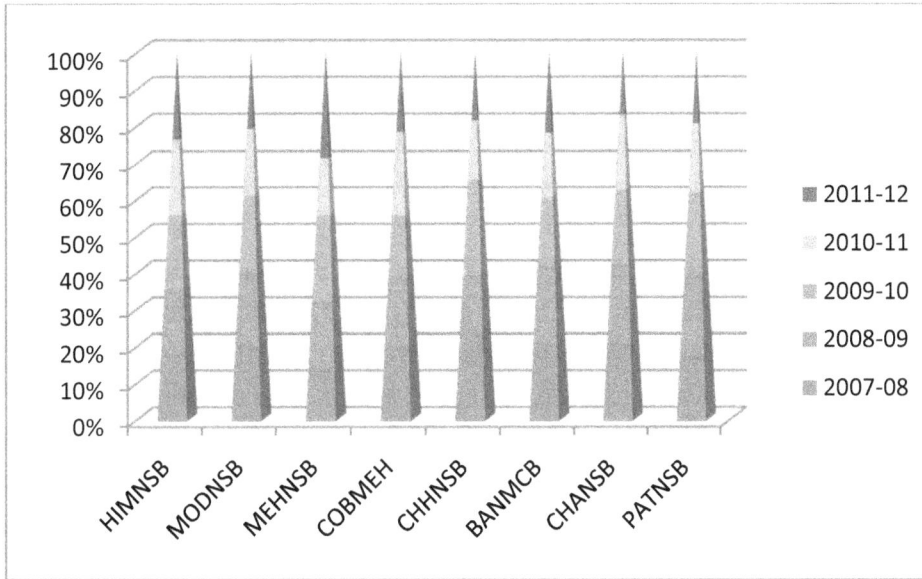

It can be observed from the above table 5.7 for himmatnagar nagarik sahakari bank that Net profit to Working Funds Ratio was same 0.59% in the year 2007-08 and 2008-09 which was the lowest during all the study period. In the year 2009-10 to 2011-12 this ratio was continuously increased to 0.66%, 0.68% and 0.79% respectively. In the year 2009-10 this ratio was equal to average of all the study period and in the year 2011-12 it was the highest during all the study period. During all the study period average of this ratio was 0.66%. For all the five years of the study this ratio was lower than its average for two years, higher than its average for two years and equal to its average for remaining one year.

It is obvious from the above table 5.7 for modasa nagarik sahakari bank that Net profit to Working Funds Ratio was same 0.95% in the year 2007-08 and 2008-09. In the year 2009-10 this ratio was increased to 0.96% and in the year 2010-11 it was decreased to 0.85%. In the year 2010-11 it was the lowest during all the study period. In the year 2011-12 this ratio was increased to 1.00% which was the highest during all the study period. During all the study period average of this ratio was 0.94%. For all the five years of the study this ratio was lower than its average for one year and higher than its average in the remaining four years.

It is apparent from the above table 5.7 for mehsana nagarik sahakari bank that Net profit to Working Funds Ratio was 0.34% in the year 2007-08 which was the lowest during all the study period. In the year 2008-09 and 2009-10 this ratio was continuously increased to 0.44% and 0.57% respectively. In the year 2010-11 it was decreased to 0.38% and in the year 2011-12 it was increased to 0.71%. In the year 2011-12 this ratio was the highest during all the study period. During all the study period average of this ratio was 0.49%. For all the five years of the study this ratio was lower than its average for three years and higher than its average in the remaining two years.

It is cleared from the above table 5.7 for co-operative bank of mehsana that Net profit to Working Funds Ratio was 0.92% in the year 2007-08. In the year 2008-09 and 2009-10 this ratio was continuously decreased to 0.87% and 0.78% respectively. In the year 2009-10 it was the lowest during all the study period. In the year 2010-11 this ratio was increased to 1.04% which was the highest during all the study period. In the year 2011-12 this ratio was decreased to 1.02%. During all the study period average of this ratio was 0.93%. For all the five years of the study this ratio was lower than its average for three years and higher than its average in the remaining two years.

It isevident from the above table 5.7 for chhapi nagarik sahakari bank that Net profit to Working Funds Ratio was 0.61% in the year 2007-08. In the year 2008-09 this ratio was decreased to 0.41% which was the lowest during all the study period. In the year 2009-10 this ratio was increased to 0.66% which was the highest during all the study period. In the year 2010-11 this ratio was decreased to 0.42%. In the year 2011-12 it was increased to 0.49%. During all the study period average of this ratio was 0.52%. For all the five years of the study this ratio was lower than its average for three years and higher than its average in the remaining two years.

It can be observed from the above table 5.7 for banaskantha mercantile co-operative bank that Net profit to Working Funds Ratio was 0.55% in the year 2007-08. In the year 2008-09 this ratio was increased to 0.56%. In the year 2009-10 and 2010-11this ratio was decreased to 0.49% and 0.46% respectively. In the year 2010-11this ratio was the lowest during all the study period. In the year 2011-12it was increased to 0.59% which was the highest during all the study period. During all the study period average of this ratio was 0.53%. For all the five years of the study this ratio was lower than its average for three two years and higher than its average for three years.

It is obvious from the above table 5.7 for chanasma nagarik sahakari bank that Net profit to Working Funds Ratio was 0.84% in the year 2007-08. In the year 2008-09 this ratio was increased to 0.88% which was the highest during all the study period. In the year 2009-10 this ratio was decreased to 0.81% which was equal to average of all the study period. In the year 2010-11 this ratio was increased to 0.82%. In the year 2011-12 it was decreased to 0.71% which was the lowest during all the study period. During all the study period average of this ratio was 0.81%. For all the five years of the study this ratio was lower than its average for one year, higher than its average in remaining three years and equal to its average for remaining one year.

It is apparent from the above table 5.7 for patan nagarik sahakari bank that Net profit to Working Funds Ratio was 0.52% in the year 2007-08 which was the lowest during all the study period. In the year 2008-09 this ratio was increased to 0.68% which was the highest during all the study period. In the year 2009-10 and 2010-11 this ratio was decreased to 0.65% and 0.56% respectively. In the year 2011-12 this ratio was increased to 0.59%. During all the study period average of this ratio was 0.60%. For all the five years of the study this ratio was lower than its average for three years and higher than its average in remaining two years.

It can be seen from the above table 5.7 for all Citizen co-operative banks that average of Net profit to Working Funds Ratio during 2007-08 to 2011-12 was 0.69%. In the year 2007-08 and 2008-09 average ratios of all banks was same 0.67%. In the year 2009-10 this ratio was increased to 0.70%. In the year 2010-11 this ratio was decreased to 0.65% which was the lowest during all the study period. In the year 2011-12 this ratio was increased to 0.74% which was the highest during all the study period. For all the five years of the study average ratio of all banks was lower than its average for three years and higher than its average in remaining two years.

❖ **F test (ANOVA) Analysis**

The statements of hypothesis are as under:

- **Hypothesis between the banks:**

H_0: There is no significant difference in the net profit to working funds ratio of different Citizen Co-operative banks of North Gujarat for every financial year.

H_1: There is significant difference in the net profit to working funds ratio of different Citizen Co-operative banks of North Gujarat for every financial year.

- **Hypothesis between the years:**

H_0: There is no significant difference in the net profit to working funds ratio of every Citizen Co-operative bank of North Gujarat for different financial years.

H_1: There is significant difference in the net profit to working funds ratio of every Citizen Co-operative bank of North Gujarat for different financial years.

Table 5.7-A

Source of Variation	SS	df	MS	F
Between Banks	1.21	07	0.17	20.51
Between years	0.04	04	0.01	1.05
Error	0.24	28	0.01	
Total	1.48	39		

Table Value for df (7,28) is 2.36 at 5% level of significance.

Table Value for df (4,28) is 2.71 at 5% level of significance.

Table 5.7-A represents the difference for the banks is significant because the table value for df (7,28) is (2.36) which is lower than calculated value of 'F' (20.51). So, null hypothesis (H_0) is rejected and alternative hypothesis (H_1) is accepted. I.e. there is significant difference in the net profit to working funds ratio of different Citizen Co-operative banks of North Gujarat for every financial year.

Same way the difference for the years is not significant because the table value for df (4,28) is (2.71) which is higher than the calculated value of 'F' (1.05) for years and so here null hypothesis(H_0) is accepted and alternative hypothesis (H_1) is rejected. I.e. there is no significant difference in the net profit to working funds ratio of every Citizen Co-operative bank of North Gujarat for different financial years.

5.4.8 Net Profit to Owned Funds Ratio

The net profits include profits earned by the bank after appropriations whereas owned funds include share capital, all reserves, and surplus of Citizen Co-operative banks. Formula for the ratio of net profit to owned funds is as follows:

$$\text{Net Profit to Owned Funds Ratio} = \frac{\text{Net Profit}}{\text{Owned Funds}} *100$$

Ideally, this ratio should be high for the banks.

Net Profit to Owned Funds Ratio of selected citizen cooperative banks of North Gujarat for the study period 2007-08 to 2011-12 is presented in the table 5.8 as follows:

Table 5.8
Net Profit to Owned Funds Ratio

YEAR	HIMNSB	MODNSB	MEHNSB	COBMEH	CHHNSB	BANMCB	CHANSB	PATNSB	AVERAGE
2007-08	3.46	5.63	2.13	6.53	4.82	3.55	5.72	2.31	3.55
2008-09	3.86	5.77	3.12	6.08	3.37	3.63	6.09	3.30	4.40
2009-10	4.14	6.07	4.67	5.90	5.09	3.45	5.97	3.63	4.86
2010-11	4.39	5.63	3.06	7.32	3.21	3.22	6.34	3.67	4.61
2011-12	5.09	6.30	5.58	7.28	3.18	4.44	6.16	3.82	5.23
AVERAGE	4.19	5.88	3.71	6.62	3.94	3.66	4.91	3.34	4.53

Source: Annual reports of CCBs during year 2007-08 to 2011-12.

It can be observed from the above table 5.8 for himmatnagar nagarik sahakari bank that Net Profit to Owned Funds Ratio was 3.46% in the year 2007-08 which was the lowest during all the study period. In the year 2008-09 to 2011-12 this ratio was continuously increased to 3.86%, 4.14%, 4.39% and 5.09% respectively. In the year 2011-12 this ratio was the highest during all the study period. During all the study period average of this ratio was 4.19%. For all the five years of the study this ratio was lower than its average for three years and higher than its average for remaining two years.

It is obvious from the above table 5.8 for modasa nagarik sahakari bank that Net Profit to Owned Funds Ratio was 5.63% in the year 2007-08 which was the lowest during all the study period. In the year 2008-09 to 2009-10 this ratio was continuously increased to 5.77% and 6.07% respectively. In the year 2010-11 this ratio was decreased to 5.63% and in the year 2011-12 this ratio was increased to 6.30% which was the highest during all the study period. During all the study period average of this ratio was 5.88%. For all the five years of the study this ratio was lower than its average for three years and higher than its average for remaining two years.

It is apparent from the above table 5.8 for mehsana nagarik sahakari bank that Net Profit to Owned FundsRatio was 2.13% in the year 2007-08 which was the lowest during all the study period. In the year 2008-09 and 2009-10 this ratio was continuously increased to 3.12% and 4.67% respectively. In the year 2010-11 it was decreased to 3.06% and in the year 2011-12 it was increased to 5.58%. In the year 2011-12 this ratio was the highest during all the study period. During all the study period average of this ratio was 3.71%. For all the five years of the study this ratio was lower than its average for three years and higher than its average in the remaining two years.

It is cleared from the above table 5.8 for co-operative bank of mehsana that Net Profit to Owned FundsRatio was 6.53% in the year 2007-08. In the year 2008-09 and 2009-10 this ratio was continuously decreased to 6.08% and 5.90% respectively. In the year 2009-10 it was the lowest during all the study period. In the year 2010-11 this ratio was increased to 7.32% which was the highest during all the study period. In the year 2011-12 this ratio was decreased to 7.28%. During all the study period average of this ratio was 6.62%. For all the five years of the study this ratio was lower than its average for three years and higher than its average in the remaining two years.

It isevident from the above table 5.8 for chhapi nagarik sahakari bank that Net Profit to Owned FundsRatio was 4.82% in the year 2007-08. In the year 2008-09 this ratio was decreased to 3.37%. In the year 2009-10 this ratio was increased to 5.09% which was the highest during all the study period. In the year 2010-11 this ratio was decreased to 3.21%. In the year 2011-12 it was decreased to 3.18% which was the lowest during all the study period. During all the study period average of this ratio was 3.94%. For all the five years of the study this ratio was lower than its average for three years and higher than its average in the remaining two years.

It can be observed from the above table 5.8 for banaskantha mercantile co-operative bank that Net Profit to Owned FundsRatio was 3.55% in the year 2007-08. In the year 2008-09 this ratio was increased to 3.63%. In the year 2009-10 and 2010-11this ratio was decreased to 3.45% and 3.22% respectively. In the year 2010-11this ratio was the lowest during all the study period. In the year 2011-12it was increased to 4.44% which was the highest during all the study period. During all the study period average of this ratio was 3.66%. For all the five years of the study this ratio was lower than its average for three four years and higher than its average for one year.

It is obvious from the above table 5.8 for chanasma nagarik sahakari bank that Net Profit to Owned FundsRatio was 5.72% in the year 2007-08 which was the lowest during all the study period. In the year 2008-09 this ratio was increased to 6.09%. In the year 2009-10 this ratio was decreased to 5.97%. In the year 2010-11 this ratio was increased to 6.34% which was the highest during all the study period. In the year 2011-12 it was decreased to 6.16%. During all the study period average of this ratio was 6.05%. For all the five years of the study this ratio was lower than its average for two years and higher than its average in remaining three years.

It is apparent from the above table 5.8 for patan nagarik sahakari bank that Net Profit to Owned FundsRatio was 2.31% in the year 2007-08 which was the lowest during all the study period. In the year 2008-09 to 2011-12 this ratio was continuously increased to 3.30%, 3.63%, 3.67% and 3.82% respectively. In the year 2011-12 this ratio was the highest during all the study period. During all the study period average of this ratio was 3.34%. For all the five years of the study this ratio was lower than its average for two years and higher than its average in remaining three years.

It can be seen from the above table 5.8 for all Citizen co-operative banks that average of Net Profit to Owned FundsRatio during 2007-08 to 2011-12 was 4.67%. In the year 2007-08 average ratios of all banks was 4.27% which was the lowest during all the study period. In the year 2008-09 and 2009-10 this ratio was increased to 4.40% and 4.86% respectively. In the year 2010-11 this ratio was decreased to 4.61%. In the year 2011-12 this ratio was increased to 5.23% which was the highest during all the study period. For all the five years of the study average ratio of all banks was lower than its average for three years and higher than its average in remaining two years.

❖ F test (ANOVA) Analysis

The statements of hypothesis are as under:

- **Hypothesis between the banks:**

H_0: There is no significant difference in the net profit to owned funds ratio of different Citizen Co-operative banks of North Gujarat for every financial year.

H_1: There is significant difference in the net profit to owned funds ratio of different Citizen Co-operative banks of North Gujarat for every financial year.

- **Hypothesis between the years:**

H_0: There is no significant difference in the net profit to owned funds ratio of every Citizen Co-operative bank of North Gujarat for different financial years.

H_1: There is significant difference in the net profit to owned funds ratio of every Citizen Co-operative bank of North Gujarat for different financial years.

Table 5.8-A

Source of Variation	SS	df	MS	F
Between Banks	58.24	07	8.32	18.41
Between years	4.72	04	1.18	2.61
Error	12.65	28	0.45	
Total	75.61	39		

Table Value for df (7,28) is 2.36 at 5% level of significance.

Table Value for df (4,28) is 2.71 at 5% level of significance.

Table 5.8-A represents the difference for the banks is significant because the table value for df (7,28) is (2.36) which is lower than calculated value of 'F' (18.41). So, null hypothesis (H_o) is rejected and alternative hypothesis (H_1) is accepted. I.e. there is significant difference in the net profit to owned funds ratio of different Citizen Co-operative banks of North Gujarat for every financial year.

Same way the difference for the years is not significant because the table value for df (4,28) is (2.71) which is higher than the calculated value of 'F' (2.61) for years and so here null hypothesis(H₀) is accepted and alternative hypothesis (H₁) is rejected. I.e. there is no significant difference in the net profit to owned funds ratio of every Citizen Co-operative bank of North Gujarat for different financial years.

5.4.9 Net Profit to Shareholder's EquityRatio

This ratio is an inevitable measure of profitability. This ratio measures a bank's profitability by revealing how much profit a bank generates with the money shareholders have invested. Formula for the ratio of net profit to shareholder's equity is as follows:

$$\text{Net Profit to Shareholder's Equity Ratio} = \frac{\text{Net Profit}}{\text{Shareholder's Equity}} *100$$

Net Profit to Shareholder's Equity Ratioof selected citizen cooperative banks of North Gujarat for the study period 2007-08 to 2011-12 is presented in the table 5.9 as follows:

Table 5.9
Net Profit to Shareholder's EquityRatio

YEAR	HIMNSB	MODNSB	MEHNSB	COBMEH	CHHNSB	BANMCB	CHANSB	PATNSB	AVERAGE
2007-08	51.84	64.37	15.91	61.09	49.61	23.16	26.01	15.98	38.50
2008-09	55.93	65.80	20.63	59.94	36.05	22.96	25.39	22.06	38.60
2009-10	57.84	64.49	27.41	54.00	60.32	20.58	24.32	22.51	41.43
2010-11	38.15	55.73	16.46	53.35	37.93	17.01	26.30	22.32	33.41
2011-12	42.71	57.75	28.11	49.05	40.45	23.24	25.22	22.02	36.07
AVERAGE	49.30	61.63	21.70	55.49	44.87	21.39	25.45	20.98	37.60

Source: Annual reports of CCBs during year 2007-08 to 2011-12.

It can be observed from the above table 5.9 for himmatnagar nagarik sahakari bank that Net Profit to Shareholder's Equity Ratio was 51.84% in the year 2007-08. In the year 2008-09 and 2009-10 this ratio was continuously increased to 55.93% and 57.84% respectively. In the year 2009-10 this ratio was the highest during all the study period. . In the year 2010-11 this ratio was decreased to 38.15% which was the lowest during all the study period. In the year 2011-12 this ratio was increased to 42.71%. During all the study period average of this ratio was 49.30%. For all the five years of the study this ratio was lower than its average for two years and higher than its average for remaining three years.

It is obvious from the above table 5.9 for modasa nagarik sahakari bank that Net Profit to Shareholder's Equity Ratio was 64.37% in the year 2007-08. In the year 2008-09 this ratio was increased to 65.80% which was the highest during all the study period.

In the year 2009-10 and 2010-11 this ratio was decreased to 64.49% and 55.73% respectively. In the year 2010-11 this ratio was the lowest during all the study period. In the year 2011-12 this ratio was increased to 57.75%. During all the study period average of this ratio was 61.63%. For all the five years of the study this ratio was lower than its average for two years and higher than its average for remaining three years.

It is apparent from the above table 5.9 for mehsana nagarik sahakari bank that Net Profit to Shareholder's Equity Ratio was 15.91% in the year 2007-08 which was the lowest during all the study period. In the year 2008-09 and 2009-10 this ratio was continuously increased to 20.63% and 27.41% respectively. In the year 2010-11 it was decreased to 16.46% and in the year 2011-12 it was increased to 28.11%. In the year 2011-12 this ratio was the highest during all the study period. During all the study period average of this ratio was 21.70%. For all the five years of the study this ratio was lower than its average for three years and higher than its average in the remaining two years.

It is cleared from the above table 5.9 for co-operative bank of mehsana that Net Profit to Shareholder's Equity Ratio was 61.09% in the year 2007-08 which was the highest during all the study period. In the year 2008-09 to 2011-12 this ratio was continuously decreased to 59.94%, 54.00%, 53.35% and 49.05% respectively. In the year 2011-12 it was the lowest during all the study period. During all the study period average of this ratio was 55.49%. For all the five years of the study this ratio was lower than its average for three years and higher than its average in the remaining two years.

It isevident from the above table 5.9 for chhapi nagarik sahakari bank that Net Profit to Shareholder's Equity Ratio was 49.61% in the year 2007-08. In the year 2008-09 this ratio was decreased to 36.05% which was the lowest during all the study period. In the year 2009-10 this ratio was increased to 60.32% which was the highest during all the study period. In the year 2010-11 this ratio was decreased to 37.93%. In the year 2011-12 it was increased to 40.45%. During all the study period average of this ratio was 44.87%. For all the five years of the study this ratio was lower than its average for three years and higher than its average in the remaining two years.

It can be observed from the above table 5.9 for banaskantha mercantile co-operative bank that Net Profit to Shareholder's Equity Ratio was 23.16% in the year 2007-08. In the year 2008-09 this ratio was increased to 22.96%. In the year 2009-10 and 2010-11this ratio was decreased to 20.58% and 17.01% respectively. In the year 2010-11this ratio was the lowest during all the study period. In the year 2011-12 it was increased to 23.24% which was the highest during all the study period. During all the study period average of this ratio was 21.39%. For all the five years of the study this ratio was lower than its average for three two years and higher than its average for three years.

It is obvious from the above table 5.9 for chanasma nagarik sahakari bank that Net Profit to Shareholder's Equity Ratio was 26.01% in the year 2007-08. In the year 2008-09 and 2009-10 this ratio was decreased to 25.39% and 24.32% respectively. In the year 2009-10 this ratio was the lowest during all the study period. In the year 2010-

11this ratio was increased to 26.30% which was the highest during all the study period. In the year 2011-12 it was decreased to 25.22%. During all the study period average of this ratio was 25.45%. For all the five years of the study this ratio was lower than its average for three years and higher than its average in remaining two years.

It is apparent from the above table 5.9 for patan nagarik sahakari bank that Net Profit to Shareholder's Equity Ratio was 15.98% in the year 2007-08 which was the lowest during all the study period. In the year 2008-09 and 2009-10 this ratio was continuously increased to 22.06% and 22.51% respectively. In the year 2009-10 this ratio was the highest during all the study period. In the year 2010-11and 2011-12 this ratio was decreased to 22.32% and 22.02% respectively. During all the study period average of this ratio was 20.98%. For all the five years of the study this ratio was lower than its average for one year and higher than its average in remaining four years.

It can be seen from the above table 5.9 for all Citizen co-operative banks that average of Net Profit to Shareholder's Equity Ratio during 2007-08 to 2011-12 was 37.60%. In the year 2007-08 average ratios of all banks was same 38.50%. In the year 2008-09 and 2009-10 this ratio was increased to 38.60% and 41.43% respectively. In the year 2009-10 this ratio was the highest during all the study period. In the year 2010-11 this ratio was decreased to 33.41% which was the lowest during all the study period. In the year 2011-12 this ratio was increased to 36.07%. For all the five years of the study average ratio of all banks was lower than its average for two years and higher than its average in remaining three years.

❖ F test (ANOVA) Analysis

The statements of hypothesis are as under:
- **Hypothesis between the banks:**

H_0:   There is no significant difference in the net profit to shareholder's equity ratio of different Citizen Co-operative banks of North Gujarat for every financial year.

H_1:   There is significant difference in the net profit to shareholder's equity ratio of different Citizen Co-operative banks of North Gujarat for every financial year.

- **Hypothesis between the years:**

H_0:   There is no significant difference in the net profit to shareholder's equity ratio of every Citizen Co-operative bank of North Gujarat for different financial years.

H_1:   There is significant difference in the net profit to shareholder's equity ratio of every Citizen Co-operative bank of North Gujarat for different financial years.

Table 5.9-A

Source of Variation	SS	df	MS	F
Between Banks	10131.65	07	1447.38	51.49
Between years	291.45	04	72.86	2.59
Error	787.06	28	28.11	
Total	11210.16	39		

Table Value for df (7,28) is 2.36 at 5% level of significance.

Table Value for df (4,28) is 2.71 at 5% level of significance.

Table 5.9-A represents the difference for the banks is significant because the table value for df (7,28) is (2.36) which is lower than calculated value of 'F' (51.49). So, null hypothesis (H_o) is rejected and alternative hypothesis (H_1) is accepted. I.e. there is significant difference in the net profit to shareholder's equity ratio of different Citizen Co-operative banks of North Gujarat for every financial year.

Same way the difference for the years is not significant because the table value for df (4,28) is (2.71) which is higher than the calculated value of 'F' (2.59) for years and so here null hypothesis(H_o) is accepted and alternative hypothesis (H_1) is rejected. I.e. there is no significant difference in the net profit to shareholder's equity ratio of every Citizen Co-operative bank of North Gujarat for different financial years.

5.5   Conclusion

In this chapter researcher has tried to analyze profitability of selected Citizen co-operative banks of north Gujarat. For an analysis of profitability various nine ratios were calculated from the annual reports of Citizen Co-operative bank of North Gujarat. The profitability of different Citizen Co-operative banks was analyzed with reference to its components such as spread and burden. Profitability ratios invite the serious attention of the bank management to put an integrated effort to correct the financial performance.

In the analysis of profitability, profit and loss account and balance sheet of selected Citizen co-operative banks has been analyzed with the help of various nine ratios and "F" test (ANOVA) of all ratios proves that there is no uniformity in profitability of different Citizen Co-operative banks of North Gujarat for every financial year. Majority ratios also prove that there is uniformity in profitability of every Citizen Co-operative banks of North Gujarat for different financial year.

References

1. S. B chodhary, "Analysis of company financial statement" Bombay, Asian Publishing House. (1964) p.123.
2. Peter Drucker, "Practice of Management"London, Mercury Books. (1961) p.65.
3. Samuelson Paul, "Economics"New York, McGraw Hill Book Co., (1979) p.602.
4. Eric Koher, "A Dictionary for Accounting" New Delhi, Prantice Hall of India Pvt. Ltd., (1972) p.345.
5. Dividsons, Sidney; Stickney, Clyde P. and weil, Romon L, "Financial Accounting- An Introduction to concept,Method and Uses" U.S.A., The Dreden Press, (1982) p.8.
6. Bion B. Howard and Miller Upton, "Introduction to business finance" New York, McGraw Hill. (1953) p.150.
7. H. Chatraborty, "Management Accountancy" Calcutta, Navbharat Publishers. (1976) p.585.
8. S.C. Kuchhal, "Financial Management- An Analytical and Conceptual Approach", Allahabad, Chitanya Publishing House. (1977) p.71.
9. V. S. Murty, "Management Finance" Bombay, Vakils feffer and simons Ltd., (1978) p.79.

Chapter-6
Analysis of Productivity

6.1   Introduction

Productivity is a vital indicator of economic performance of an economic system. Productivity is not an end in itself. In fact, it is a mechanism for improving the material quality of life. Productivity is fundamental to progress throughout the world. It is at the heart of economic growth and development, improvements in standards of living and quality of life.

The performance of co-operative banks in term of profitability and productivity has been the main concern of all the stakeholders involved in this entrepreneurship. It is a globally well recognized fact that the growth of any financial institution like banks depends upon their productivity and profitability which are directly interrelated to each other. Therefore, in this chapter, the key parameter have been discussed which is the productivity of the selected Citizen co-operative banks of North Gujarat.

6.2   Concept of Productivity

The concept of productivity is much wider in scope as it comprises human resources whose skills can be utilized differently for achieving desired results in the process of production. Definition Productivity is defined as the goods and services produced per unit of labour, capital or both. The ratio of output to labour and capital is a total productivity measure. In simple words, productivity is the output per unit of input employed. The basic definition of productivity is: "Productivity is the relationship between changes in output and per unit of input. It is generally defined in terms of the efficiency with which inputs are transformed into useful output within the production process."[1] This relationship can be expressed as follows:

Productivity = Total Output/Total Input

According to **C.B. Gupta,** "Productivity refers to the physical relationship between the quantity produced (output) and the quantity of resources used in the course of production (input)."[2]**Kopleman** has defined productivity as, "the relationship between physical output of one or more of the associated physical inputs used in production. When single input is used to measure productivity, it is called 'factor productivity' and when all factors are combined together for the purpose, it is known as 'total factor productivity."[3]

"Productivity is the basic mission of any bank to provide the maximum welfare for the maximum number. Productivity as measure of efficiency and effectiveness and as a means of improving the quality of the life is generic from achieving the highest outputs from the limited resources. Productivity implies the certainty of being able to do better than yesterday and keeping the tempo continuously to improve upon. Such continuous improvements are to be generated through the research for new techniques, methods, processes, materials, software, and expertise coupled with vision and dedicated leadership having the ultimate faith in the welfare of human system."[4]

Productivity is simply the ratio of output to input. When this ratio is calculated in the base year it indicates the changes in productivity efficiency over the base year. As the input consist of a number of production factors and elements. Productivity can be determined separately for each of these factors. Both the output and the input may be expressed in terms of physical units or in terms of money. "Productivity is usually defined as a ratio of output produced per unit of resources consumed by the process. Productivity is a measure of performance in producing and distributing goods and service: Value added, or sales minues purchase divided by workers employed."[5]

6.3   Measurement of Productivity

Productivity is measured as the ratio between the output of a given commodity or service and the inputs used for that product. Productivity ratio is the ratio of output of wealthy produced to the input of resources used in the process. The objective behind measuring productivity is to improve the economic performance. Thus, in the context of banking, productivity can be improved by improving profit.

The productivity concept as applied in manufacturing industries cannot be applied in service sector like bank. Bank provides various types of services like acceptance of deposits, borrowings of loans and advances, creation of credit, foreign exchange business, merchant banking activity, remittance of funds etc. Thus, bank is a multi-product service industry that's why it is complicated to measure the output of banks. As banking is basically a service industry, quantitative specification of real output and input is hard to define and determine. So, the level of productivity of banks is commonly measured at the level of branches and employees, which are the two important wheels on which banking industry moves.

Here, researcher has been made an attempt to measure the productivity of the selected Citizen co-operative banks of North Gujarat throughthe following indicators:

(i) The indicators measure output considering number of employees i.e. Productivity per Employee.

(ii) The indicators measure output considering number of branches i.e. Productivity per Branch.

6.4 Productivity per Employee

Productivity is the ratio of output to input. In other words, productivity is the relationship between output of goods and services and the inputs of human and physical resources. Thus, productivity is measured not only for physical resources but also for human resources. Employee productivity ratio means measurement of employees' efficiency or skills.

6.4.1 Deposits per Employee

This ratio reveals the deposit-collection capacity of an employee. Higher the deposit per employee ratio, higher the productivity per employee. Formula for the ratio of deposit per employee is as follows:

$$\text{Deposits per Employee} = \frac{\text{Total Deposits}}{\text{No. of Employees}}$$

Deposits per Employee of selected citizen cooperative banks of North Gujarat for the study period 2007-08 to 2011-12 is presented in the table 6.1as follows:

Table 6.1

Deposits per Employee

(Rs. In Lakhs)

YEAR	HIMNSB	MODNSB	MEHNSB	COBMEH	CHHNSB	BANMCB	CHANSB	PATNSB	AVERAGE
2007-08	87.34	139.89	89.66	222.16	156.98	99.75	132.56	122.93	131.41
2008-09	101.20	158.91	103.83	273.97	88.86	109.21	133.29	152.89	140.27

2009-10	102.92	178.95	127.93	325.51	185.94	133.69	149.61	219.15	177.96
2010-11	113.70	207.85	142.25	338.69	207.11	131.85	178.26	265.73	198.18
2011-12	119.36	236.70	148.83	378.81	180.31	155.47	240.64	312.83	221.62
AVERAGE	104.91	184.46	122.50	307.83	163.84	125.99	166.87	214.71	173.89

Source: Annual reports of CCBs during year 2007-08 to 2011-12.

It can be observed from the above table 6.1 for himmatnagar nagarik sahakari bank that Deposits per Employeewas 87.34 lakhs in the year 2007-08 which was the lowest during all the study period. In the year 2008-09 to 2011-12 this ratio was continuously increased to 101.20, 102.92, 113.70 and 119.36 lakhs respectively. In the year 2011-12 this ratio was the highest during all the study period. During all the study period average of this ratio was 104.91 lakhs. For all the five years of the study this ratio was lower than its average for three years and higher than its average in the remaining two years.

It is obvious from the above table 6.1 for modasa nagarik sahakari bank that Deposits per Employeewas 139.89 lakhs in the year 2007-08 which was the lowest during all the study period. In the year 2008-09 to 2011-12 this ratio was continuously increased to 158.91, 178.95, 207.85 and 236.70 lakhs respectively. In the year 2011-12 this ratio was the highest during all the study period. During all the study period average of this ratio was 184.46 lakhs. For all the five years of the study this ratio was lower than its average for three years and higher than its average in the remaining two years.

It is apparent from the above table 6.1 for mehsana nagarik sahakari bank that Deposits per Employeewas 89.66 lakhs in the year 2007-08 which was the lowest during all the study period. In the year 2008-09 to 2011-12 this ratio was continuously increased to 103.83, 127.93, 142.25 and 148.83 lakhs respectively. In the year 2011-12 this ratio was the highest during all the study period. During all the study period average of this ratio was 122.50 lakhs. For all the five years of the study this ratio was lower than its average for two years and higher than its average in the remaining three years.

It is cleared from the above table 6.1 for co-operative bank of mehsana that Deposits per Employee was 222.16 lakhs in the year 2007-08 which was the lowest during all the study period. In the year 2008-09 to 2011-12 this ratio was continuously increased to 273.97, 325.51, 338.69 and 378.81 lakhs respectively. In the year 2011-12 this ratio was the highest during all the study period. During all the study period average of this ratio was 307.83 lakhs. For all the five years of the study this ratio was lower than its average for two years and higher than its average in the remaining three years.

It isevident from the above table 6.1 for chhapi nagarik sahakari bank that Deposits per Employeewas 156.98 lakhs in the year 2007-08. In the year 2008-09 this ratio was decreased to 88.86 lakhs which was the lowest during all the study period. In the year 2009-10 and 2010-11 this ratio was increased to 185.94 and 207.11 lakhs respectively. In the year 2010-11 it was the highest during all the study period. In the year 2011-12 this ratio was decreased to 180.31 lakhs. During all the study period average of this ratio was 163.84 lakhs. For all the five years of the study this ratio was lower than its average for two years and higher than its average in the remaining three years.

It can be observed from the above table 6.1 for banaskantha mercantile co-operative bank that Deposits per Employee was 99.75 lakhs in the year 2007-08 which was the lowest during all the study period. In the year 2008-09 and 2009-10 this ratio was increased to 109.21and 133.69 lakhs respectively. In the year 2010-11 it was decreased to 131.85 lakhs and in the year 2011-12 it was increased to 155.47 lakhs. In the year 2011-12 this ratio was the highest during all the study period. During all the study period average of this ratio was 125.99 lakhs. For all the five years of the study this ratio was lower than its average for two years and higher than its average in remaining three years.

It is obvious from the above table 6.1 for chanasma nagarik sahakari bank that Deposits per Employeewas 132.56 lakhs in the year 2007-08 which was the lowest during all the study period. In the year 2008-09 to 2011-12 this ratio was continuously increased to 133.29, 149.61, 178.26 and 240.64 lakhs respectively. In the year 2011-12 this ratio was the highest during all the study period. During all the study period average of this ratio was 166.87 lakhs. For all the five years of the study this ratio was lower than its average for three years and higher than its average in the remaining two years.

It is apparent from the above table 6.1 for patan nagarik sahakari bank that Deposits per Employeewas 122.93 lakhs in the year 2007-08 which was the lowest during all the study period. In the year 2008-09 to 2011-12 this ratio was continuously increased to 152.89, 219.15, 265.73 and 312.83 lakhs respectively. In the year 2011-12 this ratio was the highest during all the study period. During all the study period average of this ratio was 214.71 lakhs. For all the five years of the study this ratio was lower than its average for two years and higher than its average in the remaining three years.

It can be seen from the above table 6.1 for all Citizen co-operative banks that average of Deposits per Employeeduring 2007-08 to 2011-12 was 173.89 lakhs. In the year 2007-08 average ratio of all banks was 131.41 lakhs which was the lowest during all the study period. In the year 2008-09 to 2011-12 this ratio was continuously increased to 140.27, 177.96, 198.18 and 221.62 lakhs respectively. In the year 2011-12 average ratio of all banks was the highest during all the study period. For all the five years of the study average ratio of all banks was lower than its average for two years and higher than its average in remaining three years.

❖ F test (ANOVA) Analysis

The statements of hypothesis are as under:

• Hypothesis between the banks:

H_0:   There is no significant difference in the deposits per employee ratio of different Citizen Co-operative banks of North Gujarat for every financial year.

H₁: There is significant difference in the deposits per employee ratio of different Citizen Co-operative banks of North Gujarat for every financial year.

- **Hypothesis between the years:**

H₀: There is no significant difference in the deposits per employee ratio of every Citizen Co-operative bank of North Gujarat for different financial years.

H₁: There is significant difference in the deposits per employee ratio of every Citizen Co-operative bank of North Gujarat for different financial years.

Table 6.1-A

Source of Variation	SS	df	MS	F
Between Banks	147809.90	07	21115.70	29.22
Between years	46556.96	04	11639.24	16.11
Error	20234.87	28	722.67	
Total	214601.73	39		

Table Value for df (7,28) is 2.36 at 5% level of significance.

Table Value for df (4,28) is 2.71 at 5% level of significance.

Table 6.1-A represents the difference for the banks is significant because the table value for df (7,28) is (2.36) which is lower than calculated value of 'F' (29.22). So, null hypothesis (H₀) is rejected and alternative hypothesis (H₁) is accepted. I.e. there is significant difference in the deposits per employee ratio of different Citizen Co-operative banks of North Gujarat for every financial year.

Same way the difference for the years is significant because the table value for df (4,28) is (2.71) which is lower than the calculated value of 'F' (16.11) for years and so here also null hypothesis(H₀) is rejected and alternative hypothesis (H₁) is accepted. I.e. there is significant difference in the deposits per employee ratio of every Citizen Co-operative bank of North Gujarat for different financial years.

6.4.2 Advances per Employee

This ratio reveals the contacts and convincing skills of the employee to disburse and invest the amount deposited. This only ultimately results in the interest earning capacity of a particular bank. The deposits cannot be maintained unless they are advanced for productive use by the people. As this entails involvement of employee time, this also is considered a ratio to measure the productivity. Again higher is the ratio, higher is the productivity. Formula for the ratio of advances per employee is as follows:

$$\text{Advances per Employee} = \frac{\textbf{Total Advances}}{\textbf{No. of Employees}}$$

Advances per Employee Ratio of selected citizen cooperative banks of North Gujarat for the study period 2007-08 to 2011-12 is presented in the table 6.2 as follows:

139

Table 6.2
Advances per Employee

(Rs. In Lakhs)

YEAR	HIMNSB	MODNSB	MEHNSB	COBMEH	CHHNSB	BANMCB	CHANSB	PATNSB	AVERAGE
2007-08	41.99	85.36	53.61	151.34	66.74	53.54	82.21	72.40	75.90
2008-09	44.88	95.00	57.17	154.32	76.75	57.52	88.65	85.05	82.42
2009-10	45.16	108.60	66.55	160.77	89.14	72.18	105.44	106.05	94.24
2010-11	60.75	117.73	81.39	210.55	100.53	82.58	122.24	114.46	111.28
2011-12	75.77	148.24	93.12	211.79	95.86	88.42	168.24	153.94	129.42
AVERAGE	53.71	110.99	70.37	177.75	85.80	70.85	113.35	106.38	98.65

Source: Annual reports of CCBs during year 2007-08 to 2011-12.

It can be observed from the above table 6.2 for himmatnagar nagarik sahakari bank that Advances per Employeewas 41.99 lakhs in the year 2007-08 which was the lowest during all the study period. In the year 2008-09 to 2011-12 this ratio was continuously increased to 44.88, 45.16, 60.75 and 75.77 lakhs respectively. In the year 2011-12 this ratio was the highest during all the study period. During all the study period average of this ratio was 53.71 lakhs. For all the five years of the study this ratio was lower than its average for three years and higher than its average in the remaining two years.

It is obvious from the above table 6.2 for modasa nagarik sahakari bank that Advances per Employeewas 85.36 lakhs in the year 2007-08 which was the lowest during all the study period. In the year 2008-09 to 2011-12 this ratio was continuously increased to 95.00, 108.60, 117.73 and 148.24 lakhs respectively. In the year 2011-12 this ratio was the highest during all the study period. During all the study period average of this ratio was 110.99 lakhs. For all the five years of the study this ratio was lower than its average for three years and higher than its average in the remaining two years.

It is apparent from the above table 6.2 for mehsana nagarik sahakari bank that Advances per Employeewas 53.61 lakhs in the year 2007-08 which was the lowest during all the study period. In the year 2008-09 to 2011-12 this ratio was continuously increased to 57.17, 66.55, 81.39 and 93.12 lakhs respectively. In the year 2011-12 this ratio was the highest during all the study period. During all the study period average of this ratio was 70.37 lakhs. For all the five years of the study this ratio was lower than its average for three years and higher than its average in the remaining two years.

It is cleared from the above table 6.2 for co-operative bank of mehsana that Advances per Employee was 151.34 lakhs in the year 2007-08 which was the lowest during all the study period. In the year 2008-09 to 2011-12 this ratio was continuously increased to 154.32, 160.77, 210.55 and 211.79 lakhs respectively. In the year 2011-12 this ratio was the highest during all the study period. During all the study period average of this ratio was 177.75 lakhs. For all the five years of the study this ratio was lower than its average for three years and higher than its average in the remaining two years.

It isevident from the above table 6.2 for chhapi nagarik sahakari bank that Advances per Employeewas 66.74 lakhs in the year 2007-08 which was the lowest during all the study period. In the year 2008-09 to 2010-11 this ratio was continuously increased to 76.75, 89.14 and 100.53 lakhs respectively. In the year 2010-11 it was the highest during all the study period. In the year 2011-12 this ratio was decreased to 95.86 lakhs. During all the study period average of this ratio was 85.80 lakhs. For all the five years of the study this ratio was lower than its average for two years and higher than its average in the remaining three years.

It can be observed from the above table 6.2 for banaskantha mercantile co-operative bank that Advances per Employee was 53.54 lakhs in the year 2007-08 which was the lowest during all the study period. In the year 2008-09 to 2011-12 this ratio was continuously increased to 57.52, 72.18, 82.58 and 88.42 lakhs respectively. In the year 2011-12 this ratio was the highest during all the study period. During all the study period average of this ratio was 70.85 lakhs. For all the five years of the study this ratio was lower than its average for two years and higher than its average in the remaining three years.

It is obvious from the above table 6.2 for chanasma nagarik sahakari bank that Advances per Employeewas 82.21 lakhs in the year 2007-08 which was the lowest during all the study period. In the year 2008-09 to 2011-12 this ratio was continuously increased to 88.65, 105.44, 122.24 and 168.24 lakhs respectively. In the year 2011-12 this ratio was the highest during all the study period. During all the study period average of this ratio was 113.35 lakhs. For all the five years of the study this ratio was lower than its average for three years and higher than its average in the remaining two years.

It is apparent from the above table 6.2 for patan nagarik sahakari bank that Advances per Employeewas 72.40 lakhs in the year 2007-08 which was the lowest during all the study period. In the year 2008-09 to 2011-12 this ratio was continuously increased to 85.05, 106.05, 114.46 and 153.94 lakhs respectively. In the year 2011-12 this ratio was the highest during all the study period. During all the study period average of this ratio was 106.38 lakhs. For all the five years of the study this ratio was lower than its average for three years and higher than its average in the remaining two years.

It can be seen from the above table 6.2 for all Citizen co-operative banks that average of Advances per Employeeduring 2007-08 to 2011-12 was 98.65 lakhs. In the year 2007-08 average ratio of all banks was 75.90 lakhs which was the lowest during all the study period. In the year 2008-09 to 2011-12 this ratio was continuously increased to 82.42, 94.24, 111.28 and 129.42 lakhs respectively. In the year 2011-12 average ratio of all banks was the highest during all the study period. For all the five years of the study average ratio of all banks was lower than its average for three years and higher than its average in the remaining two years.

❖ F test (ANOVA) Analysis

The statements of hypothesis are as under:

- **Hypothesis between the banks:**

H_0:   There is no significant difference in the advances per employee ratio of different Citizen Co-operative banks of North Gujarat for every financial year.

H_1:   There is significant difference in the advances per employee ratio of different Citizen Co-operative banks of North Gujarat for every financial year.

- **Hypothesis between the years:**

H_0:   There is no significant difference in the advances per employee ratio of every Citizen Co-operative bank of North Gujarat for different financial years.

H_1:   There is significant difference in the advances per employee ratio of every Citizen Co-operative bank of North Gujarat for different financial years.

Table 6.2-A

Source of Variation	SS	df	MS	F
Between Banks	52214.09	07	7459.16	65.91
Between years	15256.66	04	3814.17	33.70
Error	3168.78	28	113.17	
Total	70639.53	39		

Table Value for df (7,28) is 2.36 at 5% level of significance.

Table Value for df (4,28) is 2.71 at 5% level of significance.

Table 6.2-A represents the difference for the banks is significant because the table value for df (7,28) is (2.36) which is lower than calculated value of 'F' (65.91). So, null hypothesis (H_o) is rejected and alternative hypothesis (H_1) is accepted. I.e. there is significant difference in the advances per employee ratio of different Citizen Co-operative banks of North Gujarat for every financial year.

Same way the difference for the years is significant because the table value for df (4,28) is (2.71) which is lower than the calculated value of 'F' (33.70) for years and so here also null hypothesis(H_o) is rejected and alternative hypothesis (H_1) is accepted. I.e. there is significant difference in the advances per employee ratio of every Citizen Co-operative bank of North Gujarat for different financial years.

6.4.3 Business per Employee

Deposit collection and the advance disbursement are the two basic activities of any given bank. The productivity of any bank in fact relates to the creation and delivery of capital. Here creation means deposits and delivery means advances. Both together are the net measure of productivity. Here, Business is equal to **aggregate deposits plus aggregate advances**. If this ratio is higher, the employee of the bank is better and the productivity of the bank is more. Formula for the ratio of businessper employee is as follows:

$$\text{Business per Employee} = \frac{\text{Total Business}}{\text{No. of Employees}}$$

142

Business per Employee Ratio of selected citizen cooperative banks of North Gujarat for the study period 2007-08 to 2011-12 is presented in the table 6.3 as follows:

Table 6.3

Business per Employee

(Rs. In Lakhs)

YEAR	HIMNSB	MODNSB	MEHNSB	COBMEH	CHHNSB	BANMCB	CHANSB	PATNSB	AVERAGE
2007-08	129.32	225.26	143.28	373.51	223.72	153.28	214.77	195.33	207.31
2008-09	146.09	253.91	161.00	428.29	165.61	166.73	221.94	237.94	222.69
2009-10	148.09	287.55	194.48	486.28	275.08	205.87	255.05	325.21	272.20
2010-11	174.45	325.58	223.65	549.25	307.64	214.43	300.51	380.19	309.46
2011-12	195.13	384.94	241.95	590.60	276.17	243.89	408.87	466.77	351.04
AVERAGE	158.62	295.45	192.87	485.58	249.64	196.84	280.23	321.09	272.54

Source: Annual reports of CCBs during year 2007-08 to 2011-12.

Chart 6.1

Chart Showing Business per Employee Ratio

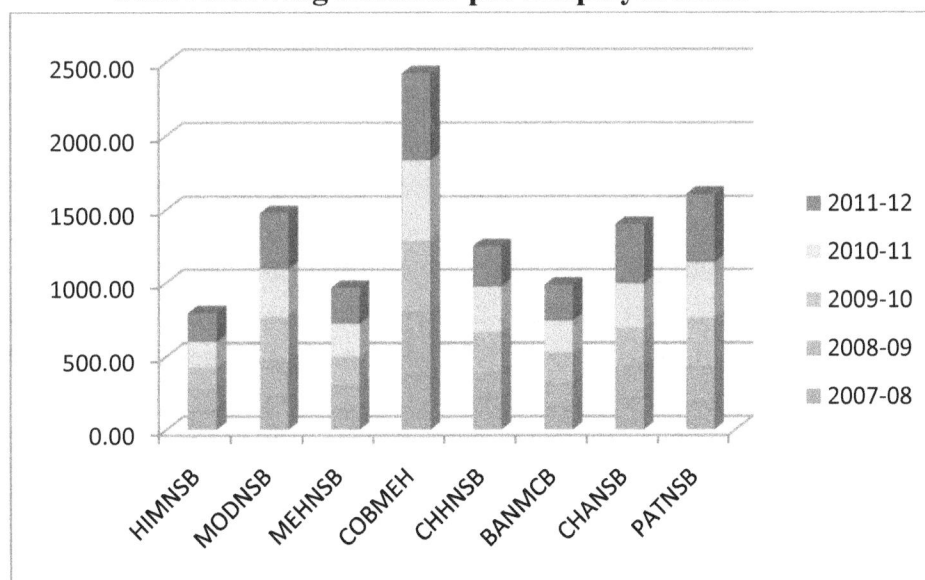

It can be observed from the above table 6.3 for himmatnagar nagarik sahakari bank that Business per Employeewas 129.32 lakhs in the year 2007-08 which was the lowest during all the study period. In the year 2008-09 to 2011-12 this ratio was continuously increased to 146.09, 148.09, 174.45 and 195.13 lakhs respectively. In the year 2011-12 this ratio was the highest during all the study period. During all the study period average of this ratio was 158.62 lakhs. For all the five years of the study this ratio was lower than its average for three years and higher than its average in the remaining two years.

It is obvious from the above table 6.3 for modasa nagarik sahakari bank that Business per Employeewas 225.26 lakhs in the year 2007-08 which was the lowest during all the study period. In the year 2008-09 to 2011-12 this ratio was continuously increased to 253.91, 287.55, 325.58 and 384.94 lakhs respectively. In the year 2011-12 this ratio was the highest during all the study period. During all the study period average of this ratio was 295.45 lakhs. For all the five years of the study this ratio was lower than its average for three years and higher than its average in the remaining two years.

It is apparent from the above table 6.3 for mehsana nagarik sahakari bank that Business per Employeewas 143.28 lakhs in the year 2007-08 which was the lowest during all the study period. In the year 2008-09 to 2011-12 this ratio was continuously increased to 161.00, 194.48, 223.65 and 241.95 lakhs respectively. In the year 2011-12 this ratio was the highest during all the study period. During all the study period average of this ratio was 192.87 lakhs. For all the five years of the study this ratio was lower than its average for two years and higher than its average in the remaining three years.

It is cleared from the above table 6.3 for co-operative bank of mehsana that Business per Employee was 373.51 lakhs in the year 2007-08 which was the lowest during all the study period. In the year 2008-09 to 2011-12 this ratio was continuously increased to 428.29, 486.28, 549.25 and 590.60 lakhs respectively. In the year 2011-12 this ratio was the highest during all the study period. During all the study period average of this ratio was 485.58 lakhs. For all the five years of the study this ratio was lower than its average for two years and higher than its average in the remaining three years.

It isevident from the above table 6.3 for chhapi nagarik sahakari bank that Business per Employeewas 223.72 lakhs in the year 2007-08. In the year 2008-09 this ratio was decreased to 165.61 lakhs which was the lowest during all the study period. In the year 2009-10 and 2010-11 this ratio was continuously increased to 275.08 and 307.64 lakhs respectively. In the year 2010-11 it was the highest during all the study period. In the year 2011-12 this ratio was decreased to 276.17 lakhs. During all the study period average of this ratio was 249.64 lakhs. For all the five years of the study this ratio was lower than its average for two years and higher than its average in the remaining three years.

It can be observed from the above table 6.3 for banaskantha mercantile co-operative bank that Business per Employee was 153.28 lakhs in the year 2007-08 which was the lowest during all the study period. In the year 2008-09 to 2011-12 this ratio was continuously increased to 166.73, 205.87, 214.43 and 243.89 lakhs respectively. In the year 2011-12 this ratio was the highest during all the study period. During all the study period average of this ratio was 196.84 lakhs. For all the five years of the study this ratio was lower than its average for two years and higher than its average in the remaining three years.

It is obvious from the above table 6.3 for chanasma nagarik sahakari bank that Business per Employeewas 214.77 lakhs in the year 2007-08 which was the lowest during all the study period. In the year 2008-09 to 2011-12 this ratio was continuously increased to 221.94, 255.05, 300.51 and 408.87 lakhs respectively. In the year 2011-12 this ratio was the highest during all the study period. During all the study period average of this ratio was 280.23 lakhs. For all the five years of the study this ratio was lower than its average for three years and higher than its average in the remaining two years.

It is apparent from the above table 6.3 for patan nagarik sahakari bank that Business per Employeewas 195.33 lakhs in the year 2007-08 which was the lowest during all the study period. In the year 2008-09 to 2011-12 this ratio was continuously increased to 237.94, 325.21, 380.19 and 466.77 lakhs respectively. In the year 2011-12 this ratio was the highest during all the study period. During all the study period average of this ratio was 321.09 lakhs. For all the five years of the study this ratio was lower than its average for two years and higher than its average in the remaining three years.

It can be seen from the above table 6.3 for all Citizen co-operative banks that average of Business per Employeeduring 2007-08 to 2011-12 was 272.54 lakhs. In the year 2007-08 average ratio of all banks was 207.31 lakhs which was the lowest during all the study period. In the year 2008-09 to 2011-12 this ratio was continuously increased to 222.69, 272.20, 309.46 and 351.04 lakhs respectively. In the year 2011-12 average ratio of all banks was the highest during all the study period. For all the five years of the study average ratio of all banks was lower than its average for three years and higher than its average in the remaining two years.

❖ F test (ANOVA) Analysis

The statements of hypothesis are as under:

• Hypothesis between the banks:

H_0:   There is no significant difference in the business per employee ratio of different Citizen Co-operative banks of North Gujarat for every financial year.

H_1:   There is significant difference in the business per employee ratio of different Citizen Co-operative banks of North Gujarat for every financial year.

• Hypothesis between the years:

H_0:   There is no significant difference in the business per employee ratio of every Citizen Co-operative bank of North Gujarat for different financial years.

H_1:   There is significant difference in the business per employee ratio of every Citizen Co-operative bank of North Gujarat for different financial years.

Table 6.3-A

Source of Variation	SS	df	MS	F
Between Banks	369545.20	07	52792.17	45.38
Between years	114130.09	04	28532.52	24.53
Error	32569.96	28	1163.21	
Total	516245.25	39		

Table Value for df (7,28) is 2.36 at 5% level of significance.

Table Value for df (4,28) is 2.71 at 5% level of significance.

Table 6.3-A represents the difference for the banks is significant because the table value for df (7,28) is (2.36) which is lower than calculated value of 'F' (45.38). So, null hypothesis (H_o) is rejected and alternative hypothesis (H_1) is accepted. I.e. there is significant difference in the business per employee ratio of different Citizen Co-operative banks of North Gujarat for every financial year.

Same way the difference for the years is significant because the table value for df (4,28) is (2.71) which is lower than the calculated value of 'F' (24.53) for years and so here also null hypothesis(H_o) is rejected and alternative hypothesis (H_1) is accepted. I.e. there is significant difference in the business per employee ratio of every Citizen Co-operative bank of North Gujarat for different financial years.

6.4.4 Spread per Employee

Interest on loans, advances and investments is the main source of bank's total income. The difference between interest earned and interest paid is called spread. Spread per employee indicates the amount of spread available for each employee of the bank. The larger is this ratio spread, the higher are the profits of the bank. An increasing ratio signifies better employee productivity. Formula for the ratio of spread per employee is as follows:

$$\text{Spread per Employee} = \frac{\text{Spread}}{\text{No. of Employees}}$$

Spread per Employee Ratio of selected citizen cooperative banks of North Gujarat for the study period 2007-08 to 2011-12 is presented in the table 6.4 as follows:

Table 6.4

Spread per Employee

(Rs. In Lakhs)

YEAR	HIMNSB	MODNSB	MEHNSB	COBMEH	CHHNSB	BANMCB	CHANSB	PATNSB	AVERAGE
2007-08	4.31	6.90	2.75	10.17	4.53	5.07	5.83	5.54	5.64
2008-09	4.84	7.80	3.32	10.32	4.78	5.36	5.97	7.68	6.26
2009-10	5.30	8.69	4.23	10.64	8.77	5.62	6.52	9.98	7.47
2010-11	5.81	9.23	5.37	13.08	8.41	5.94	8.09	11.35	8.41
2011-12	7.38	11.17	7.02	13.21	8.36	7.34	11.15	15.71	10.17
AVERAGE	5.53	8.76	4.54	11.48	6.97	5.87	7.51	10.05	7.59

Source: Annual reports of CCBs during year 2007-08 to 2011-12.

Chart 6.2
Chart Showing Spread per Employee Ratio

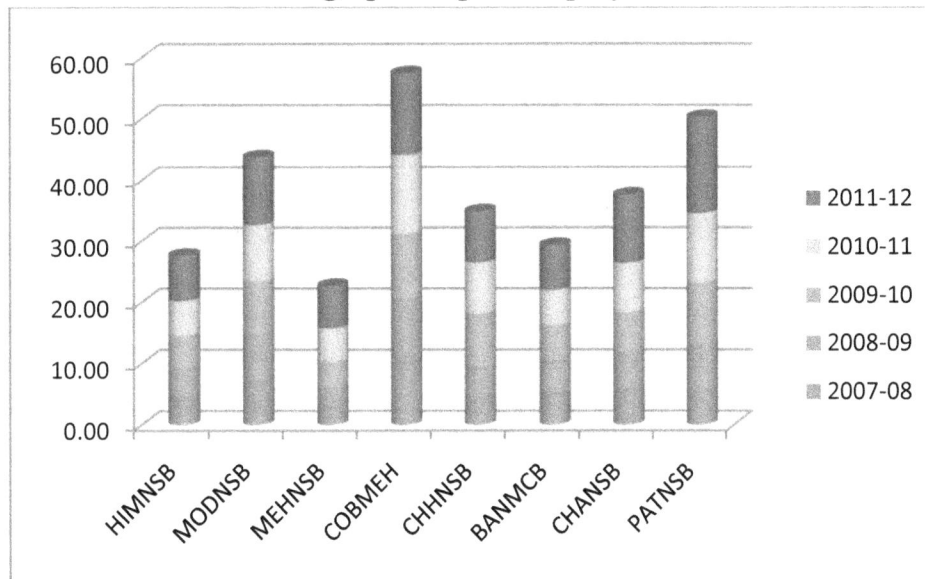

It can be observed from the above table 6.4 for himmatnagar nagarik sahakari bank that Spread per Employeewas 4.31 lakhs in the year 2007-08 which was the lowest during all the study period. In the year 2008-09 to 2011-12 this ratio was continuously increased to 4.84, 5.30, 5.81 and 7.38 lakhs respectively. In the year 2011-12 this ratio was the highest during all the study period. During all the study period average of this ratio was 5.53 lakhs. For all the five years of the study this ratio was lower than its average for three years and higher than its average in the remaining two years.

It is obvious from the above table 6.4 for modasa nagarik sahakari bank that Spread per Employeewas 6.90 lakhs in the year 2007-08 which was the lowest during all the study period. In the year 2008-09 to 2011-12 this ratio was continuously increased to 7.80, 8.69, 9.23 and 11.17 lakhs respectively. In the year 2011-12 this ratio was the highest during all the study period. During all the study period average of this ratio was 295.45 lakhs. For all the five years of the study this ratio was lower than its average for three years and higher than its average in the remaining two years.

It is apparent from the above table 6.4 for mehsana nagarik sahakari bank that Spread per Employeewas 2.75 lakhs in the year 2007-08 which was the lowest during all the study period. In the year 2008-09 to 2011-12 this ratio was continuously increased to 3.32, 4.23, 5.37 and 7.02 lakhs respectively. In the year 2011-12 this ratio was the highest during all the study period. During all the study period average of this ratio was 4.54 lakhs. For all the five years of the study this ratio was lower than its average for three years and higher than its average in the remaining two years.

It is cleared from the above table 6.4 for co-operative bank of mehsana that Spread per Employee was 10.17 lakhs in the year 2007-08 which was the lowest during all the study period. In the year 2008-09 to 2011-12 this ratio was continuously increased to 10.32, 10.64, 13.08 and 13.21 lakhs respectively. In the year 2011-12 this ratio was the highest during all the study period. During all the study period average of this ratio was 11.48 lakhs. For all the five years of the study this ratio was lower than its average for three years and higher than its average in the remaining two years.

It isevident from the above table 6.4 for chhapi nagarik sahakari bank that Spread per Employeewas 4.53 lakhs in the year 2007-08 which was the lowest during all the study period. In the year 2008-09 and 2009-10 this ratio was increased to 4.78 and 8.77 lakhs respectively. In the year 2009-10 it was the highest during all the study period. In the year 2010-11 and 2011-12 this ratio was continuously decreased to 8.41 and 8.36 lakhs respectively. During all the study period average of this ratio was 6.97 lakhs. For all the five years of the study this ratio was lower than its average for two years and higher than its average in the remaining three years.

It can be observed from the above table 6.4 for banaskantha mercantile co-operative bank that Spread per Employee was 5.07 lakhs in the year 2007-08 which was the lowest during all the study period. In the year 2008-09 to 2011-12 this ratio was continuously increased to 5.36, 5.62, 5.94 and 7.34 lakhs respectively. In the year 2011-12 this ratio was the highest during all the study period. During all the study period average of this ratio was 5.87 lakhs. For all the five years of the study this ratio was lower than its average for three years and higher than its average in the remaining two years.

It is obvious from the above table 6.4 for chanasma nagarik sahakari bank that Spread per Employeewas 5.83 lakhs in the year 2007-08 which was the lowest during all the study period. In the year 2008-09 to 2011-12 this ratio was continuously increased to 5.97, 6.52, 8.09 and 11.15 lakhs respectively. In the year 2011-12 this ratio was the highest during all the study period. During all the study period average of this ratio was 7.51 lakhs. For all the five years of the study this ratio was lower than its average for three years and higher than its average in the remaining two years.

It is apparent from the above table 6.4 for patan nagarik sahakari bank that Spread per Employeewas 5.54 lakhs in the year 2007-08 which was the lowest during all the study period. In the year 2008-09 to 2011-12 this ratio was continuously increased to 7.68, 9.98, 11.35 and 15.71 lakhs respectively. In the year 2011-12 this ratio was the highest during all the study period. During all the study period average of this ratio was 10.05 lakhs. For all the five years of the study this ratio was lower than its average for three years and higher than its average in the remaining two years.

It can be seen from the above table 6.4 for all Citizen co-operative banks that average of Spread per Employeeduring 2007-08 to 2011-12 was 7.59 lakhs. In the year 2007-08 average ratio of all banks was 5.64 lakhs which was the lowest during all the study period. In the year 2008-09 to 2011-12 this ratio was continuously increased to 6.26, 7.47, 8.41 and 10.17 lakhs respectively. In the year 2011-12 average ratio of all banks was the highest during all the study period. For all the five years of the study average ratio of all banks was lower than its average for three years and higher than its average in the remaining two years.

❖ F test (ANOVA) Analysis

The statements of hypothesis are as under:

• Hypothesis between the banks:

H_0: There is no significant difference in the spread per employee ratio of different Citizen Co-operative banks of North Gujarat for every financial year.

H_1: There is significant difference in the spread per employee ratio of different Citizen Co-operative banks of North Gujarat for every financial year.

• Hypothesis between the years:

H_0: There is no significant difference in the spread per employee ratio of every Citizen Co-operative bank of North Gujarat for different financial years.

H_1: There is significant difference in the spread per employee ratio of every Citizen Co-operative bank of North Gujarat for different financial years.

Table 6.4-A

Source of Variation	SS	df	MS	F
Between Banks	197.64	7	28.23	23.15
Between years	103.30	4	25.82	21.18
Error	34.15	28	1.22	
Total	335.08	39		

Table Value for df (7,28) is 2.36 at 5% level of significance.

Table Value for df (4,28) is 2.71 at 5% level of significance.

Table 6.4-A represents the difference for the banks is significant because the table value for df (7,28) is (2.36) which is lower than calculated value of 'F' (23.15). So, null hypothesis (H_o) is rejected and alternative hypothesis (H_1) is accepted. I.e. there is significant difference in the spread per employee ratio of different Citizen Co-operative banks of North Gujarat for every financial year.

Same way the difference for the years is significant because the table value for df (4,28) is (2.71) which is lower than the calculated value of 'F' (21.18) for years and so here also null hypothesis(H_o) is rejected and alternative hypothesis (H_1) is accepted. I.e. there is significant difference in the spread per employee ratio of every Citizen Co-operative bank of North Gujarat for different financial years.

6.4.5 Operating Expenses per Employee

Operating expenses (staff costs) include expenses made on salaries, allowances, provident fund, bonus, etc. Due to improper recognition of income and high costs, several banks suffered losses. The expenses per employee increased at periodical intervals due to wage and salary hikes, promotions, higher contribution to provident fund, etc. It is the expenditure incurred to operate a branch. The decreasing ratio signifies better employee productivity. Formula for the ratio of operatingexpensesper employee is as follows:

$$\text{Operating Expenses per Employee} = \frac{\text{Operating Expenses}}{\text{No. of Employees}}$$

Operating Expenses per Employee Ratio of selected citizen cooperative banks of North Gujarat for the study period 2007-08 to 2011-12 is presented in the table 6.5 as follows:

Table 6.5
Operating Expenses per Employee

(Rs. In Lakhs)

YEAR	HIMNSB	MODNSB	MEHNSB	COBMEH	CHHNSB	BANMCB	CHANSB	PATNSB	AVERAGE
2007-08	2.73	2.87	1.64	2.01	1.63	2.72	2.55	3.68	2.48
2008-09	3.00	3.24	1.79	2.27	1.87	2.92	2.67	4.26	2.75
2009-10	3.35	3.76	1.98	2.55	3.09	3.24	2.89	5.60	3.31
2010-11	4.03	4.53	2.30	3.06	2.85	3.55	3.26	5.97	3.69
2011-12	4.42	5.13	2.81	3.24	3.70	4.14	4.05	7.01	4.31
AVERAGE	3.51	3.91	2.10	2.63	2.63	3.31	3.08	5.30	3.31

Source: Annual reports of CCBs during year 2007-08 to 2011-12.

It can be observed from the above table 6.5 for himmatnagar nagarik sahakari bank that Operating Expenses per Employeewas 2.73 lakhs in the year 2007-08 which was the lowest during all the study period. In the year 2008-09 to 2011-12 this ratio was continuously increased to 3.00, 3.35, 4.03 and 4.42 lakhs respectively. In the year 2011-12 this ratio was the highest during all the study period. During all the study period average of this ratio was 3.51 lakhs. For all the five years of the study this ratio was lower than its average for three years and higher than its average in the remaining two years.

It is obvious from the above table 6.5 for modasa nagarik sahakari bank that Operating Expenses per Employeewas 2.87 lakhs in the year 2007-08 which was the lowest during all the study period. In the year 2008-09 to 2011-12 this ratio was continuously increased to 3.24, 3.76, 4.53 and 5.13 lakhs respectively. In the year 2011-12 this ratio was the highest during all the study period. During all the study period average of this ratio was 3.91 lakhs. For all the five years of the study this ratio was lower than its average for three years and higher than its average in the remaining two years.

It is apparent from the above table 6.5 for mehsana nagarik sahakari bank that Operating Expenses per Employeewas 1.64 lakhs in the year 2007-08 which was the lowest during all the study period. In the year 2008-09 to 2011-12 this ratio was continuously increased to 1.79, 1.98, 2.30 and 2.81 lakhs respectively. In the year 2011-12 this ratio was the highest during all the study period. During all the study period average of this ratio was 2.10 lakhs. For all the five years of the study this ratio was lower than its average for three years and higher than its average in the remaining two years.

It is cleared from the above table 6.5 for co-operative bank of mehsana that Operating Expenses per Employee was 2.01 lakhs in the year 2007-08 which was the lowest during all the study period. In the year 2008-09 to 2011-12 this ratio was continuously increased to 2.27, 2.55, 3.06 and 3.24 lakhs respectively. In the year 2011-12 this ratio was the highest during all the study period. During all the study period average of this ratio was 2.63 lakhs. For all the five years of the study this ratio was lower than its average for three years and higher than its average in the remaining two years.

It isevident from the above table 6.5 for chhapi nagarik sahakari bank that Operating Expenses per Employeewas 1.63 lakhs in the year 2007-08 which was the lowest during all the study period. In the year 2008-09 and 2009-10 this ratio was increased to 1.87 and 3.09 lakhs respectively. In the year 2010-11 this ratio was increased to 2.85 lakhs and in the year 2011-12 it was increased to 3.70 lakhs. In the year 2011-12 it was the highest during all the study period. During all the study period average of this ratio was 2.63 lakhs. For all the five years of the study this ratio was lower than its average for two years and higher than its average in the remaining three years.

It can be observed from the above table 6.5 for banaskantha mercantile co-operative bank that Operating Expenses per Employee was 2.72 lakhs in the year 2007-08 which was the lowest during all the study period. In the year 2008-09 to 2011-12 this ratio was continuously increased to 2.92, 3.24, 3.55 and 4.14 lakhs respectively. In the year 2011-12 this ratio was the highest during all the study period. During all the study period average of this ratio was 3.31 lakhs. For all the five years of the study this ratio was lower than its average for three years and higher than its average in the remaining two years.

It is obvious from the above table 6.5 for chanasma nagarik sahakari bank that Operating Expenses per Employeewas 2.55 lakhs in the year 2007-08 which was the lowest during all the study period. In the year 2008-09 to 2011-12 this ratio was continuously increased to 2.67, 2.89, 3.26 and 4.05 lakhs respectively. In the year 2011-12 this ratio was the highest during all the study period. During all the study period average of this ratio was 3.08 lakhs. For all the five years of the study this ratio was lower than its average for three years and higher than its average in the remaining two years.

It is apparent from the above table 6.5 for patan nagarik sahakari bank that Operating Expenses per Employeewas 3.68 lakhs in the year 2007-08 which was the lowest during all the study period. In the year 2008-09 to 2011-12 this ratio was continuously increased to 4.26, 5.60, 5.97 and 7.01 lakhs respectively. In the year 2011-

12 this ratio was the highest during all the study period. During all the study period average of this ratio was 5.30 lakhs. For all the five years of the study this ratio was lower than its average for two years and higher than its average in the remaining three years.

It can be seen from the above table 6.5 for all Citizen co-operative banks that average of Operating Expenses per Employeeduring 2007-08 to 2011-12 was 3.31 lakhs. In the year 2007-08 average ratio of all banks was 2.48 lakhs which was the lowest during all the study period. In the year 2008-09 to 2011-12 this ratio was continuously increased to 2.75, 3.31, 3.69 and 4.31 lakhs respectively. In the year 2009-10it was equal to average ratio of all banks during all the study period and in the year 2011-12 average ratio of all banks was the highest during all the study period. For all the five years of the study average ratio of all banks was lower than its average for two years, higher than its average for two years and equal to average ratio of all banks in the remaining one year.

❖ **F test (ANOVA) Analysis**

The statements of hypothesis are as under:

- **Hypothesis between the banks:**

H_0: There is no significant difference in the operating expenses per employee ratio of different Citizen Co-operative banks of North Gujarat for every financial year.

H_1: There is significant difference in the operating expenses per employee ratio of different Citizen Co-operative banks of North Gujarat for every financial year.

- **Hypothesis between the years:**

H_0: There is no significant difference in the operating expenses per employee ratio of every Citizen Co-operative bank of North Gujarat for different financial years.

H_1: There is significant difference in the operating expenses per employee ratio of every Citizen Co-operative bank of North Gujarat for different financial years.

Table 6.5-A

Source of Variation	SS	df	MS	F
Between Banks	34.09	07	4.87	45.42
Between years	17.25	04	4.31	40.21
Error	3.00	28	0.11	
Total	54.34	39		

Table Value for df (7,28) is 2.36 at 5% level of significance.

Table Value for df (4,28) is 2.71 at 5% level of significance.

Table 6.5-A represents the difference for the banks is significant because the table value for df (7,28) is (2.36) which is lower than calculated value of 'F' (45.42).

So, null hypothesis (H$_o$) is rejected and alternative hypothesis (H$_1$) is accepted. I.e. there is significant difference in the operating expenses per employee ratio of different Citizen Co-operative banks of North Gujarat for every financial year.

Same way the difference for the years is significant because the table value for df (4,28) is (2.71) which is lower than the calculated value of 'F' (40.21) for years and so here also null hypothesis(H$_o$) is rejected and alternative hypothesis (H$_1$) is accepted. I.e. there is significant difference in the operating expenses per employee ratio of every Citizen Co-operative bank of North Gujarat for different financial years.

6.4.6 Net Profit per Employee

Net profit is the net margin left after considering all expenses and incomes. In other words, it is the excess of income over expenditure. The net profit per employee indicates the output obtained in the form of net profit from per unit of input i.e. employees of the bank. This ratio shows the contribution of employees in the total profits of the bank, so an increase in the ratio has been considered as an indicator of better productivity. Formula for the ratio of net profit per employee is as follows:

$$\text{Net profit per Employee} = \frac{\text{Net profit}}{\text{No. of Employees}}$$

Net Profitper Employee Ratio of selected citizen cooperative banks of North Gujarat for the study period 2007-08 to 2011-12 is presented in the table 6.6 as follows:

Table 6.6
Net Profit per Employee

(Rs. In Lakhs)

YEAR	HIMNSB	MODNSB	MEHNSB	COBMEH	CHHNSB	BANMCB	CHANSB	PATNSB	AVERAGE
2007-08	0.70	1.69	0.37	2.52	1.19	0.72	1.49	1.04	1.21
2008-09	0.83	1.98	0.57	2.89	0.89	0.79	1.54	1.64	1.39
2009-10	0.93	2.24	0.89	3.04	1.61	0.83	1.56	2.11	1.65
2010-11	1.04	2.26	0.67	4.22	1.13	0.78	1.87	2.20	1.77
2011-12	1.26	2.93	1.33	4.60	1.07	1.14	2.12	2.76	2.15
AVERAGE	0.95	2.22	0.77	3.45	1.18	0.85	1.71	1.95	1.63

Source: Annual reports of CCBs during year 2007-08 to 2011-12.

Chart 6.3
Chart Showing Net Profit per Employee Ratio

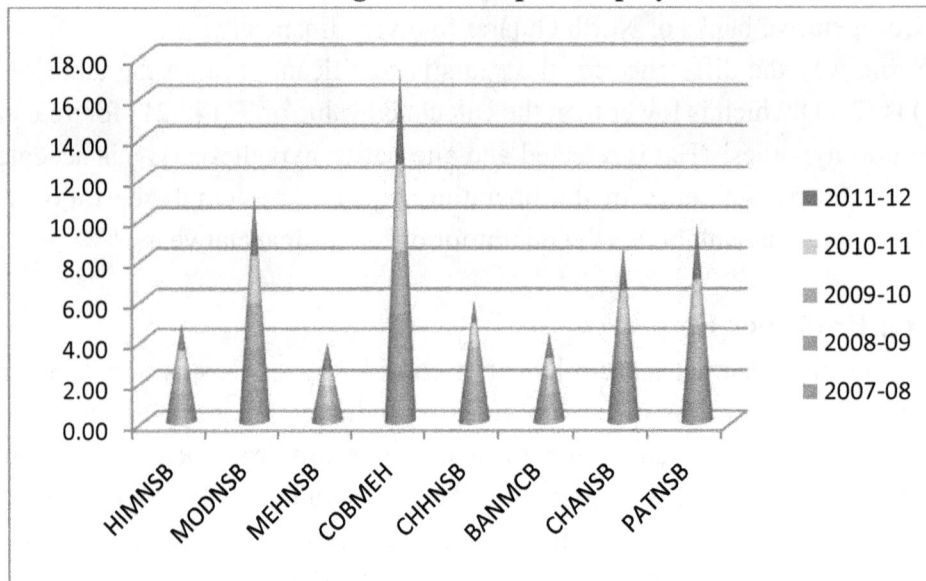

It can be observed from the above table 6.6 for himmatnagar nagarik sahakari bank that Net Profit per Employeewas 0.70 lakhs in the year 2007-08 which was the lowest during all the study period. In the year 2008-09 to 2011-12 this ratio was continuously increased to 0.83, 0.93, 1.04 and 1.26 lakhs respectively. In the year 2011-12 this ratio was the highest during all the study period. During all the study period average of this ratio was 0.95 lakhs. For all the five years of the study this ratio was lower than its average for three years and higher than its average in the remaining two years.

It is obvious from the above table 6.6 for modasa nagarik sahakari bank that Net Profit per Employeewas 1.69 lakhs in the year 2007-08 which was the lowest during all the study period. In the year 2008-09 to 2011-12 this ratio was continuously increased to 1.98, 2.24, 2.26 and 2.93 lakhs respectively. In the year 2011-12 this ratio was the highest during all the study period. During all the study period average of this ratio was 2.22 lakhs. For all the five years of the study this ratio was lower than its average for two years and higher than its average in the remaining three years.

It is apparent from the above table 6.6 for mehsana nagarik sahakari bank that Net Profit per Employeewas 0.37 lakhs in the year 2007-08 which was the lowest during all the study period. In the year 2008-09 to 2009-10 this ratio was continuously increased to 0.57 and 0.89 lakhs respectively. In the year 2010-11 this ratio was decreased to 0.67 lakhs and in the year 2011-12 this ratio was increased to 1.33 lakhs. In the year 2011-12 this ratio was the highest during all the study period. During all the study period average of this ratio was 0.77 lakhs. For all the five years of the study this ratio was lower than its average for three years and higher than its average in the remaining two years.

It is cleared from the above table 6.6 for co-operative bank of mehsana that Net Profit per Employee was 2.52 lakhs in the year 2007-08 which was the lowest during all the study period. In the year 2008-09 to 2011-12 this ratio was continuously increased to 2.89, 3.04, 4.22 and 4.60 lakhs respectively. In the year 2011-12 this ratio was the highest during all the study period. During all the study period average of this ratio was 3.45 lakhs. For all the five years of the study this ratio was lower than its average for three years and higher than its average in the remaining two years.

It isevident from the above table 6.6 for chhapi nagarik sahakari bank that Net Profit per Employeewas 1.19 lakhs in the year 2007-08. In the year 2008-09 this ratio was decreased to 0.89 lakhs which was the lowest during all the study period. In the year 2009-10 this ratio was increased to 1.61 lakhs which was the highest during all the study period. In the year 2010-11 and 2011-12 this ratio was continuously decreased to 1.13 and 1.07 lakhs respectively. During all the study period average of this ratio was 1.18 lakhs. For all the five years of the study this ratio was lower than its average for three years and higher than its average in the remaining two years.

It can be observed from the above table 6.6 for banaskantha mercantile co-operative bank that Net Profit per Employee was 0.72 lakhs in the year 2007-08 which was the lowest during all the study period. In the year 2008-09 and 2009-10 this ratio was continuously increased to 0.79 and 0.83 lakhs respectively. In the year 2010-11 this ratio was decreased to 0.78 lakhs and in the year 2011-12 it was increased to 1.14 lakhs. In the year 2011-12 this ratio was the highest during all the study period. During all the study period average of this ratio was 0.85 lakhs. For all the five years of the study this ratio was lower than its average for four years and higher than its average in the remaining one year.

It is obvious from the above table 6.6 for chanasma nagarik sahakari bank that Net Profit per Employeewas 1.49 lakhs in the year 2007-08 which was the lowest during all the study period. In the year 2008-09 to 2011-12 this ratio was continuously increased to 1.54, 1.56, 1.87 and 2.12 lakhs respectively. In the year 2011-12 this ratio was the highest during all the study period. During all the study period average of this ratio was 1.71 lakhs. For all the five years of the study this ratio was lower than its average for three years and higher than its average in the remaining two years.

It is apparent from the above table 6.6 for patan nagarik sahakari bank that Net Profit per Employeewas 1.04 lakhs in the year 2007-08 which was the lowest during all the study period. In the year 2008-09 to 2011-12 this ratio was continuously increased to 1.64, 2.11, 2.20 and 2.76 lakhs respectively. In the year 2011-12 this ratio was the highest during all the study period. During all the study period average of this ratio was 1.95 lakhs. For all the five years of the study this ratio was lower than its average for three years and higher than its average in the remaining two years.

It can be seen from the above table 6.6 for all Citizen co-operative banks that average of Net Profit per Employeeduring 2007-08 to 2011-12 was 1.63 lakhs. In the year 2007-08 average ratio of all banks was 1.21 lakhs which was the lowest during all the study period. In the year 2008-09 to 2011-12 this ratio was continuously increased to 1.39, 1.65, 1.77 and 2.15 lakhs respectively. In the year 2011-12 average ratio of all banks was the highest during all the study period. For all the five years of the study average ratio of all banks was lower than its average for two years and higher than its average in remaining three years.

❖ F test (ANOVA) Analysis

The statements of hypothesis are as under:

• Hypothesis between the banks:

H_0:   There is no significant difference in the net profit per employee ratio of different Citizen Co-operative banks of North Gujarat for every financial year.

H_1:   There is significant difference in the net profit per employee ratio of different Citizen Co-operative banks of North Gujarat for every financial year.

• Hypothesis between the years:

H_0:   There is no significant difference in the net profit per employee ratio of every Citizen Co-operative bank of North Gujarat for different financial years.

H_1:   There is significant difference in the net profit per employee ratio of every Citizen Co-operative bank of North Gujarat for different financial years.

Table 6.6-A

Source of Variation	SS	df	MS	F
Between Banks	28.95	07	4.14	38.42
Between years	4.17	04	1.04	9.69
Error	3.01	28	0.11	
Total	36.14	39		

Table Value for df (7,28) is 2.36 at 5% level of significance.

Table Value for df (4,28) is 2.71 at 5% level of significance.

Table 6.6-A represents the difference for the banks is significant because the table value for df (7,28) is (2.36) which is lower than calculated value of 'F' (38.42). So, null hypothesis (H_o) is rejected and alternative hypothesis (H_1) is accepted. I.e. there is significant difference in the net profit per employee ratio of different Citizen Co-operative banks of North Gujarat for every financial year.

Same way the difference for the years is significant because the table value for df (4,28) is (2.71) which is lower than the calculated value of 'F' (6.69) for years and so here also null hypothesis(H_o) is rejected and alternative hypothesis (H_1) is accepted. I.e. there is significant difference in the net profit per employee ratio of every Citizen Co-operative bank of North Gujarat for different financial years.

6.5   Productivity per Branch

While evaluating the results in terms of infrastructural facilities utilized by the banks at various locations and places, again six indicators of productivity ratios have been used by the researcher as under:

6.5.1 Deposits per Branch

A Branch is the initial organizational unit in any bank with similar environment and clientele. This also follows the similar policies, methodologies and structure in a particular bank. In order to smoothen out the individual differences, this seems to be a better unit for measuring productivity. It reflects the organizational effectiveness of the bank. Higher the deposit per branch, better the system of collection and vice-versa. Formula for the ratio of deposit per branch is as follows:

$$\text{Deposits per Branch} = \frac{\text{Total Deposits}}{\text{No. of Branches}}$$

Deposits per BranchRatio of selected citizen cooperative banks of North Gujarat for the study period 2007-08 to 2011-12 is presented in the table 6.7 as follows:

Table 6.7
Deposits per Branch

(Rs. In Lakhs)

YEAR	HIMNSB	MODNSB	MEHNSB	COBMEH	CHHNSB	BANMCB	CHANSB	PATNSB	AVERAGE
2007-08	1694.37	2937.74	1178.44	1888.38	837.24	1196.95	1369.77	1843.91	1618.35
2008-09	1963.35	3178.15	1349.73	2328.78	473.90	1310.49	1377.36	2140.46	1765.28
2009-10	1996.73	3489.56	1644.76	2766.85	991.69	1292.35	1546.00	2739.43	2058.42
2010-11	2205.73	3949.21	1768.02	2878.90	1104.59	1384.40	1723.22	3321.61	2291.96
2011-12	2315.66	4142.30	1849.70	3219.88	1202.03	1632.42	2085.52	3441.15	2486.08
AVERAGE	2035.17	3539.39	1558.13	2616.56	921.89	1363.32	1620.37	2697.31	2044.02

Source: Annual reports of CCBs during year 2007-08 to 2011-12.

It can be observed from the above table 6.7 for himmatnagar nagarik sahakari bank that Deposits per Branchwas 1694.37 lakhs in the year 2007-08 which was the lowest during all the study period. In the year 2008-09 to 2011-12 this ratio was continuously increased to 1963.35, 1996.73, 2205.73 and 2315.66 lakhs respectively. In the year 2011-12 this ratio was the highest during all the study period. During all the study period average of this ratio was 2035.17 lakhs. For all the five years of the study this ratio was lower than its average for three years and higher than its average in the remaining two years.

It is obvious from the above table 6.7 for modasa nagarik sahakari bank that Deposits per Branchwas 2937.14 lakhs in the year 2007-08 which was the lowest during all the study period. In the year 2008-09 to 2011-12 this ratio was continuously increased to 3178.15, 3489.56, 3949.21 and 4142.30 lakhs respectively. In the year 2011-12 this ratio was the highest during all the study period. During all the study period average of this ratio was 3539.39 lakhs. For all the five years of the study this ratio was lower than its average for three years and higher than its average in the remaining two years.

It is apparent from the above table 6.7 for mehsana nagarik sahakari bank that Deposits per Branchwas 1178.44 lakhs in the year 2007-08 which was the lowest during all the study period. In the year 2008-09 to 2011-12 this ratio was continuously increased to 1349.73, 1644.76, 1768.02 and 1849.70 lakhs respectively. In the year 2011-12 this ratio was the highest during all the study period. During all the study period average of this ratio was 1558.13 lakhs. For all the five years of the study this ratio was lower than its average for two years and higher than its average in the remaining three years.

It is cleared from the above table 6.7 for co-operative bank of mehsana that Deposits per Branch was 1888.38 lakhs in the year 2007-08 which was the lowest during all the study period. In the year 2008-09 to 2011-12 this ratio was continuously increased to 2328.78, 2766.85, 2878.90 and 3219.88 lakhs respectively. In the year 2011-12 this ratio was the highest during all the study period. During all the study period average of this ratio was 2616.56 lakhs. For all the five years of the study this ratio was lower than its average for two years and higher than its average in the remaining three years.

It isevident from the above table 6.7 for chhapi nagarik sahakari bank that Deposits per Branchwas 837.24 lakhs in the year 2007-08. In the year 2008-09 this ratio was decreased to 473.90 lakhs which was the lowest during all the study period. In the year 2009-10 to 2011-12this ratio was continuously increased to 991.69, 1104.59 and 1202.03 lakhs respectively. In the year 2011-12 it was the highest during all the study period. During all the study period average of this ratio was 163.84 lakhs. For all the five years of the study this ratio was lower than its average for two years and higher than its average in the remaining three years.

It can be observed from the above table 6.7 for banaskantha mercantile co-operative bank that Deposits per Branch was 1196.95 lakhs in the year 2007-08 which was the lowest during all the study period. In the year 2008-09 this ratio was increased to 1310.49 lakhs and in the year 2009-10 this ratio was decreased to 1292.35 lakhs. In the year 2010-11 and 2011-12 this ratio was increased to 1384.40 and 1632.42 lakhs respectively. In the year 2011-12 this ratio was the highest during all the study period. During all the study period average of this ratio was 1363.32 lakhs. For all the five years of the study this ratio was lower than its average for three years and higher than its average in the remaining two years.

It is obvious from the above table 6.7 for chanasma nagarik sahakari bank that Deposits per Branchwas 1369.77 lakhs in the year 2007-08 which was the lowest during all the study period. In the year 2008-09 to 2011-12 this ratio was continuously increased to 1377.36, 1546.00, 1723.22 and 2085.52 lakhs respectively. In the year 2011-12 this ratio was the highest during all the study period. During all the study period average of this ratio was 1620.37 lakhs. For all the five years of the study this ratio was lower than its average for three years and higher than its average in the remaining two years.

It is apparent from the above table 6.7 for patan nagarik sahakari bank that Deposits per Branchwas 1843.91 lakhs in the year 2007-08 which was the lowest during all the study period. In the year 2008-09 to 2011-12 this ratio was continuously increased to 2140.46, 2739.43, 3321.61 and 3441.15 lakhs respectively. In the year 2011-12 this ratio was the highest during all the study period. During all the study period average of this ratio was 2697.31 lakhs. For all the five years of the study this ratio was lower than its average for two years and higher than its average in the remaining three years.

It can be seen from the above table 6.7 for all Citizen co-operative banks that average of Deposits per Branchduring 2007-08 to 2011-12 was 2044.02 lakhs. In the year 2007-08 average ratio of all banks was 1618.35lakhs which was the lowest during all the study period. In the year 2008-09 to 2011-12 this ratio was continuously increased to 1765.28, 2058.42, 2291.96 and 2486.08 lakhs respectively. In the year 2011-12 average ratio of all banks was the highest during all the study period. For all the five years of the study average ratio of all banks was lower than its average for two years and higher than its average in remaining three years.

❖ F test (ANOVA) Analysis

The statements of hypothesis are as under:
- **Hypothesis between the banks:**

H_0: There is no significant difference in the deposits per branch ratio of different Citizen Co-operative banks of North Gujarat for every financial year.

H_1: There is significant difference in the deposits per branch ratio of different Citizen Co-operative banks of North Gujarat for every financial year.

- **Hypothesis between the years:**

H_0: There is no significant difference in the deposits per branch ratio of every Citizen Co-operative bank of North Gujarat for different financial years.

H_1: There is significant difference in the deposits per branch ratio of every Citizen Co-operative bank of North Gujarat for different financial years.

Table 6.7-A

Source of Variation	SS	df	MS	F
Between Banks	25644425.98	07	3663489.43	79.39
Between years	4127955.62	04	1031988.90	22.36
Error	1292131.39	28	46147.55	
Total	31064512.98	39		

Table Value for df (7,28) is 2.36 at 5% level of significance.

Table Value for df (4,28) is 2.71 at 5% level of significance.

Table 6.7-A represents the difference for the banks is significant because the table value for df (7,28) is (2.36) which is lower than calculated value of 'F' (79.39). So, null hypothesis (H₀) is rejected and alternative hypothesis (H₁) is accepted. I.e. there is significant difference in the deposits per branch ratio of different Citizen Co-operative banks of North Gujarat for every financial year.

Same way the difference for the years is significant because the table value for df (4,28) is (2.71) which is lower than the calculated value of 'F' (22.36) for years and so here also null hypothesis(H₀) is rejected and alternative hypothesis (H₁) is accepted. I.e. there is significant difference in the deposits per branch ratio of every Citizen Co-operative bank of North Gujarat for different financial years.

6.5.2 Advances per Branch

In addition to employee skills, the loan policies as well as interest rates etc. of a particular bank also affect advances. This ratio reflects this aspect of the bank. Higher the advances per branch, better the advance policies and hence the productivity. Formula for the ratio of advances per branch is as follows:

$$\text{Advances per Branch} = \frac{\text{Total Advances}}{\text{No. of Branches}}$$

Advances per BranchRatio of selected citizen cooperative banks of North Gujarat for the study period 2007-08 to 2011-12 is presented in the table 6.8 as follows:

Table 6.8

Advances per Branch

(Rs. In Lakhs)

YEAR	HIMNSB	MODNSB	MEHNSB	COBMEH	CHHNSB	BANMCB	CHANSB	PATNSB	AVERAGE
2007-08	814.53	1792.62	704.62	1286.42	355.95	642.45	849.48	1085.98	941.51
2008-09	870.76	1900.10	743.22	1311.69	409.34	690.30	916.01	1190.69	1004.01
2009-10	876.19	2117.75	855.64	1366.52	475.41	697.71	1089.50	1325.65	1100.55
2010-11	1178.62	2236.86	1011.61	1789.68	536.14	867.06	1181.67	1430.79	1279.05
2011-12	1469.95	2594.23	1157.41	1800.23	639.08	928.42	1458.05	1693.33	1467.59
AVERAGE	1042.01	2128.31	894.50	1510.91	483.18	765.19	1098.94	1345.28	1158.54

Source: Annual reports of CCBs during year 2007-08 to 2011-12.

It can be observed from the above table 6.8 for himmatnagar nagarik sahakari bank that Advances per Branchwas 814.53 lakhs in the year 2007-08 which was the lowest during all the study period. In the year 2008-09 to 2011-12 this ratio was continuously increased to 870.76, 876.19, 1178.62 and 1469.95 lakhs respectively. In the year 2011-12 this ratio was the highest during all the study period. During all the study period average of this ratio was 1042.01 lakhs. For all the five years of the study this ratio was lower than its average for three years and higher than its average in the remaining two years.

It is obvious from the above table 6.8 for modasa nagarik sahakari bank that Advances per Branchwas 1792.62 lakhs in the year 2007-08 which was the lowest during all the study period. In the year 2008-09 to 2011-12 this ratio was continuously increased to 1900.10, 2117.75, 2236.86 and 2594.23 lakhs respectively. In the year 2011-12 this ratio was the highest during all the study period. During all the study period average of this ratio was 2128.31 lakhs. For all the five years of the study this ratio was lower than its average for three years and higher than its average in the remaining two years.

It is apparent from the above table 6.8 for mehsana nagarik sahakari bank that Advances per Branchwas 704.62 lakhs in the year 2007-08 which was the lowest during all the study period. In the year 2008-09 to 2011-12 this ratio was continuously increased to 743.22, 855.64, 1011.61 and 1157.41 lakhs respectively. In the year 2011-12 this ratio was the highest during all the study period. During all the study period average of this ratio was 894.50 lakhs. For all the five years of the study this ratio was lower than its average for three years and higher than its average in the remaining two years.

It is cleared from the above table 6.8 for co-operative bank of mehsana that Advances per Branch was 1286.42 lakhs in the year 2007-08 which was the lowest during all the study period. In the year 2008-09 to 2011-12 this ratio was continuously increased to 1311.69, 1366.52, 1789.68 and 1800.23 lakhs respectively. In the year 2011-12 this ratio was the highest during all the study period. During all the study period average of this ratio was 1510.91 lakhs. For all the five years of the study this ratio was lower than its average for three years and higher than its average in the remaining two years.

It isevident from the above table 6.8 for chhapi nagarik sahakari bank that Advances per Branchwas 355.95 lakhs in the year 2007-08 which was the lowest during all the study period. In the year 2008-09 to 2011-12 this ratio was continuously increased to 409.34, 475.41, 536.14 and 639.08 lakhs respectively. In the year 2011-12 this ratio was the highest during all the study period. During all the study period average of this ratio was 483.18 lakhs. For all the five years of the study this ratio was lower than its average for three years and higher than its average in the remaining two years.

It can be observed from the above table 6.8 for banaskantha mercantile co-operative bank that Advances per Branch was 642.45 lakhs in the year 2007-08 which was the lowest during all the study period. In the year 2008-09 to 2011-12 this ratio was continuously increased to 690.30, 697.71, 867.06 and 928.42 lakhs respectively. In the year 2011-12 this ratio was the highest during all the study period. During all the study period average of this ratio was 765.19 lakhs. For all the five years of the study this ratio was lower than its average for three years and higher than its average in the remaining two years.

It is obvious from the above table 6.8 for chanasma nagarik sahakari bank that Advances per Branchwas 849.48 lakhs in the year 2007-08 which was the lowest during all the study period. In the year 2008-09 to 2011-12 this ratio was continuously increased to 916.01, 1089.50, 1181.67 and 1458.05 lakhs respectively. In the year 2011-12 this ratio was the highest during all the study period. During all the study period average of this ratio was 1098.94 lakhs. For all the five years of the study this ratio was lower than its average for three years and higher than its average in the remaining two years.

It is apparent from the above table 6.8 for patan nagarik sahakari bank that Advances per Branchwas 1085.98 lakhs in the year 2007-08 which was the lowest during all the study period. In the year 2008-09 to 2011-12 this ratio was continuously increased to 1190.69, 1325.65, 1430.79 and 1663.33 lakhs respectively. In the year 2011-12 this ratio was the highest during all the study period. During all the study period average of this ratio was 1345.28 lakhs. For all the five years of the study this ratio was lower than its average for three years and higher than its average in the remaining two years.

It can be seen from the above table 6.8 for all Citizen co-operative banks that average of Advances per Branchduring 2007-08 to 2011-12 was 1158.54 lakhs. In the year 2007-08 average ratio of all banks was 941.51 lakhs which was the lowest during all the study period. In the year 2008-09 to 2011-12 this ratio was continuously increased to 1004.01, 1100.55, 1279.05 and 1467.59 lakhs respectively. In the year 2011-12 average ratio of all banks was the highest during all the study period. For all the five years of the study average ratio of all banks was lower than its average for three years and higher than its average in the remaining two years.

❖ F test (ANOVA) Analysis

The statements of hypothesis are as under:

• Hypothesis between the banks:

H_0:   There is no significant difference in the advances per branch ratio of different Citizen Co-operative banks of North Gujarat for every financial year.

H_1:   There is significant difference in the advances per branch ratio of different Citizen Co-operative banks of North Gujarat for every financial year.

• Hypothesis between the years:

H_0:   There is no significant difference in the advances per branch ratio of every Citizen Co-operative bank of North Gujarat for different financial years.

H_1:   There is significant difference in the advances per branch ratio of every Citizen Co-operative bank of North Gujarat for different financial years.

Table 6.8-A

Source of Variation	SS	df	MS	F
Between Banks	8985876	07	1283697	173.36
Between years	1475040	04	368760	49.80
Error	207329	28	7404.61	
Total	10668245	39		

Table Value for df (7,28) is 2.36 at 5% level of significance.

Table Value for df (4,28) is 2.71 at 5% level of significance.

Table 6.8-A represents the difference for the banks is significant because the table value for df (7,28) is (2.36) which is lower than calculated value of 'F' (173.36). So, null hypothesis (H_o) is rejected and alternative hypothesis (H_1) is accepted. I.e. there is significant difference in the advances per branch ratio of different Citizen Co-operative banks of North Gujarat for every financial year.

Same way the difference for the years is significant because the table value for df (4,28) is (2.71) which is lower than the calculated value of 'F' (49.80) for years and so here also null hypothesis(H_o) is rejected and alternative hypothesis (H_1) is accepted. I.e. there is significant difference in the advances per branch ratio of every Citizen Co-operative bank of North Gujarat for different financial years.

6.5.3 Business per Branch

Business per branch is also considered as an important indicator in measuring the productivity of a bank. It implies the total volume of business in the form of its deposits and loans and advances to priority sectors for capital formation and strengthening the financial status of the borrower. Advances and deposits of a branch together reflect the overall banking system and its productivity. An increase in the ratio indicates proper utilization of bank resources that in turn leads to increased management productivity. Formula for the ratio of business per branch is as follows:

$$\text{Business per Branch} = \frac{\text{Total Business}}{\text{No. of Branches}}$$

Business per BranchRatio of selected citizen cooperative banks of North Gujarat for the study period 2007-08 to 2011-12 is presented in the table 6.9 as follows:

Table 6.9

Business per Branch

Rs. In Lakhs)

YEAR	HIMNSB	MODNSB	MEHNSB	COBMEH	CHHNSB	BANMCB	CHANSB	PATNSB	AVERAGE
2007-08	2508.90	4730.36	1883.07	3174.80	1193.19	1839.40	2219.25	2929.88	2559.86
2008-09	2834.11	5078.25	2092.95	3640.47	883.24	2000.79	2293.37	3331.15	2769.29
2009-10	2872.92	5607.31	2500.41	4133.37	1467.10	1990.06	2635.50	4065.07	3158.97
2010-11	3384.35	6186.07	2779.63	4668.58	1640.73	2251.46	2904.89	4752.40	3571.01
2011-12	3785.62	6736.53	3007.10	5020.11	1841.11	2560.85	3543.58	5134.48	3953.67
AVERAGE	3077.18	5667.70	2452.63	4127.47	1405.07	2128.51	2719.32	4042.59	3202.56

Source: Annual reports of CCBs during year 2007-08 to 2011-12.

Chart 6.4
Chart Showing Business per Branch Ratio

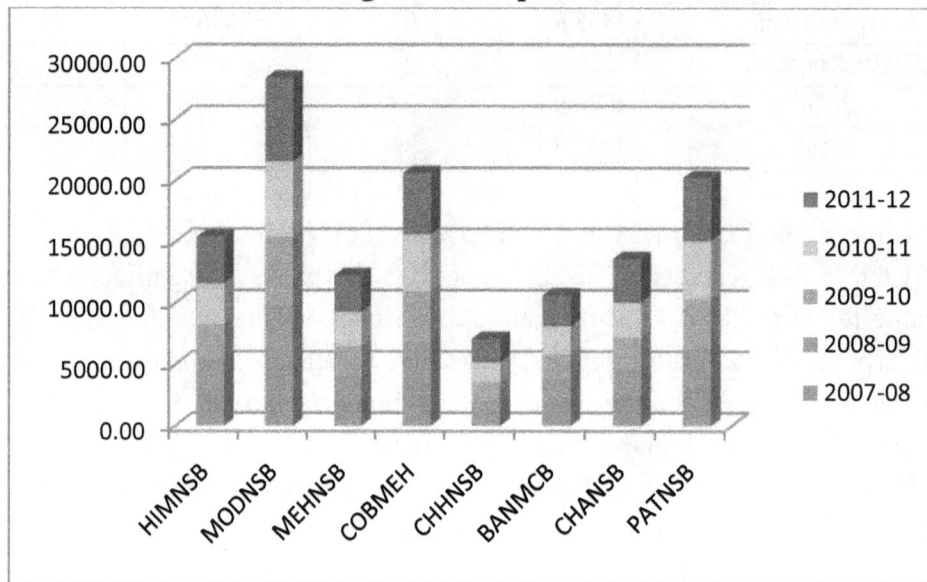

It can be observed from the above table 6.9 for himmatnagar nagarik sahakari bank that Business per Branchwas 2508.90 lakhs in the year 2007-08 which was the lowest during all the study period. In the year 2008-09 to 2011-12 this ratio was continuously increased to 2834.11, 2872.92, 3384.35 and 3785.62 lakhs respectively. In the year 2011-12 this ratio was the highest during all the study period. During all the study period average of this ratio was 3077.18 lakhs. For all the five years of the study this ratio was lower than its average for three years and higher than its average in the remaining two years.

It is obvious from the above table 6.9 for modasa nagarik sahakari bank that Business per Branchwas 4730.36 lakhs in the year 2007-08 which was the lowest during all the study period. In the year 2008-09 to 2011-12 this ratio was continuously increased to 5078.25, 5607.31, 6186.07 and 6736.53 lakhs respectively. In the year 2011-12 this ratio was the highest during all the study period. During all the study period average of this ratio was 5667.70 lakhs. For all the five years of the study this ratio was lower than its average for three years and higher than its average in the remaining two years.

It is apparent from the above table 6.9 for mehsana nagarik sahakari bank that Business per Branchwas 1883.07 lakhs in the year 2007-08 which was the lowest during all the study period. In the year 2008-09 to 2011-12 this ratio was continuously increased to 2092.95, 2500.41, 2779.63 and 3007.10 lakhs respectively. In the year 2011-12 this ratio was the highest during all the study period. During all the study period average of this ratio was 2452.63 lakhs. For all the five years of the study this ratio was lower than its average for two years and higher than its average in the remaining three years.

It is cleared from the above table 6.9 for co-operative bank of mehsana that Business per Branch was 3174.80 lakhs in the year 2007-08 which was the lowest during all the study period. In the year 2008-09 to 2011-12 this ratio was continuously increased to 3640.47, 4133.37, 4668.58 and 5020.11 lakhs respectively. In the year 2011-12 this ratio was the highest during all the study period. During all the study period average of this ratio was 4127.47 lakhs. For all the five years of the study this ratio was lower than its average for two years and higher than its average in the remaining three years.

It isevident from the above table 6.9 for chhapi nagarik sahakari bank that Business per Branchwas 1193.19 lakhs in the year 2007-08. In the year 2008-09 this ratio was decreased to 883.24 lakhs which was the lowest during all the study period. In the year 2009-10 to 2011-12 this ratio was continuously increased to 1467.10, 1640.73 and 1841.11 lakhs respectively. In the year 2011-12 it was the highest during all the study period. During all the study period average of this ratio was 1405.07 lakhs. For all the five years of the study this ratio was lower than its average for two years and higher than its average in the remaining three years.

It can be observed from the above table 6.9 for banaskantha mercantile co-operative bank that Business per Branch was 1839.40 lakhs in the year 2007-08 which was the lowest during all the study period. In the year 2008-09 this ratio was increased to 2000.79 lakhs and in the year 2009-10 this ratio was decreased to 1990.06 lakhs. In the year 2010-11 and 2011-12 this ratio was increased to 2251.46 and 2560.85 lakhs respectively. In the year 2011-12 this ratio was the highest during all the study period. During all the study period average of this ratio was 2128.51 lakhs. For all the five years of the study this ratio was lower than its average for three years and higher than its average in the remaining two years.

It is obvious from the above table 6.9 for chanasma nagarik sahakari bank that Business per Branchwas 2219.25 lakhs in the year 2007-08 which was the lowest during all the study period. In the year 2008-09 to 2011-12 this ratio was continuously increased to 2293.37, 2635.50, 2904.89 and 3543.58 lakhs respectively. In the year 2011-12 this ratio was the highest during all the study period. During all the study period average of this ratio was 2719.32 lakhs. For all the five years of the study this ratio was lower than its average for three years and higher than its average in the remaining two years.

It is apparent from the above table 6.9 for patan nagarik sahakari bank that Business per Branchwas 2929.88 lakhs in the year 2007-08 which was the lowest during all the study period. In the year 2008-09 to 2011-12 this ratio was continuously increased to 3331.15, 4065.07, 4752.40 and 5134.48 lakhs respectively. In the year 2011-12 this ratio was the highest during all the study period. During all the study period average of this ratio was 4042.59 lakhs. For all the five years of the study this ratio was lower than its average for two years and higher than its average in the remaining three years.

It can be seen from the above table 6.9 for all Citizen co-operative banks that average of Business per Branchduring 2007-08 to 2011-12 was 3202.56 lakhs. In the year 2007-08 average ratio of all banks was 2559.86 lakhs which was the lowest during all the study period. In the year 2008-09 to 2011-12 this ratio was continuously increased to 2769.29, 3158.97, 3571.01 and 3953.67 lakhs respectively. In the year 2011-12 average ratio of all banks was the highest during all the study period. For all the five years of the study average ratio of all banks was lower than its average for three years and higher than its average in remaining two years.

❖ **F test (ANOVA) Analysis**

The statements of hypothesis are as under:

- **Hypothesis between the banks:**

H_0: There is no significant difference in the business per branch ratio of different Citizen Co-operative banks of North Gujarat for every financial year.

H_1: There is significant difference in the business per branch ratio of different Citizen Co-operative banks of North Gujarat for every financial year.

- **Hypothesis between the years:**

H_0: There is no significant difference in the business per branch ratio of every Citizen Co-operative bank of North Gujarat for different financial years.

H_1: There is significant difference in the business per branch ratio of every Citizen Co-operative bank of North Gujarat for different financial years.

Table 6.9-A

Source of Variation	SS	df	MS	F
Between Banks	64171063.06	07	9167295	140.60
Between years	10420952.76	04	2605238	39.96
Error	1825667.24	28	65202.40	
Total	76417683.07	39		

Table Value for df (7,28) is 2.36 at 5% level of significance.

Table Value for df (4,28) is 2.71 at 5% level of significance.

Table 6.9-A represents the difference for the banks is significant because the table value for df (7,28) is (2.36) which is lower than calculated value of 'F' (140.60). So, null hypothesis (H_0) is rejected and alternative hypothesis (H_1) is accepted. I.e. there is significant difference in the business per branch ratio of different Citizen Co-operative banks of North Gujarat for every financial year.

Same way the difference for the years is significant because the table value for df (4,28) is (2.71) which is lower than the calculated value of 'F' (39.96) for years and so here also null hypothesis(H_o) is rejected and alternative hypothesis (H_1) is accepted. I.e. there is significant difference in the business per branch ratio of every Citizen Co-operative bank of North Gujarat for different financial years.

6.5.4 Spread per Branch

Spread is an item of income. It is the difference between interest received and interest paid. It is an important determinant of profitability.

An increase in the ratio depicts the more money left at disposal after meeting operational and administrative expenses. Formula for the ratio of Spread per branch is as follows:

$$\text{Spread per Branch} = \frac{\text{Spread}}{\text{No. of Branches}}$$

Spread per BranchRatio of selected citizen cooperative banks of North Gujarat for the study period 2007-08 to 2011-12 is presented in the table 6.10 as follows:

Table 6.10
Spread per Branch

(Rs. In Lakhs)

YEAR	HIMNSB	MODNSB	MEHNSB	COBMEH	CHHNSB	BANMCB	CHANSB	PATNSB	AVERAGE
2007-08	83.54	145.00	36.09	86.45	24.18	60.89	60.29	83.11	72.44
2008-09	93.80	156.06	43.21	87.73	25.51	64.36	61.65	107.53	79.98
2009-10	102.74	169.40	54.38	90.41	46.78	54.29	67.41	124.71	88.77
2010-11	112.80	175.39	66.70	111.14	44.87	62.39	78.24	141.86	99.17
2011-12	143.13	195.55	87.24	112.31	55.71	77.05	96.68	172.82	117.56
AVERAGE	107.20	168.28	57.52	97.61	39.41	63.79	72.85	126.01	91.58

Source: Annual reports of CCBs during year 2007-08 to 2011-12.

Chart 6.5
Chart Showing Spread per Branch Ratio

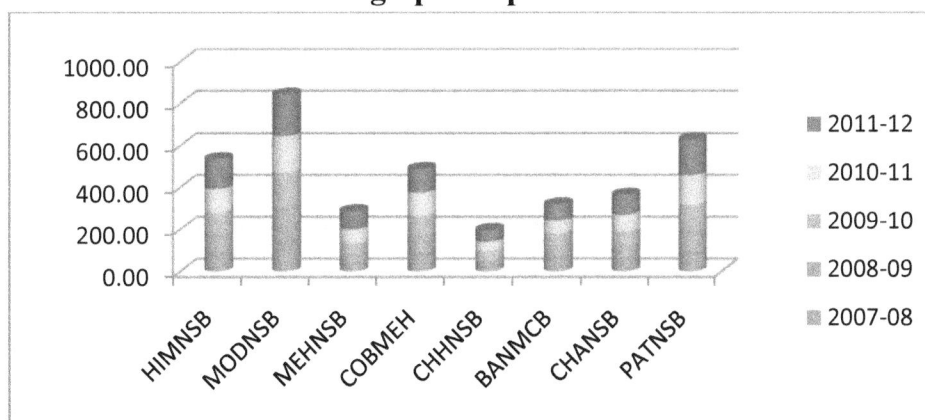

It can be observed from the above table 6.10 for himmatnagar nagarik sahakari bank that Spread per Branchwas 83.54 lakhs in the year 2007-08 which was the lowest during all the study period. In the year 2008-09 to 2011-12 this ratio was continuously increased to 93.80, 102.74, 112.80 and 143.13 lakhs respectively. In the year 2011-12 this ratio was the highest during all the study period. During all the study period average of this ratio was 107.20 lakhs. For all the five years of the study this ratio was lower than its average for three years and higher than its average in the remaining two years.

It is obvious from the above table 6.10 for modasa nagarik sahakari bank that Spread per Branchwas 145.00 lakhs in the year 2007-08 which was the lowest during all the study period. In the year 2008-09 to 2011-12 this ratio was continuously increased to 156.06, 169.40, 175.39 and 195.55 lakhs respectively. In the year 2011-12 this ratio was the highest during all the study period. During all the study period average of this ratio was 168.28 lakhs. For all the five years of the study this ratio was lower than its average for two years and higher than its average in the remaining three years.

It is apparent from the above table 6.10 for mehsana nagarik sahakari bank that Spread per Branchwas 36.09 lakhs in the year 2007-08 which was the lowest during all the study period. In the year 2008-09 to 2011-12 this ratio was continuously increased to 43.21, 54.38, 66.70 and 87.24 lakhs respectively. In the year 2011-12 this ratio was the highest during all the study period. During all the study period average of this ratio was 57.52 lakhs. For all the five years of the study this ratio was lower than its average for three years and higher than its average in the remaining two years.

It is cleared from the above table 6.10 for co-operative bank of mehsana that Spread per Branch was 86.45 lakhs in the year 2007-08 which was the lowest during all the study period. In the year 2008-09 to 2011-12 this ratio was continuously increased to 87.73, 90.41, 111.14 and 112.31 lakhs respectively. In the year 2011-12 this ratio was the highest during all the study period. During all the study period average of this ratio was 97.61 lakhs. For all the five years of the study this ratio was lower than its average for two years and higher than its average in the remaining three years.

It isevident from the above table 6.10 for chhapi nagarik sahakari bank that Spread per Branchwas 24.18 lakhs in the year 2007-08 which was the lowest during all the study period. In the year 2008-09 and 2009-10 this ratio was continuously increased to 25.51 and 46.78 lakhs respectively. In the year 2010-11 this ratio was decreased to 44.87 lakhs. In the year 2011-12 this ratio was increased to 55.71 lakhs which was the highest during all the study period. During all the study period average of this ratio was 39.41 lakhs. For all the five years of the study this ratio was lower than its average for two years and higher than its average in the remaining three years.

It can be observed from the above table 6.10 for banaskantha mercantile co-operative bank that Spread per Branch was 60.89 lakhs in the year 2007-08. In the year 2008-09 this ratio was increased to 64.36 lakhs and in the year 2009-10 this ratio was decreased to 54.29 lakhs. In the year 2009-10 this ratio was the lowest during all the study period. In the year 2010-11 and 2011-12 this ratio was increased to 62.39 and 77.05 lakhs respectively. In the year 2011-12 this ratio was the highest during all the study period. During all the study period average of this ratio was 63.79 lakhs. For all the five years of the study this ratio was lower than its average for three years and higher than its average in the remaining two years.

It is obvious from the above table 6.10 for chanasma nagarik sahakari bank that Spread per Branchwas 60.29 lakhs in the year 2007-08 which was the lowest during all the study period. In the year 2008-09 to 2011-12 this ratio was continuously increased to 61.65, 67.41, 78.24 and 96.68 lakhs respectively. In the year 2011-12 this ratio was the highest during all the study period. During all the study period average of this ratio was 72.85 lakhs. For all the five years of the study this ratio was lower than its average for three years and higher than its average in the remaining two years.

It is apparent from the above table 6.10 for patan nagarik sahakari bank that Spread per Branchwas 83.11 lakhs in the year 2007-08 which was the lowest during all the study period. In the year 2008-09 to 2011-12 this ratio was continuously increased to 107.53, 124.71, 141.86 and 172.82 lakhs respectively. In the year 2011-12 this ratio was the highest during all the study period. During all the study period average of this ratio was 126.01 lakhs. For all the five years of the study this ratio was lower than its average for three years and higher than its average in the remaining two years.

It can be seen from the above table 6.10 for all Citizen co-operative banks that average of Spread per Branchduring 2007-08 to 2011-12 was 91.58 lakhs. In the year 2007-08 average ratio of all banks was 72.44 lakhs which was the lowest during all the study period. In the year 2008-09 to 2011-12 this ratio was continuously increased to 79.98, 88.77, 99.17 and 117.56 lakhs respectively. In the year 2011-12 average ratio of all banks was the highest during all the study period. For all the five years of the study average ratio of all banks was lower than its average for three years and higher than its average in remaining two years.

❖ F test (ANOVA) Analysis

The statements of hypothesis are as under:

• Hypothesis between the banks:

H_0:   There is no significant difference in the spread per branch ratio of different Citizen Co-operative banks of North Gujarat for every financial year.

H_1:   There is significant difference in the spread per branch ratio of different Citizen Co-operative banks of North Gujarat for every financial year.

• Hypothesis between the years:

H_0:   There is no significant difference in the spread per branch ratio of every Citizen Co-operative bank of North Gujarat for different financial years.

H_1:   There is significant difference in the spread per branch ratio of every Citizen Co-operative bank of North Gujarat for different financial years.

Table 6.10-A

Source of Variation	SS	df	MS	F
Between Banks	61765.42	07	8823.63	97.28
Between years	9929.88	04	2482.47	27.37
Error	2539.69	28	90.70	
Total	74234.98	39		

Table Value for df (7,28) is 2.36 at 5% level of significance.

Table Value for df (4,28) is 2.71 at 5% level of significance.

Table 6.10-A represents the difference for the banks is significant because the table value for df (7,28) is (2.36) which is lower than calculated value of 'F' (97.28). So, null hypothesis (H_o) is rejected and alternative hypothesis (H_1) is accepted. I.e. there is significant difference in the spread per branch ratio of different Citizen Co-operative banks of North Gujarat for every financial year.

Same way the difference for the years is significant because the table value for df (4,28) is (2.71) which is lower than the calculated value of 'F' (27.37) for years and so here also null hypothesis(H_o) is rejected and alternative hypothesis (H_1) is accepted. I.e. there is significant difference in the spread per branch ratio of every Citizen Co-operative bank of North Gujarat for different financial years.

6.5.5 Operating Expenses per Branch

Operating expenses (staff costs) include expenses made on salaries, allowances, provident fund, bonus, etc. Due to improper recognition of income and high costs, several banks suffered losses. If the expense per branch is high, lower will be the profit per branch. Formula for the ratio of operating expenses per branch is as follows:

$$\text{Operating Expenses per Branch} = \frac{\text{Operating Expenses}}{\text{No. of Branches}}$$

Operating Expenses per BranchRatio of selected citizen cooperative banks of North Gujarat for the study period 2007-08 to 2011-12 is presented in the table 6.11 as follows:

Table 6.11
Operating Expenses per Branch

(Rs. In Lakhs)

YEAR	HIMNSB	MODNSB	MEHNSB	COBMEH	CHHNSB	BANMCB	CHANSB	PATNSB	AVERAGE
2007-08	52.89	60.23	21.57	17.09	8.68	32.63	26.36	55.22	34.33
2008-09	58.17	64.79	23.22	19.32	9.98	34.99	27.60	59.64	37.22
2009-10	64.93	73.42	25.46	21.64	16.47	31.32	29.83	69.95	41.63
2010-11	78.26	86.13	28.57	26.01	15.21	37.27	31.48	74.67	47.20
2011-12	85.84	89.80	34.88	27.50	24.65	43.46	35.10	77.13	52.30
AVERAGE	68.02	74.87	26.74	22.31	15.00	35.93	30.07	67.32	42.53

Source: Annual reports of CCBs during year 2007-08 to 2011-12.

It can be observed from the above table 6.11 for himmatnagar nagarik sahakari bank that Operating Expenses per Branchwas 52.89 lakhs in the year 2007-08 which was the lowest during all the study period. In the year 2008-09 to 2011-12 this ratio was continuously increased to 58.17, 64.93, 78.26 and 85.84 lakhs respectively. In the year 2011-12 this ratio was the highest during all the study period. During all the study period average of this ratio was 68.02 lakhs. For all the five years of the study this ratio was lower than its average for three years and higher than its average in the remaining two years.

It is obvious from the above table 6.11 for modasa nagarik sahakari bank that Operating Expenses per Branchwas 60.23 lakhs in the year 2007-08 which was the lowest during all the study period. In the year 2008-09 to 2011-12 this ratio was continuously increased to 64.79, 73.42, 86.13 and 89.80 lakhs respectively. In the year 2011-12 this ratio was the highest during all the study period. During all the study period average of this ratio was 74.87 lakhs. For all the five years of the study this ratio was lower than its average for three years and higher than its average in the remaining two years.

It is apparent from the above table 6.11 for mehsana nagarik sahakari bank that Operating Expenses per Branchwas 21.57 lakhs in the year 2007-08 which was the lowest during all the study period. In the year 2008-09 to 2011-12 this ratio was continuously increased to 23.22, 25.46, 28.57 and 34.88 lakhs respectively. In the year 2011-12 this ratio was the highest during all the study period. During all the study period average of this ratio was 26.74 lakhs. For all the five years of the study this ratio was lower than its average for three years and higher than its average in the remaining two years.

It is cleared from the above table 6.11 for co-operative bank of mehsana that Operating Expenses per Branch was 17.09 lakhs in the year 2007-08 which was the lowest during all the study period. In the year 2008-09 to 2011-12 this ratio was continuously increased to 19.32, 21.64, 26.01 and 27.50 lakhs respectively. In the year 2011-12 this ratio was the highest during all the study period. During all the study period average of this ratio was 22.31 lakhs. For all the five years of the study this ratio was lower than its average for three years and higher than its average in the remaining two years.

It isevident from the above table 6.11 for chhapi nagarik sahakari bank that Operating Expenses per Branchwas 8.68 lakhs in the year 2007-08 which was the lowest during all the study period. In the year 2008-09 and 2009-10 this ratio was continuously increased to 9.98 and 16.47 lakhs respectively. In the year 2010-11 this ratio was decreased to 15.21 lakhs. In the year 2011-12 this ratio was increased to 24.65 lakhs which was the highest during all the study period. During all the study period average of this ratio was 15.00 lakhs. For all the five years of the study this ratio was lower than its average for two years and higher than its average in the remaining three years.

It can be observed from the above table 6.11 for banaskantha mercantile co-operative bank that Operating Expenses per Branch was 32.63 lakhs in the year 2007-08. In the year 2008-09 this ratio was increased to 34.99 lakhs and in the year 2009-10 this ratio was decreased to 31.32 lakhs. In the year 2009-10 this ratio was the lowest during all the study period. In the year 2010-11 and 2011-12 this ratio was increased to 37.27 and 43.46 lakhs respectively. In the year 2011-12 this ratio was the highest during all the study period. During all the study period average of this ratio was 35.93 lakhs. For all the five years of the study this ratio was lower than its average for three years and higher than its average in the remaining two years.

It is obvious from the above table 6.11 for chanasma nagarik sahakari bank that Operating Expenses per Branchwas 26.36 lakhs in the year 2007-08 which was the lowest during all the study period. In the year 2008-09 to 2011-12 this ratio was continuously increased to 27.60, 29.83, 31.48 and 35.10 lakhs respectively. In the year 2011-12 this ratio was the highest during all the study period. During all the study period average of this ratio was 30.07 lakhs. For all the five years of the study this ratio was lower than its average for three years and higher than its average in the remaining two years.

It is apparent from the above table 6.11 for patan nagarik sahakari bank that Operating Expenses per Branchwas 55.22 lakhs in the year 2007-08 which was the lowest during all the study period. In the year 2008-09 to 2011-12 this ratio was continuously increased to 59.64, 69.95, 74.67 and 77.13 lakhs respectively. In the year 2011-12 this ratio was the highest during all the study period. During all the study period average of this ratio was 67.32 lakhs. For all the five years of the study this ratio was lower than its average for two years and higher than its average in the remaining three years.

It can be seen from the above table 6.11 for all Citizen co-operative banks that average of Operating Expenses per Branchduring 2007-08 to 2011-12 was 42.53 lakhs. In the year 2007-08 average ratio of all banks was 34.33 lakhs which was the lowest during all the study period. In the year 2008-09 to 2011-12 this ratio was continuously increased to 37.22, 41.63, 47.20 and 52.30 lakhs respectively. In the year 2011-12 average ratio of all banks was the highest during all the study period. For all the five years of the study average ratio of all banks was lower than its average for three years and higher than its average in remaining two years.

❖ F test (ANOVA) Analysis

The statements of hypothesis are as under:

- **Hypothesis between the banks:**

H_0:   There is no significant difference in the operating expenses per branch ratio of different Citizen Co-operative banks of North Gujarat for every financial year.

H_1: There is significant difference in the operating expenses per branch ratio of different Citizen Co-operative banks of North Gujarat for every financial year.

- **Hypothesis between the years:**

H_0: There is no significant difference in the operating expenses per branch ratio of every Citizen Co-operative bank of North Gujarat for different financial years.

H_1: There is significant difference in the operating expenses per branch ratio of every Citizen Co-operative bank of North Gujarat for different financial years.

Table 6.11-A

Source of Variation	SS	df	MS	F
Between Banks	19625.34	07	2803.62	138.25
Between years	1707.52	04	426.88	21.05
Error	567.83	28	20.28	
Total	21900.69	39		

Table Value for df (7,28) is 2.36 at 5% level of significance.

Table Value for df (4,28) is 2.71 at 5% level of significance.

Table 6.11-A represents the difference for the banks is significant because the table value for df (7,28) is (2.36) which is lower than calculated value of 'F' (138.25). So, null hypothesis (H_o) is rejected and alternative hypothesis (H_1) is accepted. I.e. there is significant difference in the operating expenses per branch ratio of different Citizen Co-operative banks of North Gujarat for every financial year.

Same way the difference for the years is significant because the table value for df (4,28) is (2.71) which is lower than the calculated value of 'F' (21.05) for years and so here also null hypothesis(H_o) is rejected and alternative hypothesis (H_1) is accepted. I.e. there is significant difference in the operating expenses per branch ratio of every Citizen Co-operative bank of North Gujarat for different financial years.

6.5.6 Net Profit per Branch

The net profit per branch ratio establishes the relationship between the contributions of each branch in generating net profit of the business. Net profit is the net result of all the operational activities after considering all indirect expenses. The increase in the net profit per branch ratio implies better efficiency of each management unit in earning profits. Formula for the ratio of net profit per branch is as follows:

$$\text{Net profit per Branch} = \frac{\text{Net profit}}{\text{No. of Branches}}$$

Net profit per BranchRatio of selected citizen cooperative banks of North Gujarat for the study period 2007-08 to 2011-12 is presented in the table 6.12 as follows:

Table 6.12
Net Profit per Branch

(Rs. In Lakhs)

YEAR	HIMNSB	MODNSB	MEHNSB	COBMEH	CHHNSB	BANMCB	CHANSB	PATNSB	AVERAGE
2007-08	13.60	35.46	4.84	21.39	6.34	8.69	15.35	15.54	15.15
2008-09	16.01	39.53	7.37	24.56	4.75	9.50	15.87	22.96	17.57
2009-10	18.01	43.61	11.49	25.85	8.58	8.00	16.09	26.43	19.76
2010-11	20.25	42.89	8.33	35.83	6.05	8.16	18.04	27.49	20.88
2011-12	24.40	51.23	16.49	39.08	7.11	12.00	18.38	30.36	24.88
AVERAGE	18.45	42.54	9.70	29.34	6.57	9.27	16.75	24.56	19.65

Source: Annual reports of CCBs during year 2007-08 to 2011-12.

Chart 6.6
Chart Showing Net Profit per BranchRatio

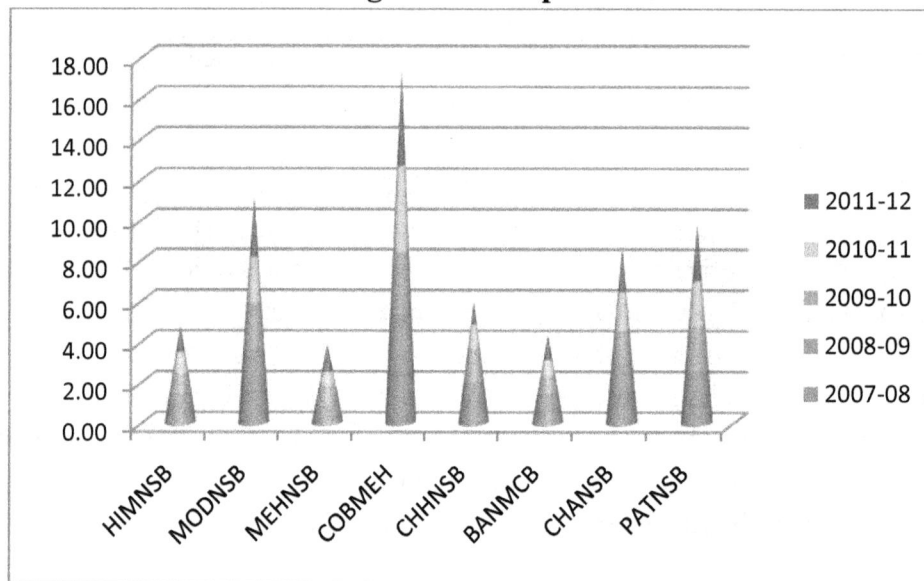

It can be observed from the above table 6.12 for himmatnagar nagarik sahakari bank that Net Profit per Branchwas 13.60 lakhs in the year 2007-08 which was the lowest during all the study period. In the year 2008-09 to 2011-12 this ratio was continuously increased to 16.01, 18.01, 20.25 and 24.40 lakhs respectively. In the year 2011-12 this ratio was the highest during all the study period. During all the study period average of this ratio was 18.45 lakhs. For all the five years of the study this ratio was lower than its average for three years and higher than its average in the remaining two years.

It is obvious from the above table 6.12 for modasa nagarik sahakari bank that Net Profit per Branchwas 35.46 lakhs in the year 2007-08 which was the lowest during all the study period. In the year 2008-09 and 2009-10 this ratio was continuously increased to 39.53 and 43.61 lakhs respectively. In the year 2010-11 this ratio was decreased to 42.89 lakhs and in the year 2011-12 this ratio was increased to 51.23 lakhs.

In the year 2011-12 this ratio was the highest during all the study period. During all the study period average of this ratio was 42.54 lakhs. For all the five years of the study this ratio was lower than its average for two years and higher than its average in the remaining three years.

It is apparent from the above table 6.12 for mehsana nagarik sahakari bank that Net Profit per Branchwas 4.84 lakhs in the year 2007-08 which was the lowest during all the study period. In the year 2008-09 and 2009-10 this ratio was continuously increased to 7.37 and 11.49 lakhs respectively. In the year 2010-11 this ratio was decreased to 8.33 lakhs and in the year 2011-12 this ratio was increased to 16.49 lakhs. In the year 2011-12 this ratio was the highest during all the study period. During all the study period average of this ratio was 9.70 lakhs. For all the five years of the study this ratio was lower than its average for three years and higher than its average in the remaining two years.

It is cleared from the above table 6.12 for co-operative bank of mehsana that Net Profit per Branch was 21.39 lakhs in the year 2007-08 which was the lowest during all the study period. In the year 2008-09 to 2011-12 this ratio was continuously increased to 24.56, 25.85, 35.83 and 39.08 lakhs respectively. In the year 2011-12 this ratio was the highest during all the study period. During all the study period average of this ratio was 29.34 lakhs. For all the five years of the study this ratio was lower than its average for three years and higher than its average in the remaining two years.

It isevident from the above table 6.12 for chhapi nagarik sahakari bank that Net Profit per Branchwas 6.34 lakhs in the year 2007-08. In the year 2008-09 this ratio was decreased to 4.75 lakhs which was the lowest during all the study period. In the year 2009-10 this ratio was increased to 8.58 lakhs which was the highest during all the study period. In the year 2010-11 this ratio was decreased to 6.05 lakhs and in the year 2011-12 this ratio was increased to 7.11 lakhs. During all the study period average of this ratio was 6.57 lakhs. For all the five years of the study this ratio was lower than its average for three years and higher than its average in the remaining two years.

It can be observed from the above table 6.12 for banaskantha mercantile co-operative bank that Net Profit per Branch was 8.69 lakhs in the year 2007-08. In the year 2008-09 this ratio was increased to 9.50 lakhs and in the year 2009-10 this ratio was decreased to 8.00 lakhs which was the lowest during all the study period. In the year 2010-11and 2011-12 this ratio was continuously increased to 8.16 and 12.00 lakhs respectively. In the year 2011-12 this ratio was the highest during all the study period. During all the study period average of this ratio was 9.27 lakhs. For all the five years of the study this ratio was lower than its average for three years and higher than its average in the remaining two years.

It is obvious from the above table 6.12 for chanasma nagarik sahakari bank that Net Profit per Branchwas 15.35 lakhs in the year 2007-08 which was the lowest during all the study period. In the year 2008-09 to 2011-12 this ratio was continuously increased to 15.87, 16.09, 18.04 and 18.38 lakhs respectively. In the year 2011-12 this ratio was the highest during all the study period. During all the study period average of this ratio was 16.75 lakhs. For all the five years of the study this ratio was lower than its average for three years and higher than its average in the remaining two years.

It is apparent from the above table 6.12 for patan nagarik sahakari bank that Net Profit per Branchwas 15.54 lakhs in the year 2007-08 which was the lowest during all the study period. In the year 2008-09 to 2011-12 this ratio was continuously increased to 22.96, 26.43, 27.49 and 30.36 lakhs respectively. In the year 2011-12 this ratio was the highest during all the study period. During all the study period average of this ratio was 24.56 lakhs. For all the five years of the study this ratio was lower than its average for two years and higher than its average in the remaining three years.

It can be seen from the above table 6.12 for all Citizen co-operative banks that average of Net Profit per Branchduring 2007-08 to 2011-12 was 19.65 lakhs. In the year 2007-08 average ratio of all banks was 15.15 lakhs which was the lowest during all the study period. In the year 2008-09 to 2011-12 this ratio was continuously increased to 17.57, 19.76, 20.88 and 24.88 lakhs respectively. In the year 2011-12 average ratio of all banks was the highest during all the study period. For all the five years of the study average ratio of all banks was lower than its average for two years and higher than its average in remaining three years.

❖ F test (ANOVA) Analysis

The statements of hypothesis are as under:

- ### Hypothesis between the banks:

H_0:   There is no significant difference in the net profit per branch ratio of different Citizen Co-operative banks of North Gujarat for every financial year.

H_1:   There is significant difference in the net profit per branch ratio of different Citizen Co-operative banks of North Gujarat for every financial year.

- ### Hypothesis between the years:

H_0:   There is no significant difference in the net profit per branch ratio of every Citizen Co-operative bank of North Gujarat for different financial years.

H_1:   There is significant difference in the net profit per branch ratio of every Citizen Co-operative bank of North Gujarat for different financial years.

Table 6.12A

Source of Variation	SS	df	MS	F
Between Banks	5149.49	07	735.64	83.06
Between years	427.64	04	106.91	12.07
Error	248.00	28	8.86	
Total	5825.13	39		

Table Value for df (7,28) is 2.36 at 5% level of significance.

Table Value for df (4,28) is 2.71 at 5% level of significance.

Table 6.12-A represents the difference for the banks is significant because the table value for df (7,28) is (2.36) which is lower than calculated value of 'F' (83.06).

176

So, null hypothesis (H$_o$) is rejected and alternative hypothesis (H$_1$) is accepted. I.e. there is significant difference in the net profit per branch ratio of different Citizen Co-operative banks of North Gujarat for every financial year.

Same way the difference for the years is significant because the table value for df (4,28) is (2.71) which is lower than the calculated value of 'F' (12.07) for years and so here also null hypothesis(H$_o$) is rejected and alternative hypothesis (H$_1$) is accepted. I.e. there is significant difference in the net profit per branch ratio of every Citizen Co-operative bank of North Gujarat for different financial years.

6.5   Conclusion

In this chapter researcher has tried to analyze **productivity** of selected Citizen co-operative banks of north Gujarat. For an analysis of **productivity** various twelve ratios were calculated from the annual reports of Citizen Co-operative bank of North Gujarat. The **productivity** of different Citizen Co-operative banks was analyzed with reference to its components such as ratios per employees and ratios per branches.

In the analysis of **productivity**, profit and loss account and balance sheet of selected Citizen co-operative banks has been analyzed with the help of various twelve ratios and "F" test (ANOVA) of all ratios proves that there is no uniformity in **productivity** of different Citizen Co-operative banks of North Gujarat for every financial year and there is no uniformity in **productivity** of every Citizen Co-operative banks of North Gujarat for different financial year.

In the analysis of employee productivity; results of Citizen Co-operative bank of North Gujarat was found exceptionally good. All variables such as, net-profit per employee, business per employee and spread per employee have shown desirable results except total operating expenditure per employee.Further, similar trend has been visible in the results of branch productivity. The net profit per branch, business per branch and spread per branch has shown a remarkable increase during the study period. However, an increase in the total operating expenditure per branch reflects that bank must take serious steps to exercise control over undesirable expenditure.

References

1. Jagwant Singh, "Indian Banking Industry: Growth and Trends in Productivity"New Delhi, Deep and Deep Publications. (1993) p.21.
2. C.B. Gupta, "Production, Productivity and Cost Effectiveness" New Delhi, Sultan Chand &.Co. (1990) p.4.3.
3. Richard E. Kopleman, "Managing Productivity Organizations" New Delhi, McGraw Hill Book Company, (1986) p.3.
4. R. P. Mohanty, "managing technology forstrategic advantages" The Economic Times, Thursday 9th Jan.(1992) p.14.
5. Gordon K.C.Chen and Robert E. Mcgarrah, "productivity management Text and cases" New York, International editions Holt Saunders CBS college publication. (1982) p.3.

Chapter-7
Analysis of Assets and Debts

7.1   Introduction

The banks, acting as financial intermediaries, accept deposits from investors, which make up the liability side of their balance sheet, and lend funds to borrowers, which form the assets on their balance sheet. If a bank builds up a sufficiently large asset and liability base, it will be able to meet the needs of both investors and borrowers, as it can maintain liquidity to meet investors' requirements, as well as create long term assets to meet the needs of borrowers. The importance of assets and debts in co-operative banks is inevitable and needs due care attention during the course of operation. The attention would help the bank to get into liquidation and can survive in the long run successfully. Therefore, in this chapter, the researcher has tried to do analyze of assets and debts of the selected Citizen co-operative banks of North Gujarat.

7.2 Concept of Assets and Debts

A balance sheet is a financial report that shows the value of a company's assets, liabilities, and owner's equity at a specific period of time, usually at the end of an accounting period, such as a quarter or a year. A balance sheet is often described as a 'snapshot of a company's financial condition.'[1] The balance sheet is also known as the 'statement of condition'[2], the 'statement of financial position', the 'statement of assets and liabilities', and the 'statement of worth.'[3] Further, **P.G. Hastings** says: "The balance sheet reveals the property owned by the business, the assets and the debts owned by the company, the liabilities."[4]

Assets are the lifeline for any business. Any business cannot work efficiently without sufficient assets. An asset is anything that can be sold for value. "An **asset** is an economic resource. Anything tangible or intangible that is capable of being owned or controlled to produce value and that is held to have positive economic value is considered an asset. Simply stated, assets represent value of ownership that can be converted into cash."[5] Assets are items that are owned and have value. Assets would include cash, investments, money that is owed to the person or entity (accounts receivable), inventory of items for sale, supplies, pre-paid expenses, land, land improvements (buildings), equipment, etc.

A liability (debt) is an obligation that must eventually be paid, and, hence, it is a claim on assets. Liabilities are obligations or items that are owed to others. Liabilities are the accounting opposite of assets. Liabilities would include accounts payable, accrued interest and principle on bonds issued, accrued interest and principal on mortgages outstanding, etc. The owner's equity in a bank is often referred to as bank capital, which is what is left when all assets have been sold and all liabilities have been paid. The relationship of the assets, liabilities, and owner's equity of a bank is shown by the equation: **Assets = Liabilities + Equity**

7.3 Measurement of Assets and Debts

Banking is a business of money transaction. It is a service providing unit. By providing banking services it receives interest and non-interest income. Accepting deposits and advancing loan is a primary function of a bank. Banking business cannot be compared with other productive units. So, measurement indicators of a firm for assets and debts can be applied to the bank with some changes. For measurement of assets and debts of Citizen co-operative banks of North Gujarat, seventeen ratios have been used, viz., owned funds to working funds ratio, total deposits to working funds ratio, total advances to working funds ratio etc.

7.4   Analysis of Assets and Debts

Researcher has been made an attempt to analyze the assets and debts of the selected Citizen co-operative banks of North Gujarat through the following ratios:

7.4.1   Owned Funds to Working Funds Ratio

Owned funds include share capital, all reserves, and surplus of Citizen Co-operative banks.The working funds denote the total of the balance sheet items except contra items. By this ratio we can know proportion of Owned funds against bank's working funds. The higher this ratio indicates the bank uses less borrowed capital. Thus, a high ratio is desirable. Formula for the ratio of owned funds to working funds is as follows:

$$\text{Owned Funds to Working Funds Ratio} = \frac{\text{Owned Funds}}{\text{Working Funds}} * 100$$

Gujarat for the study period 2007-08 to 2011-12 is presented in the table 7.1 as follows:

Table 7.1
Owned Funds to Working Funds Ratio

YEAR	HIMNSB	MODNSB	MEHNSB	COBMEH	CHHNSB	BANMCB	CHANSB	PATNSB	AVERAGE
2007-08	17.02	16.97	16.02	14.16	12.57	15.40	14.73	22.36	16.15
2008-09	15.40	16.48	14.10	14.24	12.22	15.34	14.41	20.76	15.37
2009-10	16.00	15.89	12.21	13.30	13.04	14.09	13.59	17.92	14.50
2010-11	15.59	15.10	12.43	14.24	13.00	14.43	12.98	15.26	14.13
2011-12	15.50	15.81	12.63	14.07	15.30	13.26	11.52	15.49	14.20
AVERAGE	15.90	16.05	13.48	14.00	13.22	14.50	13.45	18.36	14.87

Source: Annual reports of CCBs during year 2007-08 to 2011-12.

It can be observed from the above table 7.1 for himmatnagar nagarik sahakari bank that Owned Funds to Working Funds Ratio was 17.02% in the year 2007-08which was the highest during all the study period. In the year 2008-09 this ratio decreased to 15.40% which was the lowest during all the study period. In the year 2009-10 this ratio was increased to 16.00%. In the year 2010-11and 2011-12 this ratio was decreased to 15.59%and 15.50% respectively. During all the study period average of this ratio was 15.90%. For all the five years of the study this ratio was lower than its average for three years and higher than its average in the remaining two years.

It is obvious from the above table 7.1 for modasa nagarik sahakari bank that Owned Funds to Working Funds Ratio was 16.97% in the year 2007-08 which was the highest during all the study period. In the year 2008-09 to 2010-11 this ratio was continuously decreased to 16.48%,15.89% and 15.10% respectively. In the year 2010-11 this ratio was the lowest during all the study period. In the year 2011-12 this ratio was increased to 15.81%. During all the study period average of this ratio was 16.05%. For all the five years of the study this ratio was lower than its average for three years and higher than its average in the remaining two years.

It is apparent from the above table 7.1 for mehsana nagarik sahakari bank that Owned Funds to Working Funds Ratio was 16.02% in the year 2007-08 which was the highest during all the study period. In the year 2008-09 and 2009-10 this ratio was continuously decreased to 14.10% and 12.21% respectively. In the year 2009-10 this ratio was the lowest during all the study period.In the year 2010-11 and2011-12 this ratio was continuously increased to 12.43% and 12.63% respectively. During all the study period average of this ratio was 13.48%. For all the five years of the study this ratio was lower than its average for three years and higher than its average in the remaining two years.

It is cleared from the above table 7.1 for co-operative bank of mehsana that Owned Funds me to Working Funds Ratio was 14.16% in the year 2007-08. In the year 2008-09 this ratio was increased to 14.24%. In the year 2009-10 this ratio was decreased to 13.30% which was the lowest during all the study period. In the year 2010-11 this ratio was increased to 14.24%. In the year 2008-09 and 2010-11 this ratio was the highest during all the study period. In the year 2011-12 this ratio was decreased to 14.07%. During all the study period average of this ratio was 14.00%. For all the five years of the study this ratio was lower than its average for one year and higher than its average in the remaining four years.

It isevident from the above table 7.1 for chhapi nagarik sahakari bank that Owned Funds to Working Funds Ratio was 12.57% in the year 2007-08.In the year 2008-09 this ratio was decreased to 12.22% which was the lowest during all the study period. In the year 2009-10 this ratio was increased to 13.04% and in the year 2010-11 it was decreased to 13.00%. In the year 2011-12 this ratio was increased to 15.30%which was the highest during all the study period. During all the study period average of this ratio was 13.22%. For all the five years of the study this ratio was lower than its average for four years and higher than its average in the remaining one year.

It can be observed from the above table 7.1 for banaskantha mercantile co-operative bank that Owned Funds to Working Funds Ratio was 15.40% in the year 2007-08which was the highest during all the study period. In the year 2008-09 and 2009-10 this ratio was continuously decreased to 15.34% and 14.09% respectively. In the year 2010-11 this ratio was increased to 14.43%. In the year 2011-12 it was decreased to 13.26%which was the lowest during all the study period. During all the study period average of this ratio was 14.50%. For all the five years of the study this ratio was lower than its average for three years and higher than its average in remaining two years.

It is obvious from the above table 7.1 for chanasma nagarik sahakari bank that Owned Funds to Working Funds Ratio was 14.73% in the year 2007-08 which was the highest during all the study period. In the year 2008-09 to 2011-12 this ratio was continuously decreased to 14.41%, 13.59%, 12.98% and 11.52% respectively. In the year 2011-12 this ratio was the lowest during all the study period. During all the study period average of this ratio was 13.45%. For all the five years of the study this ratio was lower than its average for two years and higher than its average in remaining three years.

It is apparent from the above table 7.1 for patan nagarik sahakari bank that Owned Funds to Working Funds Ratio was 22.36% in the year 2007-08which was the highest during all the study period. In the year 2008-09 to 2010-11 this ratio was continuously decreased to 20.76%, 17.92% and 15.26% respectively. In the year 2010-11 this ratio wasthe lowest during all the study period. In the year 2011-12 this ratio was increased to 15.49%. During all the study period average of this ratio was 18.36%. For all the five years of the study this ratio was lower than its average for three years and higher than its average in remaining two years.

It can be seen from the above table 7.1 for all Citizen co-operative banks that average of Owned Funds to Working Funds Ratio during 2007-08 to 2011-12 was 14.87%. In the year 2007-08 average ratio of all banks was 16.15%which was the highest during all the study period. In the year 2008-09 to 2010-11 this ratio was continuously decreased to 15.37%, 14.50% and 14.13% respectively. In the year 2010-11 it was the lowest during all the study period. In the year 2011-12 this ratio was increased to 14.20%. For all the five years of the study average ratio of all banks was lower than its average for three years and higher than its average in remaining two years.

❖ F test (ANOVA) Analysis

The statements of hypothesis are as under:

• Hypothesis between the banks:

H_0: There is no significant difference in the owned funds to working funds ratio of different Citizen Co-operative banks of North Gujarat for every financial year.

H_1: There is significant difference in the owned funds to working funds ratio of different Citizen Co-operative banks of North Gujarat for every financial year.

• Hypothesis between the years:

H_0: There is no significant difference in the owned funds to working funds ratio of every Citizen Co-operative bank of North Gujarat for different financial years.

H_1: There is significant difference in the owned funds to working funds ratio of every Citizen Co-operative bank of North Gujarat for different financial years.

Table 7.1-A

Source of Variation	SS	df	MS	F
Between Banks	110.82	07	15.83	9.67
Between years	24.25	04	6.06	3.70
Error	45.85	28	1.64	
Total	180.92	39		

Table Value for df (7,28) is 2.36 at 5% level of significance.

Table Value for df (4,28) is 2.71 at 5% level of significance.

Table 7.1-A represents the difference for the banks is significant because the table value for df (7,28) is (2.36) which is lower than calculated value of 'F' (9.67). So, null hypothesis (H_o) is rejected and alternative hypothesis (H_1) is accepted. I.e. there is significant difference in the owned funds to working funds ratio of different Citizen Co-operative banks of North Gujarat for every financial year.

Same way the difference for the years is significant because the table value for df (4,28) is (2.71) which is lower than the calculated value of 'F' (3.70) for years and so here null hypothesis(H_o) is rejected and alternative hypothesis (H_1) is accepted. I.e. there is significant difference in the owned funds to working funds ratio of every Citizen Co-operative bank of North Gujarat for different financial years.

7.4.2 Term Deposits to Total Deposits Ratio

Deposit is lifeblood of banking organization which keeps the banks alive. So, it's very necessary to know the proportion of each type of deposits in total deposits, to get an idea about the financial stability of the banks. A deposit held at a financial institution that has a fixed term is called term deposit. These are generally short-term with maturities ranging anywhere from a month to a few years. An increasing ratio indicates the increasing faith of the public towards the bank. Formula for the ratio of term deposits to total deposits is as follows:

$$\text{Term Deposits to Total Deposits Ratio} = \frac{\text{Term Deposits}}{\text{Total Deposits}} * 100$$

Term Deposits to Total Deposits Ratioof selected citizen cooperative banks of North Gujarat for the study period 2007-08 to 2011-12 is presented in the table 7.2 as follows:

Table 7.2

Term Deposits to Total Deposits Ratio

YEAR	HIMNSB	MODNSB	MEHNSB	COBMEH	CHHNSB	BANMCB	CHANSB	PATNSB	AVERAGE
2007-08	56.69	72.30	53.94	71.85	20.15	44.43	69.74	73.25	57.79
2008-09	58.61	72.65	56.92	77.62	23.52	48.25	70.71	74.28	60.32
2009-10	53.05	72.33	57.12	71.09	25.78	45.54	70.29	73.96	58.65
2010-11	46.30	67.81	56.12	73.69	29.61	41.97	69.01	68.51	56.63
2011-12	47.52	68.01	59.16	74.24	29.03	46.29	69.88	64.30	57.31
AVERAGE	52.43	70.62	56.65	73.70	25.62	45.30	69.93	70.86	58.14

Source: Annual reports of CCBs during year 2007-08 to 2011-12.

It can be observed from the above table 7.2 for himmatnagar nagarik sahakari bank that Term Deposits to Total Deposits Ratio was 56.69% in the year 2007-08.In the year 2008-09 this ratio increased to 58.61% which was the highest during all the study period. In the year 2009-10 and 2010-11 this ratio was continuouslydecreased to 53.05%and 46.30% respectively. In the year 2010-11 this ratio was the lowest during all the study period.In the year 2011-12 this ratio was increased to 47.52%. During all the study period average of this ratio was 52.43%. For all the five years of the study this ratio was lower than its average for two years and higher than its average in the remaining three years.

It is obvious from the above table 7.2 for modasa nagarik sahakari bank that Term Deposits to Total Deposits Ratio was 72.30% in the year 2007-08.In the year 2008-09 this ratio increased to 72.65% which was the highest during all the study period. In the year 2009-10 and 2010-11 this ratio was continuouslydecreased to 72.33%and 67.81% respectively. In the year 2010-11 this ratio was the lowest during all the study period.In the year 2011-12 this ratio was increased to 68.01%. During all the study period average of this ratio was 70.62%. For all the five years of the study this ratio was lower than its average for two years and higher than its average in the remaining three years.

It is apparent from the above table 7.2 for mehsana nagarik sahakari bank that Term Deposits to Total Deposits Ratio was 53.94% in the year 2007-08 which was the lowest during all the study period. In the year 2008-09 and 2009-10 this ratio was continuously increased to 56.92% and 57.12% respectively. In the year 2010-11 this ratio was decreased to 56.12% and in the year 2011-12it was increased to 59.16%.In the year 2011-12 this ratio was the highest during all the study period. During all the study period average of this ratio was 56.65%. For all the five years of the study this ratio was lower than its average for two years and higher than its average in the remaining three years.

It is cleared from the above table 7.2 for co-operative bank of mehsana that Term Deposits to Total Deposits Ratio was 71.85% in the year 2007-08. In the year 2008-09 this ratio was increased to 77.62%which was the highest during all the study period. In the year 2009-10 this ratio was decreased to 71.09% which was the lowest during all the study period. In the year 2010-11 and 2011-12 this ratio wascontinuously increased to 73.69%and 74.24% respectively. During all the study period average of this ratio was 73.70%. For all the five years of the study this ratio was lower than its average three years and higher than its average in the remaining two years.

It isevident from the above table 7.2 for chhapi nagarik sahakari bank that Term Deposits to Total Deposits Ratio was 20.15% in the year 2007-08%which was the lowest during all the study period.In the year 2008-09 to 2010-11 this ratio was continuously increased to 23.52%, 25.78% and 29.61% respectively.In the year 2010-11 this ratio was the highest during all the study period. In the year 2011-12 this ratio was decreased to 29.03%.During all the study period average of this ratio was 25.62%. For all the five years of the study this ratio was lower than its average for two years and higher than its average in the remaining three years.

It can be observed from the above table 7.2 for banaskantha mercantile co-operative bank that Term Deposits to Total Deposits Ratio was 44.43% in the year 2007-08.In the year 2008-09 this ratio was increased to 48.25%which was the highest during all the study period. In the year 2009-10and 2010-11 this ratio was continuously decreased to 45.54% and 41.97% respectively.In the year 2010-11 this ratio was the lowest during all the study period. In the year 2011-12 this ratio was increased to 46.29%.During all the study period average of this ratio was 45.30%. For all the five years of the study this ratio was lower than its average for two years and higher than its average in the remaining three years.

It is obvious from the above table 7.2 for chanasma nagarik sahakari bank that Term Deposits to Total Deposits Ratio was 69.74% in the year 2007-08. In the year 2008-09 this ratio was increased to 70.71%which was the highest during all the study period. In the year 2009-10and 2010-11 this ratio was continuously decreased to 70.29% and 69.01% respectively.In the year 2010-11 this ratio was the lowest during all the study period. In the year 2011-12 this ratio was increased to 69.88%.During all the study period average of this ratio was 69.93%. For all the five years of the study this ratio was lower than its average for three years and higher than its average in the remaining two years.

It is apparent from the above table 7.2 for patan nagarik sahakari bank that Term Deposits to Total Deposits Ratio was 73.25% in the year 2007-08.In the year 2008-09 this ratio was increased to 74.28%which was the highest during all the study period. In the year 2009-10to 2011-12 this ratio was continuously decreased to 73.96%, 68.51%and 64.30% respectively.In the year 2011-12 this ratio was the lowest during all the study period. During all the study period average of this ratio was 70.86%. For all the five years of the study this ratio was lower than its average for two years and higher than its average in the remaining three years.

It can be seen from the above table 7.2 for all Citizen co-operative banks that average of Term Deposits to Total Deposits Ratio during 2007-08 to 2011-12 was 58.14%. In the year 2007-08 average ratio of all banks was 57.79%.In the year 2008-09 this ratio was increased to 60.32%which was the highest during all the study period. In the year 2009-10and 2010-11 this ratio was continuously decreased to 58.65% and 56.63% respectively.In the year 2010-11 this ratio was the lowest during all the study period. In the year 2011-12 this ratio was increased to 57.31%. For all the five years of the study average ratio of all banks was lower than its average for three years and higher than its average in remaining two years.

❖ **F test (ANOVA) Analysis**

The statements of hypothesis are as under:

- **Hypothesis between the banks:**

H₀: There is no significant difference in the term deposits to total deposits ratio of different Citizen Co-operative banks of North Gujarat for every financial year.

H₁: There is significant difference in the term deposits to total deposits ratio of different Citizen Co-operative banks of North Gujarat for every financial year.

- **Hypothesis between the years:**

H₀: There is no significant difference in the term deposits to total deposits ratio of every Citizen Co-operative bank of North Gujarat for different financial years.

H₁: There is significant difference in the term deposits to total deposits ratio of every Citizen Co-operative bank of North Gujarat for different financial years.

Table 7.2-A

Source of Variation	SS	df	MS	F
Between Banks	9779.24	07	1397.03	140.36
Between years	64.90	04	16.23	1.63
Error	278.69	28	9.95	
Total	10122.83	39		

Table Value for df (7,28) is 2.36 at 5% level of significance.

Table Value for df (4,28) is 2.71 at 5% level of significance.

Table 7.2-A represents the difference for the banks is significant because the table value for df (7,28) is (2.36) which is lower than calculated value of 'F' (140.36). So, null hypothesis (H₀) is rejected and alternative hypothesis (H₁) is accepted. I.e. there is significant difference in the term deposits to total deposits ratio of different Citizen Co-operative banks of North Gujarat for every financial year.

Same way the difference for the years is not significant because the table value for df (4,28) is (2.71) which is higher than the calculated value of 'F' (1.63) for years and so here null hypothesis(H₀) is accepted and alternative hypothesis (H₁) is rejected. I.e. there is no significant difference in the term deposits to total deposits ratio of every Citizen Co-operative bank of North Gujarat for different financial years.

7.4.3 Saving Deposits to Total Deposits Ratio

The Savings deposits promote thrift among the people. Individuals and Non-profit institutions can hold the savings deposit. The savings account holder gets the advantage of liquidity and small income in the form of interest. The higher this ratio indicates the bank focuses in higher collection of Savings deposits. Formula for the ratio of saving deposits to total deposits is as follows:

$$\text{Saving Deposits to Total Deposits Ratio} = \frac{\text{Saving Deposits}}{\text{Total Deposits}} *100$$

North Gujarat for the study period 2007-08 to 2011-12 is presented in the table 7.3 as follows:

Table 7.3

Saving Deposits to Total Deposits Ratio

YEAR	HIMNSB	MODNSB	MEHNSB	COBMEH	CHHNSB	BANMCB	CHANSB	PATNSB	AVERAGE
2007-08	34.81	23.48	27.92	19.03	22.30	35.86	23.61	24.59	26.45
2008-09	34.27	23.86	26.70	17.26	23.04	35.98	22.00	23.54	25.83
2009-10	39.01	24.68	27.96	21.59	23.58	35.73	22.03	21.87	27.06
2010-11	43.64	27.21	31.85	19.17	22.36	37.36	24.46	24.87	28.86
2011-12	41.90	27.71	28.91	19.53	25.03	35.80	21.36	27.46	28.46
AVERAGE	38.73	25.39	28.67	19.32	23.26	36.14	22.69	24.47	27.33

Source: Annual reports of CCBs during year 2007-08 to 2011-12.

It can be observed from the above table 7.3 for himmatnagar nagarik sahakari bank that Saving Deposits to Total Deposits Ratio was 34.81% in the year 2007-08. In the year 2008-09 this ratio decreased to 34.27% which was the lowest during all the study period. In the year 2009-10 and 2010-11 this ratio was continuously increased to 39.01%and 43.64% respectively. In the year 2010-11 this ratio was the highest during all the study period. In the year 2011-12 this ratio was decreased to 41.90%. During all the study period average of this ratio was 38.73%. For all the five years of the study this ratio was lower than its average for two years and higher than its average in the remaining three years.

It is obvious from the above table 7.3 for modasa nagarik sahakari bank that Saving Deposits to Total Deposits Ratio was 23.48% in the year 2007-08 which was the lowest during all the study period. In the year 2008-09 to 2011-12 this ratio was continuously increased to 23.86%,24.68%, 27.21% and 27.71% respectively. In the year 2011-12 this ratio was the highest during all the study period. During all the study period average of this ratio was 25.39%. For all the five years of the study this ratio was lower than its average for three years and higher than its average in the remaining two years.

It is apparent from the above table 7.3 for mehsana nagarik sahakari bank that Saving Deposits to Total Deposits Ratio was 27.92% in the year 2007-08. In the year 2008-09 this ratio was decreased to 26.70%which was the lowest during all the study period. In the year 2009-10 and 2010-11 this ratio was continuously increased to 27.96% and 31.85% respectively. In the year 2010-11this ratio was the highest during all the study period.In the year 2011-12 this ratio wasdecreased to 28.91%. During all the study period average of this ratio was 28.67%. For all the five years of the study this ratio was lower than its average for two years and higher than its average in the remaining three years.

It is cleared from the above table 7.3 for co-operative bank of mehsana that Saving Deposits to Total Deposits Ratio was 19.03% in the year 2007-08. In the year

2008-09 this ratio was decreased to 17.26%which was the lowest during all the study period. In the year 2009-10 this ratio was increased to 21.59%which was the highest during all the study period. In the year 2010-11 this ratio was decreased to 19.17%. In the year 2011-12 this ratio was increased to 19.53%. During all the study period average of this ratio was 19.32%. For all the five years of the study this ratio was lower than its average for three years and higher than its average in the remaining two years.

It isevident from the above table 7.3 for chhapi nagarik sahakari bank that Saving Deposits to Total Deposits Ratio was 22.30% in the year 2007-08which was the lowest during all the study period.In the year 2008-09 and 2009-10 this ratio was continuously increased to 23.04% and 23.58% respectively. In the year 2010-11 this ratio was decreased to 22.36%. In the year 2011-12 this ratio was increased to 25.03%which was the highest during all the study period. During all the study period average of this ratio was 23.26%. For all the five years of the study this ratio was lower than its average for three years and higher than its average in the remaining two years.

It can be observed from the above table 7.3 for banaskantha mercantile co-operative bank that Saving Deposits to Total Deposits Ratio was 35.86% in the year 2007-08.In the year 2008-09 this ratio was increased to 35.98% and in the year 2009-10 this ratio was decreased to 35.73%.In the year 2009-10 this ratio was the lowest during all the study period. In the year 2010-11 this ratio was increased to 37.36%which was the highest during all the study period. In the year 2011-12 it was decreased to 35.80%.During all the study period average of this ratio was 36.14%. For all the five years of the study this ratio was lower than its average for four years and higher than its average in remaining one year.

It is obvious from the above table 7.3 for chanasma nagarik sahakari bank that Saving Deposits to Total Deposits Ratio was 23.61% in the year 2007-08. In the year 2008-09 this ratio was decreased to 22.00% and in the year 2009-10 this ratio was increased to 22.03%. In the year 2010-11 this ratio was increased to 24.46%which was the highest during all the study period.In the year 2011-12 this ratio was decreased to 21.36% which was the lowest during all the study period. During all the study period average of this ratio was 22.69%. For all the five years of the study this ratio was lower than its average for three years and higher than its average in the remaining two years.

It is apparent from the above table 7.3 for patan nagarik sahakari bank that Saving Deposits to Total Deposits Ratio was 24.59% in the year 2007-08.In the year 2008-09 and 2009-10 this ratio was continuously decreased to 23.54%and 21.87% respectively.In the year 2009-10 this ratio was the lowest during all the study period. In the year 2010-11and 2011-12 this ratio wascontinuously increased to 24.87%and 27.46% respectively. In the year 2011-12 this ratio was the highest during all the study period. During all the study period average of this ratio was 24.47%. For all the five years of the study this ratio was lower than its average for two years and higher than its average in remaining three years.

It can be seen from the above table 7.3 for all Citizen co-operative banks that average of Saving Deposits to Total Deposits Ratio during 2007-08 to 2011-12 was

27.33%. In the year 2007-08 average ratio of all banks was 26.45%.In the year 2008-09this ratio was decreased to 25.83%which was the lowest during all the study period.In the year 2009-10 and 2010-11 this ratio was continuously increased to 27.06% and 28.86% respectively. In the year 2010-11 it was the highest during all the study period. In the year 2011-12 this ratio was decreased to 28.46%. For all the five years of the study average ratio of all banks was lower than its average for three years and higher than its average in remaining two years.

❖ F test (ANOVA) Analysis

The statements of hypothesis are as under:

• Hypothesis between the banks:

H_0: There is no significant difference in the saving deposits to total deposits ratio of different Citizen Co-operative banks of North Gujarat for every financial year.

H_1: There is significant difference in the saving deposits to total deposits ratio of different Citizen Co-operative banks of North Gujarat for every financial year.

• Hypothesis between the years:

H_0: There is no significant difference in the saving deposits to total deposits ratio of every Citizen Co-operative bank of North Gujarat for different financial years.

H_1: There is significant difference in the saving deposits to total deposits ratio of every Citizen Co-operative bank of North Gujarat for different financial years.

Table 7.3-A

Source of Variation	SS	df	MS	F
Between Banks	1618.24	07	231.18	75.51
Between years	53.83	04	13.46	4.40
Error	85.73	28	3.06	
Total	1757.80	39		

Table Value for df (7,28) is 2.36 at 5% level of significance.

Table Value for df (4,28) is 2.71 at 5% level of significance.

Table 7.3-A represents the difference for the banks is significant because the table value for df (7,28) is (2.36) which is lower than calculated value of 'F' (75.51). So, null hypothesis (H_o) is rejected and alternative hypothesis (H_1) is accepted. I.e. there is significant difference in the saving deposits to total depositsratio of different Citizen Co-operative banks of North Gujarat for every financial year.

Same way the difference for the years is significant because the table value for df (4,28) is (2.71) which is lower than the calculated value of 'F' (4.40) for years and so here null hypothesis(H_o) is rejected and alternative hypothesis (H_1) is accepted. I.e. there is significant difference in the saving deposits to total depositsratio of every Citizen Co-operative bank of North Gujarat for different financial years.

7.4.4 Current Deposits to Total Deposits Ratio

The people who need to have a liquid balance maintain these accounts. Current account deposit offers high liquidity. No interest is paid on current deposits and there are no restrictions on withdrawals from the current account. These accounts are generally kept by business firms, institutions and cooperative bodies. The higher this ratio indicates the bank focuses in higher collection of current deposits. Formula for the ratio of current deposits to total deposits is as follows:

$$\text{Current Deposits to Total Deposits Ratio} = \frac{\text{Current Deposits}}{\text{Total Deposits}} * 100$$

Current Deposits to Total Deposits Ratioof selected citizen cooperative banks of North Gujarat for the study period 2007-08 to 2011-12 is presented in the table 7.4 as follows:

Table 7.4

Current Deposits to Total Deposits Ratio

YEAR	HIMNSB	MODNSB	MEHNSB	COBMEH	CHHNSB	BANMCB	CHANSB	PATNSB	AVERAGE
2007-08	8.50	4.22	18.14	9.12	57.54	19.70	6.65	2.16	15.75
2008-09	7.11	3.50	16.38	5.12	53.44	15.78	7.29	2.18	13.85
2009-10	7.93	3.00	14.92	7.31	50.64	18.73	7.68	4.17	14.30
2010-11	10.06	4.98	12.03	7.14	48.03	20.67	6.53	6.62	14.51
2011-12	10.58	4.28	11.93	6.23	45.94	17.91	8.76	8.24	14.23
AVERAGE	8.84	3.99	14.68	6.98	51.12	18.56	7.38	4.67	14.53

Source: Annual reports of CCBs during year 2007-08 to 2011-12.

It can be observed from the above table 7.4 for himmatnagar nagarik sahakari bank that Current Deposits to Total Deposits Ratio was 8.50% in the year 2007-08.In the year 2008-09 this ratio decreased to 7.11%which was the lowest during all the study period. In the year 2009-10 to 2011-12 this ratio wascontinuously increased to 7.93%, 10.06%and 10.58% respectively.In the year 2011-12 this ratio was the highest during all the study period. During all the study period average of this ratio was 8.84%. For all the five years of the study this ratio was lower than its average for three years and higher than its average in the remaining two years.

It is obvious from the above table 7.4 for modasa nagarik sahakari bank that Current Deposits to Total Deposits Ratio was 4.22% in the year 2007-08. In the year 2008-09 and 2009-10 this ratio was continuously decreased to 3.50% and 3.00% respectively. In the year 2009-10 this ratio was the lowest during all the study period. In the year 2010-11 this ratio was increased to 4.98%which was the highest during all the study period.In the year 2011-12 this ratio was decreased to 4.28%. During all the study period average of this ratio was 3.99%. For all the five years of the study this ratio was lower than its average for two years and higher than its average in the remaining three years.

It is apparent from the above table 7.4 for mehsana nagarik sahakari bank that Current Deposits to Total Deposits Ratio was 18.14% in the year 2007-08 which was the highest during all the study period. In the year 2008-09 to 2011-12 this ratio was continuously decreased to 16.38%, 14.92%, 12.03% and 11.93% respectively. In the year 2011-12 this ratio was the lowest during all the study period.During all the study period average of this ratio was 14.68%. For all the five years of the study this ratio was lower than its average for two years and higher than its average in the remaining three years.

It is cleared from the above table 7.4 for co-operative bank of mehsana that Current Deposits to Total Deposits Ratio was 9.12% in the year 2007-08which was the highest during all the study period. In the year 2008-09 this ratio was decreased to 5.12%which was the lowest during all the study period. In the year 2009-10 this ratio was increased to 7.31%. In the year 2010-11 and 2011-12 this ratio was continuously decreased to 7.14% and 6.23% respectively.During all the study period average of this ratio was 6.98%. For all the five years of the study this ratio was lower than its average for two years and higher than its average in the remaining three years.

It isevident from the above table 7.4 for chhapi nagarik sahakari bank that Current Deposits to Total Deposits Ratio was 57.54% in the year 2007-08which was the highest during all the study period.In the year 2008-09 to 2011-12 this ratio was continuously decreased to 53.44%, 50.64%, 48.03% and 45.94% respectively. In the year 2011-12 this ratio was the lowest during all the study period.During all the study period average of this ratio was 51.12%.For all the five years of the study this ratio was lower than its average forthree years and higher than its average in the remaining two years.

It can be observed from the above table 7.4 for banaskantha mercantile co-operative bank that Current Deposits to Total DepositsRatio was 19.70% in the year 2007-08.In the year 2008-09 this ratio was decreased to 15.78%which was the lowest during all the study period. In the year 2009-10and 2010-11 this ratio was continuously increased to 18.73% and 20.67% respectively. In the year 2010-11 this ratio was the highest during all the study period. In the year 2011-12 this ratio was decreased to 17.91%.During all the study period average of this ratio was 18.56%. For all the five years of the study this ratio was lower than its average for two years and higher than its average in the remaining three years.

It is obvious from the above table 7.4 for chanasma nagarik sahakari bank that Current Deposits to Total DepositsRatio was 6.65% in the year 2007-08. In the year 2008-09 and 2009-10 this ratio was continuously increased to 7.29% and 7.68% respectively. In the year 2010-11 this ratio was decreased to 6.53% which was the lowest during all the study period. In the year 2011-12 this ratio was increased to 8.76% which was the highest during all the study period.During all the study period average of

192

this ratio was 7.38%. For all the five years of the study this ratio was lower than its average for three years and higher than its average in the remaining two years.

It is apparent from the above table 7.4 for patan nagarik sahakari bank that Current Deposits to Total DepositsRatio was 2.16% in the year 2007-08which was the lowest during all the study period. In the year 2008-09 to 2011-12 this ratio was continuously increased to 2.18%, 4.17%, 6.62% and 8.24% respectively. In the year 2011-12 this ratio wasthe highest during all the study period. During all the study period average of this ratio was 4.67%. For all the five years of the study this ratio was lower than its average for three years and higher than its average in remaining two years.

It can be seen from the above table 7.4 for all Citizen co-operative banks that average of Current Deposits to Total DepositsRatio during 2007-08 to 2011-12 was 14.53%. In the year 2007-08 average ratio of all banks was 15.75%which was the highest during all the study period. In the year 2008-09 this ratio was decreased to 13.85%which was the lowest during all the study period.In the year 2009-10and 2010-11 this ratio was continuously increased to 14.30% and 14.51% respectively. In the year 2011-12 this ratio was decreased to 14.23%. For all the five years of the study average ratio of all banks was lower than its average for four years and higher than its average in remaining one year.

❖ **F test (ANOVA) Analysis**

The statements of hypothesis are as under:

• **Hypothesis between the banks:**

H_0:   There is no significant difference in the current deposits to total deposits ratio of different Citizen Co-operative banks of North Gujarat for every financial year.

H_1:   There is significant difference in the current deposits to total deposits ratio of different Citizen Co-operative banks of North Gujarat for every financial year.

• **Hypothesis between the years:**

H_0:   There is no significant difference in the current deposits to total depositsratio of every Citizen Co-operative bank of North Gujarat for different financial years.

H_1:   There is significant difference in the current deposits to total depositsratio of every Citizen Co-operative bank of North Gujarat for different financial years.

Table 7.4-A

Source of Variation	SS	df	MS	F
Between Banks	8517.45	07	1216.78	210.39
Between years	16.84	04	4.21	0.73
Error	161.94	28	5.78	
Total	8696.23	39		

Table Value for df (7,28) is 2.36 at 5% level of significance.

Table Value for df (4,28) is 2.71 at 5% level of significance.

Table 7.4-A represents the difference for the banks is significant because the table value for df (7,28) is (2.36) which is lower than calculated value of 'F' (210.39). So, null hypothesis (H_o) is rejected and alternative hypothesis (H_1) is accepted. I.e. there is significant difference in the current deposits to total depositsratio of different Citizen Co-operative banks of North Gujarat for every financial year.

Same way the difference for the years is not significant because the table value for df (4,28) is (2.71) which is higher than the calculated value of 'F' (0.73) for years and so here null hypothesis(H_o) is accepted and alternative hypothesis (H_1) is rejected. I.e. there is no significant difference in the current deposits to total depositsratio of every Citizen Co-operative bank of North Gujarat for different financial years.

7.4.5   Total Deposits to Working Funds Ratio

Money placed into a banking institution for safekeeping is called deposits. Higher collection of deposits cause smooth running of banking business as well as indicates goodwill of the bank in society. The profitability of banks mainly depends on the capacity to collect deposits. The higher this ratio indicates the bank focuses in higher collection of deposits and increasing faith of the public towards the bank. Formula for the ratio of total deposits to working funds is as follows:

$$\text{Total Deposits to Working Funds Ratio} = \frac{\text{Total Deposits}}{\text{Working Funds}} *100$$

North Gujarat for the study period 2007-08 to 2011-12 is presented in the table 7.5 as follows:

Table 7.5

Total Deposits to Working Funds Ratio

YEAR	HIMNSB	MODNSB	MEHNSB	COBMEH	CHHNSB	BANMCB	CHANSB	PATNSB	AVERAGE
2007-08	73.36	79.10	83.11	81.61	80.10	75.39	75.13	61.27	76.13
2008-09	72.89	76.45	80.62	82.05	79.01	76.81	76.13	63.81	75.97
2009-10	73.42	76.63	81.51	83.99	76.74	78.42	77.91	67.35	77.00
2010-11	74.57	78.36	80.76	83.76	72.18	78.81	78.66	67.63	76.84
2011-12	74.92	80.47	79.08	84.34	76.80	80.09	80.54	67.04	77.91
AVERAGE	73.83	78.20	81.02	83.15	76.96	77.90	77.67	65.42	76.77

Source: Annual reports of CCBs during year 2007-08 to 2011-12.

Chart 7.1

Chart Showing Total Deposits to Working Funds Ratio

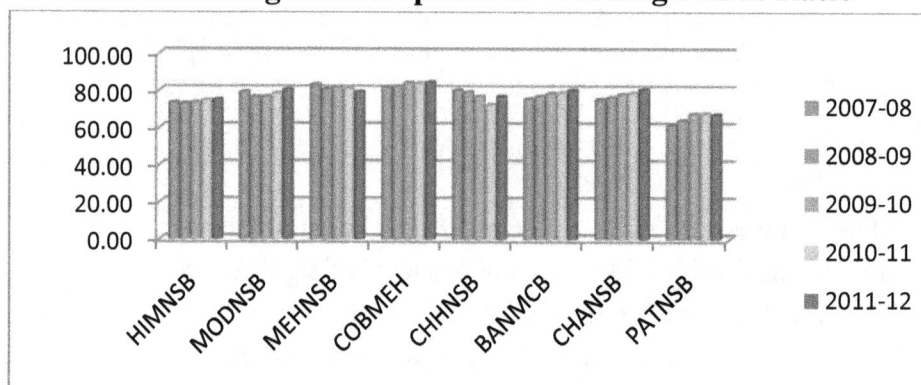

It can be observed from the above table 7.5 for himmatnagar nagarik sahakari bank that Total Deposits to Working Funds Ratio was 73.36% in the year 2007-08.In the year 2008-09 this ratio decreased to 72.89% which was the lowest during all the study period. In the year 2009-10 to 2011-12 this ratio was continuously decreased to 73.42%,74.57% and 74.92% respectively.In the year 2011-12 this ratio was the highest during all the study period. During all the study period average of this ratio was 73.83%. For all the five years of the study this ratio was lower than its average for three years and higher than its average in the remaining two years.

It is obvious from the above table 7.5 for modasa nagarik sahakari bank that Total Deposits to Working Funds Ratio was 79.10% in the year 2007-08. In the year 2008-09 this ratio decreased to 76.45% which was the lowest during all the study period. In the year 2009-10 to 2011-12 this ratio was continuously increased to 76.63%,78.36% and 80.47% respectively.In the year 2011-12 this ratio was the highest during all the study period.During all the study period average of this ratio was 78.20%. For all the five years of the study this ratio was lower than its average for two years and higher than its average in the remaining three years.

It is apparent from the above table 7.5 for mehsana nagarik sahakari bank that Total Deposits to Working Funds Ratio was 83.11% in the year 2007-08 which was the highest during all the study period. In the year 2008-09 this ratio decreased to 80.62%. In the year 2009-10 this ratio was increased to 81.51%. In the year 2010-11 and2011-12 this ratio was continuously decreased to 80.76% and 79.08% respectively. During all the study period average of this ratio was 81.02%. For all the five years of the study this ratio was lower than its average for three years and higher than its average in the remaining two years.

It is cleared from the above table 7.5 for co-operative bank of mehsana that Total Deposits to Working Funds Ratio was 81.61% in the year 2007-08which was the lowest during all the study period. In the year 2008-09 and 2009-10 this ratio was continuously increased to 82.05%and 83.99% respectively. In the year 2010-11 this ratio was decreased to 83.76%. In the year 2011-12 this ratio was increased to 84.34%which was the highest during all the study period. During all the study period average of this ratio was 83.15%. For all the five years of the study this ratio was lower than its average for two years and higher than its average in the remaining three years.

It isevident from the above table 7.5 for chhapi nagarik sahakari bank that Total Deposits to Working Funds Ratio was 80.10% in the year 2007-08which was the highest during all the study period.In the year 2008-09 to 2010-11 this ratio was continuously decreased to 79.01%, 76.74% and 72.18% respectively.In the year 2010-11 this ratio was the lowest during all the study period. In the year 2011-12 this ratio was increased to 76.80%.During all the study period average of this ratio was 76.96%. For all the five years of the study this ratio was lower than its average for three years and higher than its average in the remaining two years.

It can be observed from the above table 7.5 for banaskantha mercantile co-operative bank that Total Deposits to Working Funds Ratio was 75.39% in the year

2007-08which was the lowest during all the study period. In the year 2008-09 to 2011-12 this ratio was continuously increased to 76.81%, 78.42%, 78.81% and 80.09% respectively. In the year 2011-12 this ratio was the highest during all the study period.During all the study period average of this ratio was 77.90%. For all the five years of the study this ratio was lower than its average for two years and higher than its average in remaining three years.

It is obvious from the above table 7.5 for chanasma nagarik sahakari bank that Total Deposits to Working Funds Ratio was 75.13% in the year 2007-08 which was the lowest during all the study period. In the year 2008-09 to 2011-12 this ratio was continuously increased to 76.13%, 77.91%, 78.66% and 80.54% respectively. In the year 2011-12 this ratio was the highest during all the study period.During all the study period average of this ratio was 77.67%. For all the five years of the study this ratio was lower than its average for two years and higher than its average in remaining three years.

It is apparent from the above table 7.5 for patan nagarik sahakari bank that Total Deposits to Working Funds Ratio was 61.27% in the year 2007-08which was the lowest during all the study period. In the year 2008-09 to 2010-11 this ratio was continuously increased to 63.81%, 67.35% and 67.63% respectively.In the year 2010-11 this ratio was the highest during all the study period. In the year 2011-12 this ratio was decreased to 67.04%. During all the study period average of this ratio was 65.42%. For all the five years of the study this ratio was lower than its average for three years and higher than its average in remaining two years.

It can be seen from the above table 7.5 for all Citizen co-operative banks that average of Total Deposits to Working Funds Ratio during 2007-08 to 2011-12 was 76.77%. In the year 2007-08 average ratio of all banks was 76.13%.In the year 2008-09 this ratio was decreased to 75.97% which was the lowest during all the study period.In the year 2009-10 this ratio was increased to 77.00% and in the year 2010-11 this ratio was decreased to 76.84%.In the year 2011-12 this ratio was increased to 77.91%which was the highest during all the study period. For all the five years of the study average ratio of all banks was lower than its average for two years and higher than its average in remaining three years.

❖ **F test (ANOVA) Analysis**

The statements of hypothesis are as under:

- **Hypothesis between the banks:**

H_0:   There is no significant difference in the total deposits to working funds ratio of different Citizen Co-operative banks of North Gujarat for every financial year.

H_1:   There is significant difference in the total deposits to working funds ratio of different Citizen Co-operative banks of North Gujarat for every financial year.

- **Hypothesis between the years:**

H_0: There is no significant difference in the total deposits to working fundsratio of every Citizen Co-operative bank of North Gujarat for different financial years.

H_1: There is significant difference in the total deposits to working funds ratio of every Citizen Co-operative bank of North Gujarat for different financial years.

Table 7.5-A

Source of Variation	SS	df	MS	F
Between Banks	1001.54	07	143.08	36.55
Between years	19.20	04	4.80	1.23
Error	109.60	28	3.91	
Total	1130.35	39		

Table Value for df (7,28) is 2.36 at 5% level of significance.

Table Value for df (4,28) is 2.71 at 5% level of significance.

Table 7.5-A represents the difference for the banks is significant because the table value for df (7,28) is (2.36) which is lower than calculated value of 'F' (36.55). So, null hypothesis (H_o) is rejected and alternative hypothesis (H_1) is accepted. I.e. there is significant difference in the total deposits to working funds ratio of different Citizen Co-operative banks of North Gujarat for every financial year.

Same way the difference for the years is not significant because the table value for df (4,28) is (2.71) which is higher than the calculated value of 'F' (1.23) for years and so here null hypothesis(H_o) is accepted and alternative hypothesis (H_1) is rejected. I.e. there is no significant difference in the total deposits to working funds ratio of every Citizen Co-operative bank of North Gujarat for different financial years.

7.4.6 Other Liabilities to Working Funds Ratio

The other liabilities include bills payable, drafts payable, etc. and represents cost free funds. By this ratio we can know proportion of other liabilities against bank's working funds. With a view to safety the lower ratio indicates the good situation for the bank. Thus, a low ratio is desirable. Formula for the ratio of other liabilities to working funds is as follows:

$$\textbf{Other Liabilities to Working Funds Ratio} = \frac{\textbf{Other Liabilities}}{\textbf{Working Funds}} * 100$$

Other Liabilities to Working Funds Ratio of selected citizen cooperative banks of North Gujarat for the study period 2007-08 to 2011-12 is presented in the table 7.6 as follows:

Table 7.6
Other Liabilities to Working Funds Ratio

YEAR	HIMNSB	MODNSB	MEHNSB	COBMEH	CHHNSB	BANMCB	CHANSB	PATNSB	AVERAGE
2007-08	0.75	1.08	1.62	1.10	0.50	4.65	0.58	1.53	1.48
2008-09	0.71	1.22	1.41	1.57	0.73	4.40	0.80	1.47	1.54
2009-10	0.66	1.85	1.72	1.41	0.14	4.04	0.54	1.22	1.45
2010-11	0.47	1.28	2.02	1.51	0.43	4.15	0.46	1.41	1.47
2011-12	0.53	1.01	2.19	0.99	0.44	4.22	0.45	1.68	1.44
AVERAGE	0.62	1.29	1.79	1.32	0.45	4.29	0.57	1.46	1.47

Source: Annual reports of CCBs during year 2007-08 to 2011-12.

It can be observed from the above table 7.6 for himmatnagar nagarik sahakari bank that Other Liabilities to Working Funds Ratio was 0.75% in the year 2007-08which was the highest during all the study period.In the year 2008-09 to 2010-11 this ratio was continuously decreased to 0.71%,0.66% and 0.47% respectively.In the year 2010-11 this ratio was the lowest during all the study period. In the year 2011-12 this ratio was increased to 0.53%.During all the study period average of this ratio was 0.62%. For all the five years of the study this ratio was lower than its average for two years and higher than its average in the remaining three years.

It is obvious from the above table 7.6 for modasa nagarik sahakari bank that Other Liabilities to Working Funds Ratio was 1.08% in the year 2007-08. In the year 2008-09 and 2009-10 this ratio was continuously increased to 1.22% and 1.85% respectively. In the year 2009-10 this ratio was the highest during all the study period.In the year 2010-11and 2011-12 this ratio was continuously decreased to 1.28% and 1.01% respectively.In the year 2011-12 this ratio was the lowest during all the study period.During all the study period average of this ratio was 1.29%. For all the five years of the study this ratio was lower than its average for four years and higher than its average in the remaining one year.

It is apparent from the above table 7.6 for mehsana nagarik sahakari bank that Other Liabilities to Working Funds Ratio was 1.62% in the year 2007-08. In the year 2008-09 this ratio was decreased to 1.41%which was the lowest during all the study period. In the year 2009-10 to 2011-12 this ratio was continuously increased to 1.72%, 2.02% and 2.19% respectively. In the year 2011-12 this ratio was the highest during all the study period.During all the study period average of this ratio was 81.02%. For all the five years of the study this ratio was lower than its average for three years and higher than its average in the remaining two years.

It is cleared from the above table 7.6 for co-operative bank of mehsana that Other Liabilities to Working Funds Ratio was 1.10% in the year 2007-08.In the year 2008-09 this ratio was increased to 1.57%which was the highest during all the study period. In the year 2009-10 this ratio was decreased to 1.41% and in the year 2010-11 this ratio was increased to 1.51%. In the year 2011-12 this ratio was decreased to 0.99%which was the lowest during all the study period. During all the study period average of this ratio was 1.32%. For all the five years of the study this ratio was lower than its average for two years and higher than its average in the remaining three years.

It isevident from the above table 7.6 for chhapi nagarik sahakari bank that Other Liabilitics to Working Funds Ratio was 0.50% in the year 2007-08.In the year 2008-09 this ratio was increased to 0.73%which was the highest during all the study period. In the year 2009-10 this ratio was decreased to 0.14% which was the lowest during all the study period.In the year 2010-11 and 2011-12 this ratio was continuously increased to 0.43% and 0.44% respectively.During all the study period average of this ratio was 0.45%. For all the five years of the study this ratio was lower than its average for three years and higher than its average in the remaining two years.

It can be observed from the above table 7.6 for banaskantha mercantile co-operative bank that Other Liabilities to Working Funds Ratio was 4.65% in the year 2007-08which was the highest during all the study period.In the year 2008-09 and 2009-10 this ratio was continuously decreased to 4.40% and 4.04% respectively. In the year 2009-10 this ratio was the lowest during all the study period.In the year 2010-11 and 2011-12 this ratio was continuously increased to 4.15% and 4.22% respectively. During all the study period average of this ratio was 4.29%. For all the five years of the study this ratio was lower than its average for three years and higher than its average in the remaining two years.

It is obvious from the above table 7.6 for chanasma nagarik sahakari bank that Other Liabilities to Working Funds Ratio was 0.58% in the year 2007-08. In the year 2008-09 this ratio was increased to 0.80%which was the highest during all the study period. In the year 2009-10 to 2011-12 this ratio was continuously decreased to 0.54%, 0.46% and 0.45% respectively. In the year 2011-12 this ratio was the lowest during all the study period.During all the study period average of this ratio was 0.57%. For all the five years of the study this ratio was lower than its average for three years and higher than its average in the remaining two years.

It is apparent from the above table 7.6 for patan nagarik sahakari bank that Other Liabilities to Working Funds Ratio was 1.53% in the year 2007-08.In the year 2008-09 and 2009-10 this ratio was continuously decreased to 1.47% and 1.22% respectively.In the year 2009-10 this ratio was the lowest during all the study period. In the year 2010-11 and 2011-12 this ratio was continuously increased to 1.41%and 1.68% respectively.In the year 2011-12 this ratio was the highest during all the study period.During all the study period average of this ratio was 1.46%. For all the five years of the study this ratio was lower than its average for two years and higher than its average in remaining three years.

It can be seen from the above table 7.6 for all Citizen co-operative banks that average of Other Liabilities to Working Funds Ratio during 2007-08 to 2011-12 was 1.47%. In the year 2007-08 average ratio of all banks was 1.48%.In the year 2008-09 this ratio was increased to 1.54% which was the highest during all the study period.In the year 2009-10 this ratio was decreased to 1.45% and in the year 2010-11 this ratio was increased to 1.47%. In the year 2011-12 this ratio was decreased to 1.44%which was the lowest during all the study period.For all the five years of the study average ratio of all banks was lower than its average for three years and higher than its average in remaining two years.

❖ F test (ANOVA) Analysis

The statements of hypothesis are as under:

- **Hypothesis between the banks:**

H_0: There is no significant difference in the other liabilities to working funds ratio of different Citizen Co-operative banks of North Gujarat for every financial year.

H_1: There is significant difference in the other liabilities to working funds ratio of different Citizen Co-operative banks of North Gujarat for every financial year.

- **Hypothesis between the years:**

H_0: There is no significant difference in the other liabilities to working fundsratio of every Citizen Co-operative bank of North Gujarat for different financial years.

H_1: There is significant difference in the other liabilities to working funds ratio of every Citizen Co-operative bank of North Gujarat for different financial years.

Table 7.6-A

Source of Variation	SS	df	MS	F
Between Banks	53.45	07	7.64	124.74
Between years	0.05	04	0.01	0.22
Error	1.71	28	0.06	
Total	55.22	39		

Table Value for df (7,28) is 2.36 at 5% level of significance.

Table Value for df (4,28) is 2.71 at 5% level of significance.

Table 7.6-A represents the difference for the banks is significant because the table value for df (7,28) is (2.36) which is lower than calculated value of 'F' (124.74). So, null hypothesis (H_0) is rejected and alternative hypothesis (H_1) is accepted. I.e. there is significant difference in the other liabilities to working funds ratio of different Citizen Co-operative banks of North Gujarat for every financial year.

Same way the difference for the years is not significant because the table value for df (4,28) is (2.71) which is higher than the calculated value of 'F' (0.22) for years and so here null hypothesis(H_0) is accepted and alternative hypothesis (H_1) is rejected. I.e. there is no significant difference in the other liabilities to working funds ratio of every Citizen Co-operative bank of North Gujarat for different financial years.

7.4.7 Investments to Working Funds Ratio

Investments of citizen cooperative banks include all deposits of including investments in Government and other securities, shares and debentures, etc. By this ratio we can know proportion of investments against bank's working funds. The higher ratio indicates that the bank makes interest and dividend income by riskless safe investments. Thus, a high ratio is desirable. Formula for the ratio of investments to working funds is as follows:

$$\text{Investments to Working Funds Ratio} = \frac{\text{Investments}}{\text{Working Funds}} *100$$

Investments to Working Funds Ratio of selected citizen cooperative banks of North Gujarat for the study period 2007-08 to 2011-12 is presented in the table 7.7 as follows:

Table 7.7
Investments to Working Funds Ratio

YEAR	HIMNSB	MODNSB	MEHNSB	COBMEH	CHHNSB	BANMCB	CHANSB	PATNSB	AVERAGE
2007-08	19.65	23.98	15.18	13.16	34.29	0.03	34.74	35.86	22.11
2008-09	16.85	19.98	11.68	13.50	26.01	0.03	32.40	28.23	18.58
2009-10	17.35	18.30	14.51	13.11	23.23	0.03	29.54	33.58	18.71
2010-11	20.18	18.32	20.67	20.52	24.74	0.02	26.76	34.67	20.73
2011-12	19.81	18.77	20.68	22.77	24.58	0.02	25.75	32.56	20.62
AVERAGE	18.76	19.87	16.54	16.61	26.57	0.03	29.84	32.98	20.15

Source: Annual reports of CCBs during year 2007-08 to 2011-12.

It can be observed from the above table 7.7 for himmatnagar nagarik sahakari bank that Investments to Working Funds Ratio was 19.65% in the year 2007-08.In the year 2008-09 this ratio was decreased to 16.85%which was the lowest during all the study period.In the year 2009-10 and 2010-11 this ratio was continuously increased to 17.35% and 20.18% respectively.In the year 2010-11 this ratio was the highest during all the study period. In the year 2011-12 this ratio was decreased to 19.81%.During all the study period average of this ratio was 18.76%. For all the five years of the study this ratio was lower than its average for two years and higher than its average in the remaining three years.

It is obvious from the above table 7.7 for modasa nagarik sahakari bank that Investmentsto Working Funds Ratio was 23.98% in the year 2007-08which was the highest during all the study period. In the year 2008-09 and 2009-10 this ratio was continuously decreased to 19.98% and 18.30% respectively. In the year 2009-10 this ratio was the lowest during all the study period.In the year 2010-11and 2011-12 this ratio was continuously increased to 18.32% and 18.77% respectively.During all the study period average of this ratio was 19.87%. For all the five years of the study this ratio was lower than its average for three years and higher than its average in the remaining two years.

It is apparent from the above table 7.7 for mehsana nagarik sahakari bank that Investmentsto Working Funds Ratio was 15.18% in the year 2007-08. In the year 2008-

09 this ratio was decreased to 11.68%which was the lowest during all the study period. In the year 2009-10 to 2011-12 this ratio was continuously increased to 14.51%, 20.67% and 20.68% respectively. In the year 2011-12 this ratio was the highest during all the study period.During all the study period average of this ratio was 16.54%. For all the five years of the study this ratio was lower than its average for three years and higher than its average in the remaining two years.

It is cleared from the above table 7.7 for co-operative bank of mehsana that Investmentsto Working Funds Ratio was 13.16% in the year 2007-08.In the year 2008-09 this ratio was increased to 13.50%.In the year 2009-10 this ratio was decreased to 13.11%which was the lowest during all the study period. In the year 2010-11 and 2011-12 this ratio was continuously increased to 20.52%and 22.77% respectively. In the year 2011-12 this ratio was the highest during all the study period. During all the study period average of this ratio was 16.61%. For all the five years of the study this ratio was lower than its average for three years and higher than its average in the remaining two years.

It isevident from the above table 7.7 for chhapi nagarik sahakari bank that Investmentsto Working Funds Ratio was 34.29% in the year 2007-08which was the highest during all the study period.In the year 2008-09 and 2009-10 this ratio was continuously decreased to 26.01% and 23.23% respectively. In the year 2009-10 this ratio was the lowest during all the study period.In the year 2010-11 this ratio was increased to 24.74% and in the year 2011-12 this ratio was decreased to 24.58%..During all the study period average of this ratio was 26.57%. For all the five years of the study this ratio was lower than its average for four years and higher than its average in the remaining one year.

It can be observed from the above table 7.7 for banaskantha mercantile co-operative bank that Investments to Working Funds Ratio was same 0.03% in the year 2007-08to 2009-10 which was the equal to average ratio during all the study period.In the year 2010-11 and 2011-12 this ratio was decreased to same 0.02%. During all the study period average of this ratio was 0.03%. For all the five years of the study this ratio was lower than its average for two years and equal to its average in the remaining three years.

It is obvious from the above table 7.7 for chanasma nagarik sahakari bank that Investmentsto Working Funds Ratio was 32.74% in the year 2007-08which was the highest during all the study period. In the year 2008-09 to 2011-12 this ratio was continuously decreased to 32.40%, 29.54%, 26.76%and 25.75% respectively. In the year 2011-12 this ratio was the lowest during all the study period.During all the study period average of this ratio was 29.84%. For all the five years of the study this ratio was lower than its average for three years and higher than its average in the remaining two years.

It is apparent from the above table 7.7 for patan nagarik sahakari bank that Investmentsto Working Funds Ratio was 35.86% in the year 2007-08which was the highest during all the study period.In the year 2008-09 this ratio was decreased to

28.23% which was the lowest during all the study period. In the year 2009-10 and 2010-11 this ratiowas continuously increased to 33.58%and 34.67% respectively.In the year 2011-12 this ratio wasdecreased to 32.56%. During all the study period average of this ratio was 32.98%. For all the five years of the study this ratio was lower than its average for two years and higher than its average in remaining three years.

It can be seen from the above table 7.7 for all Citizen co-operative banks that average of Investments to Working Funds Ratio during 2007-08 to 2011-12 was 20.15%. In the year 2007-08 average ratio of all banks was 22.11%which was the highest during all the study period.In the year 2008-09 this ratio was decreased to 18.58% which was the lowest during all the study period.In the year 2009-10 and 2010-11 this ratio was increased to 18.71%and 20.73% respectively. In the year 2011-12 this ratio was decreased to 20.62%.For all the five years of the study average ratio of all banks was lower than its average for two years and higher than its average in remaining three years.

❖ F test (ANOVA) Analysis

The statements of hypothesis are as under:

• Hypothesis between the banks:

H_0: There is no significant difference in the investments to working funds ratio of different Citizen Co-operative banks of North Gujarat for every financial year.

H_1: There is significant difference in the investmentsto working funds ratio of different Citizen Co-operative banks of North Gujarat for every financial year.

• Hypothesis between the years:

H_0: There is no significant difference in the investmentsto working fundsratio of every Citizen Co-operative bank of North Gujarat for different financial years.

H_1: There is significant difference in the investmentsto working funds ratio of every Citizen Co-operative bank of North Gujarat for different financial years.

Table 7.7-A

Source of Variation	SS	df	MS	F
Between Banks	3660.84	07	522.98	52.01
Between years	71.50	04	17.87	1.78
Error	281.56	28	10.06	
Total	4013.90	39		

Table Value for df (7,28) is 2.36 at 5% level of significance.

Table Value for df (4,28) is 2.71 at 5% level of significance.

Table 7.7-A represents the difference for the banks is significant because the table value for df (7,28) is (2.36) which is lower than calculated value of 'F' (52.01). So, null hypothesis (H_o) is rejected and alternative hypothesis (H_1) is accepted. I.e. there is significant difference in the investments to working funds ratio of different Citizen Co-operative banks of North Gujarat for every financial year.

Same way the difference for the years is not significant because the table value for df (4,28) is (2.71) which is higher than the calculated value of 'F' (1.78) for years and so here null hypothesis(H_o) is accepted and alternative hypothesis (H_1) is rejected. I.e. there is no significant difference in the investments to working funds ratio of every Citizen Co-operative bank of North Gujarat for different financial years.

7.4.8   Short term Advances to Total Advances Ratio

Short term advances are granted by banks to meet the working capital needs of business. Such advances are granted by banks to its borrowers to be repaid within a short period of time not exceeding 15 months.Short term advances are normally granted against the security of tangible assets like goods in stock, shares, debentures, etc. A higher ratio indicates higher proportion of short term advances in total advances which is not good from profitability point of view. Formula for the ratio of short term advances to total advances is as follows:

$$\text{Short term Advances to Total Advances Ratio} = \frac{\text{Short term Advances}}{\text{Total Advances}} *100$$

Short term Advances to Total Advances Ratio of selected citizen cooperative banks of North Gujarat for the study period 2007-08 to 2011-12 is presented in the table 7.8 as follows:

Table 7.8
Short term Advances to Total Advances Ratio

YEAR	HIMNSB	MODNSB	MEHNSB	COBMEH	CHHNSB	BANMCB	CHANSB	PATNSB	AVERAGE
2007-08	70.45	52.73	49.31	33.90	90.27	66.31	47.02	66.86	59.61
2008-09	70.70	53.76	49.41	31.97	90.30	56.62	42.38	62.34	57.19
2009-10	65.43	51.15	50.03	26.32	87.00	46.97	44.36	62.15	54.17
2010-11	54.54	47.94	48.28	25.62	80.72	49.03	49.02	59.65	51.85
2011-12	49.60	46.12	46.99	28.13	80.35	49.49	46.33	57.39	50.55
AVERAGE	62.14	50.34	48.80	29.19	85.73	53.68	45.82	61.68	54.67

Source: Annual reports of CCBs during year 2007-08 to 2011-12.

It can be observed from the above table 7.8 for himmatnagar nagarik sahakari bank that Short term Advances to Total Advances Ratio was 70.45% in the year 2007-08.In the year 2008-09this ratio was increased to 70.70%which was the highest during all the study period.In the year 2009-10 to 2011-12 this ratio was continuously decreased to 65.43%, 54.54% and 49.60% respectively. In the year 2011-12 this ratio was the lowest during all the study period.During all the study period average of this ratio was 62.14%. For all the five years of the study this ratio was lower than its average for two years and higher than its average in the remaining three years.

It is obvious from the above table 7.8 for modasa nagarik sahakari bank that Short term Advances to Total Advances Ratio was 52.73% in the year 2007-08.In the year 2008-09this ratio was increased to 53.76%which was the highest during all the study period.In the year 2009-10 to 2011-12 this ratio was continuously decreased to 51.15%, 47.94% and 46.12% respectively. In the year 2011-12 this ratio was the lowest during all the study period. During all the study period average of this ratio was 50.34%. For all the five years of the study this ratio was lower than its average for two years and higher than its average in the remaining three years.

It is apparent from the above table 7.8 for mehsana nagarik sahakari bank that Short term Advances to Total Advances Ratio was the same 49.31% in the year 2007-08 and 2008-09. In the year 2009-10 this ratio was increased to 50.03%which was the highest during all the study period. In the year 2010-11 and 2011-12 this ratio was continuously decreased to 48.28% and 46.99% respectively. In the year 2011-12 this ratio was the lowest during all the study period.During all the study period average of this ratio was 48.80%. For all the five years of the study this ratio was lower than its average for two years and higher than its average in the remaining three years.

It is cleared from the above table 7.8 for co-operative bank of mehsana that Short term Advances to Total Advances Ratio was 33.90% in the year 2007-08which was the highest during all the study period.In the year 2008-09 to 2010-11 this ratio was continuously decreased to 31.97%, 26.32% and 25.62% respectively. In the year 2010-11 this ratio was the lowest during all the study period. In the year 2011-12 this ratio was increased to 28.13%.During all the study period average of this ratio was 29.19%. For all the five years of the study this ratio was lower than its average for threeyears and higher than its average in the remaining two years.

It isevident from the above table 7.8 for chhapi nagarik sahakari bank that Short term Advances to Total Advances Ratio was 90.27% in the year 2007-08.In the year 2008-09 this ratio was increased to 90.30%which was the highest during all the study period. In the year 2009-10 to 2011-12 this ratio was continuously decreased to 87.00%, 80.72% and 80.35% respectively. In the year 2011-12 this ratio was the lowest during all the study period.During all the study period average of this ratio was 85.73%. For all the five years of the study this ratio was lower than its average for threeyears and higher than its average in the remaining two years.

It can be observed from the above table 7.8 for banaskantha mercantile co-operative bank that Short term Advances to Total Advances Ratio was 66.31% in the year 2007-08which was the highest during all the study period.In the year 2008-09 and 2009-10 this ratio was continuously decreased to 56.62% and 46.97% respectively. In the year 2009-10 this ratio was the lowest during all the study period.In the year 2010-11 and 2011-12 this ratio was continuously increased to 49.03% and 49.49% respectively. During all the study period average of this ratio was 53.68%. For all the five years of the study this ratio was lower than its average for three years and higher than its average in the remaining two years.

It is obvious from the above table 7.8 for chanasma nagarik sahakari bank that Short term Advances to Total Advances Ratio was 47.02% in the year 2007-08. In the year 2008-09 this ratio was decreased to 42.38%which was the lowest during all the study period. In the year 2009-10 to 2010-11 this ratio was continuously increased to 44.36% and 49.02% respectively. In the year 2010-11this ratio was the highest during all the study period.In the year 2011-12 this ratio was decreased to 46.33%. During all the study period average of this ratio was 45.82%. For all the five years of the study this ratio was lower than its average for two years and higher than its average in the remaining three years.

It is apparent from the above table 7.8 for patan nagarik sahakari bank that Short term Advances to Total Advances Ratio was 66.86% in the year 2007-08 which was the highest during all the study period.In the year 2008-09 to 2011-12 this ratio was continuously decreased to 62.34%, 62.15%, 59.65% and 57.39% respectively.In the year 2011-12 this ratio was the lowest during all the study period. During all the study period average of this ratio was 61.68%. For all the five years of the study this ratio was lower than its average for two years and higher than its average in remaining three years.

It can be seen from the above table 7.8 for all Citizen co-operative banks that average of Short term Advances to Total Advances Ratio during 2007-08 to 2011-12 was 54.67%. In the year 2007-08 average ratio of all banks was 59.61%which was the highest during all the study period.In the year 2008-09 to 2011-12 this ratio was continuously decreased to 57.19%, 54.17%, 51.85% and 50.55% respectively.In the year 2011-12 this ratio was the lowest during all the study period.For all the five years of the study average ratio of all banks was lower than its average for three years and higher than its average in remaining two years.

❖ F test (ANOVA) Analysis

The statements of hypothesis are as under:

- **Hypothesis between the banks:**

H₀: There is no significant difference in the short term advances to total advances ratio of different Citizen Co-operative banks of North Gujarat for every financial year.

H₁: There is significant difference in the short term advances to total advances ratio of different Citizen Co-operative banks of North Gujarat for every financial year.

- **Hypothesis between the years:**

H₀: There is no significant difference in the short term advances to total advances ratio of every Citizen Co-operative bank of North Gujarat for different financial years.

H₁: There is significant difference in the short term advances to total advances ratio of every Citizen Co-operative bank of North Gujarat for different financial years.

Table 7.8-A

Source of Variation	SS	df	MS	F
Between Banks	9256.28	07	1322.33	83.00
Between years	446.85	04	111.71	7.01
Error	446.07	28	15.93	
Total	10149.20	39		

Table Value for df (7,28) is 2.36 at 5% level of significance.

Table Value for df (4,28) is 2.71 at 5% level of significance.

Table 7.8-A represents the difference for the banks is significant because the table value for df (7,28) is (2.36) which is lower than calculated value of 'F' (83.00). So, null hypothesis (H₀) is rejected and alternative hypothesis (H₁) is accepted. I.e. there is significant difference in the short term advances to total advances ratio of different Citizen Co-operative banks of North Gujarat for every financial year.

Same way the difference for the years is significant because the table value for df (4,28) is (2.71) which is lower than the calculated value of 'F' (7.01) for years and so here null hypothesis(H₀) is rejected and alternative hypothesis (H₁) is accepted. I.e. there is significant difference in the short term advances to total advances ratio of every Citizen Co-operative bank of North Gujarat for different financial years.

7.4.9   Medium term Advances to Total Advances Ratio

In case of medium term loan, the period ranges from 15 months to less than 5 years. Medium term loans are generally granted for heavy repairs, expansion of existing units, modernization, renovation etc. Such loans are sanctioned against the security of immovable assets. By this ratio we can know proportion of medium termadvances against bank's total advances. A higher ratio indicates medium situation of the bank from profitability and safety point of view. Formula for the ratio of medium termadvances to total advances is as follows:

$$\text{Medium term Advances to Total Advances Ratio} = \frac{\text{Medium term Advances}}{\text{Total Advances}} *100$$

Medium term Advances to Total Advances Ratio of selected citizen cooperative banks of North Gujarat for the study period 2007-08 to 2011-12 is presented in the table 7.9 as follows:

Table 7.9

Medium term Advances to Total Advances Ratio

YEAR	HIMNSB	MODNSB	MEHNSB	COBMEH	CHHNSB	BANMCB	CHANSB	PATNSB	AVERAGE
2007-08	18.36	21.72	50.69	53.52	9.73	13.57	12.85	11.12	23.95
2008-09	21.65	22.08	50.59	47.08	9.70	17.83	15.08	5.45	23.68
2009-10	25.58	28.97	49.97	43.61	13.00	27.75	19.03	16.23	28.02
2010-11	38.24	32.47	51.72	39.33	19.28	28.75	18.69	20.20	31.08
2011-12	44.02	35.11	53.01	34.39	19.65	28.68	24.51	21.28	32.58
AVERAGE	29.57	28.07	51.20	43.59	14.27	23.31	18.03	14.86	27.86

Source: Annual reports of CCBs during year 2007-08 to 2011-12.

It can be observed from the above table 7.9 for himmatnagar nagarik sahakari bank that Medium term Advances to Total Advances Ratio was 18.36% in the year 2007-08 which was the lowest during all the study period.In the year 2008-09to 2011-12 this ratio was continuously increased to 21.65%, 25.58%, 38.24% and 44.02% respectively. In the year 2011-12 this ratio was the highest during all the study period. During all the study period average of this ratio was 29.57%. For all the five years of the study this ratio was lower than its average for threeyears and higher than its average in the remaining two years.

It is obvious from the above table 7.9 for modasa nagarik sahakari bank that Medium term Advances to Total Advances Ratio was 21.72% in the year 2007-08which was the lowest during all the study period.In the year 2008-09to 2011-12 this ratio was continuously increased to 22.08%, 28.97%, 32.47% and 35.11% respectively. In the year 2011-12 this ratio was the highest during all the study period. During all the study period average of this ratio was 28.07%. For all the five years of the study this ratio was lower than its average for two years and higher than its average in the remaining three years.

It is apparent from the above table 7.9 for mehsana nagarik sahakari bank that Medium term Advances to Total Advances Ratio was the same 50.69% in the year 2007-08 and 2008-09. In the year 2009-10 this ratio was decreased to 49.97%which was the lowest during all the study period. In the year 2010-11 and 2011-12 this ratio was continuously increased to 51.72% and 53.01% respectively. In the year 2011-12 this ratio was the highest during all the study period. During all the study period average of this ratio was 51.20%. For all the five years of the study this ratio was lower than its average for threeyears and higher than its average in the remaining two years.

It is cleared from the above table 7.9 for co-operative bank of mehsana that Medium term Advances to Total Advances Ratio was 53.52% in the year 2007-08which was the highest during all the study period.In the year 2008-09to 2011-12 this ratio was continuously decreased to 47.08%, 43.61%, 39.33% and 34.39% respectively. In the year 2011-12 this ratio was the lowest during all the study period. During all the study period average of this ratio was 43.59%. For all the five years of the study this ratio was lower than its average for two years and higher than its average in the remaining three years.

It isevident from the above table 7.9 for chhapi nagarik sahakari bank that Medium term Advances to Total Advances Ratio was 9.73% in the year 2007-08.In the year 2008-09 this ratio was decreased to 9.70%which was the lowest during all the study period. In the year 2009-10 to 2011-12 this ratio was continuously increased to 13.00%, 19.28% and 19.65% respectively. In the year 2011-12 this ratio was the highest during all the study period.During all the study period average of this ratio was 14.27%. For all the five years of the study this ratio was lower than its average for threeyears and higher than its average in the remaining two years.

It can be observed from the above table 7.9 for banaskantha mercantile co-operative bank that Medium term Advances to Total Advances Ratio was 13.57% in the year 2007-08which was the lowest during all the study period.In the year 2008-09 to 2010-11 this ratio was continuously increased to 17.83%, 27.75% and 28.75% respectively. In the year 2010-11 this ratio was the highest during all the study period.In the year 2011-12 this ratio was decreased to 28.68%. During all the study period average of this ratio was 23.31%. For all the five years of the study this ratio was lower than its average for two years and higher than its average in the remaining three years.

It is obvious from the above table 7.9 for chanasma nagarik sahakari bank that Medium term Advances to Total Advances Ratio was 12.85% in the year 2007-08which was the lowest during all the study period. In the year 2008-09 and 2009-10 this ratio was increased to 15.08%and 19.03% respectively. In the year 2010-11 this ratio was decreased to 18.69%. In the year 2011-12 this ratio was increased to 24.51% which was the highest during all the study period.During all the study period average of this ratio was 18.03%. For all the five years of the study this ratio was lower than its average for two years and higher than its average in the remaining three years.

It is apparent from the above table 7.9 for patan nagarik sahakari bank that Medium term Advances to Total Advances Ratio was 11.12% in the year 2007-08. In the year 2008-09 this ratio was decreased to 5.45%which was the lowest during all the study period. In the year 2009-10 to 2011-12 this ratio was continuously increased to 16.23%, 20.20% and 21.28% respectively. In the year 2011-12 this ratio was the highest during all the study period.During all the study period average of this ratio was 14.86%.

For all the five years of the study this ratio was lower than its average for two years and higher than its average in remaining three years.

It can be seen from the above table 7.9 for all Citizen co-operative banks that average of Medium term Advances to Total Advances Ratio during 2007-08 to 2011-12 was 27.86%. In the year 2007-08 average ratio of all banks was 23.95%. In the year 2008-09 this ratio was decreased to 23.68%which was the lowest during all the study period. In the year 2009-10 to 2011-12 this ratio was continuously increased to 28.02%, 31.08% and 32.58% respectively. In the year 2011-12 this ratio was the highest during all the study period.For all the five years of the study average ratio of all banks was lower than its average for two years and higher than its average in remaining three years.

❖ **F test (ANOVA) Analysis**

The statements of hypothesis are as under:

• **Hypothesis between the banks:**

H_0: There is no significant difference in the medium term advances to total advances ratio of different Citizen Co-operative banks of North Gujarat for every financial year.

H_1: There is significant difference in the medium term advances to total advances ratio of different Citizen Co-operative banks of North Gujarat for every financial year.

• **Hypothesis between the years:**

H_0: There is no significant difference in the medium term advances to total advances ratio of every Citizen Co-operative bank of North Gujarat for different financial years.

H_1: There is significant difference in the medium term advances to total advances ratio of every Citizen Co-operative bank of North Gujarat for different financial years.

Table 7.9-A

Source of Variation	SS	df	MS	F
Between Banks	6329.24	07	904.18	28.68
Between years	523.81	04	130.95	4.15
Error	882.78	28	31.53	
Total	7735.83	39		

Table Value for df (7,28) is 2.36 at 5% level of significance.

Table Value for df (4,28) is 2.71 at 5% level of significance.

Table 7.9-A represents the difference for the banks is significant because the table value for df (7,28) is (2.36) which is lower than calculated value of 'F' (28.68). So, null hypothesis (H_o) is rejected and alternative hypothesis (H_1) is accepted. I.e. there is significant difference in the medium term advances to total advances ratio of different Citizen Co-operative banks of North Gujarat for every financial year.

Same way the difference for the years is significant because the table value for df (4,28) is (2.71) which is lower than the calculated value of 'F' (4.15) for years and so here null hypothesis(H_0) is rejected and alternative hypothesis (H_1) is accepted. I.e. there is significant difference in the medium term advances to total advances ratio of every Citizen Co-operative bank of North Gujarat for different financial years.

7.4.10 Long term Advances to Total Advances Ratio

Long-term bank advances are one way of financing major purchases or consolidating several short-term loans into one longer-term loan. Long-term advances used by consumers are mortgages, student loans, car loans, boat loans, equity loans and some personal loans. By this ratio we can know proportion of long termadvances against bank's total advances. A higher ratio indicates good situation of the bank from profitability and safety point of view. Formula for the ratio of long termadvances to total advances is as follows:

$$\text{Long termAdvances to Total Advances Ratio} = \frac{\text{Long term term Advances}}{\text{Total Advances}} * 100$$

Long term Advances to Total Advances Ratio of selected citizen cooperative banks of North Gujarat for the study period 2007-08 to 2011-12 is presented in the table 7.10 as follows:

Table 7.10

Long term Advances to Total Advances Ratio

YEAR	HIMNSB	MODNSB	MEHNSB	COBMEH	CHHNSB	BANMCB	CHANSB	PATNSB	AVERAGE
2007-08	11.19	25.55	0.00	12.58	0.00	20.11	40.13	22.02	16.45
2008-09	7.65	24.16	0.00	20.94	0.00	25.55	42.53	32.21	19.13
2009-10	8.99	19.88	0.00	30.07	0.00	25.28	36.61	21.62	17.81
2010-11	7.21	19.60	0.00	35.05	0.00	22.23	32.29	20.15	17.07
2011-12	6.38	18.77	0.00	37.47	0.00	21.84	29.16	21.33	16.87
AVERAGE	8.28	21.59	0.00	27.22	0.00	23.00	36.14	23.47	17.46

Source: Annual reports of CCBs during year 2007-08 to 2011-12.

It can be observed from the above table 7.10 for himmatnagar nagarik sahakari bank that Long term Advances to Total Advances Ratio was 11.19% in the year 2007-08 which was the highest during all the study period.In the year 2008-09 this ratio was decreased to 7.65%. In the year 2009-10 this ratio was increased to 8.99%. In the year 2010-11 and 2011-12 this ratio was continuously decreased to 7.21% and 6.38% respectively. In the year 2011-12 this ratio was the lowest during all the study period. During all the study period average of this ratio was 8.28%. For all the five years of the study this ratio was lower than its average for threeyears and higher than its average in the remaining two years.

It is obvious from the above table 7.10 for modasa nagarik sahakari bank that Long term Advances to Total Advances Ratio was 25.55% in the year 2007-08which was the highest during all the study period.In the year 2008-09to 2011-12 this ratio was continuously decreased to 24.16%, 19.88%, 19.60% and 18.77% respectively. In the year 2011-12 this ratio was the lowest during all the study period. During all the study period average of this ratio was 21.59%. For all the five years of the study this ratio was lower than its average for threeyears and higher than its average in the remaining two years.

It is apparent from the above table 7.10 for mehsana nagarik sahakari bank that Long term Advances to Total Advances Ratio was nil**(ZERO)** during the year 2007-08 to 2011-12.I.e. there is no long term advances in the mehsana nagarik sahakari bank during the study period.

It is cleared from the above table 7.10 for co-operative bank of mehsana that Long term Advances to Total Advances Ratio was 12.58% in the year 2007-08which was the lowest during all the study period.In the year 2008-09to 2011-12 this ratio was continuously increased to 20.94%, 30.07%, 35.05% and 37.47% respectively. In the year 2011-12 this ratio was the highest during all the study period. During all the study period average of this ratio was 27.22%. For all the five years of the study this ratio was lower than its average for two years and higher than its average in the remaining three years.

It isevident from the above table 7.10 for chhapi nagarik sahakari bank that Longterm Advances to Total Advances Ratio was nil**(ZERO)** during the year 2007-08 to 2011-12.I.e. there is no long term advances in the chhapi nagarik sahakari bank during the study period.

It can be observed from the above table 7.10 for banaskantha mercantile co-operative bank that Long term Advances to Total Advances Ratio was 20.11% in the year 2007-08which was the lowest during all the study period.In the year 2008-09 this ratio was increased to 25.55% which was the highest during all the study period. In the year 2009-10 this ratio was decreased to 25.28%. In the year 2010-11 and 2011-12 this ratio was continuously decreased to 22.23% and 21.84% respectively. During all the study period average of this ratio was 23.00%. For all the five years of the study this ratio was lower than its average for threeyears and higher than its average in the remaining two years.

It is obvious from the above table 7.10 for chanasma nagarik sahakari bank that Long term Advances to Total Advances Ratio was 40.13% in the year 2007-08.In the year 2008-09 this ratio was increased to 42.53% which was the highest during all the study period. In the year 2009-10 to 2011-12 this ratio was continuously decreased to 36.61%, 32.29% and 29.16% respectively. In the year 2011-12 this ratio was the lowest during all the study period.During all the study period average of this ratio was 36.14%. For all the five years of the study this ratio was lower than its average for two years and higher than its average in the remaining three years.

It is apparent from the above table 7.10 for patan nagarik sahakari bank that Long term Advances to Total Advances Ratio was 22.02% in the year 2007-08. In the year 2008-09 this ratio was increased to 32.21%which was the highest during all the study period. In the year 2009-10 to 2010-11 this ratio was continuously decreased to 21.62% and 20.15% respectively. In the year 2010-11 this ratio was the lowest during all the study period.In the year 2011-12 this ratio was decreased to 21.33%. During all the study period average of this ratio was 23.47%. For all the five years of the study this ratio was lower than its average for two years and higher than its average in remaining three years.

It can be seen from the above table 7.10 for all Citizen co-operative banks that average of Long term Advances to Total Advances Ratio during 2007-08 to 2011-12 was 17.46%. In the year 2007-08 average ratio of all banks was 16.45%which was the lowest during all the study period. In the year 2008-09 this ratio was increased to 19.13%which was the highest during all the study period.In the year 2009-10 to 2011-12 this ratio was continuously decreased to 17.81%, 17.07% and 16.87% respectively. For all the five years of the study average ratio of all banks was lower than its average for three years and higher than its average in remaining two years.

❖ F test (ANOVA) Analysis

The statements of hypothesis are as under:

• Hypothesis between the banks:

H_0:   There is no significant difference in the long term advances to total advances ratio of different Citizen Co-operative banks of North Gujarat for every financial year.

H_1:   There is significant difference in the long term advances to total advances ratio of different Citizen Co-operative banks of North Gujarat for every financial year.

• Hypothesis between the years:

H_0:   There is no significant difference in the longterm advances to total advances ratio of every Citizen Co-operative bank of North Gujarat for different financial years.

H_1:   There is significant difference in the long term advances to total advances ratio of every Citizen Co-operative bank of North Gujarat for different financial years.

Table 7.10-A

Source of Variation	SS	df	MS	F
Between Banks	6110.80	07	872.97	35.73
Between years	35.54	04	8.88	0.36
Error	684.12	28	24.43	

213

Total	6830.46	39		

Table Value for df (7,28) is 2.36 at 5% level of significance.

Table Value for df (4,28) is 2.71 at 5% level of significance.

Table 7.10-A represents the difference for the banks is significant because the table value for df (7,28) is (2.36) which is lower than calculated value of 'F' (35.73). So, null hypothesis (H_o) is rejected and alternative hypothesis (H_1) is accepted. I.e. there is significant difference in the long term advances to total advances ratio of different Citizen Co-operative banks of North Gujarat for every financial year.

Same way the difference for the years is not significant because the table value for df (4,28) is (2.71) which is higher than the calculated value of 'F' (0.36) for years and so here null hypothesis(H_o) is accepted and alternative hypothesis (H_1) is rejected. I.e. there is no significant difference in the long term advances to total advances ratio of every Citizen Co-operative bank of North Gujarat for different financial years.

7.4.11   Total Advances to Working Funds Ratio

Lending is prime function of any CCBs. Lending is popularly referred as advances or credit in banking industry. CCBs earn interest on these advances. Hence, interest on advances is the main source of income for any UCB. So, higher the advances, higher the income is.By this ratio we can know proportion of total advances against bank's working funds. A higher ratio indicates good situation of the bank from profitability and safety point of view. Formula for the ratio of total advances to working funds is as follows:

$$\text{Total Advances to Working Funds Ratio} = \frac{\text{Total Advances}}{\text{Working Funds}} *100$$

Total Advances to Working Funds Ratio of selected citizen cooperative banks of North Gujarat for the study period 2007-08 to 2011-12 is presented in the table 7.11 as follows:

Table 7.11
Total Advances to Working Funds Ratio

YEAR	HIMNSB	MODNSB	MEHNSB	COBMEH	CHHNSB	BANMCB	CHANSB	PATNSB	AVERAGE
2007-08	35.27	50.01	49.70	55.59	34.05	40.46	46.59	36.09	43.47
2008-09	32.33	47.46	44.39	46.22	35.48	40.46	50.63	35.50	41.56
2009-10	32.22	46.86	42.40	41.48	36.79	42.34	54.91	32.59	41.20
2010-11	39.85	44.38	46.21	52.07	37.00	49.36	53.94	29.13	43.99
2011-12	47.56	50.40	49.48	47.15	43.81	45.55	56.31	32.99	46.66
AVERAGE	37.44	47.82	46.44	48.50	37.43	43.63	52.47	33.26	43.38

Source: Annual reports of CCBs during year 2007-08 to 2011-12.

Chart 7.2

214

Chart Showing Total Advances to Working Funds Ratio

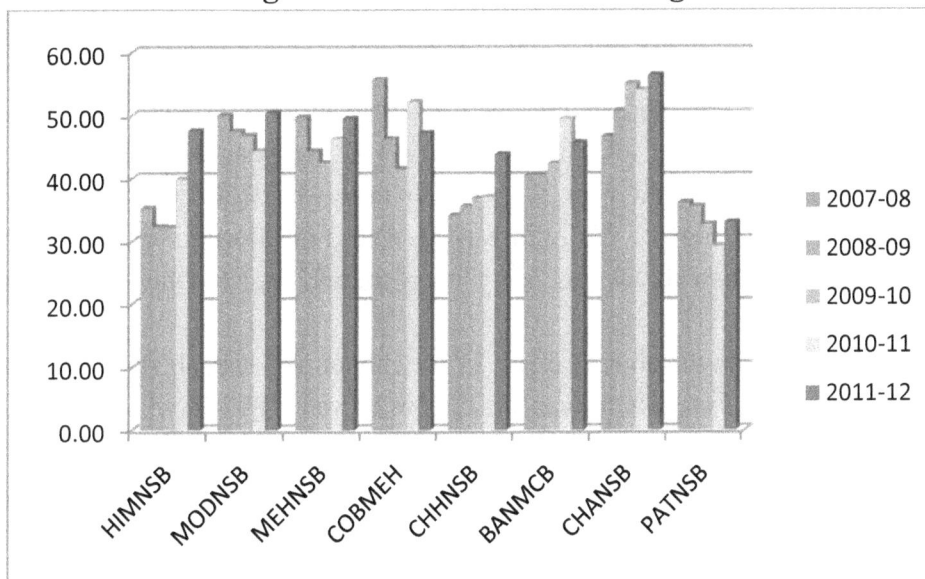

It can be observed from the above table 7.11 for himmatnagar nagarik sahakari bank that Total Advances to Working FundsRatio was 35.27% in the year 2007-08. In the year 2008-09and 2009-10 this ratio was continuously decreased to 32.33% and 32.22% respectively. In the year 2009-10 this ratio was the lowest during all the study period.In the year 2010-11 and 2011-12 this ratio was continuously increased to 39.85% and 47.56% respectively. In the year 2011-12 this ratio was the highest during all the study period. During all the study period average of this ratio was 37.44%. For all the five years of the study this ratio was lower than its average for threeyears and higher than its average in the remaining two years.

It is obvious from the above table 7.11 for modasa nagarik sahakari bank that Total Advances to Working FundsRatio was 50.01% in the year 2007-08.In the year 2008-09to 2010-11 this ratio was continuously decreased to 47.46%, 46.86% and 44.38% respectively. In the year 2010-11 this ratio was the lowest during all the study period. In the year 2011-12 this ratio was increased to 50.40%which was the highest during all the study period. During all the study period average of this ratio was 47.82%. For all the five years of the study this ratio was lower than its average for threeyears and higher than its average in the remaining two years.

It is apparent from the above table 7.11 for mehsana nagarik sahakari bank that Total Advances to Working FundsRatio was the same 47.70% in the year 2007-08 which was the highest during all the study period. In the year 2008-09and 2009-10 this ratio was continuously decreased to 44.39% and 42.40% respectively. In the year 2009-10 this ratio was the lowest during all the study period.In the year 2010-11 and 2011-12 this ratio was continuously increased to 46.21% and 49.48% respectively. During all the study period average of this ratio was 46.44%. For all the five years of the study this ratio was lower than its average for threeyears and higher than its average in the remaining two years.

It is cleared from the above table 7.11 for co-operative bank of mehsana that Total Advances to Working FundsRatio was 55.59% in the year 2007-08which was the highest during all the study period.In the year 2008-09and 2009-10 this ratio was continuously decreased to 46.22% and 41.48% respectively. In the year 2009-10 this ratio was the lowest during all the study period.In the year 2010-11 this ratio was increased to 52.07% and in the year 2011-12 this ratio was decreased to 47.15% During all the study period average of this ratio was 48.50%. For all the five years of the study this ratio was lower than its average for threeyears and higher than its average in the remaining two years.

It isevident from the above table 7.11 for chhapi nagarik sahakari bank that Total Advances to Working FundsRatio was 34.05% in the year 2007-08which was the lowest during all the study period. In the year 2008-09 to 2011-12 this ratio was continuously increased to 35.48%, 36.79%, 37.00% and 43.81% respectively. In the year 2011-12 this ratio was the highest during all the study period.During all the study period average of this ratio was 37.43%. For all the five years of the study this ratio was lower than its average for threeyears and higher than its average in the remaining two years.

It can be observed from the above table 7.11 for banaskantha mercantile co-operative bank that Total Advances to Working FundsRatio was the same 40.46% in the year 2007-08 and 2008-09which was the lowest during all the study period.In the year 2009-10 and 2010-11 this ratio was continuously increased to 42.34% and 49.36% respectively. In the year 2010-11 this ratio was the highest during all the study period.In the year 2011-12 this ratio was decreased to 45.55%. During all the study period average of this ratio was 43.63%. For all the five years of the study this ratio was lower than its average for threeyears and higher than its average in the remaining two years.

It is obvious from the above table 7.11 for chanasma nagarik sahakari bank that Total Advances to Working FundsRatio was 46.59% in the year 2007-08which was the lowest during all the study period. In the year 2008-09 and 2009-10 this ratio was increased to 50.63%and 54.91% respectively. In the year 2010-11 this ratio was decreased to 53.94%. In the year 2011-12 this ratio was increased to 56.31% which was the highest during all the study period.During all the study period average of this ratio was 52.47%. For all the five years of the study this ratio was lower than its average for two years and higher than its average in the remaining three years.

It is apparent from the above table 7.11 for patan nagarik sahakari bank that Total Advances to Working FundsRatio was 36.09% in the year 2007-08 which was the highest during all the study period. In the year 2008-09 to 2010-11 this ratio was continuously decreased to 35.50%, 32.59%and 29.13% respectively. In the year 2010-11 this ratio was the lowest during all the study period. In the year 2011-12 this ratio was increased to 32.99%. During all the study period average of this ratio was 33.26%. For all the five years of the study this ratio was lower than its average for threeyears and higher than its average in the remaining two years.

It can be seen from the above table 7.11 for all Citizen co-operative banks that average of Total Advances to Working FundsRatio during 2007-08 to 2011-12 was 43.38%. In the year 2007-08 average ratio of all banks was 43.47%. In the year 2008-09 and 2009-10 this ratio was decreased to 41.56%and 41.20% respectively. In the year 2009-10 this ratio was the lowest during all the study period. In the year 2010-11and 2011-12 this ratio was continuously increased to 43.99% and 46.66% respectively. In the year 2011-12 this ratio was the highest during all the study period.For all the five years of the study average ratio of all banks was lower than its average for two years and higher than its average in remaining three years.

❖ F test (ANOVA) Analysis

The statements of hypothesis are as under:

• Hypothesis between the banks:

H_0: There is no significant difference in the total advances to working fundsratio of different Citizen Co-operative banks of North Gujarat for every financial year.

H_1: There is significant difference in the total advances to working fundsratio of different Citizen Co-operative banks of North Gujarat for every financial year.

• Hypothesis between the years:

H_0: There is no significant difference in the total advances to working fundsratio of every Citizen Co-operative bank of North Gujarat for different financial years.

H_1: There is significant difference in the total advances to working fundsratio of every Citizen Co-operative bank of North Gujarat for different financial years.

Table 7.11-A

Source of Variation	SS	df	MS	F
Between Banks	1555.93	07	222.28	15.45
Between years	153.60	04	38.40	2.67
Error	402.89	28	14.39	
Total	2112.42	39		

Table Value for df (7,28) is 2.36 at 5% level of significance.

Table Value for df (4,28) is 2.71 at 5% level of significance.

Table 7.11-A represents the difference for the banks is significant because the table value for df (7,28) is (2.36) which is lower than calculated value of 'F' (15.45). So, null hypothesis (H_0) is rejected and alternative hypothesis (H_1) is accepted. I.e. there is significant difference in the total advances to working fundsratio of different Citizen Co-operative banks of North Gujarat for every financial year.

Same way the difference for the years is not significant because the table value for df (4,28) is (2.71) which is higher than the calculated value of 'F' (2.67) for years and so here null hypothesis(H_0) is accepted and alternative hypothesis (H_1) is rejected. I.e. there is no significant difference in the total advances to working fundsratio of every Citizen Co-operative bank of North Gujarat for different financial years.

7.4.12 NPA to Total Advances Ratio

Gross NPA ratio is the total of all loan assets that are classified as NPAas per the RBI guidelines as on a balance sheet date. Gross NPA consists of allnon-standard assets such as sub-standard, doubtful, and loss assets. This ratioreflects the quality of loans by measuring the problematic loan as a percentageof bank's total loan portfolio.It indicates the quality of credit portfolio of the banks. High gross NPAratio indicates low quality credit portfolio of the bank and vice versa.Formula for the ratio of NPA to total advances is as follows:

$$\text{NPA to Total Advances Ratio} = \frac{\text{Gross NPA}}{\text{Total Advances}} *100$$

NPA to Total Advances Ratio of selected citizen cooperative banks of North Gujarat for the study period 2007-08 to 2011-12 is presented in the table 7.12 as follows:

Table 7.12
NPA to Total Advances Ratio

YEAR	HIMNSB	MODNSB	MEHNSB	COBMEH	CHHNSB	BANMCB	CHANSB	PATNSB	AVERAGE
2007-08	16.33	3.97	12.41	3.23	6.64	1.70	3.34	8.57	7.02
2008-09	13.23	4.31	9.84	3.13	3.74	0.81	2.85	7.93	5.73
2009-10	11.89	3.45	6.35	3.30	2.24	0.31	0.95	8.54	4.63
2010-11	7.27	2.68	5.54	2.12	1.04	0.21	0.87	8.11	3.48
2011-12	5.95	3.36	3.99	2.64	0.77	0.14	2.76	6.56	3.27
AVERAGE	10.93	3.55	7.63	2.88	2.88	0.63	2.15	7.94	4.83

Source: Annual reports of CCBs during year 2007-08 to 2011-12.

It can be observed from the above table 7.12 for himmatnagar nagarik sahakari bank that NPA to Total Advances Ratio was 16.33% in the year 2007-08 which was the highest during all the study period.In the year 2008-09to 2011-12 this ratio was continuously decreased to 13.23%, 11.89%, 7.27% and 5.95% respectively. In the year 2011-12 this ratio was the lowest during all the study period. During all the study period average of this ratio was 10.93%. For all the five years of the study this ratio was lower than its average for two years and higher than its average in the remaining three years.

It is obvious from the above table 7.12 for modasa nagarik sahakari bank that NPA to Total Advances Ratio was 3.97% in the year 2007-08.In the year 2008-09this ratio was increased to 4.31% which was the highest during all the study period.In the year 2009-10 and 2010-11 this ratio was decreased to 3.45% and 2.68% respectively. In the year 2010-11 this ratio was the lowest during all the study period.In the year 2011-12 this ratio wasincreased to 3.36%. During all the study period average of this ratio was 3.55%. For all the five years of the study this ratio was lower than its average for threeyears and higher than its average in the remaining two years.

It is apparent from the above table 7.12 for mehsana nagarik sahakari bank that NPA to Total Advances Ratio was 12.41%in the year 2007-08 which was the highest during all the study period. In the year 2008-09 to 2011-12 this ratio was continuously decreased to 9.84%, 6.35%, 5.54% and 3.99% respectively. In the year 2011-12 this ratio was the lowest during all the study period. During all the study period average of this ratio was 7.63%. For all the five years of the study this ratio was lower than its average for threeyears and higher than its average in the remaining two years.

It is cleared from the above table 7.12 for co-operative bank of mehsana that NPAto Total Advances Ratio was 3.23% in the year 2007-08.which was the highest during all the study period.In the year 2008-09 this ratio was decreased to 3.13%and in the year 2009-10 this ratio was increased to 3.30%. In the year 2009-10 this ratio was the highest during all the study period. In the year 2010-11 this ratio was decreased to 2012%which was the lowest during all the study period.In the year 2011-12 this ratio was increased to 2.64%. During all the study period average of this ratio was 2.88%. For all the five years of the study this ratio was lower than its average for two years and higher than its average in the remaining three years.

It isevident from the above table 7.12 for chhapi nagarik sahakari bank that NPAto Total Advances Ratio was 6.64% in the year 2007-08 which was the highest during all the study period.In the year 2008-09 to 2011-12 this ratio was continuously decreased to 3.74%, 2.24%, 1.04% and 0.77% respectively. In the year 2011-12 this ratio was the lowest during all the study period. During all the study period average of this ratio was 2.88%. For all the five years of the study this ratio was lower than its average for threeyears and higher than its average in the remaining two years.

It can be observed from the above table 7.12 for banaskantha mercantile co-operative bank that NPA to Total Advances Ratio was 1.70% in the year 2007-08which was the highest during all the study period.In the year 2008-09 to 2011-12 this ratio was continuously decreased to 0.81%, 0.31%, 0.21% and 0.14% respectively. In the year 2011-12 this ratio was the lowest during all the study period. During all the study period average of this ratio was 0.63%. For all the five years of the study this ratio was lower than its average for threeyears and higher than its average in the remaining two years.

It is obvious from the above table 7.12 for chanasma nagarik sahakari bank that NPA to Total Advances Ratio was 3.34% in the year 2007-08which was the highest during all the study period. In the year 2008-09 to 2010-11 this ratio was continuously decreased to 2.85%,0.95%and 0.87% respectively. In the year 2010-11 this ratio wasthe lowest during all the study period. In the year 2011-12 this ratio was increased to 2.76%. During all the study period average of this ratio was 2.15%. For all the five years of the study this ratio was lower than its average for two years and higher than its average in the remaining three years.

It is apparent from the above table 7.12 for patan nagarik sahakari bank that NPA to Total Advances Ratio was 8.57% in the year 2007-08which was the highest during all the study period. In the year 2008-09 this ratio was decreased to 7.93%.In the year 2009-10 this ratio was increased to 8.54%. In the year 2010-11 and 2011-12 this ratio was continuously decreased to 8.11%and 6.56% respectively. In the year 2011-12 this ratio was the lowest during all the study period.During all the study period average of this ratio was 7.94%. For all the five years of the study this ratio was lower than its average for two years and higher than its average in remaining three years.

It can be seen from the above table 7.12 for all Citizen co-operative banks that average of NPA to Total Advances Ratio during 2007-08 to 2011-12 was 27.86%. In the year 2007-08 average ratio of all banks was 4.83%. In the year 2008-09 this ratio was decreased to 7.02%which was the highest during all the study period. In the year 2009-10 to 2011-12 this ratio was continuously decreased to 5.73%, 4.63%, 3.48% and 3.27% respectively. In the year 2011-12 this ratio was the lowest during all the study period.For all the five years of the study average ratio of all banks was lower than its average for three years and higher than its average in remaining two years.

❖ **F test (ANOVA) Analysis**

The statements of hypothesis are as under:

- **Hypothesis between the banks:**

H_0:   There is no significant difference in the NPA to total advances ratio of different Citizen Co-operative banks of North Gujarat for every financial year.

H_1:   There is significant difference in the NPAto total advances ratio of different Citizen Co-operative banks of North Gujarat for every financial year.

- **Hypothesis between the years:**

H_0:   There is no significant difference in the NPAto total advances ratio of every Citizen Co-operative bank of North Gujarat for different financial years.

H_1:   There is significant difference in the NPA to total advances ratio of every Citizen Co-operative bank of North Gujarat for different financial years.

Table 7.12-A

Source of Variation	SS	df	MS	F
Between Banks	443.66	07	63.38	23.16
Between years	79.34	04	19.84	7.25
Error	76.61	28	2.74	
Total	599.61	39		

Table Value for df (7,28) is 2.36 at 5% level of significance.

Table Value for df (4,28) is 2.71 at 5% level of significance.

Table 7.12-A represents the difference for the banks is significant because the table value for df (7,28) is (2.36) which is lower than calculated value of 'F' (23.16).

So, null hypothesis (H$_o$) is rejected and alternative hypothesis (H$_1$) is accepted. I.e. there is significant difference in the NPA to total advances ratio of different Citizen Co-operative banks of North Gujarat for every financial year.

Same way the difference for the years is significant because the table value for df (4,28) is (2.71) which is lower than the calculated value of 'F' (7.25) for years and so here null hypothesis(H$_o$) is rejected and alternative hypothesis (H$_1$) is accepted. I.e. there is significant difference in the NPA to total advances ratio of every Citizen Co-operative bank of North Gujarat for different financial years.

7.4.13   Cash and Bank to Working Funds Ratio

As cash on hand yields no returns, banks should maintain onlyminimum cash balance required for day to day business. This will also reduce thesecurity risk for the bank.Amount kept in CA with other bank and if no interest is paidincome/yield on this balance will be nil. Cash is the cash on hand at the time books are closed at the end of the fiscal year. This refers to all cash in checking, savings and short-term investment accounts.High cash and bank ratio indicates weak position from profitability point of view and good position from liquidity point of view.Formula for the ratio of cash and bank to working funds is as follows:

$$\text{Cash and Bank to Working Funds Ratio} = \frac{\text{Cash and Bank}}{\text{Working Funds}} * 100$$

f

North Gujarat for the study period 2007-08 to 2011-12 is presented in the table 7.13 as follows:

Table 7.13

Cash and Bank to Working Funds Ratio

YEAR	HIMNSB	MODNSB	MEHNSB	COBMEH	CHHNSB	BANMCB	CHANSB	PATNSB	AVERAGE
2007-08	35.64	25.14	33.74	15.60	25.01	57.36	14.41	26.52	29.18
2008-09	40.63	31.04	39.34	36.80	31.01	57.50	12.51	34.55	35.42
2009-10	40.03	30.82	38.54	43.01	30.82	55.07	11.66	30.95	35.11
2010-11	30.43	32.88	29.95	26.13	28.51	48.03	15.69	30.33	30.24
2011-12	23.54	26.54	26.25	28.99	28.99	51.79	14.98	28.88	28.74
AVERAGE	34.05	29.28	33.56	30.11	28.87	53.95	13.85	30.25	31.74

Source: Annual reports of CCBs during year 2007-08 to 2011-12.

It can be observed from the above table 7.13 for himmatnagar nagarik sahakari bank that Cash and Bankto Working FundsRatio was 35.64% in the year 2007-08. In the year 2008-09 this ratio was increased to 40.63% which was the highest during all the study period. In the year 2009-10 to 2011-12 this ratio was continuously decreased to 40.03%, 30.43% and 23.54% respectively. In the year 2011-12 this ratiowas the lowest during all the study period.During all the study period average of this ratio was 34.05%.

For all the five years of the study this ratio was lower than its average for two years and higher than its average in the remaining three years.

It is obvious from the above table 7.13 for modasa nagarik sahakari bank that Cash and Bankto Working FundsRatio was 25.14% in the year 2007-08which was the lowest during all the study period.In the year 2008-09 this ratio was increased to 31.04% and in the year 2009-10 it was decreased to 30.82%. In the year 2010-11 this ratio was increased to 32.88%which was the highest during all the study period. In the year 2011-12 this ratio was decreased to 26.54%. During all the study period average of this ratio was 29.28%. For all the five years of the study this ratio was lower than its average for two years and higher than its average in the remaining three years.

It is apparent from the above table 7.13 for mehsana nagarik sahakari bank that Cash and Bankto Working FundsRatio was the same 33.74% in the year 2007-08. In the year 2008-09 this ratio was increased to 39.34%which was the highest during all the study period. In the year 2009-10 to 20111-12 this ratio was continuously decreased to 38.54%, 29.95% and 26.25% respectively.In the year 2011-12 this ratio was the lowest during all the study period. During all the study period average of this ratio was 33.56%. For all the five years of the study this ratio was lower than its average for two years and higher than its average in the remaining three years.

It is cleared from the above table 7.13 for co-operative bank of mehsana that Cash and Bankto Working FundsRatio was 15.60% in the year 2007-08which was the lowest during all the study period.In the year 2008-09and 2009-10 this ratio was continuously increased to 36.80% and 43.01% respectively. In the year 2009-10 this ratio was the highest during all the study period.In the year 2010-11 this ratio was decreased to 26.13% and in the year 2011-12 this ratio was increased to 28.99% During all the study period average of this ratio was 30.11%. For all the five years of the study this ratio was lower than its average for threeyears and higher than its average in the remaining two years.

It isevident from the above table 7.13 for chhapi nagarik sahakari bank that Cash and Bankto Working FundsRatio was 25.01% in the year 2007-08which was the lowest during all the study period. In the year 2008-09 this ratio was increased to 31.01% which was the highest during all the study period.In the year 200-10 and 2010-11 this ratio was continuously decreased to 30.82%and 28.51% respectively. In the year 2011-12 this ratiowas increased to 28.99%. During all the study period average of this ratio was 28.87%. For all the five years of the study this ratio was lower than its average for threeyears and higher than its average in the remaining two years.

It can be observed from the above table 7.13 for banaskantha mercantile co-operative bank that Cash and Bankto Working FundsRatio was 57.36% in the year 2007-08. In the year 2008-09this ratio was increased to 57.50%which was the highest during all the study period.In the year 2009-10 and 2010-11 this ratio was continuously decreased to 55.07% and 48.03% respectively.In the year 2010-11 this ratio was the lowest during all the study period. In the year 2011-12 this ratio was increased to 51.79%. During all the study period average of this ratio was 53.95%. For all the five years of the study this ratio was lower than its average two years and higher than its average in the remaining three years.

It is obvious from the above table 7.13 for chanasma nagarik sahakari bank that Cash and Bankto Working FundsRatio was 14.41% in the year 2007-08.In the year 2008-09 and 2009-10 this ratio was continuously decreased to 12.51%and 11.66% respectively.In the year 2009-10 this ratio was the lowest during all the study period. In the year 2010-11 this ratio was increased to 15.69% which was the highest during all the study period. In the year 2011-12 this ratio was decreased to 14.98%. During all the study period average of this ratio was 13.85%. For all the five years of the study this ratio was lower than its average for two years and higher than its average in the remaining three years.

It is apparent from the above table 7.13 for patan nagarik sahakari bank that Cash and Bankto Working FundsRatio was 26.52% in the year 2007-08 which was the lowest during all the study period. In the year 2008-09 and 2009-10 this ratio was continuously increased to 34.55%and 30.95% respectively.In the year 2008-09 this ratio was the highest during all the study period. In the year 2010-11and 2011-12 this ratio was continuously decreased to 30.33% and 28.88% respectively.During all the study period average of this ratio was 30.25%. For all the five years of the study this ratio was lower than its average for two years and higher than its average in the remaining three years.

It can be seen from the above table 7.13 for all Citizen co-operative banks that average of Cash and Bankto Working FundsRatio during 2007-08 to 2011-12 was 31.74%. In the year 2007-08 average ratio of all banks was 29.18%. In the year 2008-09this ratio was increased to 35.42%which was the highest during all the study period. In the year 2009-10to 2011-12 this ratio was continuously decreased to 35.11%, 30.24% and 28.74% respectively. In the year 2011-12 this ratio was the lowest during all the study period.For all the five years of the study average ratio of all banks was lower than its average for threeyears and higher than its average in the remaining two years.

❖ **F test (ANOVA) Analysis**

The statements of hypothesis are as under:
- **Hypothesis between the banks:**

H_0:   There is no significant difference in the cash and bankto working fundsratio of different Citizen Co-operative banks of North Gujarat for every financial year.

H_1:   There is significant difference in the cash and bankto working fundsratio of different Citizen Co-operative banks of North Gujarat for every financial year.

- **Hypothesis between the years:**

H_0:   There is no significant difference in the cash and bankto working fundsratio of every Citizen Co-operative bank of North Gujarat for different financial years.

H₁: There is significant difference in the cash and bankto working fundsratio of every Citizen Co-operative bank of North Gujarat for different financial years.

Table 7.13-A

Source of Variation	SS	df	MS	F
Between Banks	4205.62	07	600.80	27.79
Between years	341.68	04	85.42	3.95
Error	605.33	28	21.62	
Total	5152.64	39		

Table Value for df (7,28) is 2.36 at 5% level of significance.

Table Value for df (4,28) is 2.71 at 5% level of significance.

Table 7.13-A represents the difference for the banks is significant because the table value for df (7,28) is (2.36) which is lower than calculated value of 'F' (27.79). So, null hypothesis (H₀) is rejected and alternative hypothesis (H₁) is accepted. I.e. there is significant difference in the cash and bankto working fundsratio of different Citizen Co-operative banks of North Gujarat for every financial year.

Same way the difference for the years is significant because the table value for df (4,28) is (2.71) which is lower than the calculated value of 'F' (3.95) for years and so here null hypothesis(H₀) is rejected and alternative hypothesis (H₁) is accepted. I.e. there is significant difference in the cash and bankto working fundsratio of every Citizen Co-operative bank of North Gujarat for different financial years.

7.4.14 Fixed Assets to Working Funds Ratio

In any financial institution, the involvement of fixed assets isminimum. Here fixed assets include land and buildings, furniture,typewriters, computers and so on. Working funds are utilized for investmentin fixed assets. Higher the ratio the more is the amount invested in fixed assets. Fromthe shareholders point of view maximum ratio is preferable. But whereas from the point of view of profitability investing more in fixed assets meansshort of money for lending operations.Formula for the ratio of fixed assets to working funds is as follows:

$$\text{Fixed Assets to Working Funds Ratio} = \frac{\textbf{Fixed Assets}}{\textbf{Working Funds}} * 100$$

Fixed Assetsto Working Funds Ratio of selected citizen cooperative banks of North Gujarat for the study period 2007-08 to 2011-12 is presented in the table 7.14 as follows:

Table 7.14
Fixed Assets to Working Funds Ratio

YEAR	HIMNSB	MODNSB	MEHNSB	COBMEH	CHHNSB	BANMCB	CHANSB	PATNSB	AVERAGE
2007-08	0.79	0.48	3.26	1.06	0.38	1.18	0.96	1.07	1.15
2008-09	0.61	0.42	2.64	0.79	0.52	1.10	1.31	0.94	1.04
2009-10	0.56	0.46	2.15	0.73	0.41	1.78	1.17	1.01	1.03
2010-11	0.51	0.65	1.86	0.88	0.34	1.78	0.98	0.98	1.00
2011-12	0.50	0.63	1.67	0.47	0.83	1.52	0.88	0.93	0.93

| AVERAGE | 0.59 | 0.53 | 2.32 | 0.79 | 0.50 | 1.47 | 1.06 | 0.99 | 1.03 |

Source: Annual reports of CCBs during year 2007-08 to 2011-12.

It can be observed from the above table 7.14 for himmatnagar nagarik sahakari bank that Fixed Assetsto Working FundsRatio was 0.79% in the year 2007-08which was the highest during all the study period. In the year 2008-09to 2011-12 this ratio was continuously decreased to 0.61%, 0.56%, 0.51% and 0.50% respectively. In the year 2011-12 this ratio was the lowest during all the study period. During all the study period average of this ratio was 0.59%. For all the five years of the study this ratio was lower than its average for threeyears and higher than its average in the remaining two years.

It is obvious from the above table 7.14 for modasa nagarik sahakari bank that Fixed Assetsto Working FundsRatio was 0.48% in the year 2007-08.In the year 2008-09 this ratio was decreased to 0.42% which was the lowest during all the study period. In the year 2009-10 and 2010-11 this ratio was continuously increased to 0.46% and 0.65% respectively.In the year 2010-11 this ratio was the highest during all the study period. In the year 2011-12 this ratio was decreased to 0.63%.During all the study period average of this ratio was 0.53%. For all the five years of the study this ratio was lower than its average for threeyears and higher than its average in the remaining two years.

It is apparent from the above table 7.14 for mehsana nagarik sahakari bank that Fixed Assetsto Working FundsRatio was the same 3.26% in the year 2007-08 which was the highest during all the study period. In the year 2008-09to 2011-12 this ratio was continuously decreased to 2.64%, 2.15%, 1.86% and 1.67% respectively. In the year 2011-12 this ratio was the lowest during all the study period.During all the study period average of this ratio was 2.32%. For all the five years of the study this ratio was lower than its average for threeyears and higher than its average in the remaining two years.

It is cleared from the above table 7.14 for co-operative bank of mehsana that Fixed Assetsto Working FundsRatio was 1.06% in the year 2007-08which was the highest during all the study period.In the year 2008-09and 2009-10 this ratio was continuously decreased to 0.79% and 0.73% respectively. In the year 2008-09this ratio was equal to the average ratio of all the study period. In the year 2010-11 this ratio was increased to 0.88% and in the year 2011-12 this ratio was decreased to 0.47%. In the year 2011-12 this ratio was the lowest during all the study period. During all the study period average of this ratio was 0.79%. For all the five years of the study this ratio was lower than its average for two years, higher than its average fortwo years and equal to its average in the remaining one year.

It isevident from the above table 7.14 for chhapi nagarik sahakari bank that Fixed Assetsto Working FundsRatio was 0.38% in the year 2007-08.In the year 2008-09 this ratio was increased to 0.52%. In the year 2009-10and 2010-11 this ratio was continuously decreased to 0.41% and 0.34% respectively. In the year 2010-11 this ratio was the lowest during all the study period.In the year 2011-12 this ratio was increased to 0.83%which was the highest during all the study period. During all the study period average of this ratio was 0.50%.For all the five years of the study this ratio was lower than its average for threeyears and higher than its average in the remaining two years.

It can be observed from the above table 7.14 for banaskantha mercantile co-operative bank that Fixed Assetsto Working FundsRatio was 1.18% in the year 2007-08. In the year 2008-09this ratio was decreased to 1.10%which was the lowest during all the study period.In the year 2009-10 and 2010-11 this ratio was the same 1.78%. In the year 2009-10 and 2010-11 this ratio was the highest during all the study period.In the year 2011-12 this ratio was decreased to 1.52%. During all the study period average of this ratio was 1.47%. For all the five years of the study this ratio was lower than its average for two years and higher than its average in the remaining three years.

It is obvious from the above table 7.14 for chanasma nagarik sahakari bank that Fixed Assetsto Working FundsRatio was 0.96% in the year 2007-08.In the year 2008-09this ratio was increased to 1.31%which was the highest during all the study period.In the year 2009-10to 2011-12 this ratio was continuously decreased to 1.17%, 0.98%and 0.88%respectively. In the year 2011-12 this ratio was the lowest during all the study period.During all the study period average of this ratio was 1.06%. For all the five years of the study this ratio was lower than its average for threeyears and higher than its average in the remaining two years.

It is apparent from the above table 7.14 for patan nagarik sahakari bank that Fixed Assetsto Working FundsRatio was 1.07% in the year 2007-08which was the highest during all the study period. In the year 2008-09this ratio was decreased to 0.94% and in the year 2009-10 this ratio was increased to 1.01%. In the year 2010-11 and2011-12 this ratio was continuously decreased to 0.98%and 0.93%respectively.In the year 2011-12 this ratio was the lowest during all the study period. During all the study period average of this ratio was 0.99%. For all the five years of the study this ratio was lower than its average for threeyears and higher than its average in the remaining two years.

It can be seen from the above table 7.14 for all Citizen co-operative banks that average of Fixed Assetsto Working FundsRatio during 2007-08 to 2011-12 was 1.03%. In the year 2007-08 average ratio of all banks was 1.15%which was the highest during all the study period. In the year 2008-09 to 2011-12 this ratio was continuously decreased to 1.04%, 1.035, 1.00% and 0.93% respectively. In the year 2009-10this ratio was equal to the average ratio of all the study period. In the year 2011-12 this ratio was the lowest during all the study period.For all the five years of the study average ratio of all banks was lower than its average for two years, higher than its average for twoyears and equal to its average in the remaining one year.

❖ F test (ANOVA) Analysis

The statements of hypothesis are as under:

- **Hypothesis between the banks:**

H_0:   There is no significant difference in the fixed assetsto working fundsratio of different Citizen Co-operative banks of North Gujarat for every financial year.

H₁: There is significant difference in the fixed assetsto working fundsratio of different Citizen Co-operative banks of North Gujarat for every financial year.

- **Hypothesis between the years:**

H₀: There is no significant difference in the fixed assetsto working fundsratio of every Citizen Co-operative bank of North Gujarat for different financial years.

H₁: There is significant difference in the fixed assetsto working fundsratio of every Citizen Co-operative bank of North Gujarat for different financial years.

Table 7.14-A

Source of Variation	SS	df	MS	F
Between Banks	13.21	07	1.89	21.54
Between years	0.20	04	0.05	0.58
Error	2.45	28	0.09	
Total	15.86	39		

Table Value for df (7,28) is 2.36 at 5% level of significance.

Table Value for df (4,28) is 2.71 at 5% level of significance.

Table 7.14-A represents the difference for the banks is significant because the table value for df (7,28) is (2.36) which is lower than calculated value of 'F' (21.54). So, null hypothesis (H₀) is rejected and alternative hypothesis (H₁) is accepted. I.e. there is significant difference in the fixed assetsto working fundsratio of different Citizen Co-operative banks of North Gujarat for every financial year.

Same way the difference for the years is not significant because the table value for df (4,28) is (2.71) which is higher than the calculated value of 'F' (0.58) for years and so here null hypothesis(H₀) is accepted and alternative hypothesis (H₁) is rejected. I.e. there is no significant difference in the fixed assetsto working fundsratio of every Citizen Co-operative bank of North Gujarat for different financial years.

7.4.15 Fixed Assets to Owned Funds Ratio

This item on the Balance Sheet displays the deployment of funds by CCBs in the various fixed assets. These fixed assets are required by the CCBs to carry its business. Mostly, Buildings, premises, furniture fixtures and fittings, vehicles, Investments made for computerization etc. are accounted here.By this ratio we can know proportion of fixed assets against bank's owned funds. A higher ratio indicates good situation of the bank from fixed assets point of view.Formula for the ratio of fixed assets to owned funds is as follows:

$$\textbf{Fixed Assets to Owned Funds Ratio} = \frac{\textbf{Fixed Assets}}{\textbf{Owned Funds}} * \textbf{100}$$

Fixed Assetsto Owned Funds Ratio of selected citizen cooperative banks of North Gujarat for the study period 2007-08 to 2011-12 is presented in the table 7.15 as follows:

Table 7.15
Fixed Assets to Owned Funds Ratio

YEAR	HIMNSB	MODNSB	MEHNSB	COBMEH	CHHNSB	BANMCB	CHANSB	PATNSB	AVERAGE
2007-08	4.66	2.84	20.34	7.46	3.00	7.64	6.51	4.77	7.15
2008-09	3.99	2.56	18.75	5.53	4.27	7.18	9.12	4.54	6.99
2009-10	3.49	2.87	17.59	5.52	3.14	12.62	8.63	5.66	7.44
2010-11	3.25	4.32	14.97	6.17	2.58	12.36	7.54	6.40	7.20
2011-12	3.22	3.96	13.24	3.34	5.45	11.45	7.60	5.98	6.78
AVERAGE	3.72	3.31	16.98	5.60	3.69	10.25	7.88	5.47	7.11

Source: Annual reports of CCBs during year 2007-08 to 2011-12.

It can be observed from the above table 7.15 for himmatnagar nagarik sahakari bank that Fixed Assetsto Owned FundsRatio was 4.66% in the year 2007-08which was the highest during all the study period. In the year 2008-09to 2011-12 this ratio was continuously decreased to 3.99%, 3.49%, 3.25% and 3.22% respectively. In the year 2011-12 this ratio was the lowest during all the study period. During all the study period average of this ratio was 3.72%. For all the five years of the study this ratio was lower than its average for threeyears and higher than its average in the remaining two years.

It is obvious from the above table 7.15 for modasa nagarik sahakari bank that Fixed Assetsto Owned FundsRatio was 2.84% in the year 2007-08.In the year 2008-09 this ratio was decreased to 2.56% which was the lowest during all the study period. In the year 2009-10 and 2010-11 this ratio was continuously increased to 2.87% and 4.32% respectively.In the year 2010-11 this ratio was the highest during all the study period. In the year 2011-12 this ratio was decreased to 3.96%.During all the study period average of this ratio was 3.31%. For all the five years of the study this ratio was lower than its average for threeyears and higher than its average in the remaining two years.

It is apparent from the above table 7.15 for mehsana nagarik sahakari bank that Fixed Assetsto Owned FundsRatio was the same 20.34% in the year 2007-08 which was the highest during all the study period. In the year 2008-09to 2011-12 this ratio was continuously decreased to 18.75%, 17.59%, 14.97% and 13.24% respectively. In the year 2011-12 this ratio was the lowest during all the study period.During all the study period average of this ratio was 16.98%. For all the five years of the study this ratio was lower than its average for two years and higher than its average in the remaining three years.

It is cleared from the above table 7.15 for co-operative bank of mehsana that Fixed Assetsto Owned FundsRatio was 7.46% in the year 2007-08which was the highest during all the study period.In the year 2008-09and 2009-10 this ratio was continuously decreased to 5.53% and 5.52% respectively. In the year 2010-11 this ratio was increased to 6.17% and in the year 2011-12 this ratio was decreased to 3.34%. In the year 2011-12 this ratio was the lowest during all the study period. During all the study period average of this ratio was 5.60%. For all the five years of the study this ratio was lower than its average for threeyears and higher than its average in the remaining two years.

It isevident from the above table 7.15 for chhapi nagarik sahakari bank that Fixed Assetsto Owned FundsRatio was 3.00% in the year 2007-08.In the year 2008-09 this ratio was increased to 4.27%. In the year 2009-10and 2010-11 this ratio was continuously decreased to 3.14% and 2.58% respectively. In the year 2010-11 this ratio was the lowest during all the study period.In the year 2011-12 this ratio was increased to 5.45%which was the highest during all the study period. During all the study period average of this ratio was 3.69%.For all the five years of the study this ratio was lower than its average for threeyears and higher than its average in the remaining two years.

It can be observed from the above table 7.15 for banaskantha mercantile co-operative bank that Fixed Assetsto Owned FundsRatio was 7.64% in the year 2007-08. In the year 2008-09this ratio was decreased to 7.18%which was the lowest during all the study period.In the year 2009-10 this ratio was increased to 12.62%which was the highest during all the study period. In the year 2010-11 and 2011-12 this ratio was continuously decreased to 12.36% and 11.45% respectively. During all the study period average of this ratio was 10.25%. For all the five years of the study this ratio was lower than its average for two years and higher than its average in the remaining three years.

It is obvious from the above table 7.15 for chanasma nagarik sahakari bank that Fixed Assetsto Owned FundsRatio was 6.51% in the year 2007-08 which was the lowest during all the study period.In the year 2008-09this ratio was increased to 9.12%which was the highest during all the study period.In the year 2009-10and 2010-11 this ratio was continuously decreased to 8.63%and 7.54%respectively. In the year 2011-12 this ratio was increased to 7.60%. During all the study period average of this ratio was 7.88%. For all the five years of the study this ratio was lower than its average for threeyears and higher than its average in the remaining two years.

It is apparent from the above table 7.15 for patan nagarik sahakari bank that Fixed Assetsto Owned FundsRatio was 4.77% in the year 2007-08.In the year 2008-09this ratiowas decreased to 4.54% which was the lowest during all the study period. In the year 2009-10 and 2010-11 this ratio was continuously increased to 5.66%and 6.40%respectively.In the year 2010-11 this ratiowas the highest during all the study period. In the year 2011-12 this ratio was decreased to 5.98%.During all the study period average of this ratio was 5.47%. For all the five years of the study this ratio was lower than its average for two years and higher than its average in the remaining three years.

It can be seen from the above table 7.15 for all Citizen co-operative banks that average of Fixed Assetsto Owned FundsRatio during 2007-08 to 2011-12 was 7.11%. In the year 2007-08 average ratio of all banks was 7.15%.In the year 2008-09this ratio was decreased to 6.99%.In the year 2009-10 this ratio was increased to 7.44% which was the highest during all the study period. In the year 2010-11 and 2011-12 this ratio was continuously decreased to 7.20% and 6.78% respectively. In the year 2011-12 this ratio was the lowest during all the study period.For all the five years of the study average ratio of all banks was lower than its average for two years and higher than its average in the remaining three years.

❖ **F test (ANOVA) Analysis**

The statements of hypothesis are as under:

- **Hypothesis between the banks:**

H_0: There is no significant difference in the fixed assetsto owned fundsratio of different Citizen Co-operative banks of North Gujarat for every financial year.

H_1: There is significant difference in the fixed assetsto owned fundsratio of different Citizen Co-operative banks of North Gujarat for every financial year.

- **Hypothesis between the years:**

H_0: There is no significant difference in the fixed assetsto owned fundsratio of every Citizen Co-operative bank of North Gujarat for different financial years.

H_1: There is significant difference in the fixed assetsto owned fundsratio of every Citizen Co-operative bank of North Gujarat for different financial years.

Table 7.15-A

Source of Variation	SS	df	MS	F
Between Banks	752.17	07	107.45	35.97
Between years	1.93	04	0.48	0.16
Error	83.64	28	2.99	
Total	837.74	39		

Table Value for df (7,28) is 2.36 at 5% level of significance.

Table Value for df (4,28) is 2.71 at 5% level of significance.

Table 7.15-A represents the difference for the banks is significant because the table value for df (7,28) is (2.36) which is lower than calculated value of 'F' (35.97). So, null hypothesis (H_0) is rejected and alternative hypothesis (H_1) is accepted. I.e. there is significant difference in the fixed assetsto owned fundsratio of different Citizen Co-operative banks of North Gujarat for every financial year.

Same way the difference for the years is not significant because the table value for df (4,28) is (2.71) which is higher than the calculated value of 'F' (0.16) for years and so here null hypothesis(H_0) is accepted and alternative hypothesis (H_1) is rejected. I.e. there is no significant difference in the fixed assetsto owned fundsratio of every Citizen Co-operative bank of North Gujarat for different financial years.

7.4.16 Other Assets to Working Funds Ratio

The figure shown in the other assets includes stationary stock, telephone deposits, security premium, etc.By this ratio we can know proportion of other assets against bank's working funds. A higher ratio indicates good situation of the bank from assets point of view.Formula for the ratio of other assets to working funds is as follows:

$$\text{Other Assets to Working Funds Ratio} = \frac{\text{Other Assets}}{\text{Working Funds}} *100$$

Other Assetsto Working Funds Ratio of selected citizen cooperative banks of North Gujarat for the study period 2007-08 to 2011-12 is presented in the table 7.16 as follows:

Table 7.16

Other Assets to Working Funds Ratio

YEAR	HIMNSB	MODNSB	MEHNSB	COBMEH	CHHNSB	BANMCB	CHANSB	PATNSB	AVERAGE
2007-08	0.04	0.85	0.74	0.98	0.55	3.23	0.63	0.59	0.95
2008-09	0.04	0.60	0.55	1.42	0.34	3.50	0.77	0.50	0.96
2009-10	0.04	0.65	0.47	1.07	0.32	3.13	0.43	0.49	0.83
2010-11	0.04	0.53	0.51	1.23	0.49	2.96	0.56	0.65	0.87
2011-12	0.30	0.49	0.28	0.73	0.66	3.02	0.30	0.92	0.84
AVERAGE	0.09	0.62	0.51	1.09	0.47	3.17	0.54	0.63	0.89

Source: Annual reports of CCBs during year 2007-08 to 2011-12.

It can be observed from the above table 7.16 for himmatnagar nagarik sahakari bank that Other Assetsto Working FundsRatio was the same 0.04% in the year 2007-08 to 2010-11which was the lowest during all the study period. In the year 2011-12 this ratio was increased to 0.30% which was the highest during all the study period. During all the study period average of this ratio was 0.09%. For all the five years of the study this ratio was lower than its average for four years and higher than its average in the remaining one year.

It is obvious from the above table 7.16 for modasa nagarik sahakari bank that Other Assetsto Working FundsRatio was 0.85% in the year 2007-08which was the highest during all the study period.In the year 2008-09 this ratio was decreased to 0.60% and in the year 2009-10 it was increased to 0.65%. In the year 2010-11 and 2011-12 this ratio was continuously decreased to 0.53% and 0.49% respectively. In the year 2011-12 this ratio was the lowest during all the study period. During all the study period average of this ratio was 0.62%. For all the five years of the study this ratio was lower than its average for threeyears and higher than its average in the remaining two years.

It is apparent from the above table 7.16 for mehsana nagarik sahakari bank that Other Assetsto Working FundsRatio was the same 0.74% in the year 2007-08 which was the highest during all the study period. In the year 2008-09and 2009-10 this ratio was continuously decreased to 0.55% and 0.47% respectively. In the year 2010-11 this ratio was increased to 0.51%. In the year 2011-12 this ratio was decreased to 0.28% which was the lowest during all the study period. During all the study period average of this ratio was 0.51%. For all the five years of the study this ratio was lower than its average for threeyears and higher than its average in the remaining two years.

It is cleared from the above table 7.16 for co-operative bank of mehsana that Other Assetsto Working FundsRatio was 0.98% in the year 2007-08.In the year 2008-09 this ratio was increased to 1.42% and in the year 2009-10 it was decreased to 1.07%.In the year 2008-09 this ratio was the highest during all the study period. In the year 2010-11 this ratio was increased to 1.23%. In the year 2011-12 this ratio was decreased to 0.73% which was the lowest during all the study period. During all the study period average of this ratio was 1.09%. For all the five years of the study this ratio was lower than its average for threeyears and higher than its average in the remaining two years.

It isevident from the above table 7.16 for chhapi nagarik sahakari bank that Other Assetsto Working FundsRatio was 0.55% in the year 2007-08.In the year 2008-09 and 2009-10 this ratio was decreased to 0.34%and 0.32% respectively. In the year 2009-10this ratio was the lowest during all the study period.In the year 2010-11 and 2011-12 this ratio was continuously increased to 0.49% and 0.66% respectively. In the year 2011-12 this ratio was the highest during all the study period.During all the study period average of this ratio was 0.47%. For all the five years of the study this ratio was lower than its average for two years and higher than its average in the remaining three years.

It can be observed from the above table 7.16 for banaskantha mercantile co-operative bank that Other Assetsto Working FundsRatio was 3.23% in theyear 2007-08. In the year 2008-09this ratio was increased to 3.50%which was the highest during all the study period.In the year 2009-10 and 2010-11 this ratio was continuously decreased to 3.13% and 2.96% respectively. In the year 2010-11 this ratio was the lowest during all the study period.In the year 2011-12 this ratio was increased to 3.02%. During all the study period average of this ratio was 3.17%. For all the five years of the study this ratio was lower than its average for threeyears and higher than its average in the remaining two years.

It is obvious from the above table 7.16 for chanasma nagarik sahakari bank that Other Assetsto Working FundsRatio was 0.63% in the year 2007-08.In the year 2008-09this ratio was increased to 0.77%which was the highest during all the study period.In the year 2008-09this ratio was decreased to 0.43%. In the year 2010-11 this ratio was increased to 0.56%. In the year 2011-12 this ratio was decreased to 0.30% which was the lowest during all the study period.During all the study period average of this ratio was 0.54%. For all the five years of the study this ratio was lower than its average for two years and higher than its average in the remaining three years.

It is apparent from the above table 7.16 for patan nagarik sahakari bank that Other Assetsto Working FundsRatio was 0.59% in the year 2007-08. In the year 2008-09 and 2009-10 this ratio was decreased to 0.50%and 0.49% respectively. In the year 2009-10this ratio was the lowest during all the study period.In the year 2010-11 and 2011-12 this ratio was continuously increased to 0.65% and 0.92% respectively. In the year 2011-12 this ratio was the highest during all the study period.During all the study period average of this ratio was 0.63%. For all the five years of the study this ratio was lower than its average for threeyears and higher than its average in the remaining two years.

It can be seen from the above table 7.16 for all Citizen co-operative banks that average of Other Assetsto Working FundsRatio during 2007-08 to 2011-12 was 0.89%. In the year 2007-08 average ratio of all banks was 0.95%. In the year 2008-09this ratio was increased to 0.96%which was the highest during all the study period. In the year 2009-10 this ratio was decreased to 0.83% which was the lowest during all the study period. In the year 2010-11 this ratio was increased to 0.87%. In the year 2011-12 this ratio was decreased to 0.84%.For all the five years of the study average ratio of all banks was lower than its average for three years and higher than its average in remaining two years.

❖ F test (ANOVA) Analysis

The statements of hypothesis are as under:

• Hypothesis between the banks:

H_0: There is no significant difference in the other assetsto working fundsratio of different Citizen Co-operative banks of North Gujarat for every financial year.

H_1: There is significant difference in the other assetsto working fundsratio of different Citizen Co-operative banks of North Gujarat for every financial year.

• Hypothesis between the years:

H_0: There is no significant difference in the other assetsto working fundsratio of every Citizen Co-operative bank of North Gujarat for different financial years.

H_1: There is significant difference in the other assetsto working fundsratio of every Citizen Co-operative bank of North Gujarat for different financial years.

Table 7.16-A

Source of Variation	SS	df	MS	F
Between Banks	32.24	07	4.61	145.36
Between years	0.13	04	0.03	1.02
Error	0.89	28	0.03	
Total	33.26	39		

Table Value for df (7,28) is 2.36 at 5% level of significance.

Table Value for df (4,28) is 2.71 at 5% level of significance.

Table 7.16-A represents the difference for the banks is significant because the table value for df (7,28) is (2.36) which is lower than calculated value of 'F' (145.36). So, null hypothesis (H$_o$) is rejected and alternative hypothesis (H$_1$) is accepted. I.e. there is significant difference in the other assetsto working fundsratio of different Citizen Co-operative banks of North Gujarat for every financial year.

Same way the difference for the years is not significant because the table value for df (4,28) is (2.71) which is higher than the calculated value of 'F' (1.02) for years and so here null hypothesis(H₀) is accepted and alternative hypothesis (H₁) is rejected. I.e. there is no significant difference in the other assetsto working fundsratio of every Citizen Co-operative bank of North Gujarat for different financial years.

7.4.17 Advances to Deposits Ratio

The ratio establishes the relation between deposits received and loansand advances made by the banks. This ratio indicates how much of advanceslent by banks done through deposits. It is the proportion of loan created bybanks from deposits received. If low-cost deposits are effectively utilized onhigh cost lending, it increases the profitability of the organization. A higher ratio reflects the ability of the bank to makeoptimal use of the deposits and lower credit deposits ratio indicates creditcreation incapability of the bank in relation to deposits, which considerablyaffect the profitability of bank.Formula for the ratio of advancesto deposits is as follows:

$$\text{Advances to Deposits Ratio} = \frac{\text{Advances}}{\text{Deposits}} *100$$

Advances to Deposits Ratio of selected citizen cooperative banks of North Gujarat for the study period 2007-08 to 2011-12 is presented in the table 7.17 as follows:

Table 7.17
Advances to Deposits Ratio

YEAR	HIMNSB	MODNSB	MEHNSB	COBMEH	CHHNSB	BANMCB	CHANSB	PATNSB	AVERAGE
2007-08	48.07	63.22	59.79	68.12	42.51	53.67	62.02	58.90	57.04
2008-09	44.35	62.09	55.06	56.33	44.90	52.67	66.50	55.63	54.69
2009-10	43.88	61.15	52.02	49.39	47.94	53.99	70.47	48.39	53.40
2010-11	53.43	56.64	57.22	62.17	51.27	62.63	68.57	43.08	56.88
2011-12	63.48	62.63	62.57	55.91	57.05	56.87	69.91	49.21	59.70
AVERAGE	50.64	61.15	57.33	58.38	48.74	55.97	67.50	51.04	56.34

Source: Annual reports of CCBs during year 2007-08 to 2011-12.

Chart 7.3
Advances to Deposits Ratio

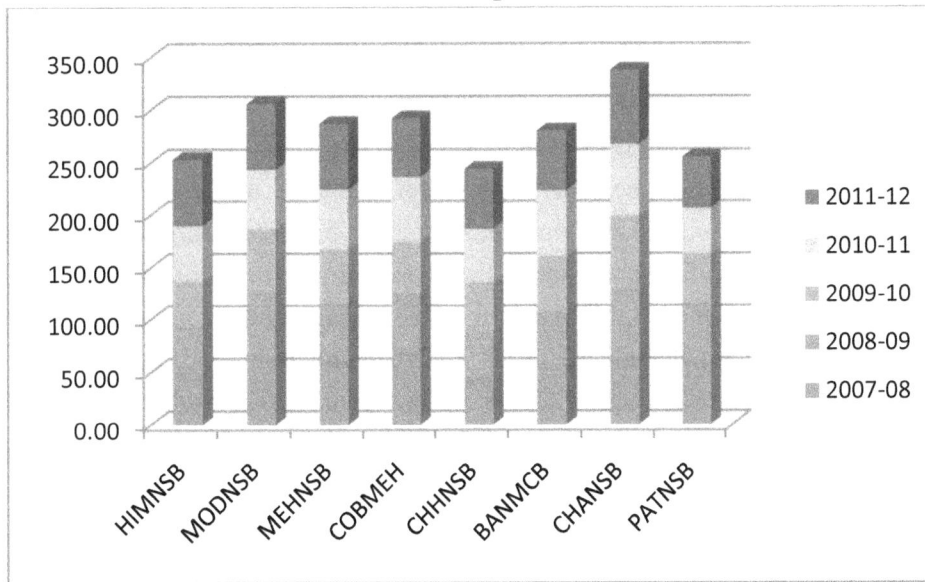

It can be observed from the above table 7.17 for himmatnagar nagarik sahakari bank that Advances to DepositsRatio was the same 48.07% in the year 2007-08.In the year 2008-09and 2009-10 this ratio was continuously decreased to 44.35% and 43.88% respectively.In the year 2009-10 this ratio was the lowest during all the study period. In the year 2010-11 and2011-12 this ratio wascontinuouslyincreased to 53.43% and 63.48% respectively. In the year 2011-12 this ratio was the highest during all the study period. During all the study period average of this ratio was 50.64%. For all the five years of the study this ratio was lower than its average for threeyears and higher than its average in the remaining two years.

It is obvious from the above table 7.17 for modasa nagarik sahakari bank that Advances to DepositsRatio was 63.22% in the year 2007-08which was the highest during all the study period.In the year 2008-09to 2010-11 this ratio was continuously decreased to 62.09%, 61.15% and 56.64% respectively.In the year 2009-10 this ratio was equal to average ratio of all the study period. In the year 2010-11 this ratio was the lowest during all the study period. In the year 2011-12 this ratio was increased to 62.63%. During all the study period average of this ratio was 61.15%. For all the five years of the study this ratio was lower than its average for one year, higher than its average for three years and equal to its average in the remaining one year.

It is apparent from the above table 7.17 for mehsana nagarik sahakari bank that Advances to DepositsRatio was the same 59.79% in the year 2007-08. In the year 2008-09and 2009-10 this ratio was continuously decreased to 55.06% and 52.02% respectively. In the year 2009-10 this ratio was the lowest during all the study period. In the year 2010-11 and 2011-12 this ratio was continuously increased to 57.22%and 62.57% respectively. In the year 2011-12 this ratio was the highest during all the study period. During all the study period average of this ratio was 57.33%. For all the five years of the study this ratio was lower than its average for threeyears and higher than its average in the remaining two years.

It is cleared from the above table 7.17 for co-operative bank of mehsana that Advances to DepositsRatio was 68.12% in the year 2007-08which was the highest during all the study period.In the year 2008-09and 2009-10 this ratio was continuously decreased to 56.33% and 49.39% respectively. In the year 2009-10 this ratio was the lowest during all the study period. In the year 2010-11 this ratio was increased to 62.17% and in the year 2011-12 it was decreased to 55.91%.During all the study period average of this ratio was 58.38%. For all the five years of the study this ratio was lower than its average for threeyears and higher than its average in the remaining two years.

It isevident from the above table 7.17 for chhapi nagarik sahakari bank that Advances to DepositsRatio was 42.51% in the year 2007-08which was the lowest during all the study period.In the year 2008-09 to 2011-12 this ratio was continuously increased to 44.90%, 47.94%, 51.27% and 57.05% respectively. In the year 2011-12 this ratio was the highest during all the study period.During all the study period average of this ratio was 48.74%. For all the five years of the study this ratio was lower than its average for threeyears and higher than its average in the remaining two years.

It can be observed from the above table 7.17 for banaskantha mercantile co-operative bank that Advances to DepositsRatio was 53.67% in theyear 2007-08. In the year 2008-09this ratio was decreased to 52.67%which was the lowest during all the study period.In the year 2009-10 and 2010-11 this ratio was continuously increased to 53.99% and 62.63% respectively. In the year 2010-11 this ratio was the highest during all the study period.In the year 2011-12 this ratio was decreased to 56.87%. During all the study period average of this ratio was 55.97%. For all the five years of the study this ratio was lower than its average for threeyears and higher than its average in the remaining two years.

It is obvious from the above table 7.17 for chanasma nagarik sahakari bank that Advances to DepositsRatio was 62.02% in the year 2007-08which was the lowest during all the study period.In the year 2008-09and 2009-10 this ratio was continuously increased to 66.50% and 70.47% respectively. In the year 2009-10 this ratio was the highest during all the study period.In the year 2010-11this ratio was decreased to 68.57% and in the year 2011-12 it was increased to 69.91%. During all the study period average of this ratio was 67.50%. For all the five years of the study this ratio was lower than its average for two years and higher than its average in the remaining three years.

It is apparent from the above table 7.17 for patan nagarik sahakari bank that Advances to DepositsRatio was 58.90% in the year 2007-08which was the highest during all the study period. In the year 2008-09 to 2010-11 this ratio was continuously decreased to 55.63%, 48.39% and 43.08% respectively. In the year 2010-11this ratio was the lowest during all the study period.In the year 2011-12 this ratio was increased to 49.21%. During all the study period average of this ratio was 51.04%. For all the five years of the study this ratio was lower than its average for threeyears and higher than its average in the remaining two years.

It can be seen from the above table 7.17 for all Citizen co-operative banks that average of Advances to DepositsRatio during 2007-08 to 2011-12 was 56.34%. In the year 2007-08 average ratio of all banks was 57.04%. In the year 2008-09and 2009-10 this ratio was continuously decreased to 54.69% and 53.40% respectively. In the year 2009-10 this ratio was the lowest during all the study period. In the year 2010-11 this ratio was increased to 56.88%. In the year 2011-12 this ratio was decreased to 59.70% which was the highest during all the study period. For all the five years of the study average ratio of all banks was lower than its average for two years and higher than its average in remaining three years.

❖ **F test (ANOVA) Analysis**

The statements of hypothesis are as under:

- **Hypothesis between the banks:**

H_0: There is no significant difference in the advances to depositsratio of different Citizen Co-operative banks of North Gujarat for every financial year.

H_1: There is significant difference in the advances to depositsratio of different Citizen Co-operative banks of North Gujarat for every financial year.

- **Hypothesis between the years:**

H_0: There is no significant difference in the advances to depositsratio of every Citizen Co-operative bank of North Gujarat for different financial years.

H_1: There is significant difference in the advances to depositsratio of every Citizen Co-operative bank of North Gujarat for different financial years.

Table 7.17-A

Source of Variation	SS	df	MS	F
Between Banks	1356.04	07	193.72	7.04
Between years	187.44	04	46.86	1.70
Error	770.26	28	27.51	
Total	2313.74	39		

Table Value for df (7,28) is 2.36 at 5% level of significance.

Table Value for df (4,28) is 2.71 at 5% level of significance.

Table 7.17-A represents the difference for the banks is significant because the table value for df (7,28) is (2.36) which is lower than calculated value of 'F' (7.04). So, null hypothesis (H_0) is rejected and alternative hypothesis (H_1) is accepted. I.e. there is significant difference in the advances to depositsratio of different Citizen Co-operative banks of North Gujarat for every financial year.

Same way the difference for the years is not significant because the table value for df (4,28) is (2.71) which is higher than the calculated value of 'F' (1.70) for years and so here null hypothesis(H_0) is accepted and alternative hypothesis (H_1) is rejected.

I.e. there is no significant difference in the advances to depositsratio of every Citizen Co-operative bank of North Gujarat for different financial years.

7.5 Conclusion

In this chapter researcher has tried to analyze **assets and debts** of selected Citizen co-operative banks of north Gujarat. For an analysis of **assets and debts** various seventeen ratios were calculated from the annual reports of Citizen Co-operative bank of North Gujarat. The **assets and debts** of different Citizen Co-operative banks were analyzed with reference to its components such as working fund ratios, deposits ratios, advances ratios etc.

In the analysis of **assets and debts**, balance sheet of selected Citizen co-operative banks has been analyzed with the help of various seventeen ratios and "F" test (ANOVA) of all ratios proves that there is no uniformity in **assets and debts** of different Citizen Co-operative banks of North Gujarat for every financial year and majority of ratios proves that there is uniformity in **assets and debts** of every Citizen Co-operative banks of North Gujarat for different financial year.

References

1. Williams, Jan R., Susan F. Haka, Mark S. Bettner and Joseph V. Carcello, "Financial & Managerial Accounting" McGraw-Hill Irwin. (2008) p.40.
2. Paul G. Hastings, "The Management of Business Finance" New Jersey, D von Norstrand Company. (1966) p.16
3. Harry G. Guthmann, "Analysis of Financial Statements" New Delhi, Prentice Hall of India Pvt. Ltd. (1964) p.20.
4. Paul G. Hastings, *op.cit., p.16*
5. Sullivan, Arthur and Steven M. Sheffrin, "Economics: Principles in action" New Jersey, Pearson Prentice Hall. (2003) p.272.

Chapter-8
Findings and Suggestions

8.1   Introduction
8.2   Findings
8.3   Suggestions

8.1   Introduction

The Co-operative banks are an important constituent of the Indian financial system.Co-operative banks have completed 100 years of existence in India. They play a very important role in the financial system. The co-operative banks in India form an integral part of our money market today.Without the help of co-operative banks, millions of people in India would be lacking the much needed financial support. Co-operative banks take active part in local communities and local development with a stronger commitment and social responsibilities. These banks are best vehicles for taking banking to doorsteps of common men, unbanked people in urban and rural areas.

Citizen Co-operative Banks are Primary Co-operative Banks organized on Co-operative basis, operating in metropolitan, urban and semi-urban areas to cater the needs of specific types or groups of members pertaining to certain class of community, small scale industrial units, trade, professions, etc.Gujarat holds second position in the development of the Citizen Co-operative Banks in India.CCBs in Gujarat have recorded commendable achievement in the entire sphere of banking operations.

The present study deals with financial analysis of Citizen Co-operative Banks of North Gujarat which are organized in financial services. For these purpose eight Citizen Co-Operative banks were selected by the researcher. For financial analysis of these banks, the data related to all the eight Citizen Co-Operative banks for the period2007-08 to 2011-12 have been collected by the researcher and various techniques of financial analysis like Ratio Analysisand statistical techniques have been applied to analyze and drew conclusion. The present study has been divided in eight chapters and chapter- wise findings have been discussed as here under.This chapter summarizes the major findings of the study. On the basisof the study, the researcher offers some suggestions for the improvement of Citizen Co-operative Banks.

8.2   Findings

The main objective of the present research was to analyze income and expenses, profitability, productivity, assets and debts of Citizen Co-operative Banks of North

Gujaratand make suggestions for effective financial management of the Citizen Co-operative banks of North Gujarat. The major findings of the study were as under:

- **Analysis of Income and Expenses**

1)   Interest Income to Total Income Ratio

F test of CCBs under the study represents the difference for the banks is significant because the table value (2.36) is lower than calculated value of 'F' (3.85)So,alternative hypothesis (H_1) is accepted and Same way the difference for the years is also significant because the table value (2.71) is lower than the calculated value of 'F' (3.55) for years, so here alsoalternative hypothesis (H_1) is accepted.I.e. there is significant difference in the interest income to total income ratio of different Citizen Co-operative banks of North Gujarat for every financial year and there is significant difference in the interest income to total income ratio of every Citizen Co-operative bank of North Gujarat for different financial years.

2)   Non-Interest Income to Total Income Ratio

F test of CCBs under the study represents the difference for the banks is significant because the table value (2.36) is lower than calculated value of 'F' (3.85)So,alternative hypothesis (H_1) is accepted and Same way the difference for the years is also significant because the table value (2.71) is lower than the calculated value of 'F' (3.55) for years, so here alsoalternative hypothesis (H_1) is accepted.I.e. there is significant difference in the non-interest income to total income ratio of different Citizen Co-operative banks of North Gujarat for every financial year and there is significant difference in the non-interest income to total income ratio of every Citizen Co-operative bank of North Gujarat for different financial years.

3)   Interest Expense to Total Expense Ratio

F test of CCBs under the study represents the difference for the banks is significant because the table value (2.36) is lower than calculated value of 'F' (4.05)So,alternative hypothesis (H_1) is accepted and Same way the difference for the years is not significant because the table value (2.71) is higher than the calculated value of 'F' (1.60) for years, so here null hypothesis(H_0) is accepted.I.e. there is significant difference in the interest expense to total expenseratio of different Citizen Co-operative banks of North Gujarat for every financial year and there is no significant difference in the interest expense to total expense ratio of every Citizen Co-operative bank of North Gujarat for different financial years.

4)   Operating Expense to Total Expense Ratio

F test of CCBs under the study represents the difference for the banks is significant because the table value (2.36) is lower than calculated value of 'F'

(52.26)So,alternative hypothesis (H₁) is accepted and Same way the difference for the years is not significant because the table value (2.71) is higher than the calculated value of 'F' (1.77) for years, so here null hypothesis(H₀) is accepted.I.e. there is significant difference in the Operatingexpense to total expenseratio of different Citizen Co-operative banks of North Gujarat for every financial year and there is no significant difference in the Operatingexpense to total expense ratio of every Citizen Co-operative bank of North Gujarat for different financial years.

5) Other Expense to Total Expense Ratio

F test of CCBs under the study represents the difference for the banks is significant because the table value (2.36) is lower than calculated value of 'F' (3.71)So,alternative hypothesis (H₁) is accepted and Same way the difference for the years is not significant because the table value (2.71) is higher than the calculated value of 'F' (0.58) for years, so here null hypothesis(H₀) is accepted.I.e. there is significant difference in the otherexpenseto total expenseratio of different Citizen Co-operative banks of North Gujarat for every financial year and there is no significant difference in the otherexpenseto total expense ratio of every Citizen Co-operative bank of North Gujarat for different financial years.

6) Net Profit to Total Income Ratio

F test of CCBs under the study represents the difference for the banks is significant because the table value (2.36) is lower than calculated value of 'F' (22.83)So,alternative hypothesis (H₁) is accepted and Same way the difference for the years is not significant because the table value (2.71) is higher than the calculated value of 'F' (0.41) for years, so here null hypothesis(H₀) is accepted.I.e. there is significant difference in the net Profit to total incomeratio of different Citizen Co-operative banks of North Gujarat for every financial year and there is no significant difference in the net Profit to total incomeratio of every Citizen Co-operative bank of North Gujarat for different financial years.

In the analysis of income and expenses above six ratios and "F" test (ANOVA) of all ratios proves that there is no uniformity in income and expenses of different Citizen Co-operative banks of North Gujarat for every financial year.

• Analysis of Profitability
1) Interest Income to Working Funds Ratio

F test of CCBs under the study represents the difference for the banks is significant because the table value (2.36) is lower than calculated value of 'F' (8.29)So,alternative hypothesis (H₁) is accepted and Same way the difference for the years is not significant because the table value (2.71) is higher than the calculated value of 'F' (1.92) for years, so here null hypothesis(H₀) is accepted.I.e. there is significant difference in the interest income to working funds ratio of different Citizen Co-operative banks of North Gujarat for every financial year and there is no significant difference in the interest income to working funds ratio of every Citizen Co-operative bank of North Gujarat for different financial years.

2) Interest Expense to Working Funds Ratio

F test of CCBs under the study represents the difference for the banks is significant because the table value (2.36) is lower than calculated value of 'F' (6.23)So,alternative hypothesis (H_1) is accepted and Same way the difference for the years is not significant because the table value (2.71) is higher than the calculated value of 'F' (1.54) for years, so here null hypothesis(H_o) is accepted.I.e. there is significant difference in the interest expenseto working funds ratio of different Citizen Co-operative banks of North Gujarat for every financial year and there is no significant difference in the interest expenseto working funds ratio of every Citizen Co-operative bank of North Gujarat for different financial years.

3) Spread to Working Funds Ratio

F test of CCBs under the study represents the difference for the banks is significant because the table value (2.36) is lower than calculated value of 'F' (5.08)So,alternative hypothesis (H_1) is accepted and Same way the difference for the years is not significant because the table value (2.71) is higher than the calculated value of 'F' (2.70) for years, so here null hypothesis(H_o) is accepted.I.e. there is significant difference in the spreadto working funds ratio of different Citizen Co-operative banks of North Gujarat for every financial year and there is no significant difference in the spreadto working funds ratio of every Citizen Co-operative bank of North Gujarat for different financial years.

4) Non-Interest Income to Working Funds Ratio

F test of CCBs under the study represents the difference for the banks is significant because the table value (2.36) is lower than calculated value of 'F' (4.77)So,alternative hypothesis (H_1) is accepted and Same way the difference for the years is also significant because the table value (2.71) is lower than the calculated value of 'F' (4.04) for years, so here alsoalternative hypothesis (H_1) is accepted.I.e. there is significant difference in the non-Interest Income to working funds ratio of different Citizen Co-operative banks of North Gujarat for every financial year and there is significant difference in the non-Interest Income to working funds ratio of every Citizen Co-operative bank of North Gujarat for different financial years.

5) Non-Interest Expense to Working Funds Ratio

F test of CCBs under the study represents the difference for the banks is significant because the table value (2.36) is lower than calculated value of 'F'

(6.41)So,alternative hypothesis (H₁) is accepted and Same way the difference for the years is not significant because the table value (2.71) is higher than the calculated value of 'F' (1.73) for years, so here null hypothesis(H₀) is accepted.I.e. there is significant difference in the non-interest expenseto working funds ratio of different Citizen Co-operative banks of North Gujarat for every financial year and there is no significant difference in the non-interest expenseto working funds ratio of every Citizen Co-operative bank of North Gujarat for different financial years.

6)   **Burden to Working Funds Ratio**

F test of CCBs under the study represents the difference for the banks is significant because the table value (2.36) is lower than calculated value of 'F' (5.19)So,alternative hypothesis (H₁) is accepted and Same way the difference for the years is not significant because the table value (2.71) is higher than the calculated value of 'F' (2.41) for years, so here null hypothesis(H₀) is accepted.I.e. there is significant difference in the burdento working funds ratio of different Citizen Co-operative banks of North Gujarat for every financial year and there is no significant difference in the burdento working funds ratio of every Citizen Co-operative bank of North Gujarat for different financial years.

7)   **Net Profit to Working Funds Ratio**

F test of CCBs under the study represents the difference for the banks is significant because the table value (2.36) is lower than calculated value of 'F' (20.51)So,alternative hypothesis (H₁) is accepted and Same way the difference for the years is not significant because the table value (2.71) is higher than the calculated value of 'F' (1.05) for years, so here null hypothesis(H₀) is accepted.I.e. there is significant difference in the net profitto working funds ratio of different Citizen Co-operative banks of North Gujarat for every financial year and there is no significant difference in the net profitto working funds ratio of every Citizen Co-operative bank of North Gujarat for different financial years.

8)   **Net Profit to Owned Funds Ratio**

F test of CCBs under the study represents the difference for the banks is significant because the table value (2.36) is lower than calculated value of 'F' (18.41)So,alternative hypothesis (H₁) is accepted and Same way the difference for the years is not significant because the table value (2.71) is higher than the calculated value of 'F' (2.61) for years, so here null hypothesis(H₀) is accepted.I.e. there is significant difference in the net profit to owned funds ratio of different Citizen Co-operative banks of North Gujarat for every financial year and there is no significant difference in the net profit to owned funds ratio of every Citizen Co-operative bank of North Gujarat for different financial years.

9)   **Net Profit to Shareholder's EquityRatio**

F test of CCBs under the study represents the difference for the banks is significant because the table value (2.36) is lower than calculated value of 'F' (51.49)So,alternative hypothesis (H_1) is accepted and Same way the difference for the years is not significant because the table value (2.71) is higher than the calculated value of 'F' (2.59) for years, so here null hypothesis(H_0) is accepted.I.e. there is significant difference in the net profit to shareholder's equityratio of different Citizen Co-operative banks of North Gujarat for every financial year and there is no significant difference in the net profit to shareholder's equityratio of every Citizen Co-operative bank of North Gujarat for different financial years.

In the analysis of profitability various nine ratios and "F" test (ANOVA) of all ratios proves that there is no uniformity in profitability of different Citizen Co-operative banks of North Gujarat for every financial year.

- **Analysis of Productivity**

1)   **Deposits per Employee**

F test of CCBs under the study represents the difference for the banks is significant because the table value (2.36) is lower than calculated value of 'F' (29.22)So,alternative hypothesis (H_1) is accepted and Same way the difference for the years is also significant because the table value (2.71) is lower than the calculated value of 'F' (16.11) for years, so here alsoalternative hypothesis (H_1) is accepted.I.e. there is significant difference in the deposits per employee ratio of different Citizen Co-operative banks of North Gujarat for every financial year and there is significant difference in the deposits per employee ratio of every Citizen Co-operative bank of North Gujarat for different financial years.

2)   **Advances per Employee**

F test of CCBs under the study represents the difference for the banks is significant because the table value (2.36) is lower than calculated value of 'F' (65.91)So,alternative hypothesis (H_1) is accepted and Same way the difference for the years is also significant because the table value (2.71) is lower than the calculated value of 'F' (33.70) for years, so here alsoalternative hypothesis (H_1) is accepted.I.e. there is significant difference in the advances per employee ratio of different Citizen Co-operative banks of North Gujarat for every financial year and there is significant difference in the advances per employee ratio of every Citizen Co-operative bank of North Gujarat for different financial years.

3)   **Business per Employee**

F test of CCBs under the study represents the difference for the banks is significant because the table value (2.36) is lower than calculated value of 'F'

(45.38)So,alternative hypothesis (H₁) is accepted and Same way the difference for the years is also significant because the table value (2.71) is lower than the calculated value of 'F' (24.53) for years, so here alsoalternative hypothesis (H₁) is accepted.I.e. there is significant difference in the business per employee ratio of different Citizen Co-operative banks of North Gujarat for every financial year and there is significant difference in the business per employee ratio of every Citizen Co-operative bank of North Gujarat for different financial years.

4) **Spread per Employee**

F test of CCBs under the study represents the difference for the banks is significant because the table value (2.36) is lower than calculated value of 'F' (23.15)So,alternative hypothesis (H₁) is accepted and Same way the difference for the years is also significant because the table value (2.71) is lower than the calculated value of 'F' (21.18) for years, so here alsoalternative hypothesis (H₁) is accepted.I.e. there is significant difference in the spread per employee ratio of different Citizen Co-operative banks of North Gujarat for every financial year and there is significant difference in the spread per employee ratio of every Citizen Co-operative bank of North Gujarat for different financial years.

5) **Operating Expenses per Employee**

F test of CCBs under the study represents the difference for the banks is significant because the table value (2.36) is lower than calculated value of 'F' (45.42)So,alternative hypothesis (H₁) is accepted and Same way the difference for the years is also significant because the table value (2.71) is lower than the calculated value of 'F' (40.21) for years, so here alsoalternative hypothesis (H₁) is accepted.I.e. there is significant difference in the operating expenses per employee ratio of different Citizen Co-operative banks of North Gujarat for every financial year and there is significant difference in the operating expensesper employee ratio of every Citizen Co-operative bank of North Gujarat for different financial years.

6) **Net Profit per Employee**

F test of CCBs under the study represents the difference for the banks is significant because the table value (2.36) is lower than calculated value of 'F' (38.42)So,alternative hypothesis (H₁) is accepted and Same way the difference for the years is also significant because the table value (2.71) is lower than the calculated value of 'F' (6.69) for years, so here alsoalternative hypothesis (H₁) is accepted.I.e. there is significant difference in the net profitper employee ratio of different Citizen Co-operative banks of North Gujarat for every financial year and there is significant difference in the net profitper employee ratio of every Citizen Co-operative bank of North Gujarat for different financial years.

7) **Deposits per Branch**

F test of CCBs under the study represents the difference for the banks is significant because the table value (2.36) is lower than calculated value of 'F' (79.39) So, alternative hypothesis (H_1) is accepted and Same way the difference for the years is also significant because the table value (2.71) is lower than the calculated value of 'F' (22.36) for years, so here also alternative hypothesis (H_1) is accepted. I.e. there is significant difference in the deposits per branchratio of different Citizen Co-operative banks of North Gujarat for every financial year and there is significant difference in the deposits per branchratio of every Citizen Co-operative bank of North Gujarat for different financial years.

8) **Advances per Branch**

F test of CCBs under the study represents the difference for the banks is significant because the table value (2.36) is lower than calculated value of 'F' (173.36) So, alternative hypothesis (H_1) is accepted and Same way the difference for the years is also significant because the table value (2.71) is lower than the calculated value of 'F' (49.80) for years, so here also alternative hypothesis (H_1) is accepted. I.e. there is significant difference in the advances per branchratio of different Citizen Co-operative banks of North Gujarat for every financial year and there is significant difference in the advances per branchratio of every Citizen Co-operative bank of North Gujarat for different financial years.

9) **Business per Branch**

F test of CCBs under the study represents the difference for the banks is significant because the table value (2.36) is lower than calculated value of 'F' (140.60) So, alternative hypothesis (H_1) is accepted and Same way the difference for the years is also significant because the table value (2.71) is lower than the calculated value of 'F' (39.96) for years, so here also alternative hypothesis (H_1) is accepted. I.e. there is significant difference in the business per branchratio of different Citizen Co-operative banks of North Gujarat for every financial year and there is significant difference in the business per branchratio of every Citizen Co-operative bank of North Gujarat for different financial years.

10) **Spread per Branch**

F test of CCBs under the study represents the difference for the banks is significant because the table value (2.36) is lower than calculated value of 'F' (97.28) So, alternative hypothesis (H_1) is accepted and Same way the difference for the years is also significant because the table value (2.71) is lower than the calculated value of 'F' (27.37) for years, so here also alternative hypothesis (H_1) is accepted. I.e. there is significant difference in the spread per branchratio of different Citizen Co-operative banks of North Gujarat for every financial year and there is significant difference in the spread per branchratio of every Citizen Co-operative bank of North Gujarat for different financial years.

11) Operating Expenses per Branch

F test of CCBs under the study represents the difference for the banks is significant because the table value (2.36) is lower than calculated value of 'F' (138.25) So, alternative hypothesis (H_1) is accepted and Same way the difference for the years is also significant because the table value (2.71) is lower than the calculated value of 'F' (21.05) for years, so here also alternative hypothesis (H_1) is accepted. I.e. there is significant difference in the operating expenses per branchratio of different Citizen Co-operative banks of North Gujarat for every financial year and there is significant difference in the operating expenses per branchratio of every Citizen Co-operative bank of North Gujarat for different financial years.

12) Net Profit per Branch

F test of CCBs under the study represents the difference for the banks is significant because the table value (2.36) is lower than calculated value of 'F' (83.06) So, alternative hypothesis (H_1) is accepted and Same way the difference for the years is also significant because the table value (2.71) is lower than the calculated value of 'F' (12.07) for years, so here also alternative hypothesis (H_1) is accepted. I.e. there is significant difference in the net profitper branchratio of different Citizen Co-operative banks of North Gujarat for every financial year and there is significant difference in the net profitper branchratio of every Citizen Co-operative bank of North Gujarat for different financial years.

In the analysis of **productivity** various twelve ratios and "F" test (ANOVA) of all ratios proves that there is no uniformity in **productivity** of different Citizen Co-operative banks of North Gujarat for every financial year and there is no uniformity in **productivity** of every Citizen Co-operative banks of North Gujarat for different financial year.

• Analysis of Assets and Debts

1) Owned Funds to Working Funds Ratio

F test of CCBs under the study represents the difference for the banks is significant because the table value (2.36) is lower than calculated value of 'F' (9.67) So, alternative hypothesis (H_1) is accepted and Same way the difference for the years is also significant because the table value (2.71) is lower than the calculated value of 'F' (3.70) for years, so here also alternative hypothesis (H_1) is accepted. I.e. there is significant difference in the owned funds to working funds ratio of different Citizen Co-operative banks of North Gujarat for every financial year and there is significant difference in the owned funds to working funds ratio of every Citizen Co-operative bank of North Gujarat for different financial years.

2) Term Deposits to Total Deposits Ratio

F test of CCBs under the study represents the difference for the banks is significant because the table value (2.36) is lower than calculated value of 'F' (140.36)So,alternative hypothesis (H_1) is accepted and Same way the difference for the years is not significant because the table value (2.71) is higher than the calculated value of 'F' (1.63) for years, so here null hypothesis(H_0) is accepted.I.e. there is significant difference in the term deposits to total depositsratio of different Citizen Co-operative banks of North Gujarat for every financial year and there is no significant difference in the term deposits to total depositsratio of every Citizen Co-operative bank of North Gujarat for different financial years.

3) Saving Deposits to Total Deposits Ratio

F test of CCBs under the study represents the difference for the banks is significant because the table value (2.36) is lower than calculated value of 'F' (75.51) So, alternative hypothesis (H_1) is accepted and Same way the difference for the years is also significant because the table value (2.71) is lower than the calculated value of 'F' (4.40) for years, so here also alternative hypothesis (H_1) is accepted. I.e. there is significant difference in the saving deposits to total deposits ratio of different Citizen Co-operative banks of North Gujarat for every financial year and there is significant difference in the saving deposits to total deposits ratio of every Citizen Co-operative bank of North Gujarat for different financial years.

4) Current Deposits to Total Deposits Ratio

F test of CCBs under the study represents the difference for the banks is significant because the table value (2.36) is lower than calculated value of 'F' (210.39)So,alternative hypothesis (H_1) is accepted and Same way the difference for the years is not significant because the table value (2.71) is higher than the calculated value of 'F' (0.73) for years, so here null hypothesis(H_0) is accepted.I.e. there is significant difference in the current deposits to total depositsratio of different Citizen Co-operative banks of North Gujarat for every financial year and there is no significant difference in the current deposits to total depositsratio of every Citizen Co-operative bank of North Gujarat for different financial years.

5) Total Deposits to Working Funds Ratio

F test of CCBs under the study represents the difference for the banks is significant because the table value (2.36) is lower than calculated value of 'F' (36.55)So,alternative hypothesis (H_1) is accepted and Same way the difference for the years is not significant because the table value (2.71) is higher than the calculated value of 'F' (1.23) for years, so here null hypothesis(H_0) is accepted.I.e. there is significant difference in the total deposits to working fundsratio of different Citizen Co-operative banks of North Gujarat for every financial year and there is no significant difference in the total deposits to working fundsratio of every Citizen Co-operative bank of North Gujarat for different financial years.

6) Other Liabilities to Working Funds Ratio

F test of CCBs under the study represents the difference for the banks is significant because the table value (2.36) is lower than calculated value of 'F' (124.74)So,alternative hypothesis (H_1) is accepted and Same way the difference for the years is not significant because the table value (2.71) is higher than the calculated value of 'F' (0.22) for years, so here null hypothesis(H_o) is accepted.I.e. there is significant difference in the other liabilities to working fundsratio of different Citizen Co-operative banks of North Gujarat for every financial year and there is no significant difference in the other liabilities to working fundsratio of every Citizen Co-operative bank of North Gujarat for different financial years.

7) Investments to Working Funds Ratio

F test of CCBs under the study represents the difference for the banks is significant because the table value (2.36) is lower than calculated value of 'F' (52.01)So,alternative hypothesis (H_1) is accepted and Same way the difference for the years is not significant because the table value (2.71) is higher than the calculated value of 'F' (1.78) for years, so here null hypothesis(H_o) is accepted.I.e. there is significant difference in the investments to working fundsratio of different Citizen Co-operative banks of North Gujarat for every financial year and there is no significant difference in the investments to working fundsratio of every Citizen Co-operative bank of North Gujarat for different financial years.

8) Short term Advances to Total Advances Ratio

F test of CCBs under the study represents the difference for the banks is significant because the table value (2.36) is lower than calculated value of 'F' (83.00) So, alternative hypothesis (H_1) is accepted and Same way the difference for the years is also significant because the table value (2.71) is lower than the calculated value of 'F' (7.01) for years, so here also alternative hypothesis (H_1) is accepted. I.e. there is significant difference in the short term advances to total advances ratio of different Citizen Co-operative banks of North Gujarat for every financial year and there is significant difference in the short term advances to total advances ratio of every Citizen Co-operative bank of North Gujarat for different financial years.

9) Medium term Advances to Total Advances Ratio

F test of CCBs under the study represents the difference for the banks is significant because the table value (2.36) is lower than calculated value of 'F' (28.68) So, alternative hypothesis (H_1) is accepted and Same way the difference for the years is also significant because the table value (2.71) is lower than the calculated value of 'F'

(4.15) for years, so here also alternative hypothesis (H₁) is accepted. I.e. there is significant difference in the medium term advances to total advances ratio of different Citizen Co-operative banks of North Gujarat for every financial year and there is significant difference in the medium term advances to total advancesratio of every Citizen Co-operative bank of North Gujarat for different financial years.

10) Long term Advances to Total Advances Ratio

F test of CCBs under the study represents the difference for the banks is significant because the table value (2.36) is lower than calculated value of 'F' (35.73)So,alternative hypothesis (H₁) is accepted and Same way the difference for the years is not significant because the table value (2.71) is higher than the calculated value of 'F' (0.36) for years, so here null hypothesis(Hₒ) is accepted.I.e. there is significant difference in the long term advances to total advances ratio of different Citizen Co-operative banks of North Gujarat for every financial year and there is no significant difference in the long term advances to total advances ratio of every Citizen Co-operative bank of North Gujarat for different financial years.

11) Total Advances to Working Funds Ratio

F test of CCBs under the study represents the difference for the banks is significant because the table value (2.36) is lower than calculated value of 'F' (15.45)So,alternative hypothesis (H₁) is accepted and Same way the difference for the years is not significant because the table value (2.71) is higher than the calculated value of 'F' (2.67) for years, so here null hypothesis(Hₒ) is accepted.I.e. there is significant difference in the total advances to working fundsratio of different Citizen Co-operative banks of North Gujarat for every financial year and there is no significant difference in the total advances to working fundsratio of every Citizen Co-operative bank of North Gujarat for different financial years.

12) NPA to Total Advances Ratio

F test of CCBs under the study represents the difference for the banks is significant because the table value (2.36) is lower than calculated value of 'F' (23.16) So, alternative hypothesis (H₁) is accepted and Same way the difference for the years is also significant because the table value (2.71) is lower than the calculated value of 'F' (7.25) for years, so here also alternative hypothesis (H₁) is accepted. I.e. there is significant difference in the NPA to total advances ratio of different Citizen Co-operative banks of North Gujarat for every financial year and there is significant difference in the NPA to total advances ratio of every Citizen Co-operative bank of North Gujarat for different financial years.

13) Cash and Bank to Working Funds Ratio

F test of CCBs under the study represents the difference for the banks is significant because the table value (2.36) is lower than calculated value of 'F' (27.79)

So, alternative hypothesis (H₁) is accepted and Same way the difference for the years is also significant because the table value (2.71) is lower than the calculated value of 'F' (3.95) for years, so here also alternative hypothesis (H₁) is accepted. I.e. there is significant difference in the cash and bankto working fundsratio of different Citizen Co-operative banks of North Gujarat for every financial year and there is significant difference in the cash and bankto working fundsratio of every Citizen Co-operative bank of North Gujarat for different financial years.

14) Fixed Assets to Working Funds Ratio

F test of CCBs under the study represents the difference for the banks is significant because the table value (2.36) is lower than calculated value of 'F' (21.54)So,alternative hypothesis (H₁) is accepted and Same way the difference for the years is not significant because the table value (2.71) is higher than the calculated value of 'F' (0.58) for years, so here null hypothesis(H₀) is accepted.I.e. there is significant difference in the fixed assetsto working fundsratio of different Citizen Co-operative banks of North Gujarat for every financial year and there is no significant difference in the fixed assetsto working fundsratio of every Citizen Co-operative bank of North Gujarat for different financial years.

15) Fixed Assets to Owned Funds Ratio

F test of CCBs under the study represents the difference for the banks is significant because the table value (2.36) is lower than calculated value of 'F' (35.97)So,alternative hypothesis (H₁) is accepted and Same way the difference for the years is not significant because the table value (2.71) is higher than the calculated value of 'F' (0.16) for years, so here null hypothesis(H₀) is accepted.I.e. there is significant difference in the fixed assetsto owned fundsratio of different Citizen Co-operative banks of North Gujarat for every financial year and there is no significant difference in the fixed assetsto owned fundsratio of every Citizen Co-operative bank of North Gujarat for different financial years.

16) Other Assets to Working Funds Ratio

F test of CCBs under the study represents the difference for the banks is significant because the table value (2.36) is lower than calculated value of 'F' (145.36)So,alternative hypothesis (H₁) is accepted and Same way the difference for the years is not significant because the table value (2.71) is higher than the calculated value of 'F' (1.02) for years, so here null hypothesis(H₀) is accepted.I.e. there is significant difference in the other assetsto working fundsratio of different Citizen Co-operative banks of North Gujarat for every financial year and there is no significant difference in the other assetsto working fundsratio of every Citizen Co-operative bank of North Gujarat for different financial years.

17) Advances to Deposits Ratio

F test of CCBs under the study represents the difference for the banks is significant because the table value (2.36) is lower than calculated value of 'F' (7.04)So,alternative hypothesis (H₁) is accepted and Same way the difference for the years is not significant because the table value (2.71) is higher than the calculated value of 'F' (1.70) for years, so here null hypothesis(H₀) is accepted.I.e. there is significant difference in the advances to depositsratio of different Citizen Co-operative banks of North Gujarat for every financial year and there is no significant difference in the advances to depositsratio of every Citizen Co-operative bank of North Gujarat for different financial years.

In the analysis of **assets and debts**various seventeen ratios and "F" test (ANOVA) of all ratios proves that there is no uniformity in **assets and debts** of different Citizen Co-operative banks of North Gujarat for every financial year,

8.3   Suggestions

By referring all these findings, there are some suggestions by the researcher for better performance of the banks. These suggestions are as under:

1)   It has been found that non-interest income in the Patan Nagarik Sahakari Bank Ltd. was negligible in the bank's total income. So bank should try to improve income from commission, exchange and brokerage and other receipts including income from non-banking assets.Many state level competitive exams are conducted by different agencies/commissions. The agencies organizing these exams should authorize CCBs to collect challan for thesame. This will also increase bank's non-fund based income.

2)   The net profit of majority of the CCBs under study has declined over the period of study. Hence, the banks should try to increase their deposit base by introducing innovative deposit schemes other than the existing ones.

3)   To improve profitability of the CCBs, it is suggested that the management of the CCBs should try to reduce operating cost by exercising efficient control over their cost of external funds and increasing operating income by utilizing funds to their full capacity.

4)   To exercise efficient control over their cost of external funds, CCBs should try to obtain more low cost funds. For the reduction and control of cost, techniques like budgetary control, standard costing and value analysis should be implemented.

5)   It has been suggested that operating expenses in the Himmatnagar Nagarik Sahakari Bank Ltd. showed higher trend in compare of all other banks. So, bank should take immediate steps to control operating expenses.

6)   It has been found that otherexpenses in the Co-operative Bank of Mehsana Ltd. were higher than average of all banks for all the study period. So bank should make try to reduce otherexpenses.

7)   It has been seen that interest expense to working funds ratio in the Chanasma Nagarik Sahakari Bank Ltd. was higher than average of all banks for all the study period. So the bank should make efforts to reduce cost of interest expenses.

8)   It has been suggested that burden in the Himmatnagar Nagarik Sahakari Bank Ltd. was shows higher trend in compare of all other banks. So, bank should take immediate steps to control operating expenses. Therefore, bank should make an effort to improve management of burden. To reduce the burden, either the interest income should be increased or the non-interest expenditure should be reduced or by both.

9)   It has been found that net profit per employeein the Co-operative Bank of Mehsana Ltd. was lower than average of all banks for all the study period. So the bank should make concerted efforts to increase net profit per employee.

10)   It has been found that business per branch ratio in the Chhapi Nagarik Sahakari Bank Ltd. was lower than average of all banks for all the study period. So bank should try to make proper utilization of bank resources.

11)   It has been observed that operating expenses branch ratio in the Modasa Nagarik Sahakari Bank Ltd. reflects that bank must take serious steps to exercise control over undesirable expenditure.

12)   The major of the CCBs under study have shown heavy dependence on term deposits as compared to any other type of deposits. For reducing the dependence of these banks on fixed deposits, it is suggested that special attention should be paid by these banks to mobilize more and more savings and current depositswith a view to reducingthe cost of funds.

13)   Long term advances to total advances ratio in Mehsana Nagarik Sahakari Bank and Chhapi Nagarik Sahakari Bank shows that there were no long term advances in these banks over the period of the study. So it is suggested that these banks should work upon every possibility to start and increase long term advances. Also these banks shouldactively participate and organize **Loan Melas** to disburse more loans.

14)   Himmatnagar, patan and mehsana nagarik sahakari banks are extremely sensitive to recovery management. Average **NPA** to total advances ratio in these banks was higher than average of other banks. Hence, in these banks, there is a great need to

establish a **Recovery Management Cell** at the branch level and a **NPAManagement Committee** at the Head Office level for timely management of loans. Also there is a great need to trainand motivate the recovery employees for better results.

15)   Cash and Bank to Working Funds Ratio in the Chanasma Nagarik Sahakari Bank was too lower than average of all other banks from liquidity point of view. So it is suggested that bank should increase cash on hand and deposits in other banks to improve liquidity position.

16)   From the other liabilities to working fundsratio, it can be concluded that the pressure of external debt on the working funds of all CCBs is low, which indicates the ability of these banks to manage their debt well. Parallel to this conclusion, it can alsobe made out that the banks have maintained a good solvency status.

17)   Majority of the CCBs have very low fixed assets to owned fundsratio, which means that the owned fundsof these banks is more than the fixed assets. Thus, creditors have sufficient margin of safety and the solvency of these banks is satisfactory. Hence, it is suggested that the banks should try to increase their owned fundsin order to improve the margin of safety for the creditors.

18)   It was found that the proportion of investments held by all these banks is very low. Hence, it is suggested that all these banks should make more investment in financial instruments such as mutual funds, commodities, property,financial derivatives etc. which are likely to give goodreturns.

19)   As co-operative banks are constituted with the objective of helping the members and serving society, hence there is a great need of conducting**Social Audit** in all these banks.

20)   The banks should apply the latest development in information and computer technology for customers to cope with several threats, pressures and competition from foreign as well as private banks.

21)   Bank's employees should be polite, impersonal and helpful. The grievances of the customers must be solved as early aspossible.

BIBLIOGRAPHY
BOOKS

Agrawal, M.R. (2003).**Financial Management.** RBSA Publishers.

Amey,L.R. and Egginton,D.A.(1975). **Management Accounting- A Conceptual Approach.**London : longman Group Ltd.

Bedi R.D. (1971). **Theory, History and Practice of Co-operation.**Meerut : Loyal Book Depot.

Calvert,H. (1933).**The Law and Practice of Co-operation.**Calcutta : Thacker Spink & Co.

Chatraborty, H. (1976).**Management Accountancy.**Calcutta : Navbharat Publishers.

Chodhary,S. B. (1964).**Analysis of company financial statement.**Bombay : Asian Publishing House.

Dennis Campbell (2009). **Comaprative Law Year Book of International Business.** Vol. 31, Wolters Kluwer.

Dividsons, Sidney; Stickney, Clyde P. and weil, Romon L, (1982).**Financial Accounting- an introduction to concept, method and uses.** U.S.A., The Dreden Press.

Drucker,Peter(1961). Practice of Management.London ; Mercury Books.

Fay, C.R. (1948). **Co-operation at Home and Abroad.** Vol.II, 1908-1938, London : Staples Press Limited.

Gerstenberg,Charles W.**Financial Organisation and Management of Business.** IVth Ed., New Delhi : Asia Publishing House.

Gole,V.L.(1966). **Fitzerald's Analysis and Interpretation of Financial Statements.** Butterworth's.

Gordon K.C.Chen and Mcgarrah,Robert E. (1982).**Productivity management Text and cases.** New York : International editions Holt Saunders CBS college publication.

Gupta,C.B. (1990). **Production, Productivity and Cost Effectiveness.** New Delhi : Sultan Chand &.Co.

Guthmann,Harry G.(1976).**Analysis of Financial Statements.** New Delhi : Prentice Hall of India Pvt. Ltd.

Hastings, Paul G. (1966). **The Management of Business Finance.** New Jersey :D von Norstrand Company.

Hough, Eleanor M.; Plunkeet, Horace; and Das, K. Madhava (1959). **The Co-operative Movement in India.**Bombay : Oxford University Press.

Howard, Bion B. and Upton,(1953).Miller Introduction to business finance. New York : McGraw Hill.

Kamat, G.S. (1978). **New Dimensions of Cooperative Management.**Mumbai : Himalaya Publishing House.

Kennedy,R.D. and McMllen,S.Y. (1968). **Financial statements form Analysis and interpretation.**Illinois : Richard D. Irwin Inc.

Koher, Eric (1972).**A Dictionary for Accounting.** New Delhi : Prantice Hall of India Pvt. Ltd.

Kopleman, Richard E. (1986).**Managing Productivity Organizations.** New Delhi : McGraw Hill Book Company.

Krishnaswami, O.R. (1978). **Fundamentals of Co-operation.** New Delhi : Sultan Chand & Company Ltd.

Kuchhal,S.C. (1977). Financial Management- An Analytical and Conceptual Approach. Allahabad : Chitanya Publishing House.

Kulkarni, K.R. and Mehta, V.L. (1958). **Theory & Practice of Co-operation in India and Abroad.**Bombay : Co-operator's Book Depot.

Kulshrestha,N.K. **Theory and Practice of Management Accounting.** 1st Ed., Aligarh : Navman Prakashan.

Kulshrestha,N.K. (1970). An Approach to Management Accounting. Aligarh :Navman Prakashan.

Mamoria, C.B. and Saksena R.D. (1973). **Co-operation in India.** Allahabad : Kitab Mahal.

Moore,Carl L. **Managerial Accounting.** 1st Ed., London : Anold Publishers Ltd.

Murty,V. S. (1978). **Management Finance.**Bombay :Vakils feffer and simons Ltd.

Needless,Belverd E.(1988). **Financial and Management accounting.** Honghton Mittin Co.

Paton and Paton,(1964). Corporation Accounts and Statements New York : McMillan.

Paul,Samuelson (1979).**Economics.**New York : McGraw Hill Book Co.

Sayers,R.S. (1972).Modern Banking. 7th Ed., London ; Oxford University Press.

Singh, Jagwant (1993).**Indian Banking Industry: Growth and Trends in Productivity.**New Delhi ; Deep and Deep Publications.

Sullivan, Arthur and Steven M. Sheffrin, (2003).**Economics: Principles in action.** New Jersey : Pearson Prentice Hall.

Tamini, K.K. (1976). **Cooperative Organisation and Management.**New Delhi : WAFM, Farmers Welfare Trust Society.

Vyas,M.R. (1991).**Financial performance of rural banks.**Jaipur : Arihant Publishers.

Weston,J.F. and Brigham, E.F.(1971).**Essentials of Managerial Finance.** 2nd ed., New York : Holt, Rinehart and Winston.

Williams, Jan R., Haka,Susan F. Bettner, Mark S. and Carcello,Joseph V. (2008). **Financial & Managerial Accounting.** McGraw-Hill Irwin.

Yukinori Miyahara, **The Development and Role of Co-op Societies in Japan- Special Reference to Agricultural Co-operavites.** Edited by Chinchankar P.Y. & Namjoshi M.V. (1977). **Co-operation and the Dynamics of Change.** Bombay : Somaiya Pub.

UNPUBLISHED Ph.D. THESIS

Amandeep,(1991).Profits and Profitability of Indian Nationalised Banks.Chandigarh : Panjab University.

Koringa,N.H.(2008).**A Study of Operational Performance and Efficiency Management of District Co-operative Purchase-Sales Unions Limited.**Rajkot : Saurashtra University.

Kshatriya,A.B. (2012).**A Comparative Analysis on Performance Appraisal of Mahila Co-operative Banks of Gujarat.**Rajkot : Saurashtra University.

Nathwani,Nirmal (2004).**The Study of Financial Performance of Banking Sector of India.**Rajkot : Saurashtra University.

Padmini,E.V.K.(1997). **Funds Management of District Co-operative Banks in Kerala.**Cochin : Cochin University of science and technology.

Patel,R.R. (2005).**Operational Efficiency of District Central Co-operative Banks in Gujarat - A Comparative Study.**Rajkot : Saurashtra University.

Ramani,V.K. (2009).**Financial Performance of selected Foreign Banks in India.**Rajkot : Saurashtra University.

Sardhara,B. L. (2005).**Financial Analysis of District Co-operative Banks.**Rajkot : Saurashtra University.

Vashist, A.K.(1987). **Performance appraisal of commercial banks in India.**An Shimla : Himachal Pradesh University.

JOURNALS

Agale, S.V. (February, 2012). **Progress of District Central Cooperative Banks in Maharashtra.** International Referred Research Journal, Vol. III, Issue-29, pp.14-15, ISSN-0975-3486, RNI-RAJBIL 2009/30097.

Bhatt, M.S. and Bhat Showkat, (summer 2013). **Ahmad Financial Performance and Efficiency of Cooperative Banks In Jammu & Kashmir.** Journal of Co-Operative Accounting and Reporting, V2, N1, pp.16-36.

Chander, Ramesh and Chandel, Jai Kishan (2011, Nov.-Apr.). **An Evaluation of Financial Performance and Viability of Cooperative Banks - A Study of Four DCCBs in Haryana.**Kaim Journal of Management and Research vol.3, No.2, pp.1-12.

Das, S.K. (2012, Jul.-Dec.). **State Cooperative Banking in Northeast India: Financial and Operational Viability Analysis.** Journal of North East India Studies, Vol. 2, No. 1, pp. 13-32.

Deshmukh, P.V. (2013, May). **The Performance of Cooperative Banking in India.** Indian Journal of Applied Research, Vol. 3, Issue 5, pp.160-162.

Gnanasekaran, E. Anbalgan, M. and Abdul Nazar, (2012, March). N. **A study on the Urban Cooperative Banks Success and growth in Vellore District-Statistical Analysis.** International Journal of Advanced Research in Computer Science and Software Engineering, Vol. 2, Issue 3, pp.434-437.

Gowd Talla, Narayana Bethapudi, Anand and Reddeppa Reddy G, **An Analytical Study on Financial Performance of Dharmavaram Urban Cooperative Bank, A.P. India.**Abhinav,Vol. NO.2, Issue no.8, pp.1-13.

Gupta, Jyoti and Jain, Suman (2012). **A study on Cooperative Banks in India with special reference to Lending Practices.** European Journal of Education and Learning, Vol.12, pp.1-9.

Gupta, V.K. Pawan kumar, and Goyal, A. (2013, July). **Financial Analysis of Indian Oil Corporation Limited.** International Journal of Research In Commerce & Management, Vol. 4, Issue no. 07, pp.46-52.

Jagtap, P.A. (2013, June).**Financial Analysis of Rajarambapu Co-Op. Bank Ltd., Peth, Dist. Sangli-A Case Study.**Advances in Management, Vol. 6 (6),pp.60-64.

Khandare, V.B. (2012, October). **Some Issues in Customers Services of Urban Cooperative Banks: A Case Study of Beed District.** International Journal of Social Science & Interdisciplinary ResearchVol.1 Issue 10, pp.145-152.

K.V.S.N. Jawahar Babu and Selkhar, Muniraja B. (2012, July-Aug). **The Emerging Urban Co-Operative Banks (Ucbs) In India: Problems and Prospects.** Journal of Business and Management, Vol. 2, Issue 5, PP 01-05.

Mohanty, R.P. (1992). **Managing technology for strategic advantages.** The Economic Times, Thursday 9th Jan.

Padmaja, B., BhanuKiran, C. and Rao, Rama Prasada C.H.,(2013, June). **An Empirical Study on Financial Performance of Anantapur Urban Cooperative Bank.** International Journal of Current Research,Vol. 5, Issue, 06, pp.1451-1456.

Pandya, B.H. (2012, January). **Financial Analysis of Tata Steel Ltd.- A Case Study.** International Journal of Research in Commerce & Management, Vol. 3, Issue NO. 1, pp.93-97.

Pareek, Shachi (2012, June). **Profitability Performance Analysis of Urban Co-operative Banks in Jaipur District.** International Indexed & Referred Research Journal, Vol. III, Issue-33, pp.24-25.

Patel, R.K. (2012, June). **Financial Performance of Urban Co-operative Bank.**Contemporary Research in India, Vol.: 2, Issue: 2, pp.263-266.

Patel, R.K. (2012). **Growth Of Urban Co-Operative Banks In India.** The Clute Institute International Academic Conference Las Vegas, Nevada, USA, pp. 882-891.

Patel, R.K. (2012, June). **Multi-Factor Evaluation and Forecasting of the Performance of Urban Co-Operative Banks in Ahmedabad.** Contemporary Research in India, Vol. 2, Issue: 2, pp.71-80.

Petropoulos, Dimitrios P. and Kyriazopoulos, George Profitability, (2010). **Efficiency and Liquidity of the Co-Operative Banks in Greece.** International Conference on Applied Economics, pp.603-607.

Ramachandran, A and Siva Shanmugam,D. (May, 2012). **An Empirical Study on the Financial Performance of Selected Scheduled Urban Cooperative Banks in**

India. Asian Journal of Research in Banking and Finance Volume 2, Issue 5, pp.1-24, ISSN: 2249-7323.

Rao, J.J. (1982). **A study of Personnel Management in Selected Primary Agricultural Cooperative Societies in Orissa.** Indian Journal of Commerce Vol. XXXI No. 11.

Rasal, R.G. (2011, July). **Performance of District Central Cooperative Banks During Post-reform period with special reference to Ahmednagar District Central Cooperative Bank.** Indian Streams Research Journal, Vol. - I, ISSUE-V.

Renuka R. and Elamathi C., (2013, Aug.). **Development of Cooperative Banking in India.** Indian Journal of Applied Research, Vol. 3, Issue 8, pp.115-118.

Sanjay Kantidas, (2012, March). **Operational and Financial Performance Analysis of Meghalaya Cooperative apex Bank.** Journal on Banking Financial Services & Insurance Research. Vol.2, Issue 3, pp.20-39.

Sant, Seema and Chaudhari, P.T. (2012, May). **A Study of the Profitability of Urban Cooperative Banks.** International Journal of Multidisciplinary Research, Vol.2 Issue 5, pp.124-134.

Shirasi, R.S. (2012, June). **A Study of Financial Working and Operational Performance of Urban Co-operative Banks in Pune District.** Indian Streams Research Journal. Vol.1, pp.1-4.

Solanke, S.S. and Agrawal, S.R. (2012, October). **Problems faced by co-operative banks and perspectives in the Indian Economy.** International Journal of Commerce, Business and Management, Vol. 1, No.2, pp.53-54.

Soni, Anilkumar and Saluja, HarjinderSingh (2013, March). **Financial Ratio Analysis of DCC Bank Limited Rajnandgaon A Case Study.** International Journal of Accounting and Financial Management Research, Vol. 3, Issue 1, pp.93-105.

Thirupathi, Kanchu (2012, October). Performance Evaluation of DCCBs in India-A Study.Asia Pacific Journal of Marketing & Management Review, Vol.1, No. 2, pp.169-180.

Uppal,R.K.(June,2005).**Profitability Behaviour of Major Banks in the Post Economic Reforms Era.** A Research Journal of Humanities & Social Sciences, Vol.3.

REPORTS

- Annual reports of selected **Citizen Co-operative banks of North Gujarat** (2007-2012).
- Reserve Bank of India. (2007-2012), **Trend and Progress of Banking in India.**
- The Agricultural Co-operatives and Farming Reforms in Japan (1 & 2), The Tokyo Foundation, Jan.14, 2009.
- Tentative conclusions on objectives of Financial Statements of Business Enterprise.

WEBSITES

- www.Co-op.Societies_Russian history.encyclopedia.com.htm.2004.
- **"History of Consumer Co-op Movement in Japan"**,(http://jccu.coop/eng/ aboutus/history.php), Assessed on 2014.
- http://en.wikipedia.org/wiki/Danish_cooperative_movement
- www.**inflibnet**.ac.in/
- **etheses.saurashtrauniversity**.edu/
- http://www.indiancooperative.com
- http://www.nafcub.org

www.ingramcontent.com/pod-product-compliance
Lightning Source LLC
Chambersburg PA
CBHW051408200326
41520CB00023B/7157